Art is Magic

A children's book
for adults by
Jeremy Deller

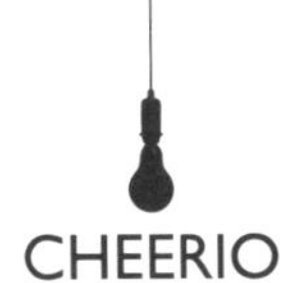

CHEERIO

5 Art…

7 Chapter 1
Music is Prophecy

19 Chapter 2
Stonehenge is a mirror

26 Neolithic T-shirts

29 Chapter 3
My 'Stairway to Heaven'
The Battle of Orgreave

39 Chapter 4
It's time to lose control
The public and public art

62 *Wir haben die Schnauze voll*

65 Chapter 5
Queen Victoria with her face smashed in
Jeremy and Mary Beard in conversation about public statuary

76 Memorial plaques

79 Chapter 6
Don't fuck with bats

84 Brexit T-shirts

87 Chapter 7
'I see your intricate subtlety Martin'
Depeche Mode and their fans

94 *Bom Bom's Dream*

97 Chapter 8
Warning! Graphic Content
A picture essay

111 Chapter 9
How to make a critic cry
A conversation with Alan Kane about *Folk Archive* and other bits and bobs

126 I ♥ Ed Hall

Worship the Chameleon!, Knokke, Belgium, 2021. I was asked to create a public sculpture in a seaside town in Belgium which was clearly crying out for a giant chameleon slide. This magical creature was expertly hand-sculpted by René at K&S Decor.

131 Chapter 10
A pub called The Curator

147 Chapter 11
The Reactionary Ravers
An interview with Daniel Scott

154 *The Deliverers*

157 Chapter 12
VALHALLA IN W12
Glam, Adrian Street and William Blake

166 10 years in Eden

170 Happiness is a Steel Band

175 Chapter 13
Benny Hill with the sound turned down
A brush with Andy Warhol

181 Chapter 14
A Range Rover crushed
and made into a bench
English Magic in Venice

192 *GraciechesterbeckyjonnynaomisakeemaIllyr*

195 Chapter 15
The Factory comes to Seven Sisters
Jonny Banger in conversation

203 Chapter 16
I burnt Rupert Murdoch
A cover version

208 *Monarchs of the Glen*

211 Chapter 17
Iggy Pop Life Class

219 Chapter 18
Lest I forget

235 Afterword
Odds and Socks
CHEERIO interview with Jeremy Deller

238 What makes the world go round

250 Notes

254 Thanks

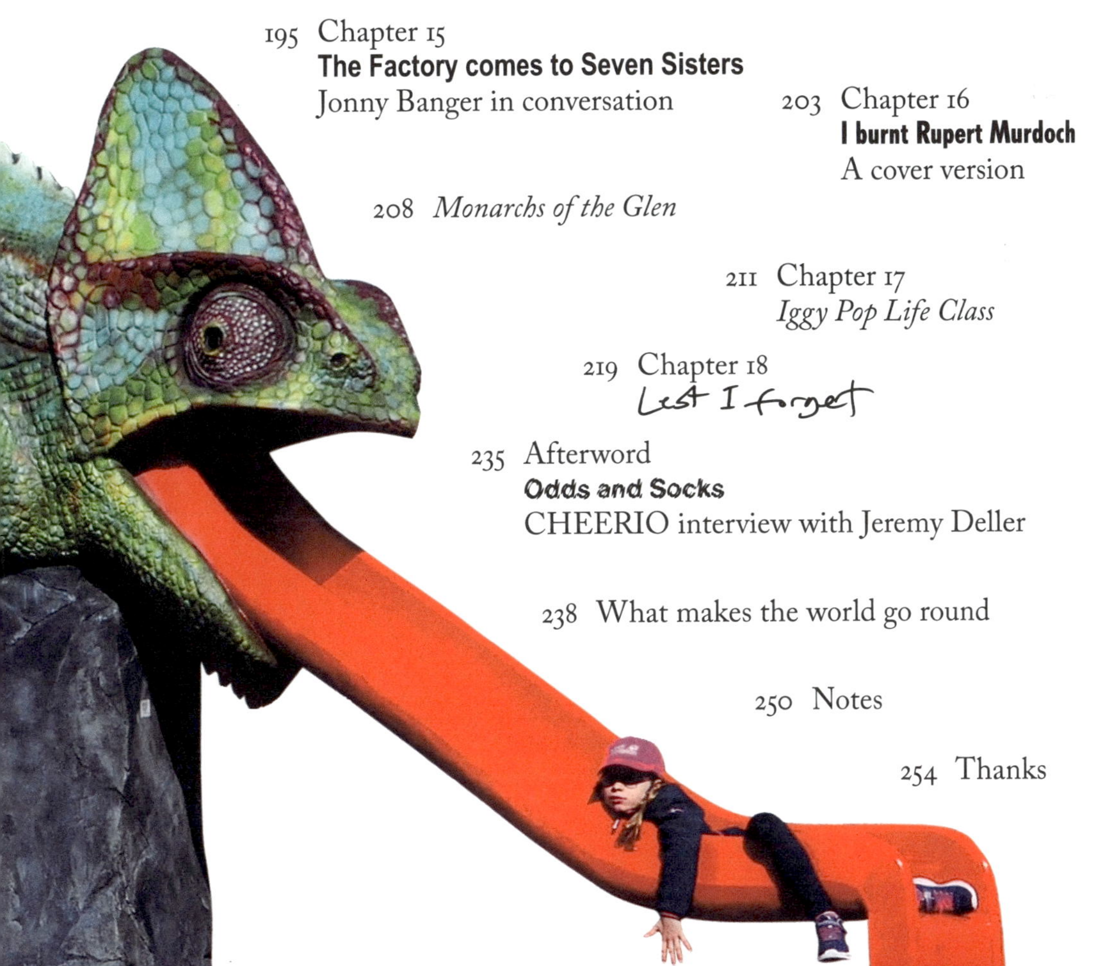

FAN STIC
N

Spring & Summer 2013 – £6.00 / $14.99

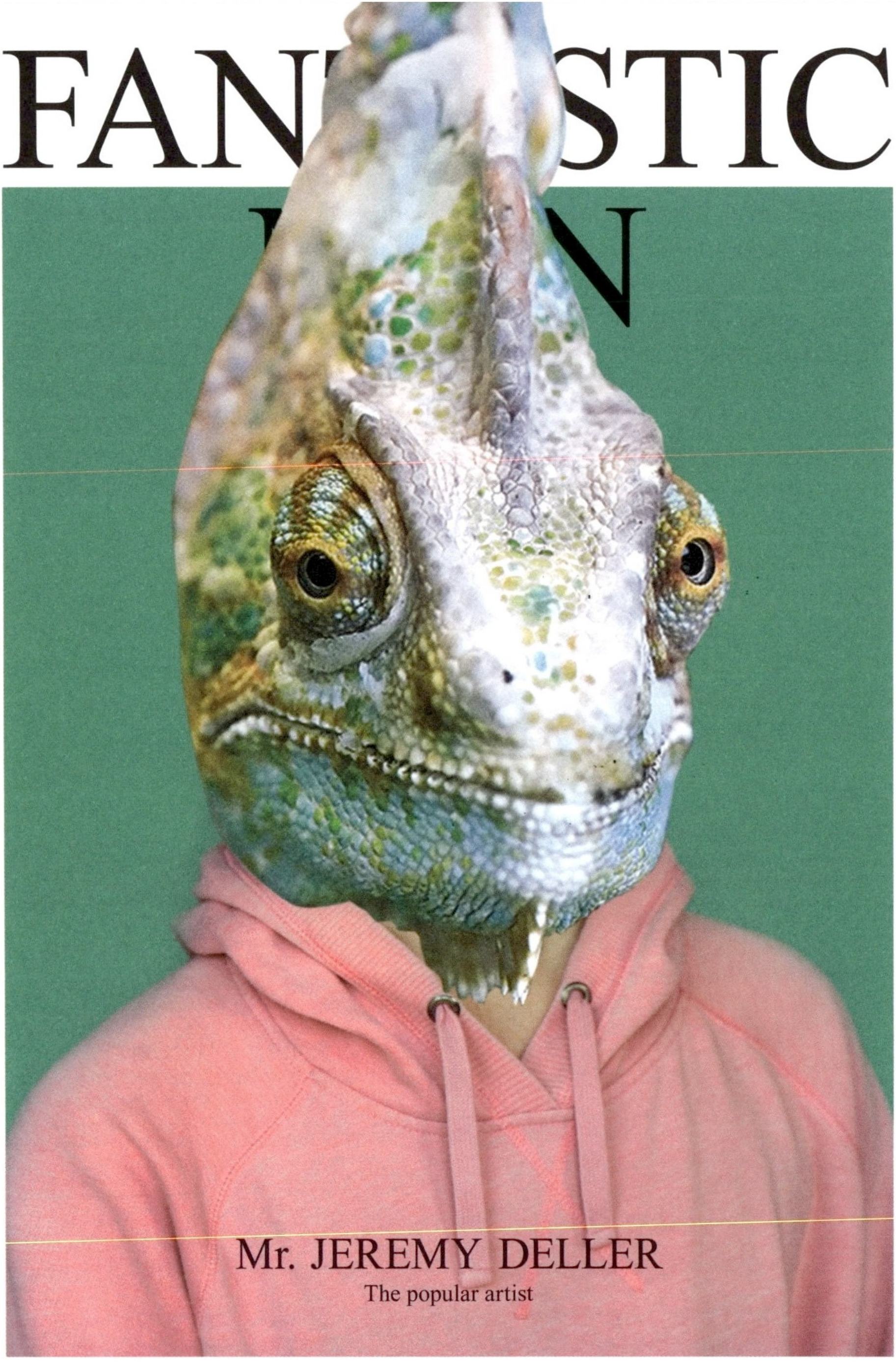

Mr. JEREMY DELLER

The popular artist

Art

… is a way of staying engaged and in love with the world. It is also a form of magic, its alchemical power transforming reality, if only for a moment, making the mundane profound. It does things that are not logical and can trick us. It can be deeply absurd and even stupid at times.

I've written all the text in this book in the only voice I know. I hope it gives the inside track on some of the projects I've worked on and attempts to explain what I was trying to do. I am not an optimistic person by nature, but I have done my best to be upbeat. Having said that, I find the act of writing mortifying, in the truest sense. When I have to do it, I quite literally feel as though I am slowly dying. I'd like to thank my editor and collaborator Daniel Scott for keeping me alive in this process.

Just for the record, you should know that this book had many other titles, all of which fell by the wayside for a variety of reasons. If you don't like the current title of the book, feel free to call it any of these:

- *Animal Vegetable Pop Music* (I have always liked this, but it proved divisive. Like Marmite, which I love)
- *Thirty Years of Hurt* (a bit too self-pitying)
- *You Can't Do That* (was once said to me by an artist when I told him about *The Battle of Orgreave*)
- *That's Not Art* (this has been said to me a few times)
- *Call That Art?* (see above)
- *Things I Like* (the title of my children's book about bats, and Marmite)
- *Everybody in the Place* (I made a film with this title and it's too confusing)
- *What's the Point of That?* (too negative)
- *What Were You Thinking?* (this title was dropped very close to printing)
- *Mid-Career Crisis* (maybe too apt)

You get the idea.

← Part of a series of collaged animal heads on original covers I made for the tenth anniversary of the magazine *Fantastic Man* in 2015. Original photograph by Alasdair McLellan. More on page 101.

Do you remember the

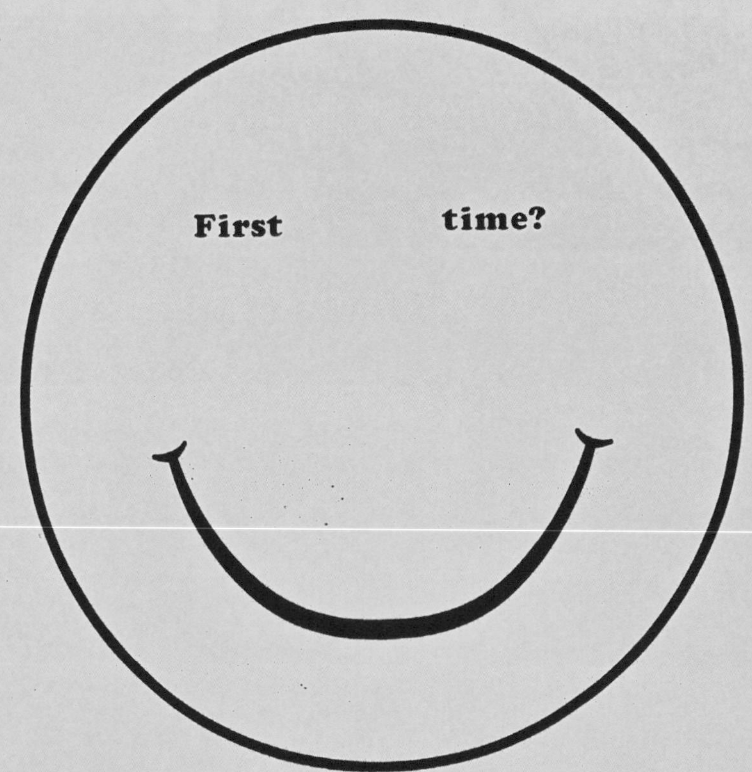

'Acid House' Memories and Memorabilia from the Archives of the Institute of Popular Music.

The Tate Gallery Liverpool

12 October - 14 December 1996.

Admission Free. Open Daily 10-6 (except Sundays 1-6)
Tel (0151 709 3223) Recorded Information (0151 709 0507)

A North West Arts presentation in conjunction with the Institute of Popular Music.

Chapter 1

Music is Prophecy

The title of this chapter is a quote by the theorist Jacques Attali and refers to moments when music leads, and history follows. Rock 'n' roll did this and so did the Beatles, both showing us the future. Showing us a new way to be. In the post-war United Kingdom, the NHS was the hardware and fifteen years later the Beatles were the software for a country trying to find a new place in the world. Music was my way of understanding and dealing with the world growing up; it was the window that I looked out of. This is perhaps less true now, but the work I make about or with music still has that quality about it. Here are a few such projects.

Exhibition posters, 1994–96

In 1994, I was unemployed and enrolled on a screen-printing class at the London College of Printing (now the London College of Communication). I was allowed to use the facilities for two days a week and, in addition, have access to the twelve computers kept in a special room. This combination led to a series of posters for speculative exhibitions about music and popular culture. In a sense I was giving myself a graphic design assignment. Among these were

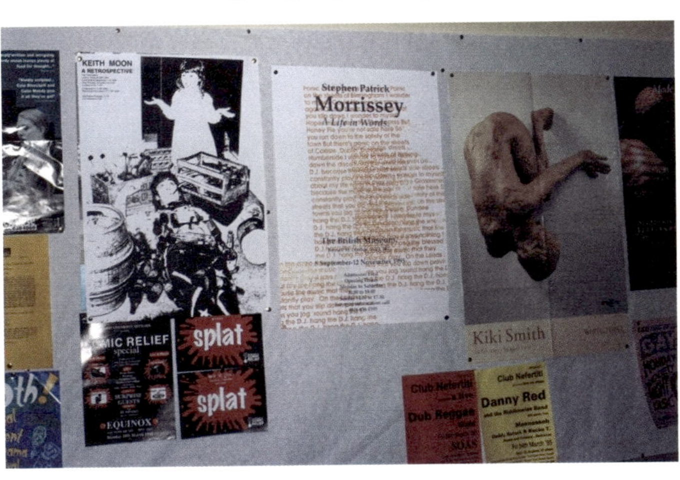

Posters I made for a speculative Morrissey lyrics exhibition at the British Museum and a Keith Moon retrospective at Tate Britain, pinned up at the Courtauld Institute of Art common room in 1996.

← One of a number of posters made in 1996 as an exercise to imagine an exhibition of the future. They arose from many impulses but mainly my love of popular culture and music and its relationship to 'high culture'.

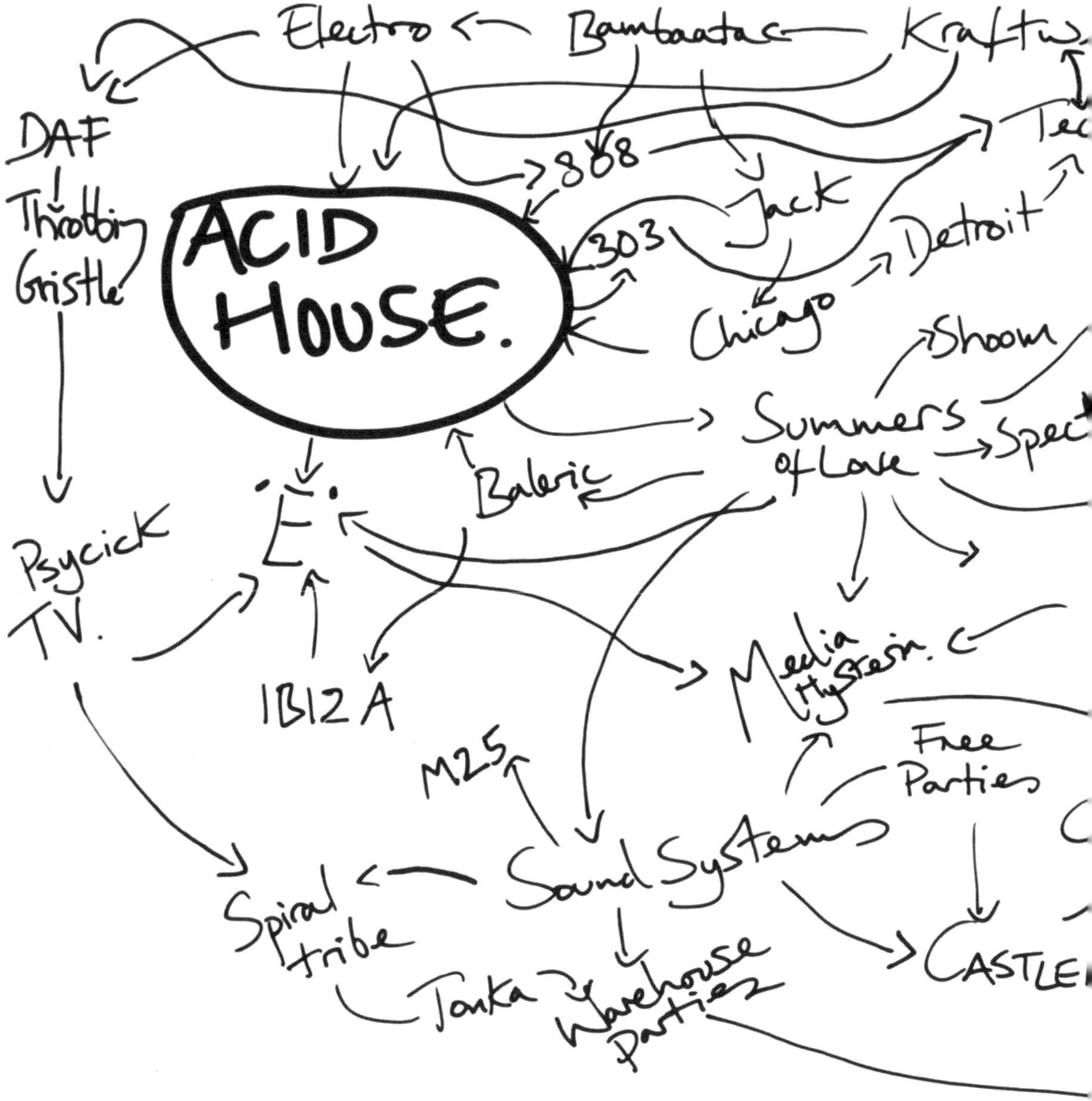

Electro
Bambaataa
Kraftw
DAF
Throbbing Gristle
808
Tec
Jack
ACID HOUSE.
303
Detroit
Chicago
Shoom
Summers of Love
Spec
Baleric
E
Psycick TV.
IBIZA
Media Hysteria.
M25
Free Parties
Sound Systems
Spiral tribe
Tonka
Warehouse Parties
CASTLE

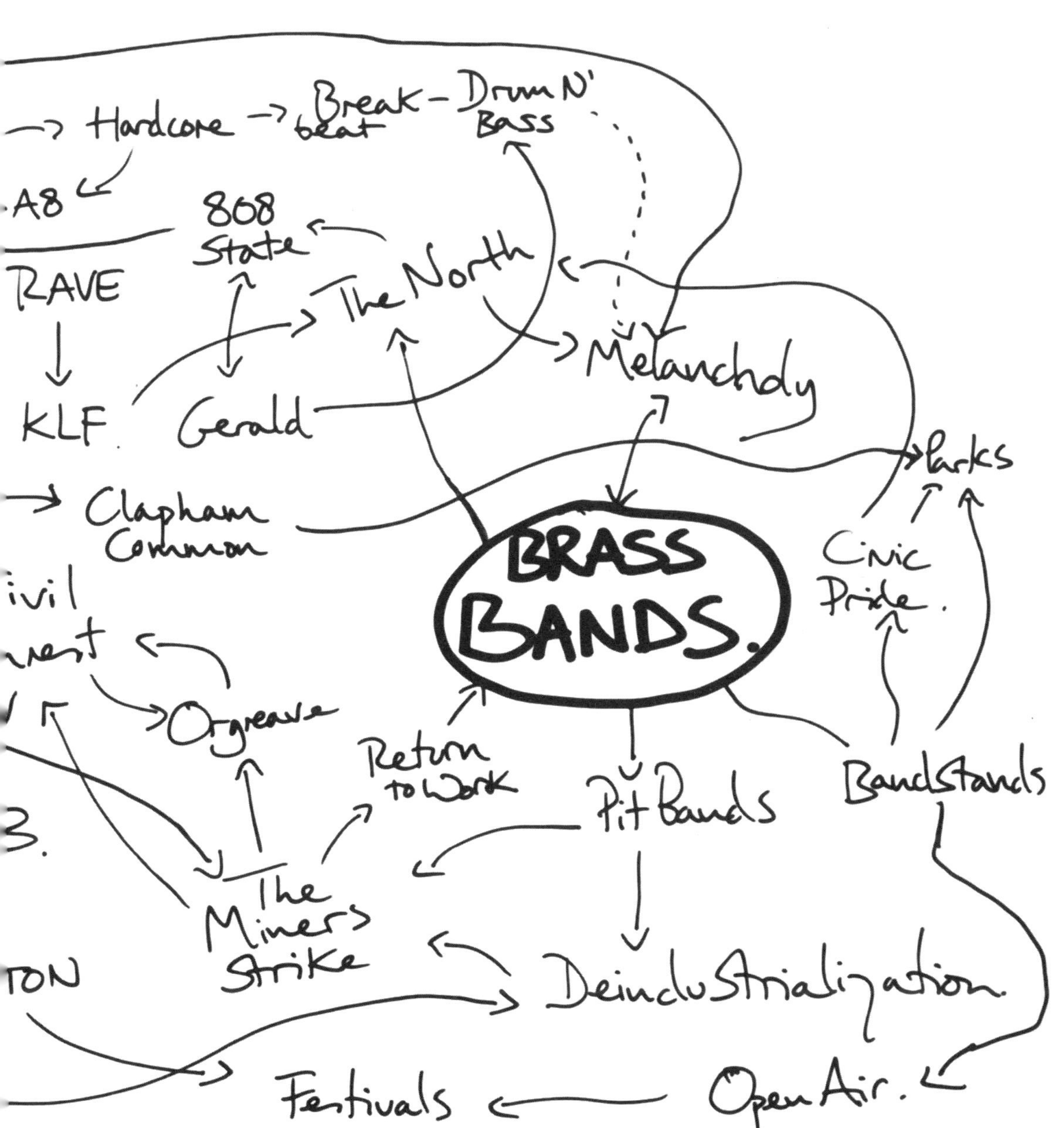

The History of the World, original drawing, 1996. I had this diagram more or less as a vision simultaneously with the words Acid Brass being put together. It was an attempt to explain the changes in twentieth-century Britain through music. Popular culture can nudge or drive the course of history and I think this happened in the late 1980s when the phenomenon of rave sped history up. It's also an illustration more or less of how my mind works.

posters for shows about rave, Joy Division and David Bowie – subjects I thought worthy of examination in a museum, even though it seemed unlikely at the time. I was also thinking about how many music movements shared similar names with art-historical movements: Gothic, Modernism and Romanticism. I made a few copies of each and then put them up in places like student common rooms, among genuine exhibition posters.

***Acid Brass*, 1997**

... is a brass band playing acid house anthems, a piece of too-soon nostalgia for a recently passed moment. It was an attempt to explain the history of twentieth-century Britain through music, from the industrial music of a brass band to the post-industrial land and soundscape of digitally made dance music. The *History of the World* diagram on the previous spread explains this better than I can.

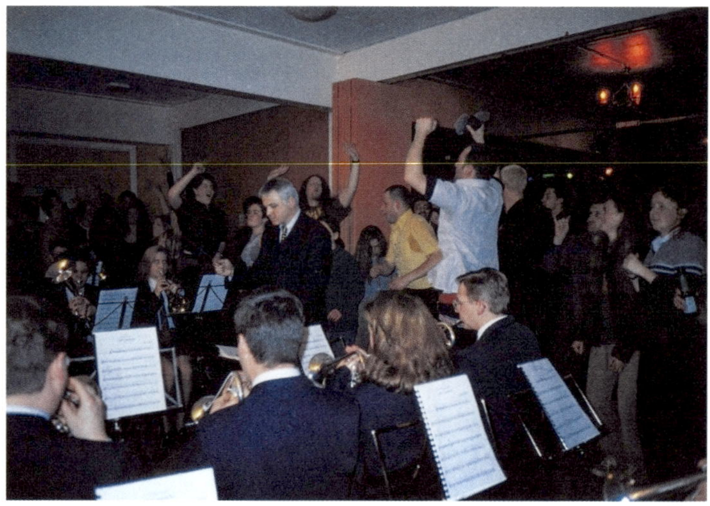

Acid Brass performance at Cardiff Art College when things got a bit out of hand in a good way, 1999.

Though I wasn't an active participant in acid house early on, it was clearly a socially significant movement. Some music reflects the times in which it is made whereas some music points to the future – acid house did the latter. I also have a thing about cover versions, which can tell profound stories of change and evolution in the simplest and most pleasurable way. Art, too, is a cover version of a reality.

It's one thing to have an idea and another to make it happen. I was recommended to approach the Williams Fairey Brass Band, who, at that point, were ranked number one in the fiercely contested hierarchy of UK brass bands. The call I made to the manager was into unknown territory. I didn't want to mention the type of music by name as its reputation had been trashed by the media, so I described it as 'contemporary electronic music'. John, the manager, responded: 'We'll give it a go once and then see what happens.'

That one call and the subsequent experience taught me that the public are more or less up for doing things, sometimes just out of curiosity, which is what makes the world go round for an artist like myself.

Brass bands are very adaptable: they can play all sorts of music, from ABBA covers to Beethoven. Little fazes them; in a sense, also, many of the players were young and the opportunity to finally play music to people their own age was welcome. When I first saw the band play in Birmingham, a woman was happily knitting in the middle of the front row, while other audience members slept.

Personally, working with the brass band liberated me: it constituted a shift from *making things* to *making things happen*. I was shocked at how easy and enjoyable the process was, and for a few years we went on an adventure together. The first concert, at the Liverpool Institute for Performing Arts, was nerve-wracking. The band looked wary as they shuffled on, sizing up the audience, which would never be the case at their regular concerts. Nobody really knew what was going to happen – but as soon as they started playing, I realised that everything was going to be okay. I'm sure some of the audience went to laugh at the band – or the idea, at least.

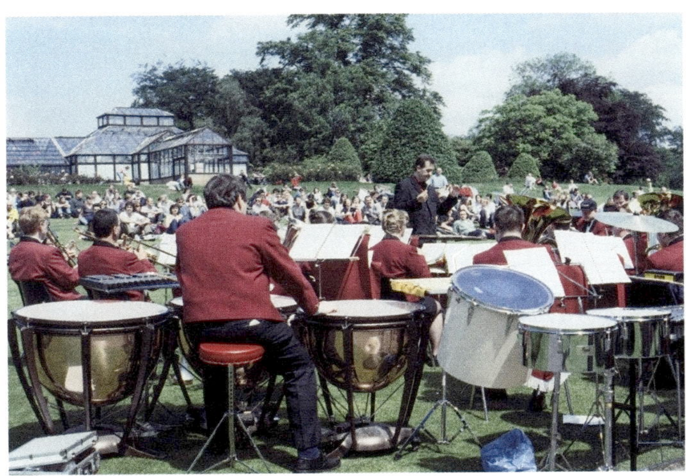

A deceptively civilised photograph of the Acid Brass concert at the Botanic Gardens in Glasgow, 1997.

Subsequent concerts were raucous. There was something about seeing thirty musicians onstage playing music that they loved which drove the crowd almost insane. It was as though a primal switch had been flipped. The communality of the concerts is as good for me as it gets, as it resonates with the communality of the rave and trade unionism.

Everybody in the Place, 2018
Music documentaries are one of my favourite things, to the point where I organised a twenty-four-hour music documentary festival in Helsinki, Finland in 2014 called The 24-hour Rockshow. We screened classics and rare films, from midday on Saturday to midday on Sunday. The best in their genre tend to be the ones made at the time, following a band on tour or documenting a festival or specific gig. Films which were later used as research material for *This Is Spinal Tap*.

Everybody in the Place is, more or less, the *History of the World* mind map made into a film; the map is basically the script. I had been carrying this film around in my head for twenty-five years to some extent. It's a film about the relationship between history and popular culture and, in this instance, how dance music sped history and change along. I had been commissioned to make a twenty-minute film about London's clubbing and dance culture in the 1980s which I didn't want to do for several reasons. One was that I had spent quite a bit of that decade not being able to get into the very clubs I was being asked to make a documentary about.

The main reason, however, was that the story of rave is a national one, with its most interesting aspects happening outside the capital, often in the countryside. Raves in the north had a closer connection to the political and economic landscape. In Blackburn, raves were literally held in factories which

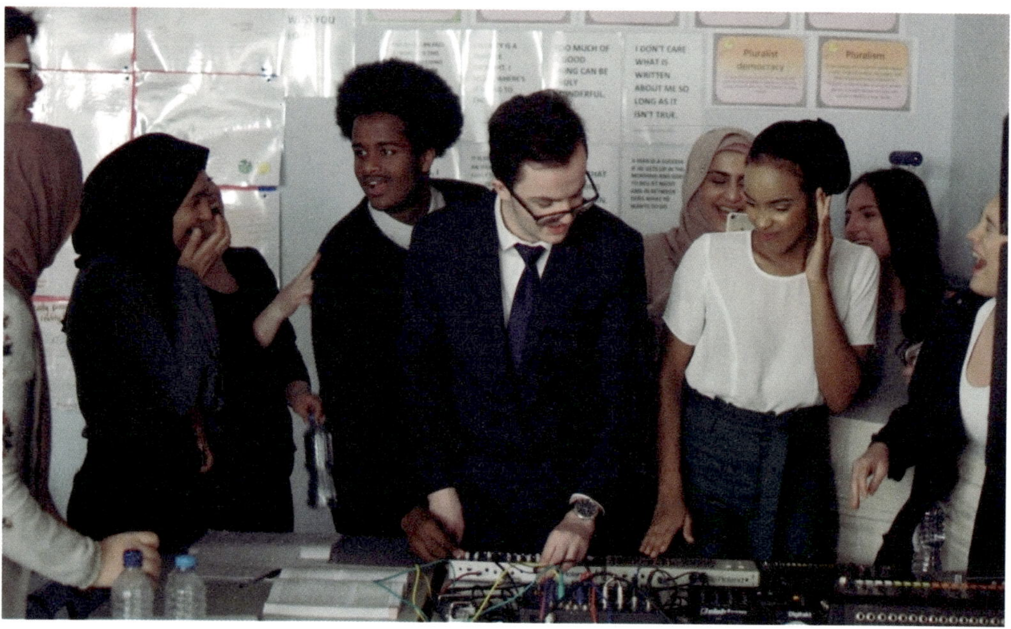

A moment during the class where we had some tech from the 1980s set up for a bit of a play about. Maybe my favourite sequence from the film.

were lying derelict as traditional industries collapsed. A factory where maybe your father or older brother worked, and where you were maybe expected to work. But instead, you go there to socialise and be deafened by music not machinery, a ritualistic dance on the ruins of our industrial past. It blows my mind that in 1984–5 the police were preventing striking miners from picketing pits by setting up roadblocks and stopping vehicles, while only three or four years later using the same tactics on young people (who may well have been relatives of these pickets) who were seeking parties and pleasure, rather than a picket line. I don't think this could have been predicted in 1985.

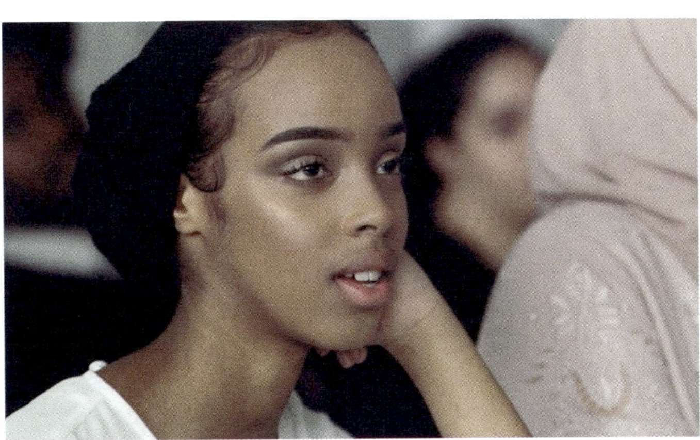

'No one's watching each other, we have technology so if we were to see someone dancing or doing something a bit different, we'd instantly record them but in these parties there is no technology, so they are just in their own space, whereas it's a bit more controlled now I think.'

A student's reaction to watching the footage of parties from the late 1980s.

Raves in the southeast seemed to be more concerned with entertainment. The footage from the south had a very different feel, with 20-year-olds arriving in Jaguars as opposed to people walking miles along rainy dual carriageways. So, I wanted to place this moment in a historical and social context and give it the respect (if that is the right word) that the music deserved. Dance music is often not taken seriously because it is seen as not having the lyrical depth, as if music should be a competition between Bob Dylan and Donna Summer. I also knew I didn't want to make a film that was all about DJs and drugs with random archive footage chucked in. There is a lucrative nostalgia industry based around men – and it is predominantly men – talking misty-eyed about their glory days at raves and gigs. It's not so different to men in their seventies and beyond being obsessed with steam trains.

In 2018, I was asked to give a talk about my work to a group of fifth and sixth form students at a school in London. I didn't really know what to expect from the students and had no idea what they would make of me or my work. As it was, I had a really great time. They were fun, engaged and asked cheeky questions. When you give a talk, you can quickly pick up the energy level in the room; an instinct probably related to our ancient selves where you would have to be able to work out if a group of strangers was hostile or not (a piece of advice: London art colleges can be perilous places at times – always best to take a hand axe).

So, when it came to make the film, I knew I wanted them to be involved in some way. I returned to give a class to a group of politics students about the relationship of dance music to British history titled 'Everybody in the Place (An Incomplete History of Britain, 1984–92)'. It is a totally subjective if not fanciful take on the subject but, as it develops, the film becomes as much about the students and their future as it is about the past and my endless reminiscing. I hope that by the end, the viewer is seeing history through their eyes as they watch and comment on an archive which was from nearly twenty years before they were born. Most of their parents were born and raised outside the UK, so there was no family memory of the events I was showing them. This meant that the students were learning about the miners' strike, the traveller movement and the phenomenon of illegal raves for the first time – a news report from the past. Their responses were revealing. For example, I was asked if the miners' strike was a dispute about climate change. The rave footage intrigued the class as it was from an era before mobile phones and social media, an almost unimaginable period. There was discussion about the countryside and how people's relationship to it during this period was being redefined as they left cities to go on a quest to find the rave. Most of the young people in the classroom had very little experience of life outside the M25, and definitely thought of themselves as Londoners first, and British citizens second.

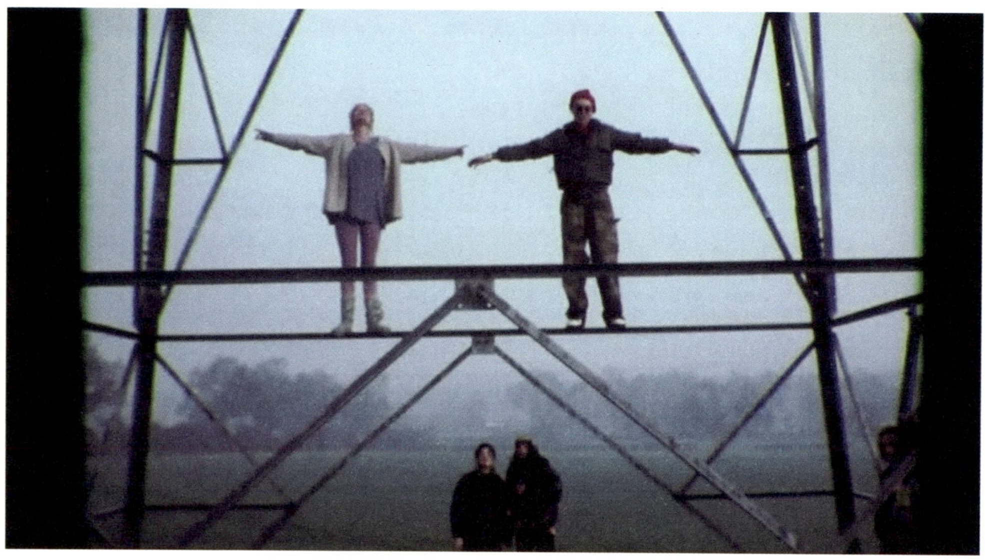

A still from Sara Sender's footage of life on the road with the Spiral Tribe sound system of which she was a member, circa 1990.

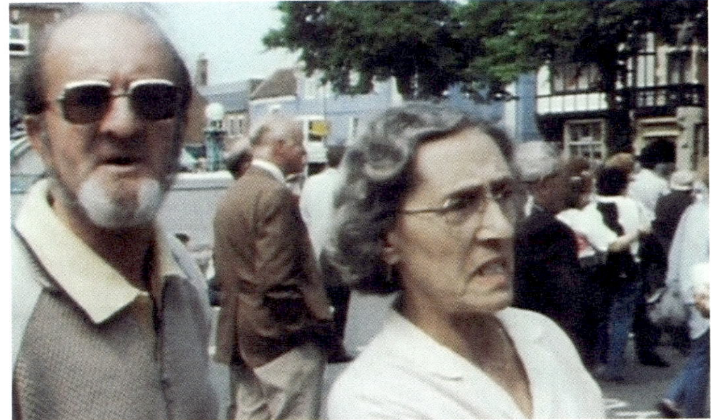

'They're all talking about South Africa and apartheid out there with the blacks but we have got it just as bad here, this a police state here now you got no freedom of speech here and got no freedom in this country.'

Members of the public defend travellers as they arrive at court in Salisbury, 1986.

The raves looked a bit out of control, an experience that is increasingly difficult to attain in an era in which social media picks over every second of your life. If anything with this film, I was trying to show the young people that the UK is possibly a more interesting place than they might think, and that the recent history of the country can be surprising. This was highlighted in a piece of archive film about the traveller movement, from 1986. The filmmaker interviews a group of older locals in Salisbury town square – hardly a hotbed of Marxism – as several handcuffed travellers arrive at court. Almost instinctively you expect a reactionary and unsympathetic response, but, in fact, they support the arrested travellers and criticise the police for their excessive use of force. My theory is that they were from a generation that had experienced the rise of fascism in the 1930s and the subsequent war, and so were totally allergic to the authoritarian turn under Margaret Thatcher.

'I don't want no bugger hassling me or chasing me about telling me what I can't or can do, it's a free country everybody do what they please, I'll share what I have with anybody, he can be the tramp in the street it doesn't bother me.'

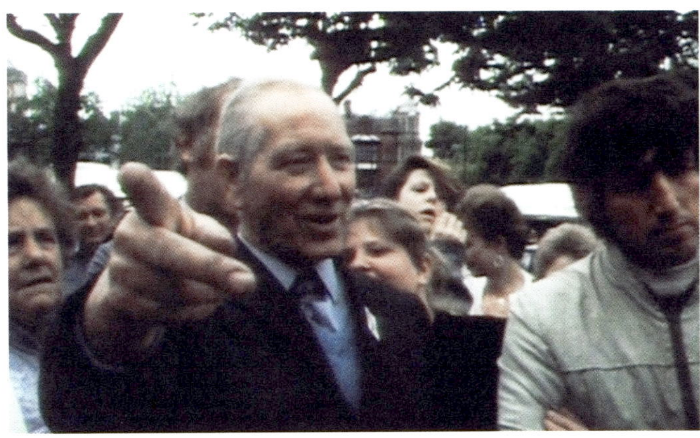

Overleaf: This was part of my script of sorts for the class – in the end I reduced it further. Without a doubt this was the most exhausting day of my life. After the teaching I hobbled home, using my bicycle as an improvised zimmer frame.

Blackburn
Replicated across the UK each with its own regional ff

Dancing on Industry :

Map of the UK.

Situation:

Infrastructure. roads-people - Spaces

The end of Industry its rites

Where deafened by ind now by music

Mill ~~foo~~ footage a bit more hardcore

Love Decade Clip. the end.

The Law - mass arrest. → Servic

Fault line digital econom

BATTLE

Industrial vs Digital. | noisy Sweaty

Industry vs Service economy . where pa of worlds worked go to par

~~Xtian - Pagan~~

SAME TIME

Xtian vs Pagan. - esp outside.

Uses of Raves — Trance / Hard

anticipate countryside. — Spiral Traveller. —
Bereft of a focusing Sound.

Traveller Movement - persecution post miners strike wounded - striking your own county. Abstract Project.
THE MUSIC WAS A FUEL - Hard - e
Country-City - tension, ~~place~~ site of conflict.
not a ~~th~~ site of peace → fundamental

city to Socialise some people never leave

go back —

PROJECTION — Abstract — Political

Sound System Culture — Free Parties..

A place of creative chaos — Class distinctions

ENGLISH RELATIONSHIP TO COUNTRYSIDE.
INDUSTRIALISE RAPIDLY // → Stonehenge
Yet → Cerne Abbas// // ✓

Who Are We

Ask ~~big~~ Questions — Fundamental

1994 CJA

CLASS DISTINCTIONS v. Raw

describe life on the Road and the parties.
down side?
Drugs?

→ Pro and anti
more support than you might think.
→ Wiltshire = S. Yorks

→ Reaction Clips.

→ CASTLEMORTON.

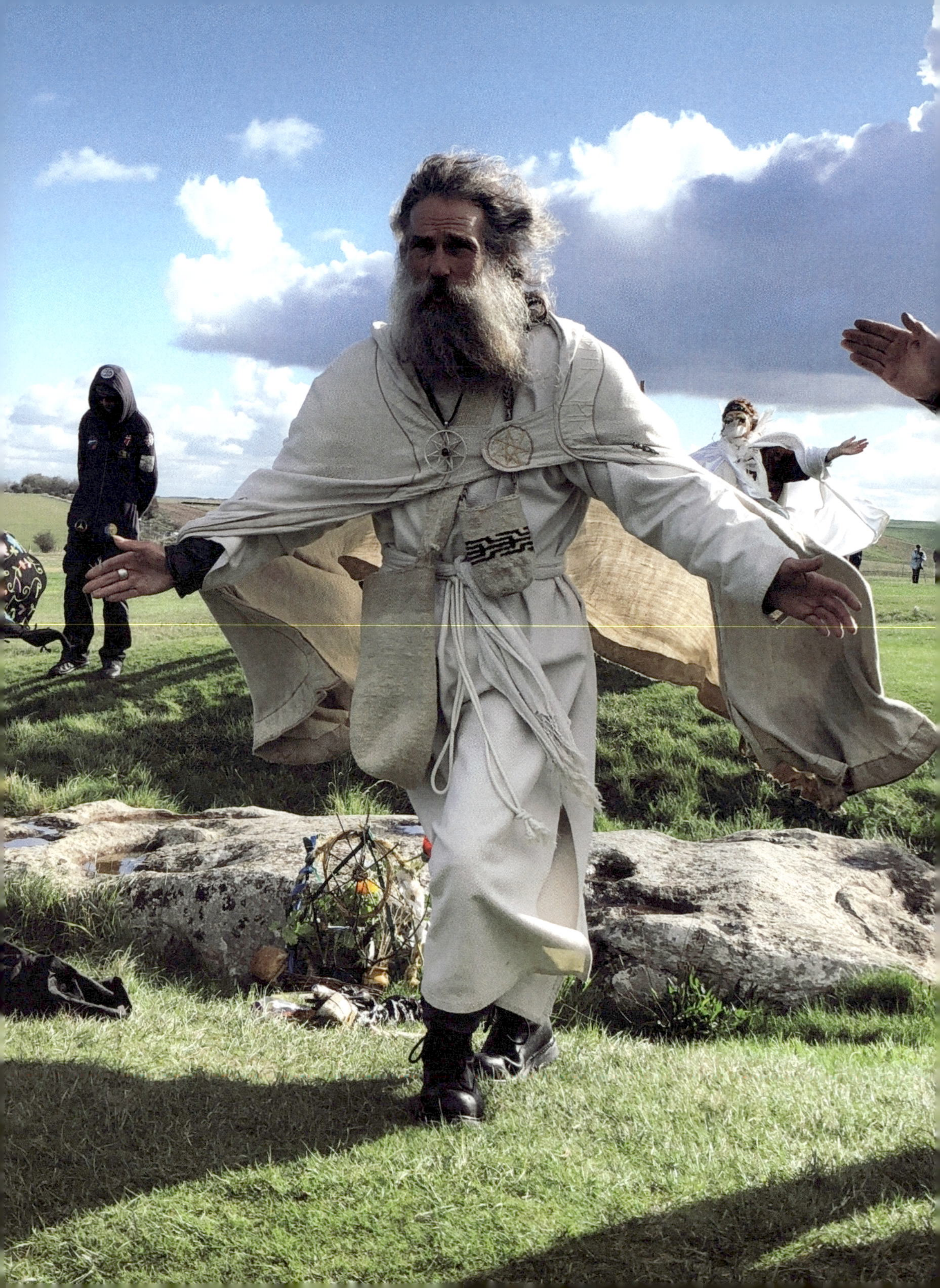

Chapter 2

Stonehenge is a mirror

Just as science fiction is as much about the present as the future, so archaeology is as much about the present as the past. A month doesn't go by in the UK without some discovery about Stonehenge being made that supposedly widens our understanding of it and so, by association, ourselves. It is a national mirror that reflects whatever it is that we are concerned about at the time. The stress and obsessions of society are encapsulated in the debate around it, sometimes at the site itself. In the 1980s, the moral panic around the traveller movement and, by association, land ownership, was played out publicly at Stonehenge. And, like many neolithic sites, we still feel drawn to them. They still function as sites of pilgrimage. Tourism is surely a form of pilgrimage. We'll never know what happened there for sure unless we master time travel.

This speculation is nevertheless a national pastime. We also look to Stonehenge to somehow unlock the secrets of life and the cosmos itself. But, of course, Stonehenge is entirely mute even though we ask a lot of it, as we project our thoughts about ourselves and the world onto it. Stonehenge is the most recognisable structure in the UK, yet it remains an enduring mystery. For our national identity to be a bit of a mystery is no bad thing, as it gives the public space to make up their own versions of who they are. The idea of multiple interpretations of a place and history goes against the instincts of nationalism and authoritarianism, where countries have their sacred founding myths which cannot be interfered with.

It was from these thoughts that *Sacrilege* (a life-size inflatable model of Stonehenge) was created in 2012. I was also trying to think what the stupidest idea that was possible to make would be, the sort of thing you might see on *The Simpsons*. It was made more or less by hand in Grantham by Inflatable World Leisure, a company which lays claim to have invented the bouncy castle. The inflatable stones were all individually painted. English Heritage organises early-morning trips for small groups to see inside the real stones and so we went incognito to work out what colour they are, in preparation for making the inflatable. It didn't occur to us that the colour of the stones changes according to the light, so our version of Stonehenge was based on a drizzly grey February morning.

← Merlin the Druid leading a ritual at Stonehenge to give thanks for it being in public ownership, 2018.

It was first inflated in Glasgow in 2012, before being absorbed into the Olympic cultural celebrations. It toured round the UK, and later went abroad where it was hammered by typhoons in Hong Kong and a heatwave in Australia. I liked the idea of Stonehenge touring – turning up in your local park unannounced and then disappearing after a day, becoming a part of folk memory. The Olympic movement can be so pompous, taking itself so seriously with all these weird rituals and hierarchies, a bit like a religion. A country or institution that can't laugh at itself is in trouble, and *Sacrilege* was my attempt to help with this situation. It allowed you to bounce about and fall over a founding myth. I was really hoping to get children into archaeology by making this: there is no way of retaining your dignity when you are leaping around on it.

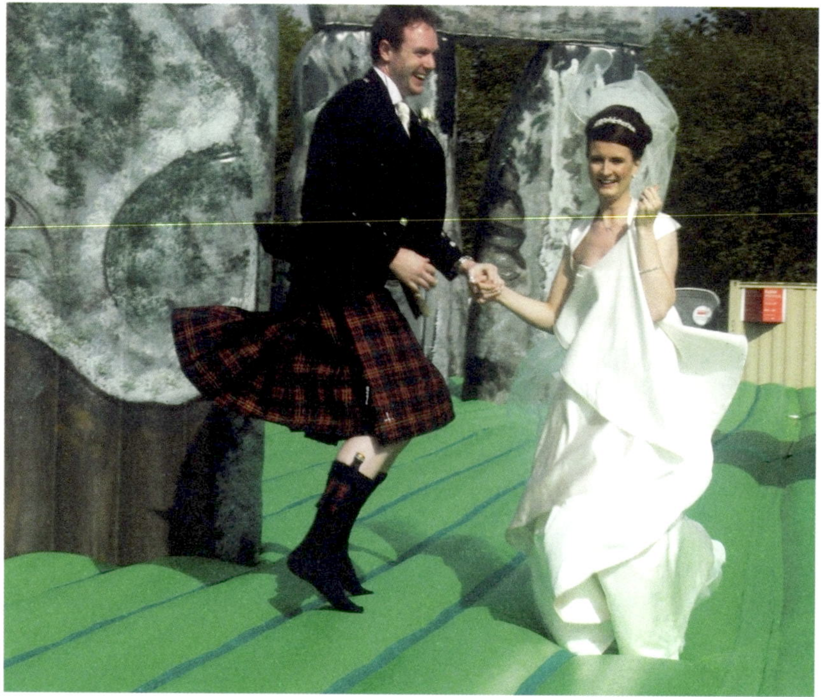

A post-ritual photo op on a copy of a ritualistic site, Glasgow.

A lot of archaeologists appreciate the more unconventional groups who are drawn to the stones. In 2018, I was asked to help orchestrate a weekend of events at Stonehenge to celebrate the 100th anniversary of it being in public ownership. *Sacrilege* was set up for the occasion, near the visitor centre – if it had been next to the stones, I think there would have been a pile-up on the A303. A small group of druids conducted a ceremony of thanks. I wasn't expecting to be so

A young visitor to *Sacrilege* in Wales ignores all health and safety protocols. →

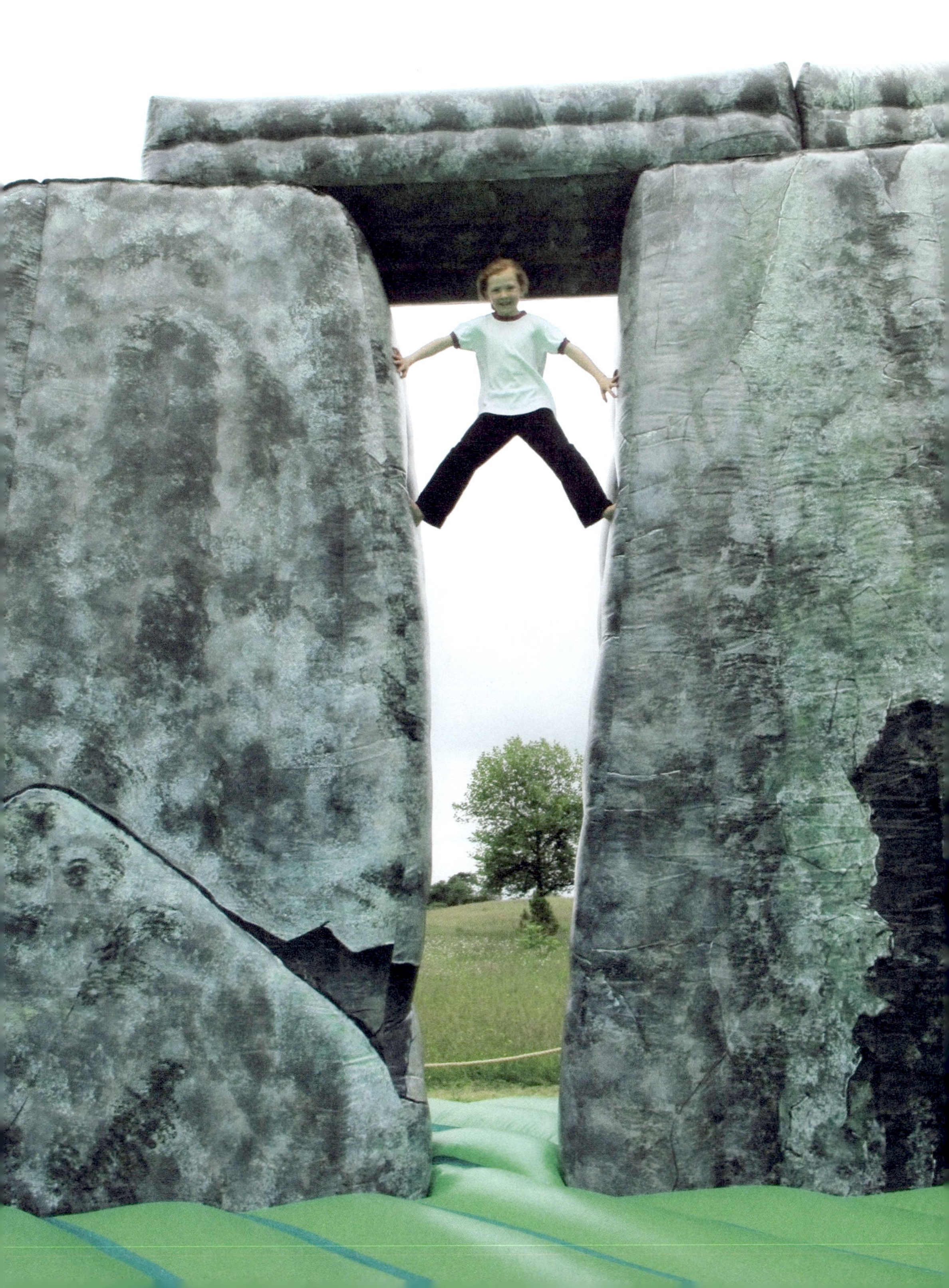

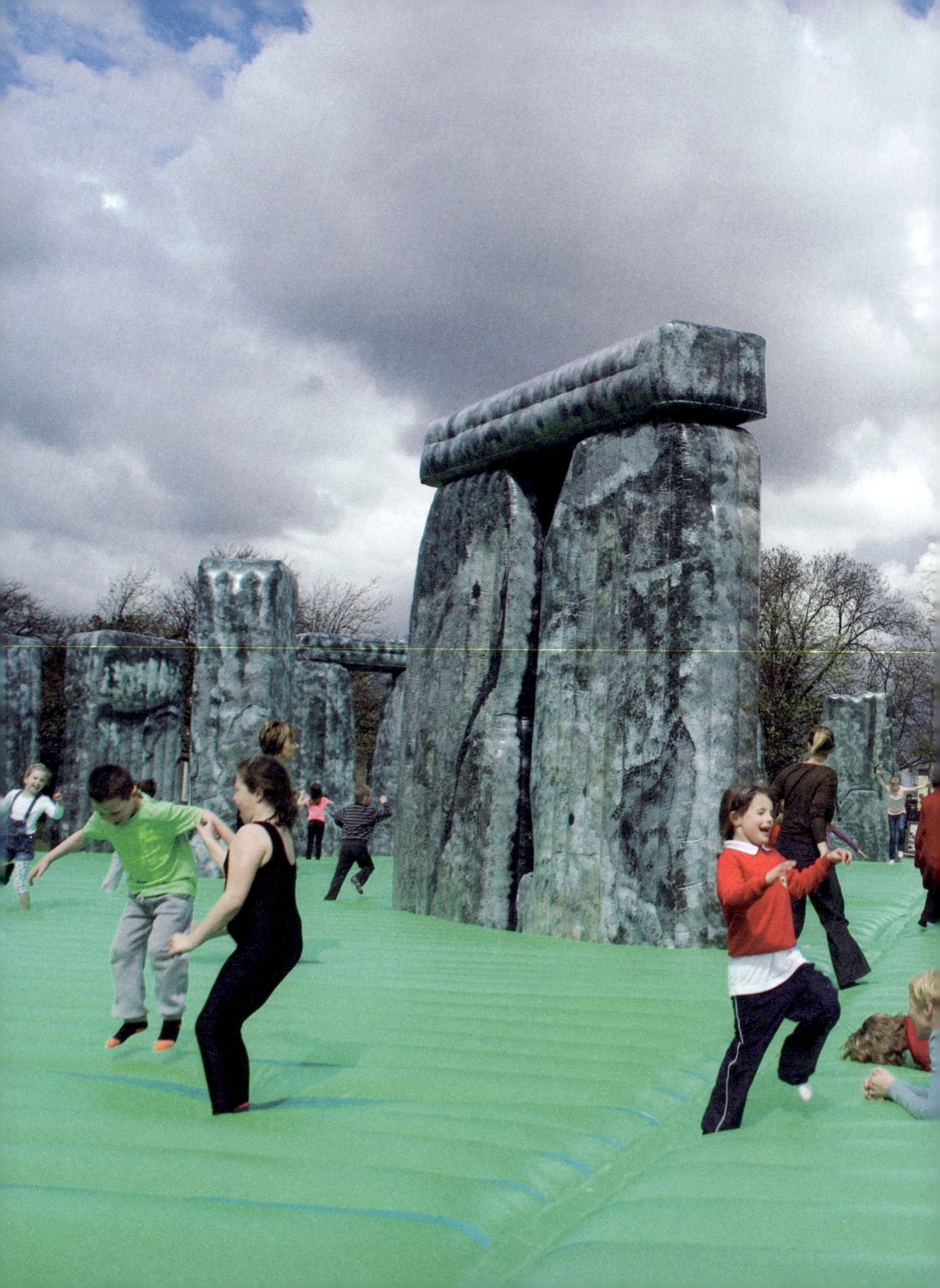

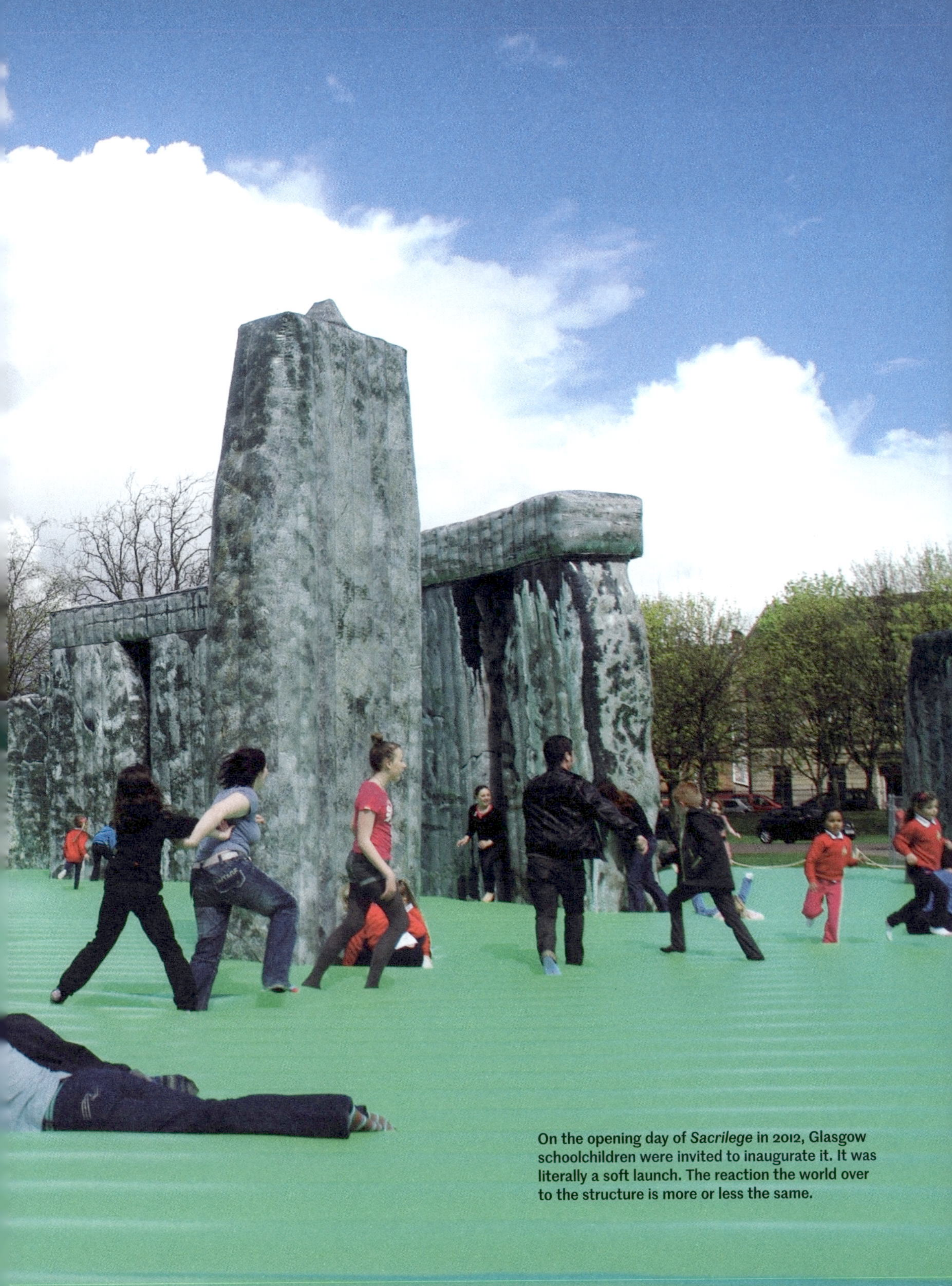

On the opening day of *Sacrilege* in 2012, Glasgow schoolchildren were invited to inaugurate it. It was literally a soft launch. The reaction the world over to the structure is more or less the same.

moved by their ritual, but it felt sincere, not theatrical in any way. After all, what the druids believe is no more made up than the beliefs of any other religion.

Personally, I'm more into smaller stone circles that have less infrastructure around them. As with ruined monasteries, they are often best experienced in bad weather. Having said that, a few years ago, I was at the Rollright Stones in Oxfordshire and, as the sun was setting, members of the local astronomical society set up their equipment to look at the stars. Soon I was looking at the rings of Saturn through a telescope in a place where maybe similar cosmic ceremonies had been held thousands of years before.

A New Dawn, an archaeologically inaccurate depiction of a smiley summer solstice, 2020.

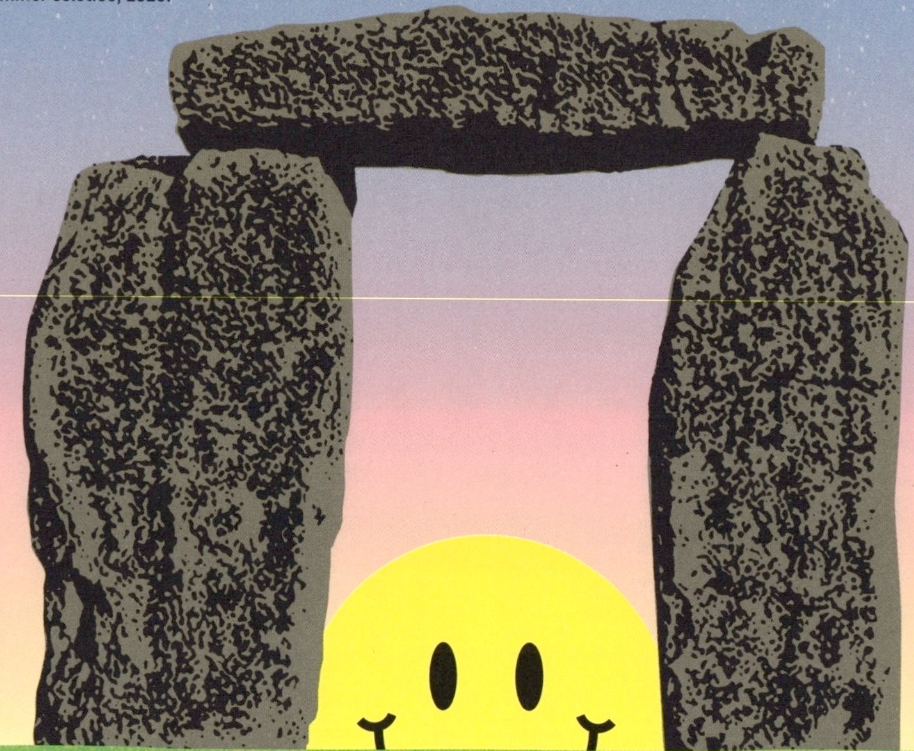

Stills from *Wiltshire Before Christ*, 2019. A mood piece about time travel. Martina is the protagonist. Filmed at Stonehenge, where the metal chariots rest. The Stonehenge site is surrounded by military land – an attack helicopter kept flying over the site when I was there one afternoon. →

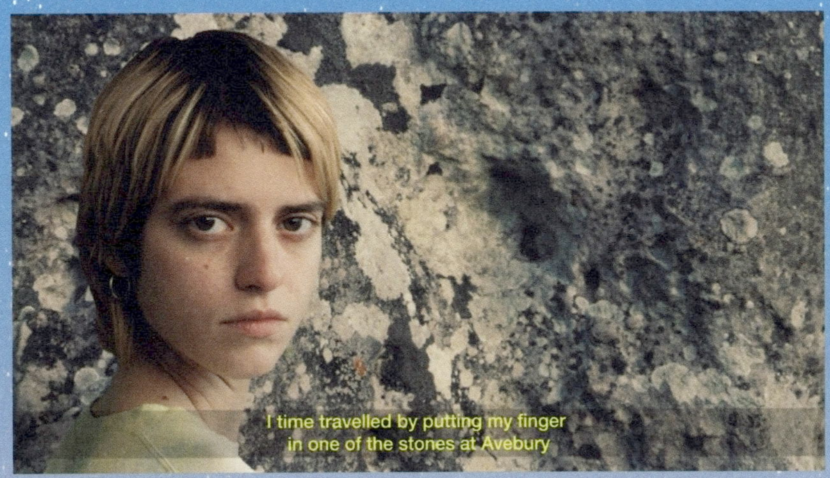
I time travelled by putting my finger
in one of the stones at Avebury

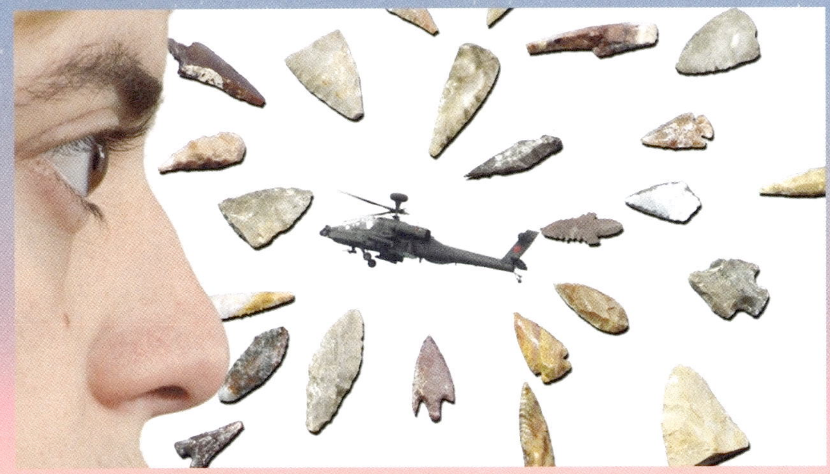

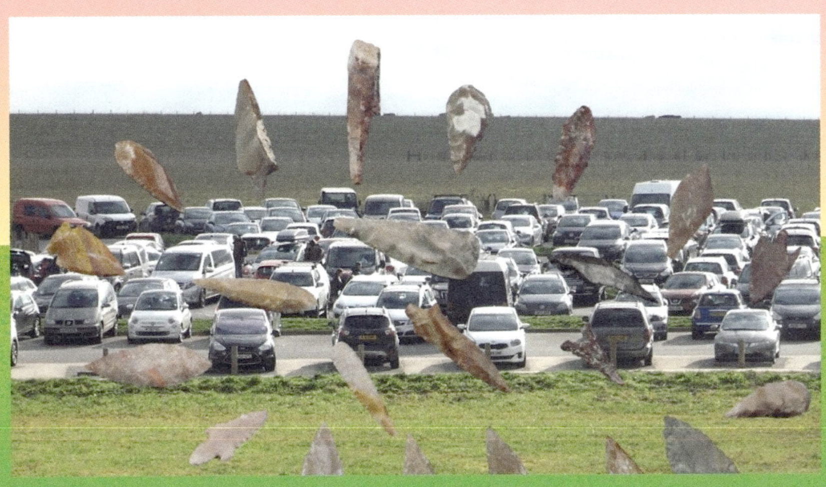

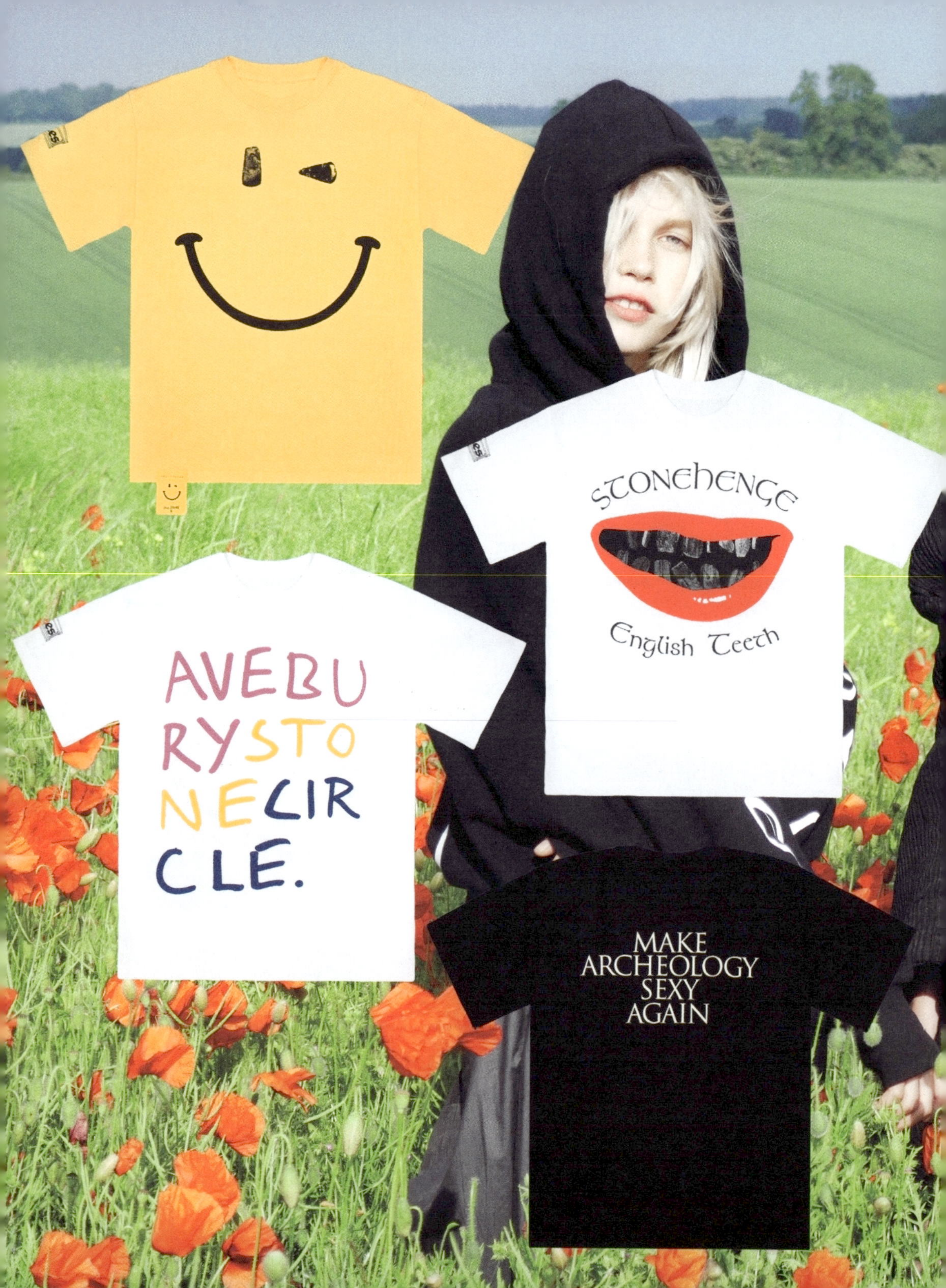
STONEHENGE
English Teeth
AVEBU
RYSTO
NECIR
CLE.
MAKE
ARCHEOLOGY
SEXY
AGAIN

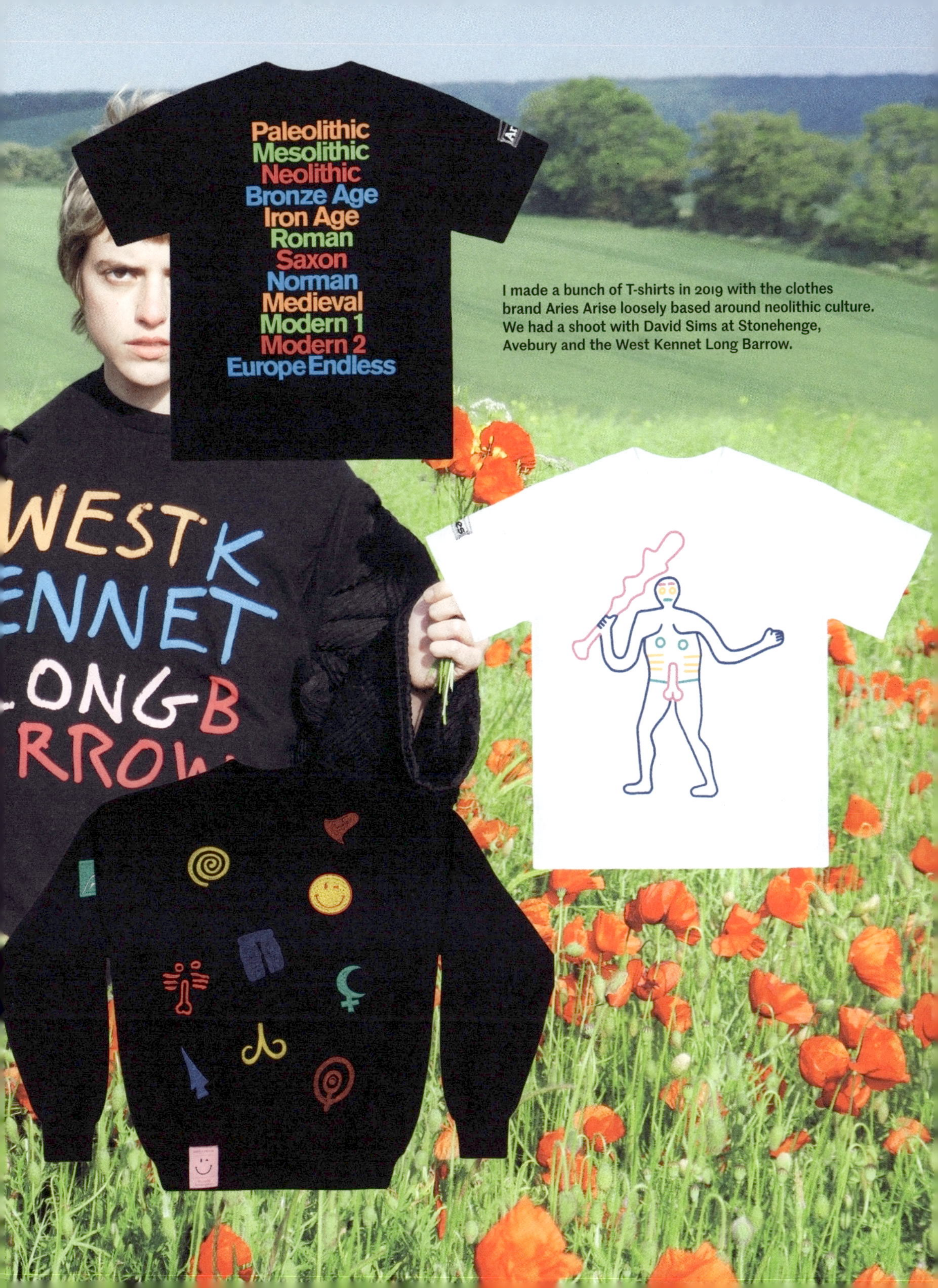

I made a bunch of T-shirts in 2019 with the clothes brand Aries Arise loosely based around neolithic culture. We had a shoot with David Sims at Stonehenge, Avebury and the West Kennet Long Barrow.

The Sealed Knot of Great Britain is proud to present

The English Civil War (part II)

Re-enacting the bloody battle of

Orgreave

This Bank Holiday Monday at Sherrif Hutton Yorks

Commencing at 1.00pm Sharp
and featuring a cast of
Thousands.

WITH THE KINGS MOUNTED TROOPS

versus

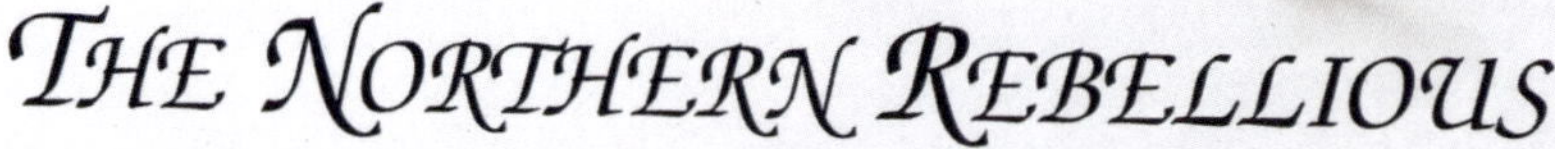

BAREBACKS.

Admission. Adults.£6.00.
Children. £.4.00
Family Ticket.£15.00.

Supported by English Heritage and the Yorkshire Tourist Board
Bringing History to Life

Chapter 3

My 'Stairway to Heaven'

The Battle of Orgreave

What are the limits of performance art? As a genre, it seems to be the most obscure to a general art audience. But what if the public can be performance artists or at least part of an artwork? This was part of the impulse to make *The Battle of Orgreave*, which is the work I always get asked questions about whenever I give a talk. It is, in fact, the one work that may outlive me.

For someone who tries to avoid confrontation and large groups of males, I certainly make a lot of work with these elements. *The Battle of Orgreave* (2001) is the most extreme example. A thousand-person re-enactment of a confrontation between police and striking miners from the 1984–5 strike. On a sunny day in June 1984, police and picketing miners ended up in a pitched battle outside the coking plant at Orgreave, near Sheffield. I experienced the miners' strike of 1984–5 through television news reports while I was at school in London. The footage from that day looked more like a medieval battle than a labour dispute, as mounted police pursued miners up a hill and down a steep railway cutting.

In 1994, I made a poster about a re-enactment of the battle. It was a semi-serious idea at that point – an attempt to see if there was a way to look at the strike and that confrontation as part of the canon of battles on British soil. I thought the form of a battle re-enactment might just be an effective way to do this as we in the UK are so used to this type of historical display. There was an absurdity built into the idea, not least because it taps into the national obsession with history and conflict to the point where, based on the way we talk about it, you'd think the Second World War had finished only last week. The event was commissioned by Artangel, formerly responsible for such projects as Rachel Whiteread's *House* and Michael Landy's *Break Down*. There was an open call for artists to send in ideas for public artworks: I proposed this idea and remember thinking that they would be mad to go with it. They called my bluff by accepting it.

The research process took about two years and consisted of travelling up to the area and talking to people who had been involved in the strike. We recruited

← This poster from 1995 was the germ of the idea for *The Battle of Orgreave*. I was thinking about the heritage industry: how it might mutate and possibly evolve. It was also meant to be absurd and confusing. I really wanted to do it but would have to wait six years to get the chance.

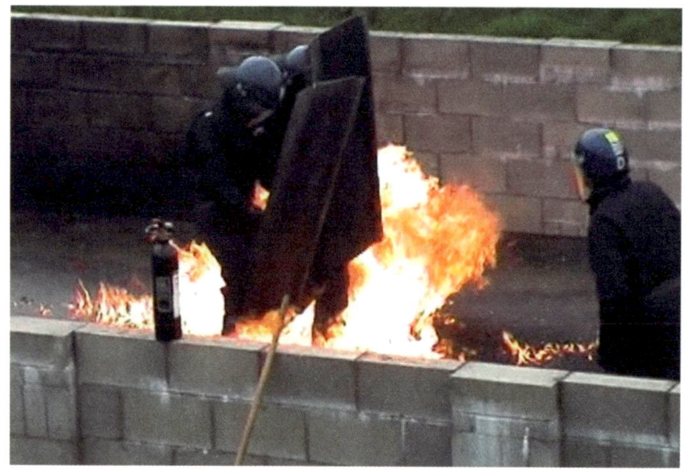

Molotov cocktail time!
Police riot training in Cheshire, 2001.

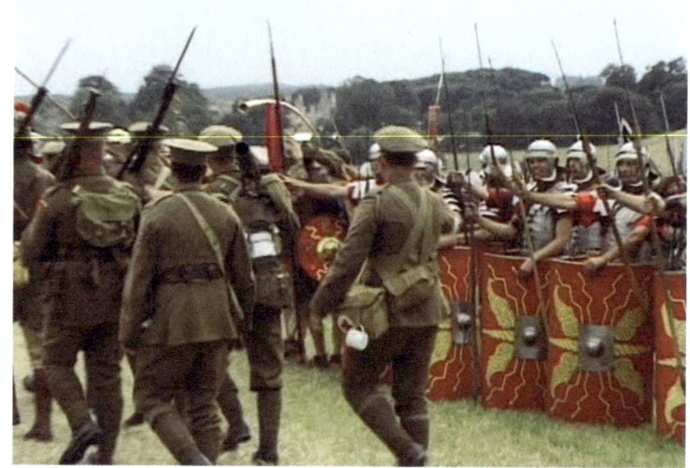

'History in Action', Kirby Hall, Northamptonshire, 2000. The climax of the weekend event was history repeating on itself and then beating itself up.

former miners from towns and villages within a thirty-mile radius of Orgreave: Barnsley, Doncaster, Sheffield, Rotherham. These meetings started off being low-key, often one-to-one in a pub or in somebody's home. The scale of these conversations gradually increased, until just before the event itself when I was meeting with fifty or more former miners at a time.

Many of the ex-miners had not seen each other during the years since the strike, so when they met up it developed into something of a reunion. I made it clear where I stood politically but they also understood the complexity of the re-enactment, in which they were being paid to recreate a day in their lives which came to represent the end of an industry that many had been born into.

Orgreave was a very public defeat, if not a humiliation, for the miners; a rout widely reported in the newspapers and TV news of the day. The strike changed from that point on, with miners avoiding large set-piece pickets and the police emboldened by this and, in a show of strength from the state, occupying whole villages.

With its sometimes uneasy mixture of war and amateur dramatics, historical re-enactment interested me. As part of my research, I went to 'History in Action', a large multi-period re-enactment event. At the end of the weekend, the different societies perform a snaking march-past saluting each other in a bizarre celebration of the history of warfare. Then all the societies convene in a field and fight each other, in a total collapse of time. It gave me an insight into their approach to history. Vikings on top of Second World War tanks attacking English Civil War Cavaliers, who in turn are attacked by a band of marauding Celts. Two thousand years of history fighting itself.

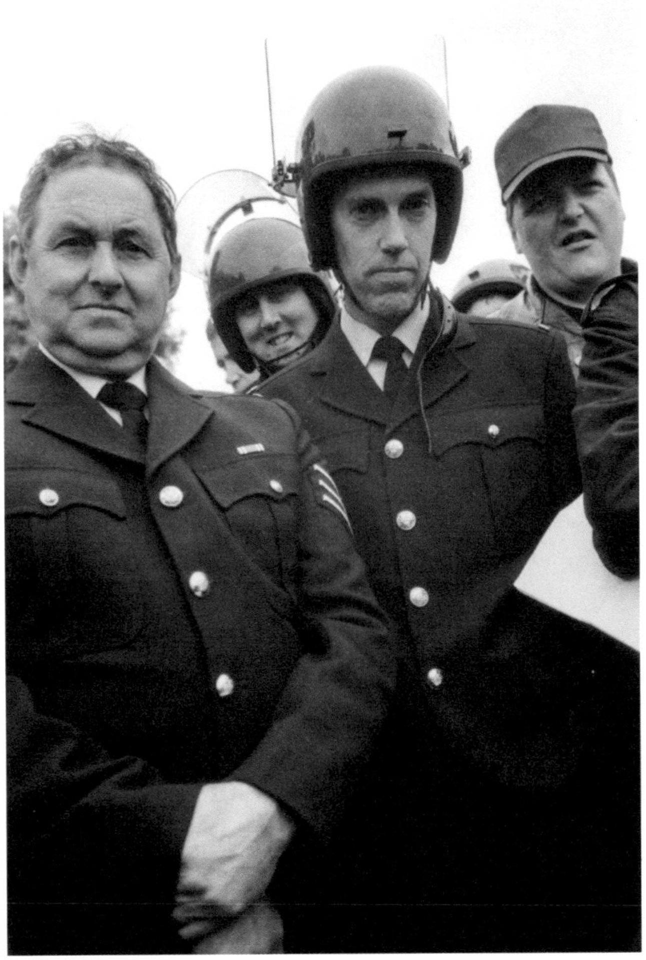

A group of re-enactors before the battle. The crash helmets denote them as members of a snatch squad – a concept derived from a more aggressive crowd-control technique known as 'colonial policing' and used by the British army and police in Northern Ireland, Cyprus, Africa, etc.

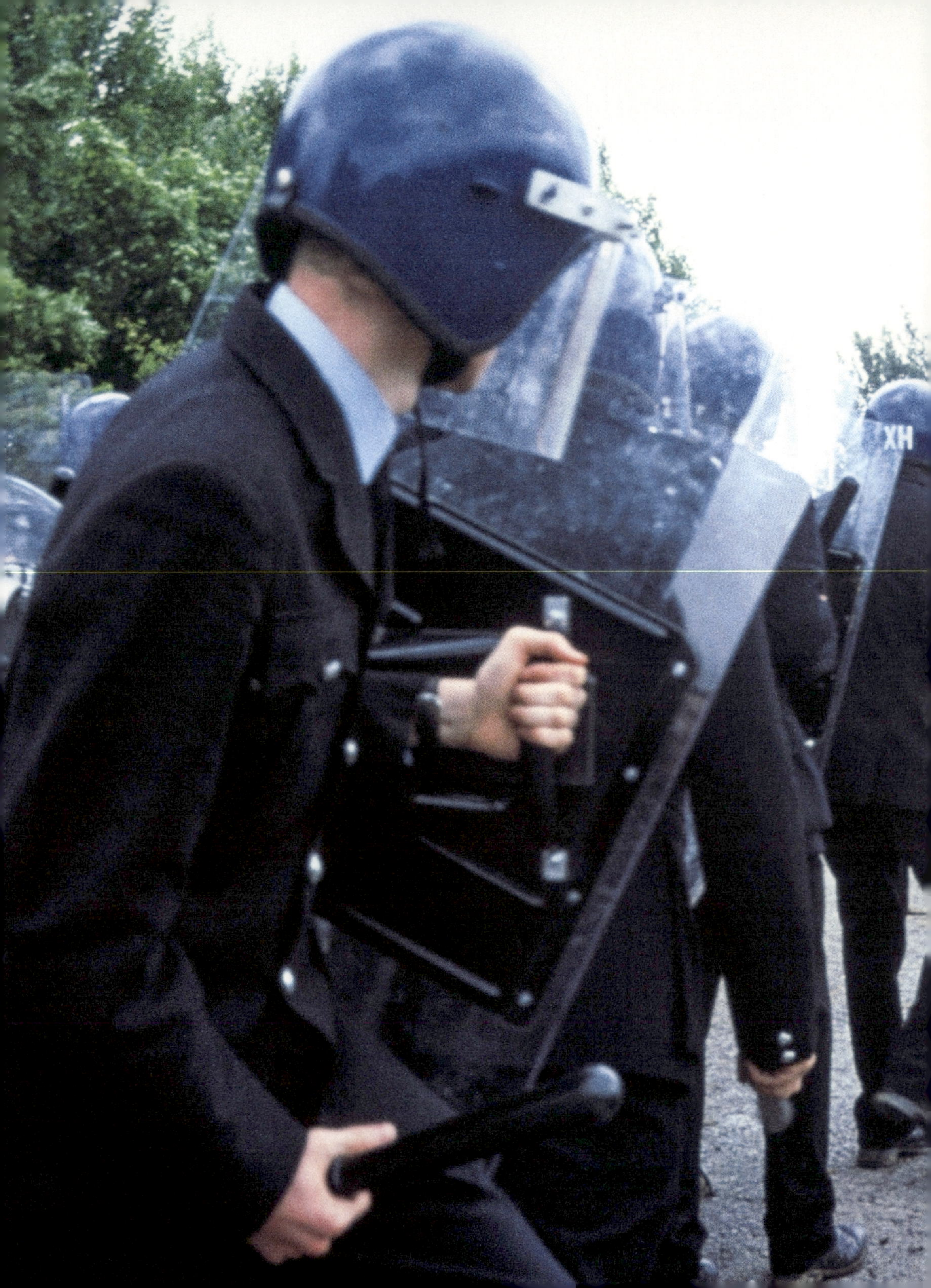
XH

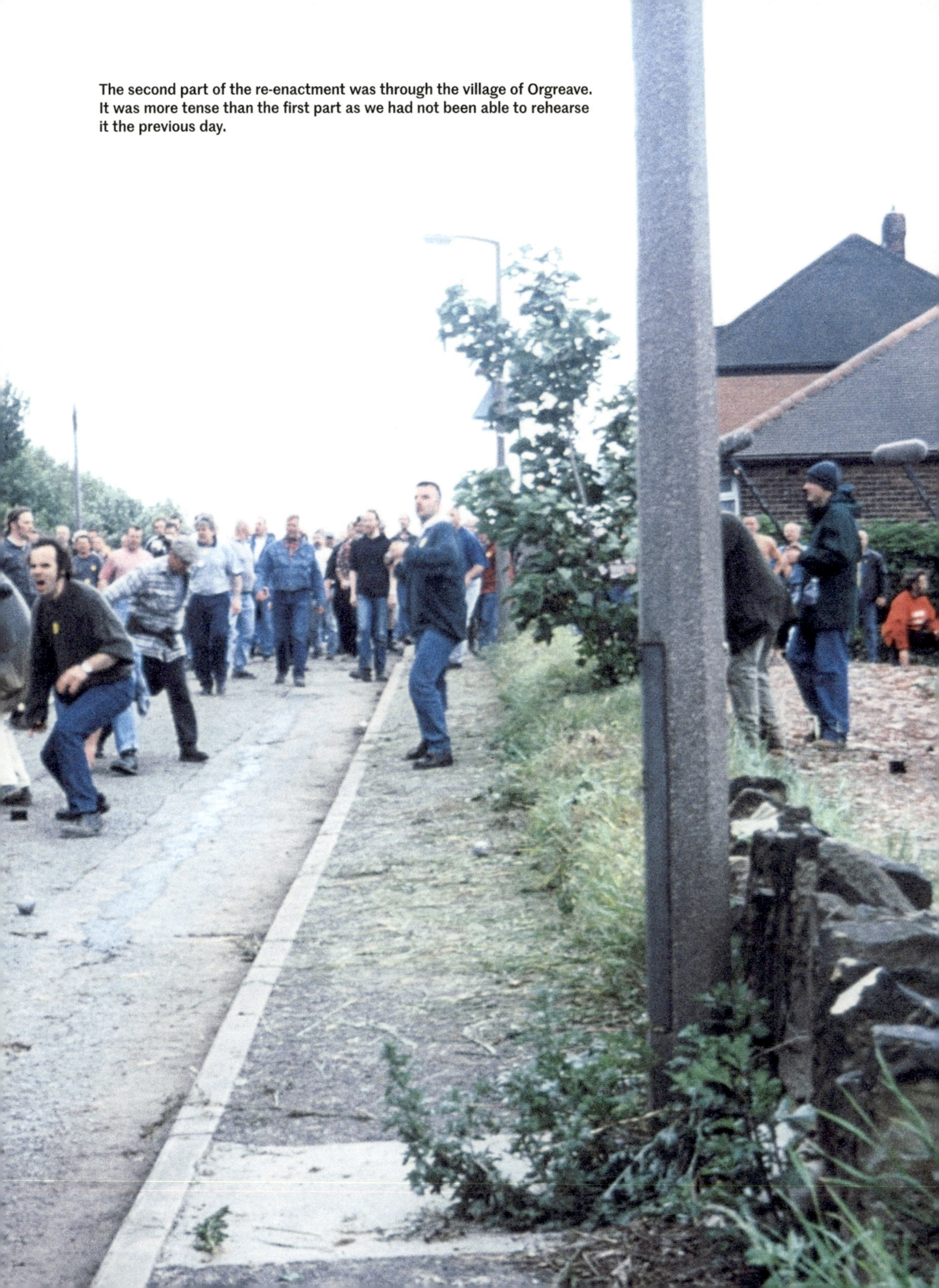

The second part of the re-enactment was through the village of Orgreave. It was more tense than the first part as we had not been able to rehearse it the previous day.

I suspected that re-enactment attracted overwhelmingly male participants, drawn to authority (i.e., both giving and taking orders), with an interest in uniforms, militaria, violence and, of course, guns. A potentially quite conservative group, with, as it turned out, some former and serving police officers in their ranks. Often re-enactments have commentators to explain the tactics and material culture of a battle. Rarely, however, is the political background to conflicts considered.

As an unscientific experiment, I brought a selection of Sunday newspapers for participants to read in the catering tent. There was a clear divide between the papers the ex-miners chose to read and the papers the re-enactors chose to read. A key figure in bringing the project to life was Howard Giles. Howard had close ties to re-enactment societies in his former role at English Heritage and worked as our recruiter. The net was cast wide, and in the credits for the film there was an incredible list of all the societies who had supplied re-enactors. Howard stressed to the participants that it was a non-political event – which it wasn't, of course, in my mind, although I suppose it depends on how you define those things. As preparation for the event, we went to a police training centre in Cheshire, where a former driving test compound was used to work through riot strategy – arresting people from within mobs, dealing with Molotov cocktails and suchlike. We hired some staff from this centre to help train those taking part on the day; I remember being slightly surprised we were able to work with them as freelancers.

The re-enactors loved being around the serving policemen. They were also fascinated by the practices of the riot police, whose techniques were probably familiar from ancient history – most notably, the continued use of shield formations and horses to break up crowds. On the rehearsal day, we ran out of time, the weather was terrible, and I nearly got trampled on by the re-enactor police horses.

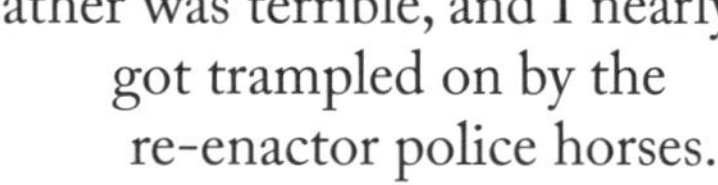

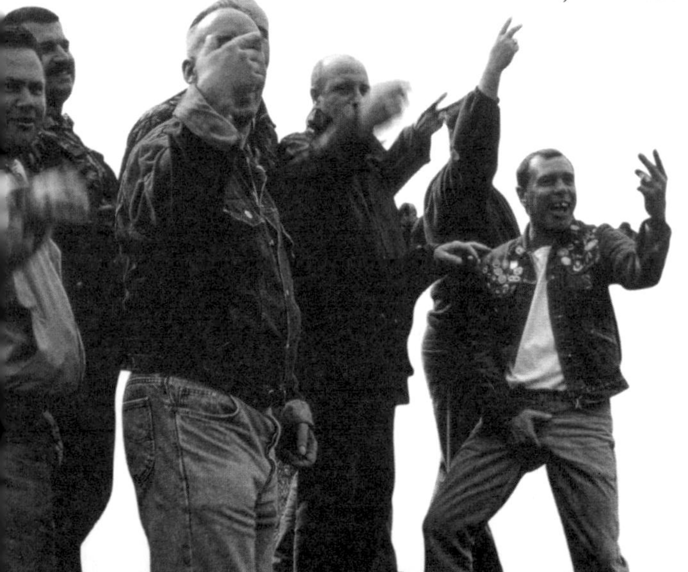

A group of ex-miners taunting the (at that point) mainly re-enactor police. In the end we had to mix re-enactors and former miners up after concerns from the re-enactment groups. The predictable realism the former miners brought to the work was a bit of a shock to many re-enactors.

The human re-enactors on the whole were wary of the ex-miners who were taking part, and a tension built up as some of them voiced concerns that the event could easily turn into a real riot. In the end this did not happen, but the re-enactors were quite taken aback by the intensity the former miners brought to their roles – not that surprising, really. When the former miners realised that the re-enactors were unnerved by them, they played up to it, adding to the overall drama. They were playing versions of their younger selves on the actual site of the riot, and this odd piece of time-travelling inevitably heightened emotions. For the re-enactment societies, this was their first and probably last experience of recreating a battle alongside the actual veterans of a conflict, many of whom were of similar ages but coming at the event from a totally different perspective.

The re-enactment was a public event, which was important for me as a form of public inquiry or, more viscerally, an autopsy of an exhumed corpse. Or even possibly as a re-enactment of a crime in its original setting. Whatever it was, it was always, in my mind at least, performance art. It was never meant to heal community wounds – however much art is heralded as being capable of achieving this. If anything, it was intended to make people angry again. It wasn't even an accurate re-enactment of the confrontation, but I guess this is almost impossible. I just thought something should happen there at that place as a memorial of sorts. In a sense, it was a very personal work despite having over a thousand people involved. It was directly related to my memories of seeing this confrontation on the news as an 18-year-old.

It was a costly project and much of the funding came from Channel 4, for whom we would film the event. The budget of £500,000 made it a very expensive hour of television, but half that amount went to paying the large number of participants. Ideally, we would have had ten times as many participants to recreate the numbers of the day but that wasn't financially feasible.

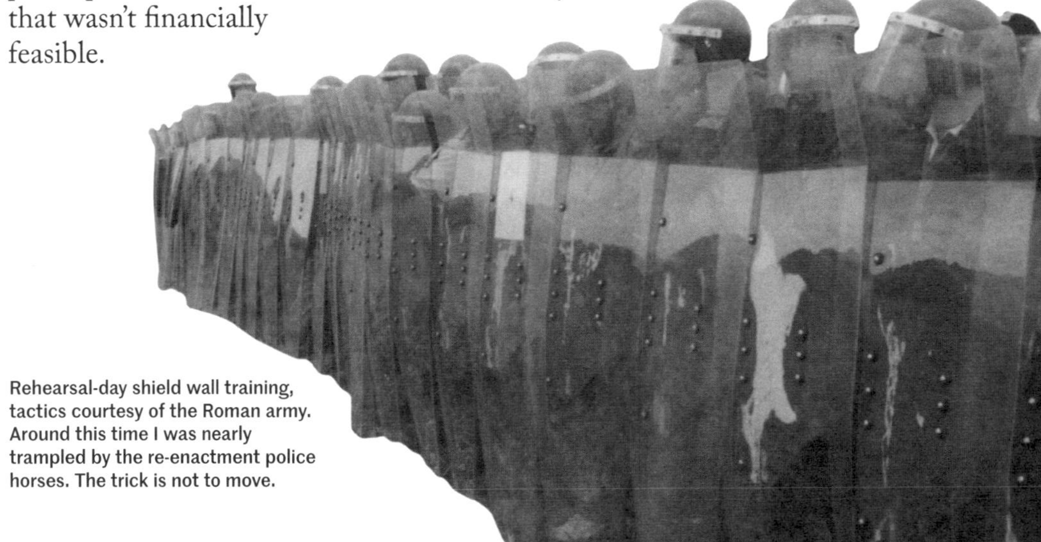

Rehearsal-day shield wall training, tactics courtesy of the Roman army. Around this time I was nearly trampled by the re-enactment police horses. The trick is not to move.

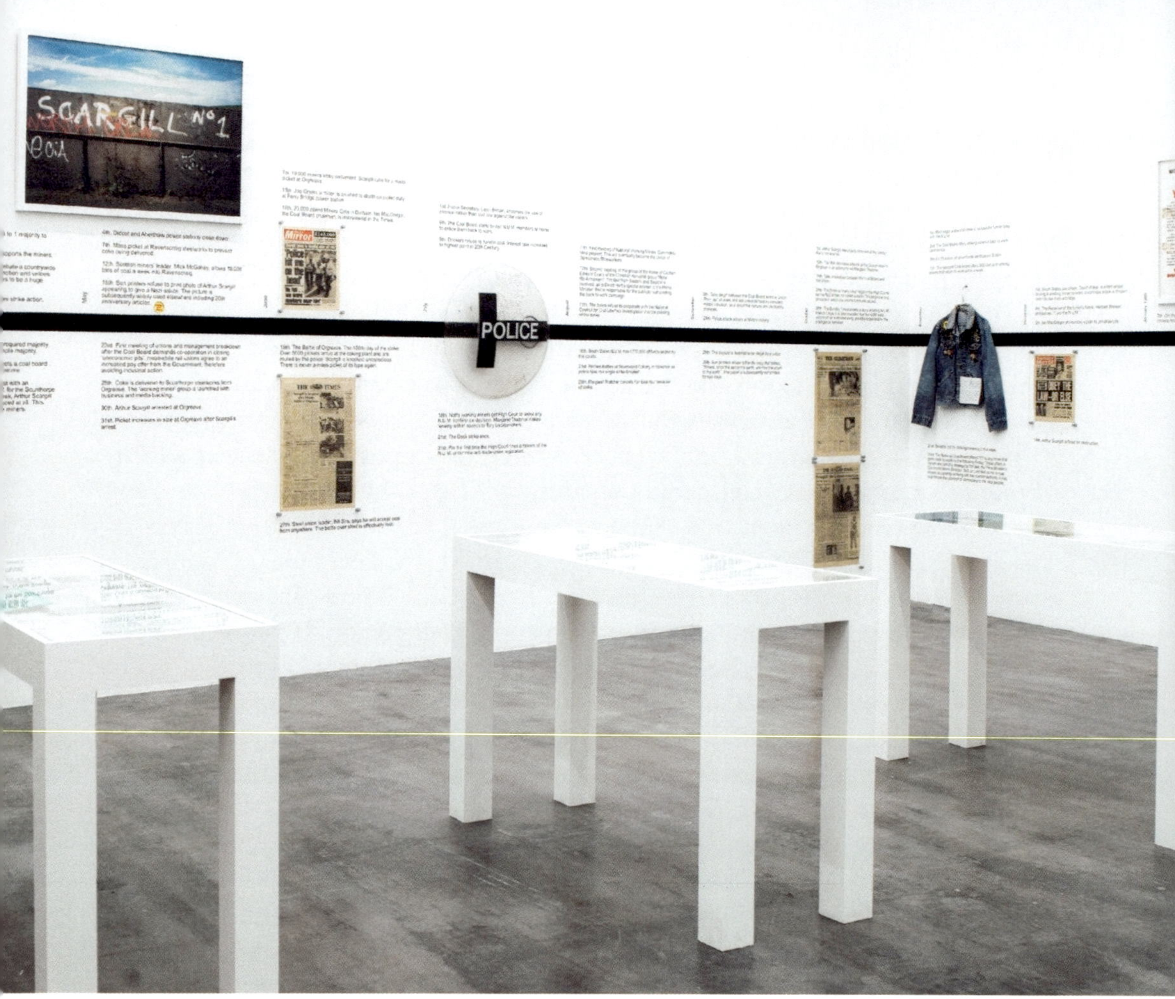

I made a study room about the strike and the re-enactment. It's shown with the film sometimes and can serve as an introduction to the conflict.

It was good that there was a film – both as a record and to ease through red tape. You can get away with a lot more regarding the police and the council if you can say you are making a film. If we had said it was an art project, it would have got mired in questions and suspicion, but doors miraculously open when you say it is going to be on the telly. Film as a kind of Trojan horse for a piece of political performance art.

We had originally asked Peter Watkins, who had made a number of political films including the peerless *Culloden*, which was a great inspiration to me, to direct. He had become totally disillusioned by British TV so, alas, was adamant he could not return to it. Mike Figgis stepped in late in the day and was totally up for what was clearly going to be a rough-and-ready improvisational shoot.

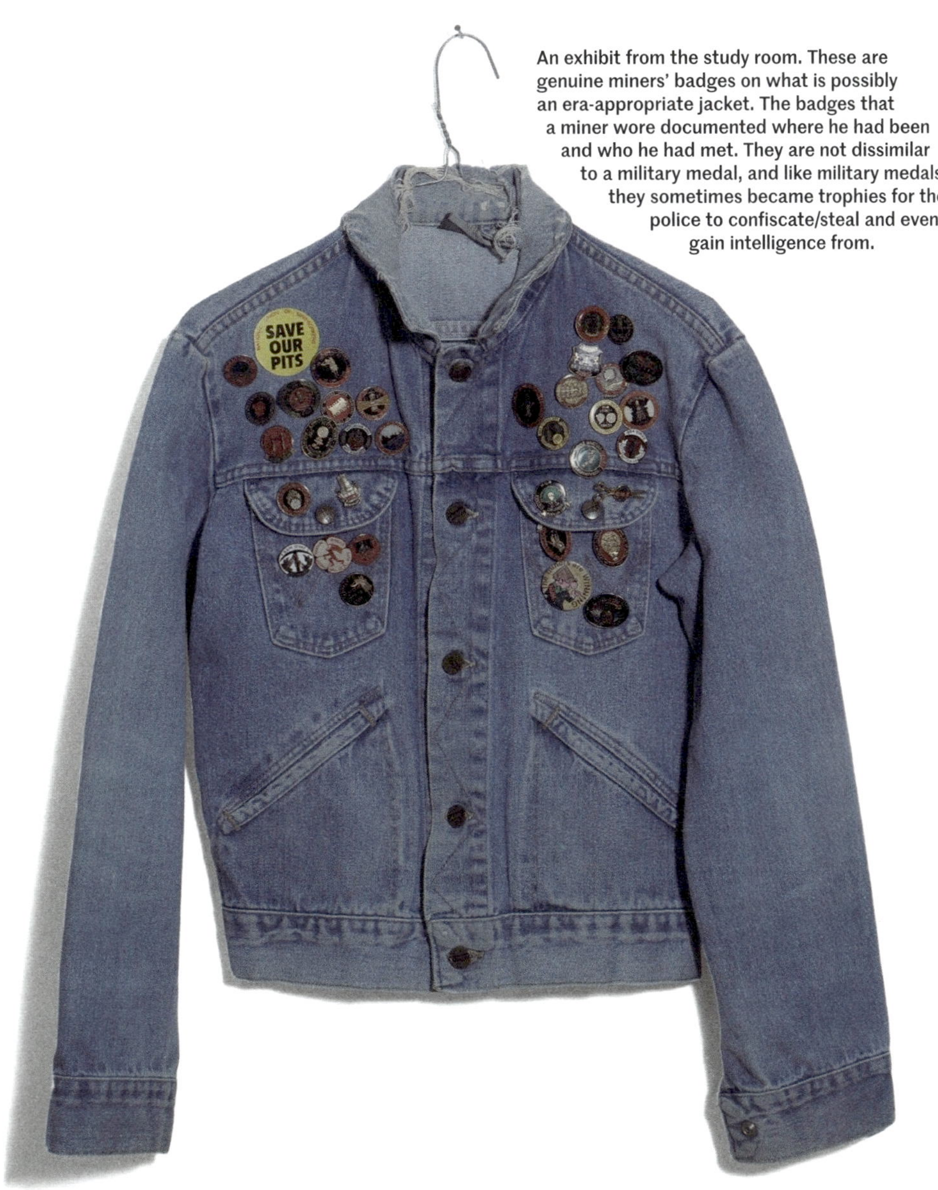

An exhibit from the study room. These are genuine miners' badges on what is possibly an era-appropriate jacket. The badges that a miner wore documented where he had been and who he had met. They are not dissimilar to a military medal, and like military medals, they sometimes became trophies for the police to confiscate/steal and even gain intelligence from.

Orgreave was out of step with most of what was going on at the time in an art world in the midst of a boom in the market and gushing media attention. *Orgreave* could not have been more different: it was unglamorous, taking place on a windy field near Sheffield where thousands of men had fought each other over a trade union dispute. Some people in London were horrified by the idea. This was not the response I received in Yorkshire.

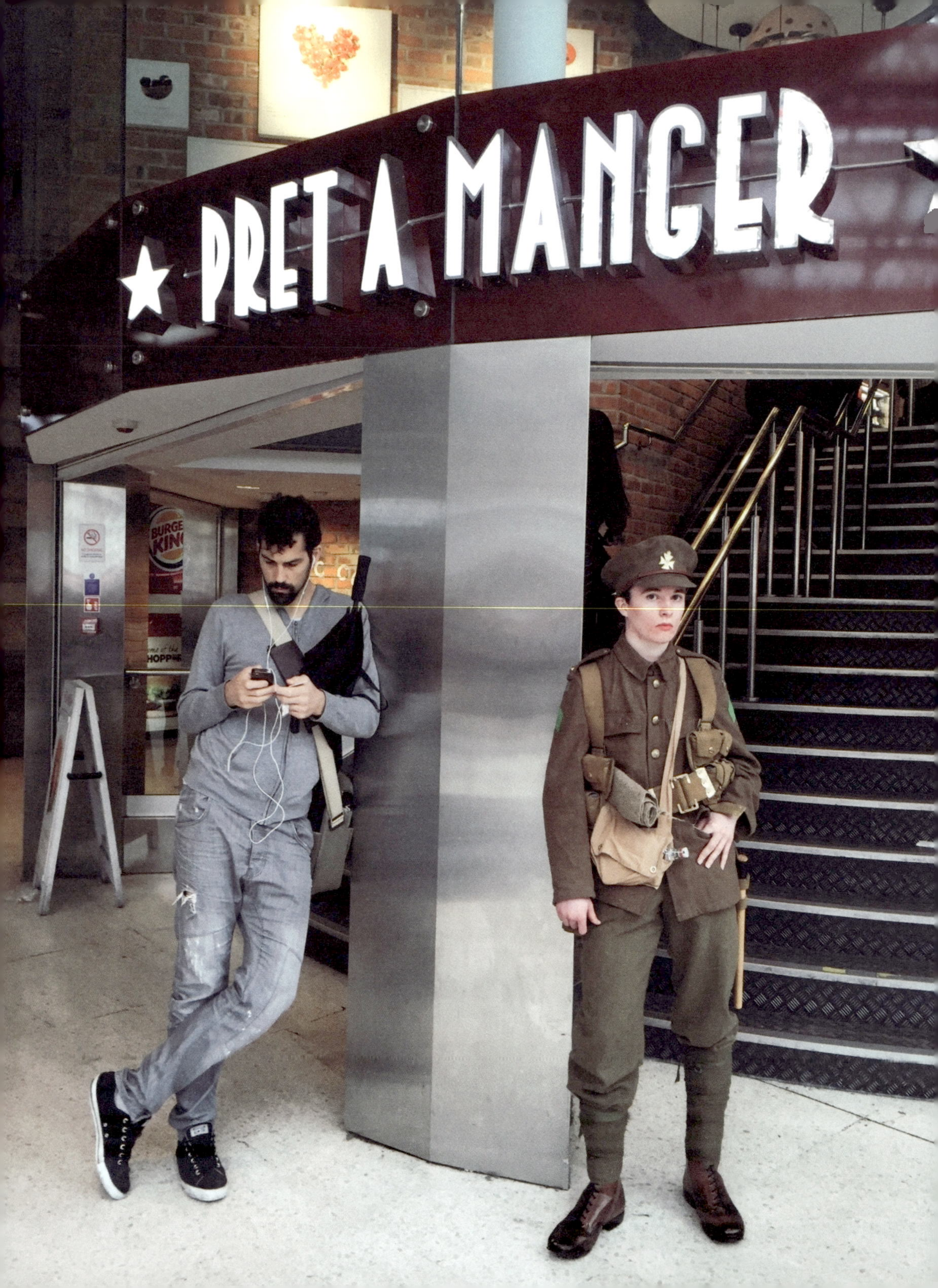
PRET A MANGER

Chapter 4

It's time to lose control

The public and public art

To some extent art is an experiment, where you introduce two elements together and then stand back and see what transpires, 'this plus this equals, what?'. Often, I look to the public to improve the work by taking it in directions that I was not expecting. In public, you can lose control of the work, as much of what takes place is simply out of your grasp – the public's response, their behaviour and, often, the weather. It is both a liberating and stressful experience. In these situations, I often enter a super-passive state and, as a result, feel disassociated from what is playing out.

***We're Here Because We're Here*, 2016**

On the first day of the Battle of the Somme, 1 July 1916, 19,000 British soldiers were killed – the worst day of losses in the history of the British army. I was approached by 14–18 NOW, the body which was commissioning work to mark the various anniversaries of the First World War, to think about how to commemorate what was essentially a human disaster.

The idea occurred to me as I asked myself, what would I like to see? Immediately, it was clear that living people had to be central to whatever it was as I didn't want a static memorial – piles of poppies, boots, guns, etc. The idea, then, was for participants to appear in groups around the country, in authentic First World War uniforms; they would 'hang out', moving through public places either on foot or by public transport. They would not act or talk. Instead, they would carry cards to hand to anyone who approached them or took their photograph, giving details of a specific soldier who died on 1 July 1916: their name, regiment and age. In essence, a printed gravestone.

I'd written notes to myself in a book as I was planning things, one of which was 'avoid sentimentality', which is almost impossible when dealing with groups of people in military uniform. Also, the public brings what they want to the work, another potential risk. The problem with the First World War is that

← 9 a.m., Waterloo. The project began at the busiest stations across the UK. For me, the juxtaposition with brand names was welcome and interesting. This participant has the ideal combination of being relaxed but also engaged with his surroundings.

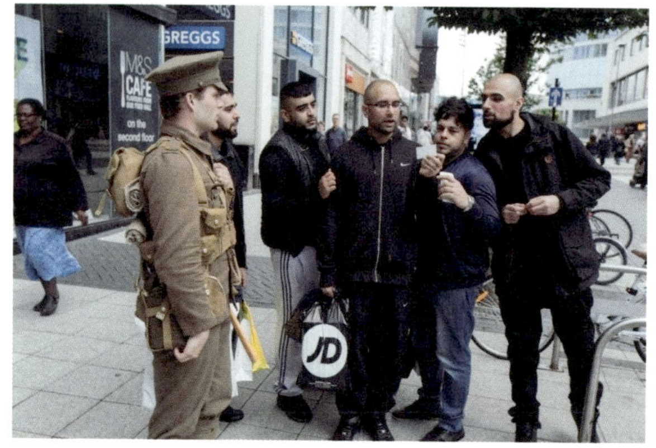

A participant gives out a card to a group of curious shoppers in Birmingham. The cards were geographically specific. In a sense, the information they gave was the equivalent of what you would read on a gravestone. A participant in Manchester gave one to a member of the public who happened to be a relative of the named soldier on it.

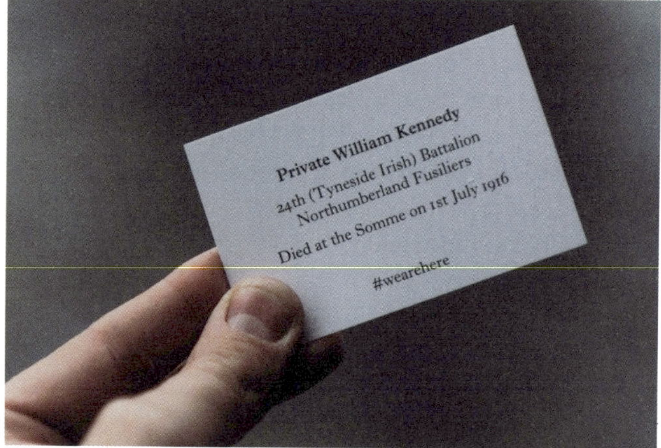

there is no one who can remember the war firsthand, so our human connection is broken and therefore easier to sentimentalise.

The final event stayed very close in spirit to the idea I had on my bike that day, and, in a sense, the intervening two years were concerned with keeping the idea intact. Jenny Waldman, who had worked on the London Olympics, coordinated the project and suggested we collaborate with the National Theatre. We met with the director Rufus Norris, who made a key suggestion at the start that the participants should not say anything at all. Speaking roles would not have worked with what we were trying to do, partly because all the participants would have needed to know the back story of their character, and also because it would have taken away much of the mystery of the encounter with an unsuspecting public. It wasn't role-playing, acting or re-enactment; although what it was was hard to define. As with *Orgreave*, we never debated whether it was theatre or art, only that it was definitely something that required the organisational skills of theatre.

It was interesting working with theatre people, as they seem to be more can-do and collaborative than artists. They are not afraid of the public and thrive when working with groups of people who tend to be slightly morose loners, speaking for myself, of course. We used a network of theatres around the country to recruit participants, our own version of army recruitment. Those who came forward didn't know what they were letting themselves in for, a little like the recruits in the First World War. Rehearsals consisted of role-playing and trust exercises, as participants got to know each other and work as units.

The team, which was often just me and Emily Lim from the National Theatre, went to every hub around the UK – from Plymouth to the Shetland Isles – and met the participants. We gave a pep talk of sorts to each group, explaining the idea and motivation for the work. The overwhelming positivity of theatre practitioners was something I was not expecting. Emily was a warm, nurturing presence, while I was the worried person at the back.

There were two big questions around the work as we were preparing. The first was what to do about pre-publicity. I didn't want any – so many experiences now are heavily trailed to the point where you are bored of something before it has even happened. Here, the work would come to the public unmediated, and their responses would not be pre-conditioned. The second was about Northern Ireland. In my opinion, it had to take place in Northern Ireland as soldiers from both the North and the Republic had fought and died at the Somme. The sight, however, of men in British uniform on the streets of Belfast and Derry was a sensitive issue. We decided to inform local politicians about the project before it began. As it was, there was a bit of swearing at the participants but little more than that.

I'm a bit of a pessimist about my work, so an inordinate amount of time was spent workshopping scenarios with a hostile public. Drunks, children, people with anti-military views and so on. As it was, we needn't have bothered. First thing in the morning, the soldiers appeared all over the country at transport hubs which would ensure that they were seen by potentially hundreds of thousands of people before 9 a.m., from where they dispersed to shopping centres, parks, town centres –

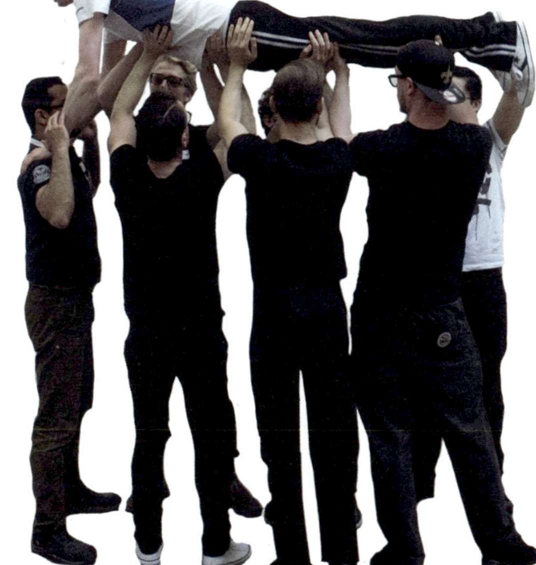

Trust exercise in rehearsals. Other activities included mass games of keepy-uppy.

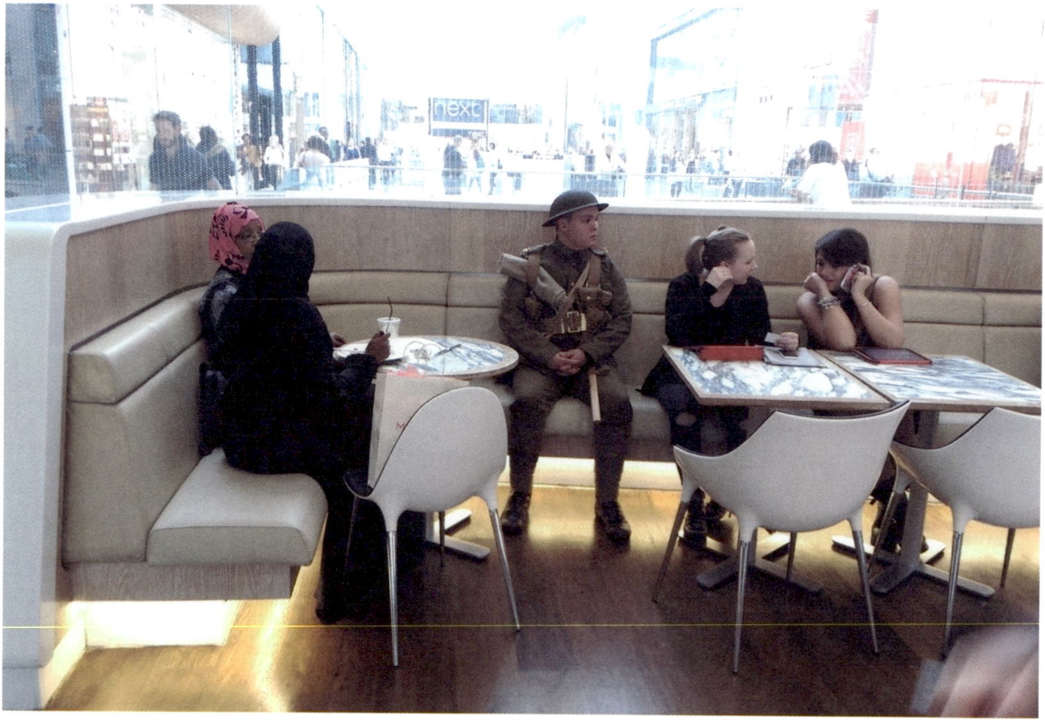

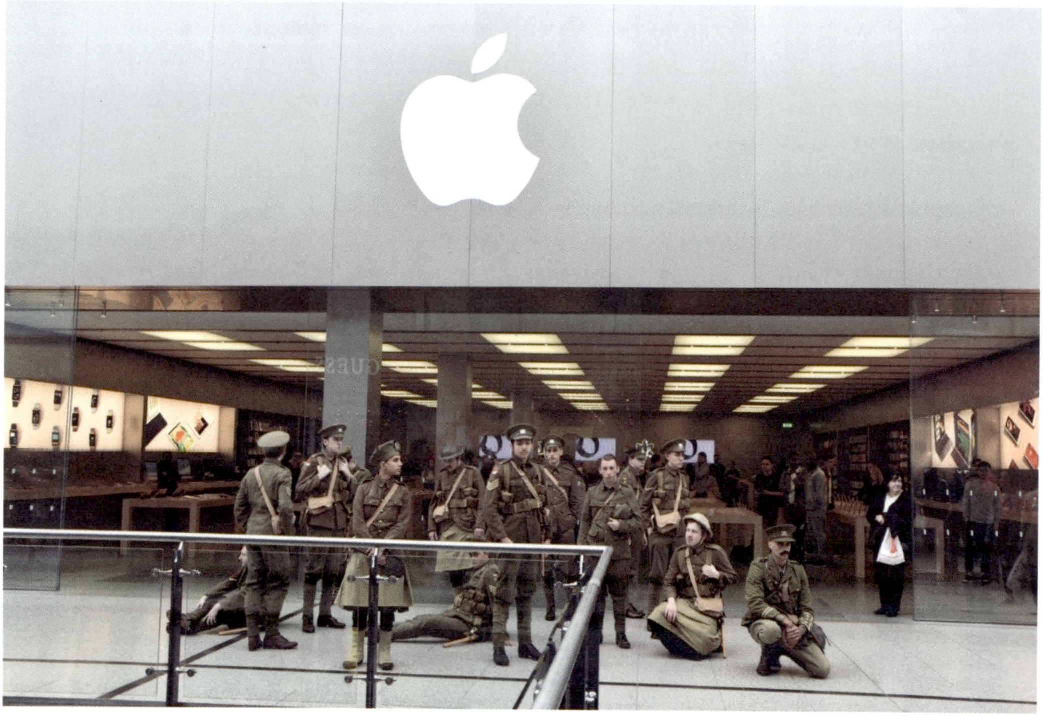

basically wherever the public would be. On the back of this there would be quite a bit of posting and sharing on social media by the public, effectively documenting the work for me. It was a viral artwork, simultaneously moving around the internet and the landscape of the UK. A work that came to you, whether you wanted it to or not, getting in the way of daily life in contemporary Britain, a country unrecognisable to that of 1916. It was the opposite of an inert war memorial which we the public have to make a conscious pilgrimage to.

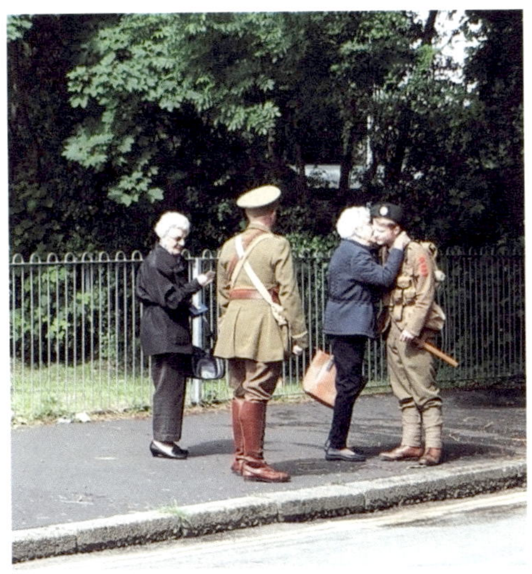

An unexpected interaction with the public. Bear in mind these women are old enough to have possibly lost a relative in the First World War. Their childhoods may have been filled with stories of fallen and injured family members.

I am sure many people saw the soldiers out of the corner of their eye and were not even certain of what they had seen. This way of experiencing the work was strangely relevant as during and after the war there was a phenomenon of members of the public claiming to have seen their dead loved ones fleetingly in the street. This public haunting or conjuring up of the dead led to a huge rise in attempts to contact the dead via mediums with all the attendant exploitation of grief that that entailed.

The unsuspecting public gave a broad range of responses to seeing the soldiers, with some crying, which we had not prepared the participants for. I suspect that the political turmoil in the UK around the time (it occurred a week after the Brexit vote) meant that the work became a way for people to express their unhappiness with what had been happening. In simple terms, it was a reminder of the sacrifice of individuals for their country a century ago.

← Shops and shopping centres were brilliant places for the participants to go to. That is where you find the public nowadays. Seeing these soldiers was meant to be visually jarring not least because they congregated in contemporary spaces. They weren't acting the role of the soldiers but were representing them; they were participants as opposed to actors. It was a subtle form of naturalistic, observational behaviour in which they were encouraged to make eye contact with the public.

We had, meanwhile, just been subjected to the spectacle of individuals willing to sacrifice their country for their political ambitions.

Apart from the stations, we didn't ask permission to go to most of the venues. I have discovered over the years that as soon as you ask people for permission for anything, you run the risk that they will refuse. We learnt our lesson having asked if we could walk through Canary Wharf and being denied. Not totally sure they would have been able to stop twenty participants dressed as soldiers. I also wanted to avoid any heritage sites such as churches, castles, war memorials, historic buildings and so on, as those seemed too obvious and comforting.

There was no hierarchy within the groups, despite the different ranks represented. As soon as people assume hierarchies, they can act as if they have power, which forms a narrative – something we wanted to avoid. I went with a group during the morning rush hour to Waterloo, the busiest station in London, and as soon as I saw the soldiers walking through the crowds of commuters, I thought that the project would work, as it simply looked so unusual. I then travelled to Milton Keynes with one of the groups but returned to Waterloo at the end of the day, when a number of other groups gathered together. This culminated with about 200 soldiers walking in circles, like a vortex, singing the circular refrain, 'We're here because we're here because we're here', an absurd nihilistic song the troops used to sing to the tune of 'Auld Lang Syne'.

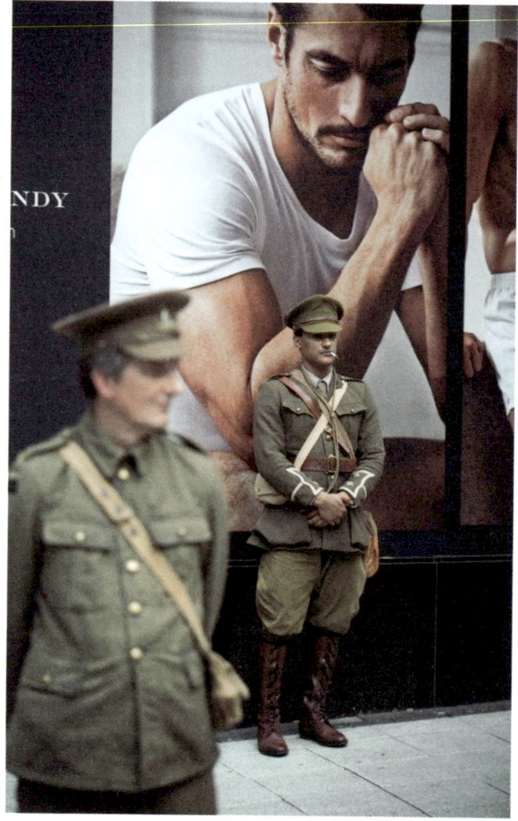

The Bullring shopping centre, Birmingham.

How is it possible
to create a
National event
art.
Intervention.

not expecting
or necessarily wanting.

1916

National Event
Dynamic figurative
Public High Vis [seen by millions]
if not Random.
Life of its own.
Living Sculpture.
Memorial
Avoid Sentimentality
unsettling
obstructive
Intervention in Daily
Life.
Corner of Eye.
or Stepping Over

These are notes for the pep talk I gave to participants when I travelled across the UK to meet every group preparing for the project. I was trying to give them an insight into my thought processes as some sort of motivation. After all, they were going to be doing this in public, not me.

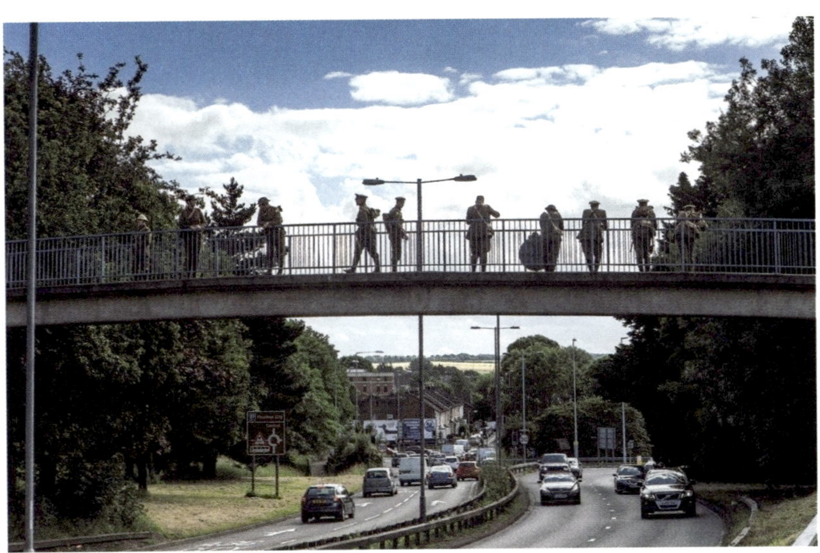

Churchill Way, Salisbury. The use of bridges and walkways was a means for the project to be seen by thousands of people.

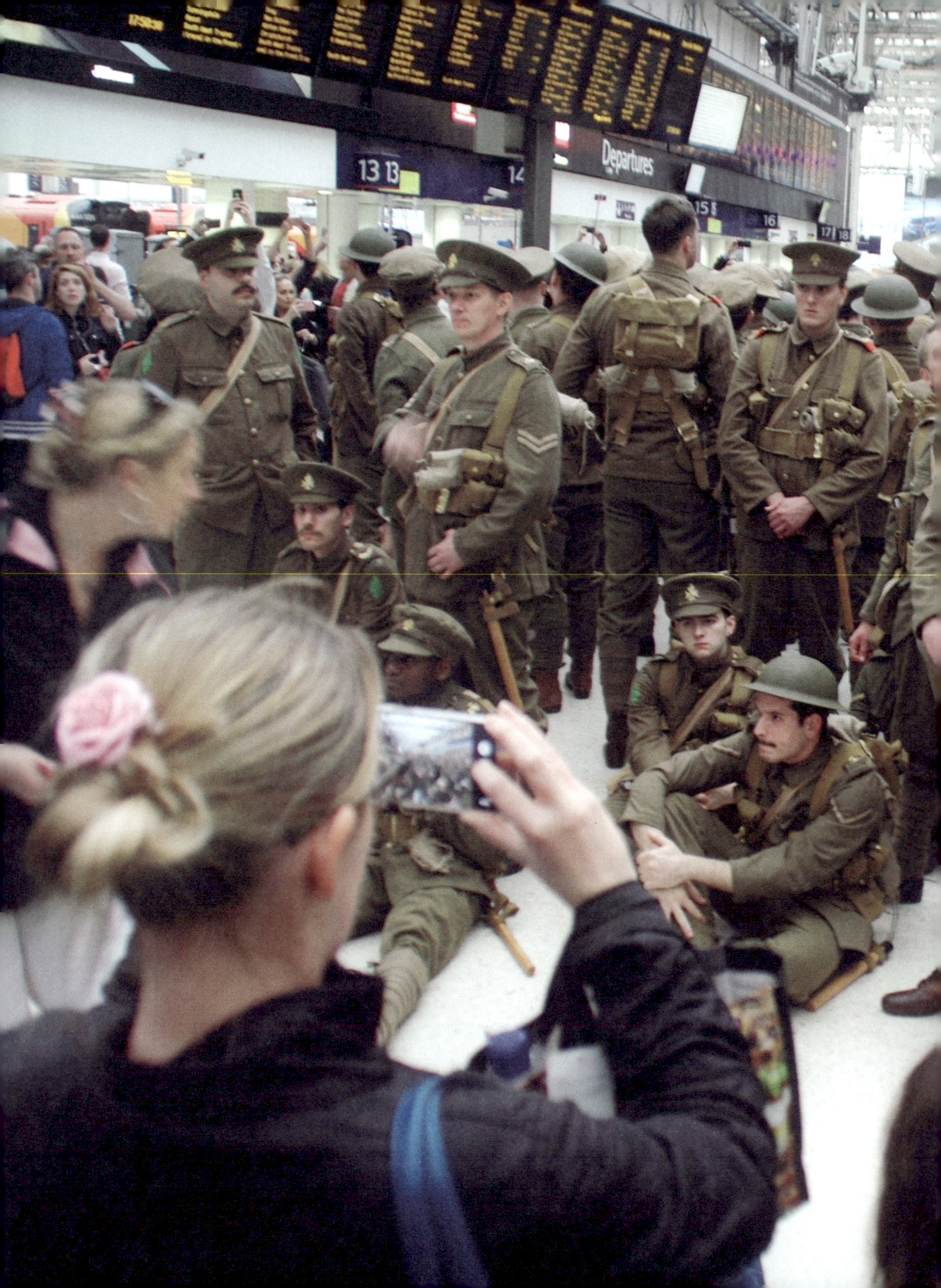
13 13
14
Departures
15
16
17 18

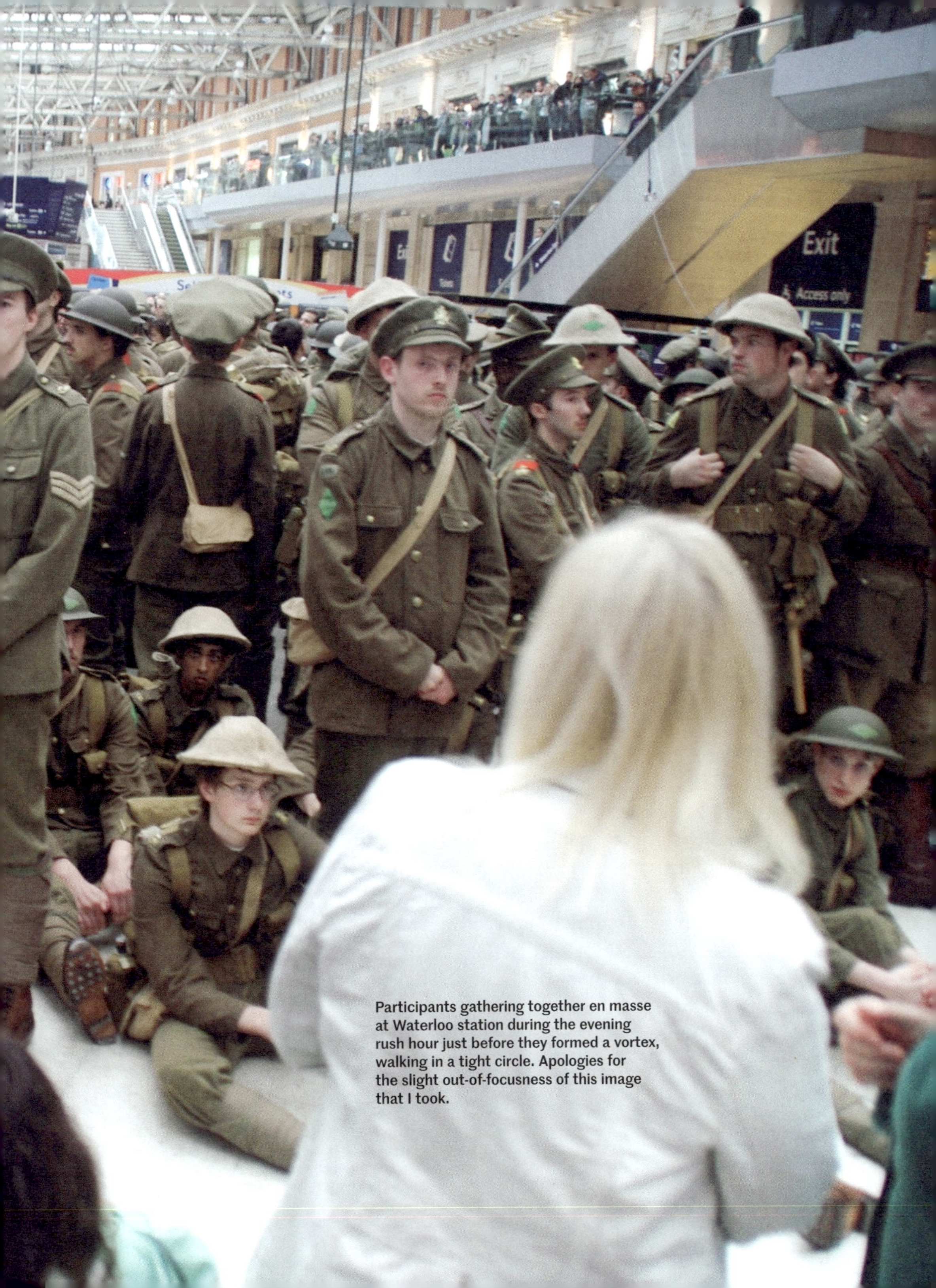

Participants gathering together en masse at Waterloo station during the evening rush hour just before they formed a vortex, walking in a tight circle. Apologies for the slight out-of-focusness of this image that I took.

It Is What It Is, 2009

Probably the most irresponsible and foolhardy work I have made to date is *It Is What It Is* – a tour of the United States with the remains of a car that had been destroyed in a bomb attack in a crowded Baghdad marketplace in 2007. We took along an American soldier, Jonathan Harvey, and Esam Pasha, an Iraqi civilian, to talk to people about the car and any 'issues' arising from it. The project was organised by Creative Time and came out of a failed attempt to have a destroyed vehicle placed on the Fourth Plinth in Trafalgar Square.

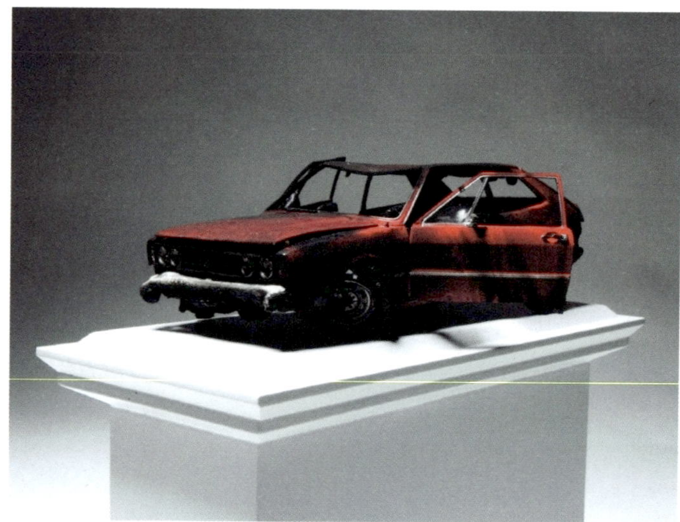

In 2007, I was shortlisted for the Fourth Plinth in Trafalgar Square. My idea was to place a vehicle destroyed in a bomb attack in Iraq on it (maquette pictured here). I wanted it to rot over its eighteen-month residency there, making an ugly mess in the square. It didn't get selected, which is hardly a surprise – it was a highly irresponsible idea.

We were driving into the unknown in a number of ways. The tour went through staunch Republican areas in the South – Texas, Alabama, Tennessee – because I was interested to meet people who did not necessarily share my opinions about the war. We established a routine of arriving in a town, setting things up in the morning then leaving in the evening, then doing the same in a new town the next day. Subsequently there were lots of discussions about religion, which Esam was happy to talk about. His breadth of knowledge was disarming for many of those he met as they assumed Iraqis were not educated at all, let alone in Christian theology, in which he excelled, being able to quote Bible verses to surprised Americans. Jonathan had worked in PsyOps (psychological operations) in Iraq and was there to represent the military. His experience of working with the civilian population in Iraq came in quite helpful on the road.

The flyer we gave out was crucial, as people were a little reluctant to ask about the car and this gave more information and also set a tone for the project and any conversation they might have. We kept things as open as possible. →

It is What it is: Conversations about Iraq
A project by Jeremy Deller
Presented by Creative Time and the New Museum

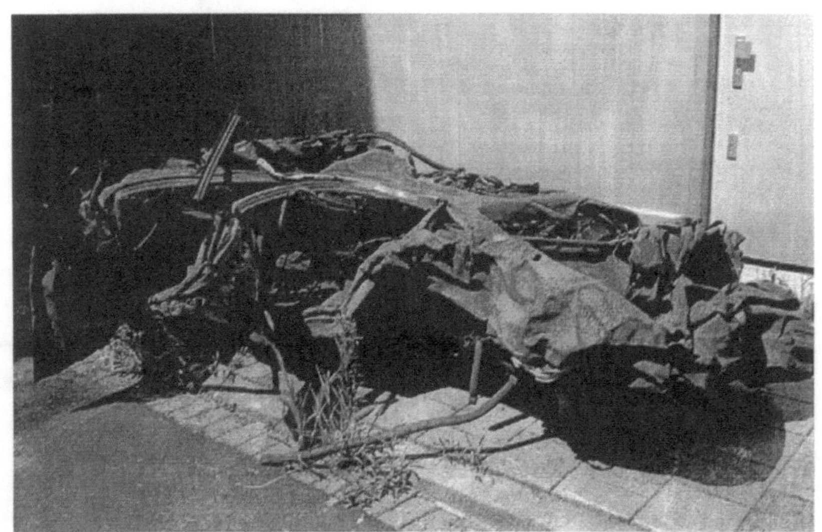

This exploded car is part of a traveling project about the ongoing situation in Iraq. The RV and car will travel from New York City to Los Angeles stopping in cities across the United States offering an opportunity to discuss Iraq itself. On hand to answer questions are Jonathan Harvey, a reservist in the military who recently served in Iraq, as well as Esam Pasha, an Iraqi artist who sought asylum in the United States in 2005. Feel free to ask them questions or look at materials from Baghdad on the tables.

More information and updates on the road at:
www.conversationsaboutiraq.org

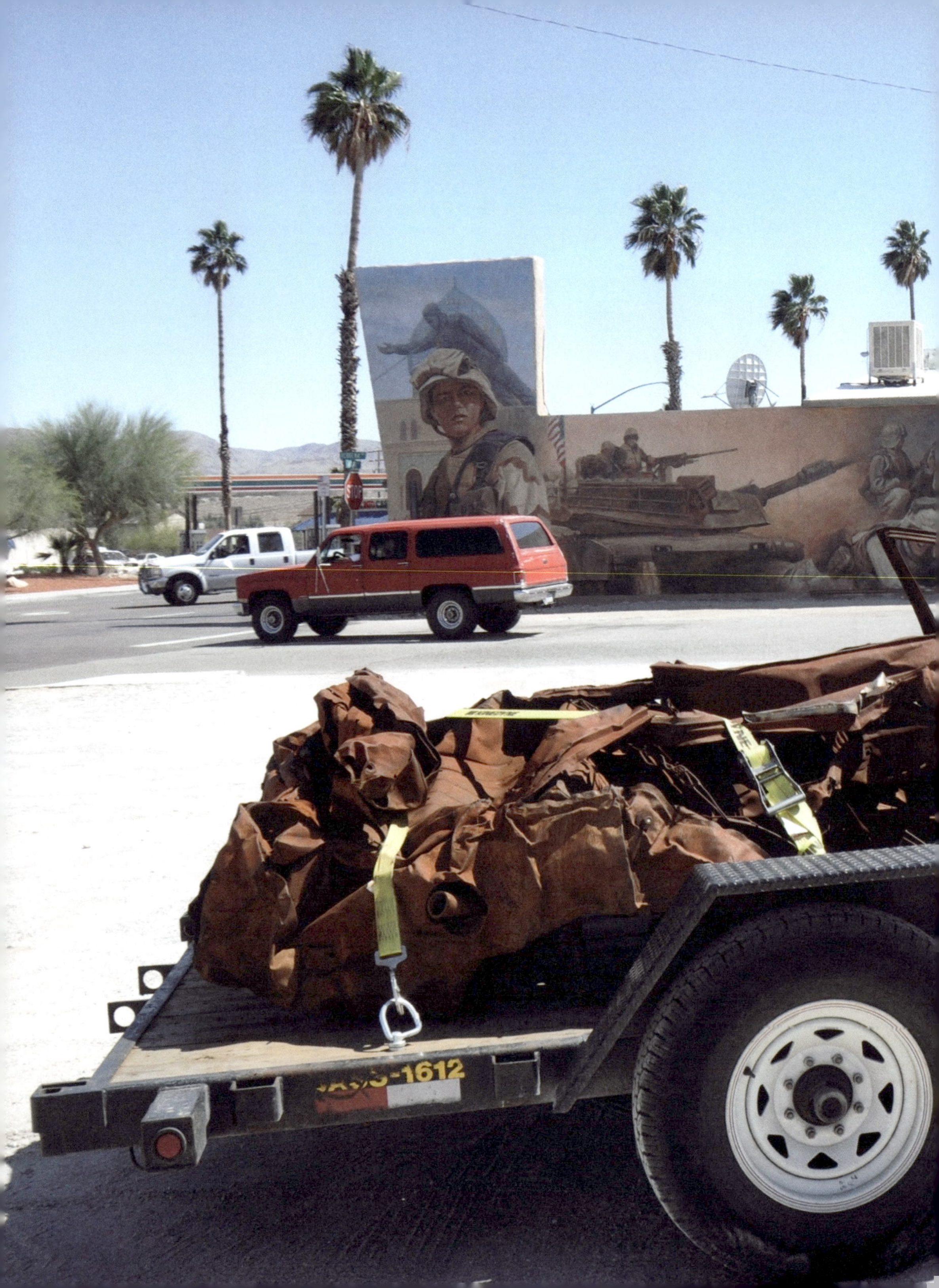
STOP
1612

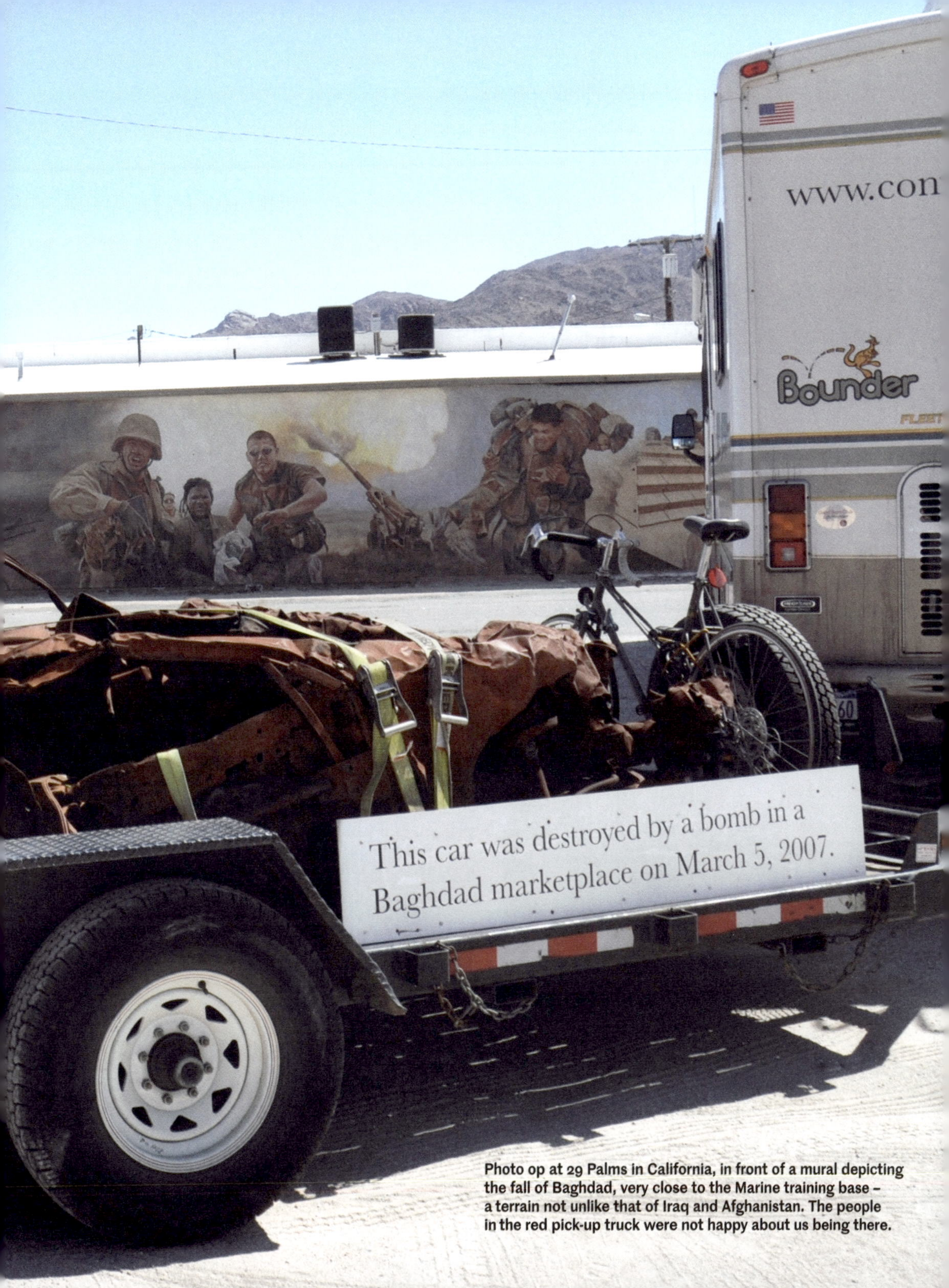

Photo op at 29 Palms in California, in front of a mural depicting the fall of Baghdad, very close to the Marine training base – a terrain not unlike that of Iraq and Afghanistan. The people in the red pick-up truck were not happy about us being there.

Transcriptions of interviews with members of the public we bumped into on the road.

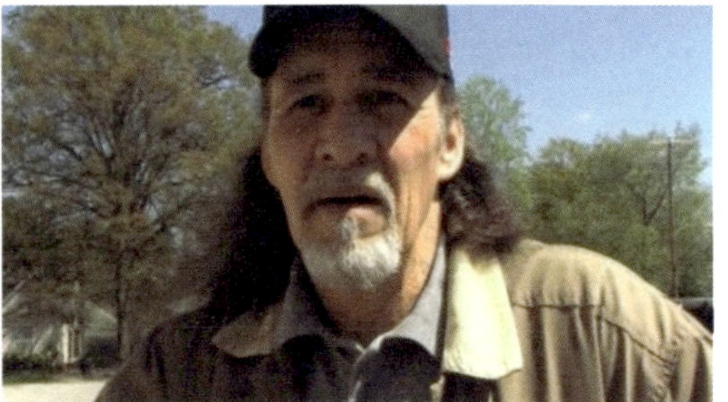

'That car over there that was blown to pieces, the people whose loved ones died in the blast, should they forgive and forget? They didn't come over here and start a war on us... Why shouldn't they hate us forever? Americans have a sense of entitlement – they think everything is owed to them. Why? People in Iraq see that every day. People around here wouldn't know how to react if every other day a bomb blew apart a car or a schoolhouse in their neighbourhood.'

Ron Hill, chef. Memphis, Tennessee

'I was a submarine sailor, a sonar tech and a navy diver. I slept in a Tomahawk Capsule for three months. I was part of the process of launching Tomahawk missiles from the Red Sea – you knew you were bringing death to someone. I kept journals the whole time we were deployed. As funny as art school may seem for a soldier it's a tough adjustment... I think I'm going to get into art therapy and work with veterans.'

John Hilger, art student and US Navy veteran. Kansas City, Missouri

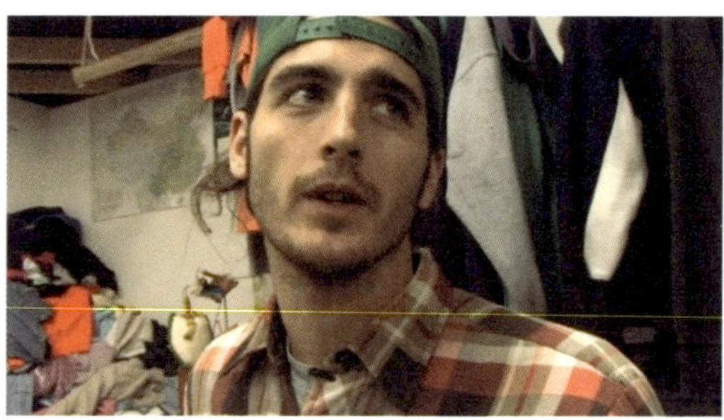

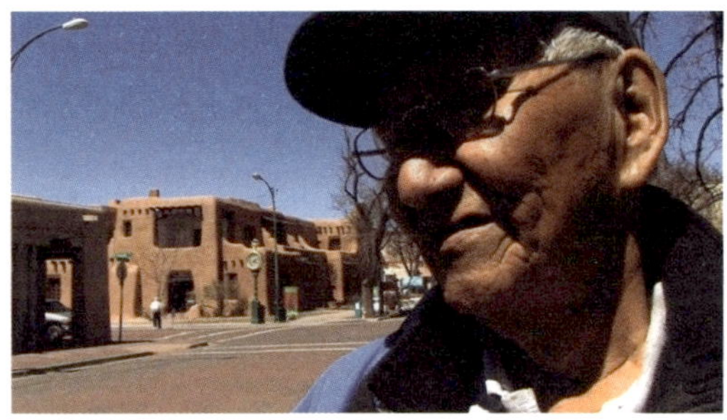

'There was a group of Native Americans that they used as scouts. We blended in – some of the natives there looked just like us. They didn't have to train us, we knew what to do, knew where to hide just like the enemy. We wore dark glasses in the day and took them off at night, and it was like daylight. When I saw the car I thought of Vietnam. They shouldn't show this in America but instead should take it to the junkyard.'

David Red Fox, Vietnam veteran. Santa Fe, New Mexico

'There was human trafficking, for want of a better word. Philippine women were being offered to high-ranking civilian and military staff as concubines. These workers lived in substandard conditions, fourteen to a trailer – we were two to a trailer – and had one outfit to wear. Their pay was about $350 a month.'

Angie Cole, former civilian contractor in the Green Zone, Baghdad. Phoenix, Arizona

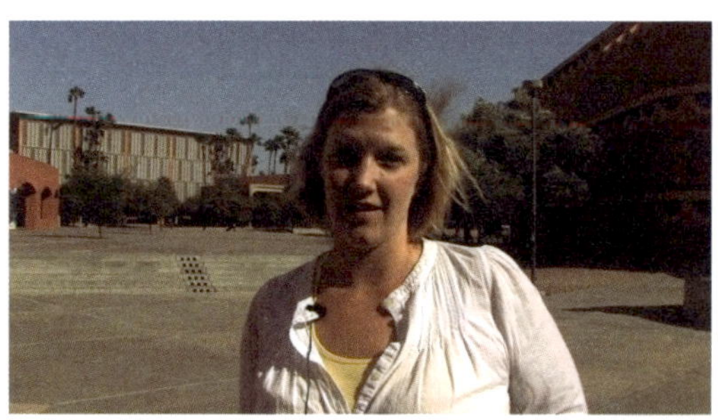

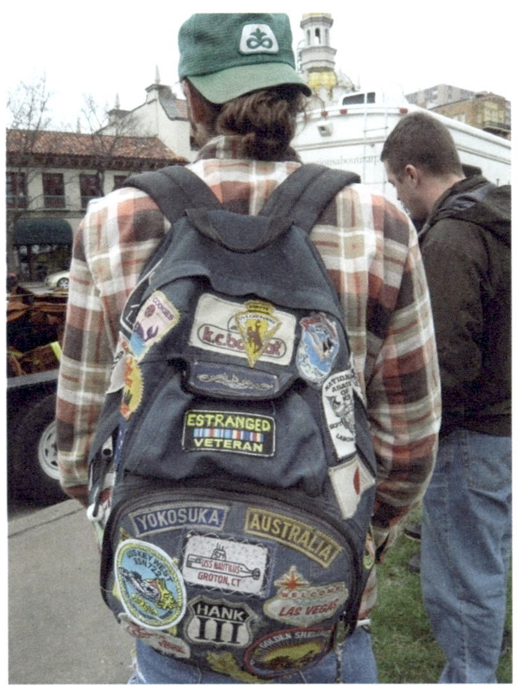

John Hilgers' backpack documenting his time in the Navy.

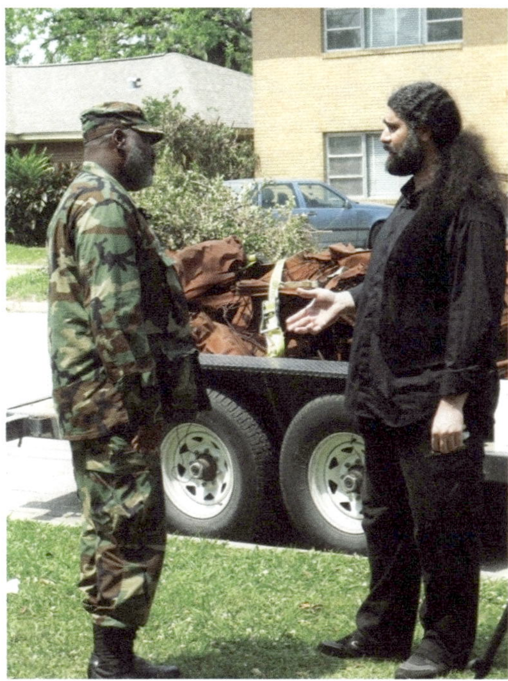

Esam talks to a veteran in Dallas, who was on his way back from a funeral and stopped by to take a look. This was typical of many of the random encounters we had. The veteran stayed for hours and talked about his time in the army and his Christian faith.

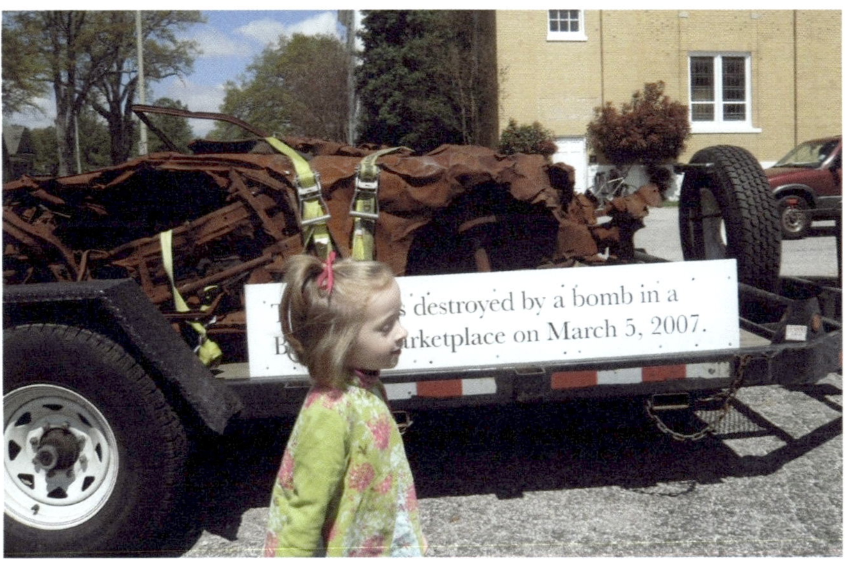

Outside the First Congregational Church, Memphis, Tennessee.

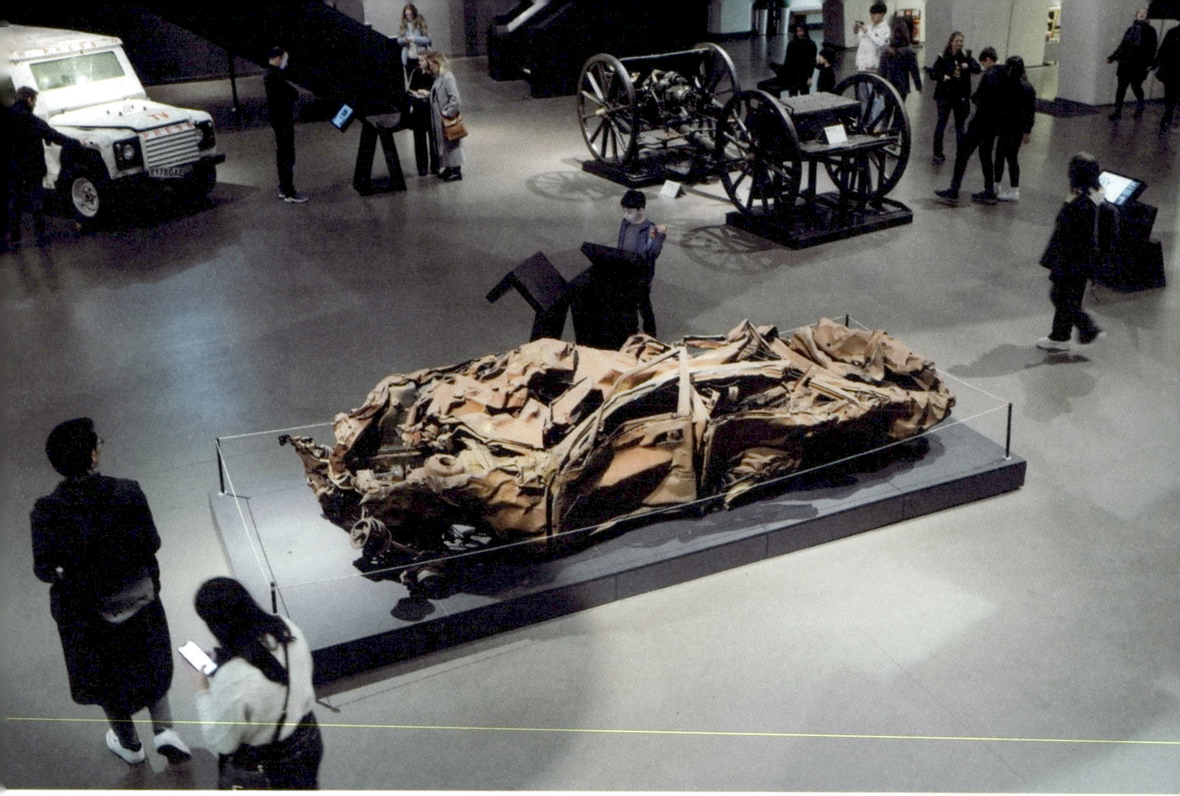

The car is now on permanent display at the Imperial War Museum in London. There is some interpretation that explains the journey across the US, but its most relevant story is what happened to it in Iraq.

The project was based around a lot of random encounters with passers-by who had no idea they would be confronted with this object. We also had no idea who these people were and what their life experiences were, so everyone was treated equally. We gave out a bland flyer that described the project in non-threatening, apolitical terms, in stark contrast to the object itself, which was full of meaning and horror. Because the project was under the auspices of a cultural organisation, we were seen as relatively neutral, which was essential. In a sense, we were taking a relic around, a sacred reminder of death.

The project was, if anything, under-documented: we made some scrappy little films, and I took photos with a camera that had a lens problem. Too much tech would have intimidated the public and made people feel that they were being used for content. Overall, we let people talk about whatever they wanted.

***Putin's Happy*, 2019**

In a sense, this film I made about Brexit, has similarities to *It Is What It Is* in its random quality of bumping into people in potentially hostile territory. It's a study of English radicalisation and paranoia and is not for the fainthearted. Many of those interviewed would never think of themselves as extremists, but that is precisely what they had gradually become over the years.

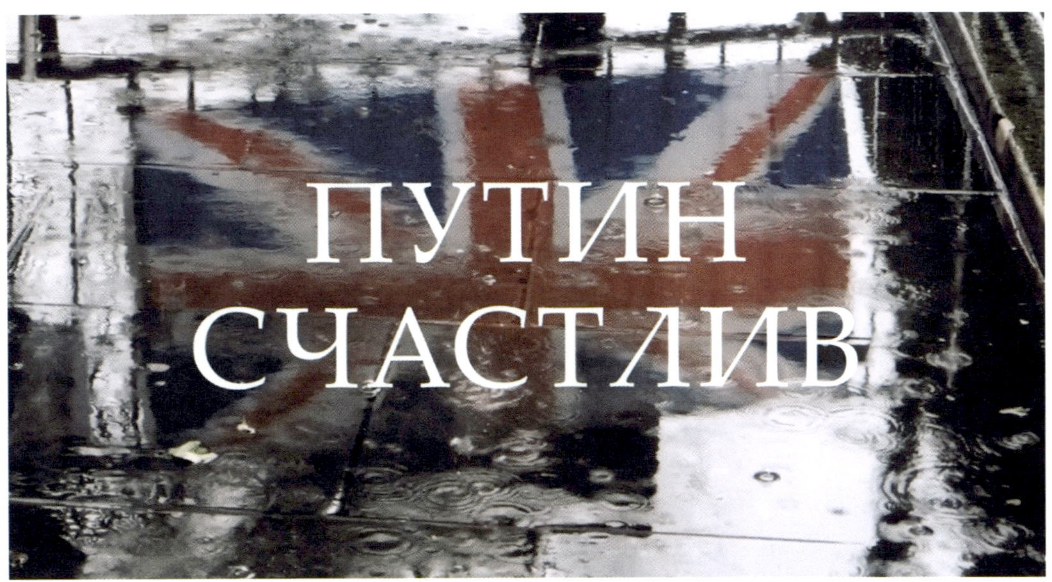

The film opens on a miserable wet day in February outside Parliament, where everyone seemed particularly angry with each other.

The film is best watched in a group: that way you can laugh at the moments of absurdity rather than be depressed by them. I had gone to Parliament Square in early 2019 during a Brexit debate and was quite unprepared for the visual and aural cacophony of the opposing sides mixing and arguing together. It was all very un-English in its passion; and arguably more American than anything else in its performative chaos, both fascinating and depressing. It felt like I was in a Hogarth print that had come to life. It really confirmed what I thought: that Brexit had sent the country insane, and clearly it would take years to de-radicalise it. I returned to the protest half a dozen times and went out of my way to speak to people who were in favour of Brexit to try to get into their heads and see if there was any common ground between them and myself. Some of these people reminded me of members of my own family. The main areas where we shared any views at all were around housing and health.

Everybody was filming and live-broadcasting themselves and people around them, so I realised that another camera was not going to attract too much

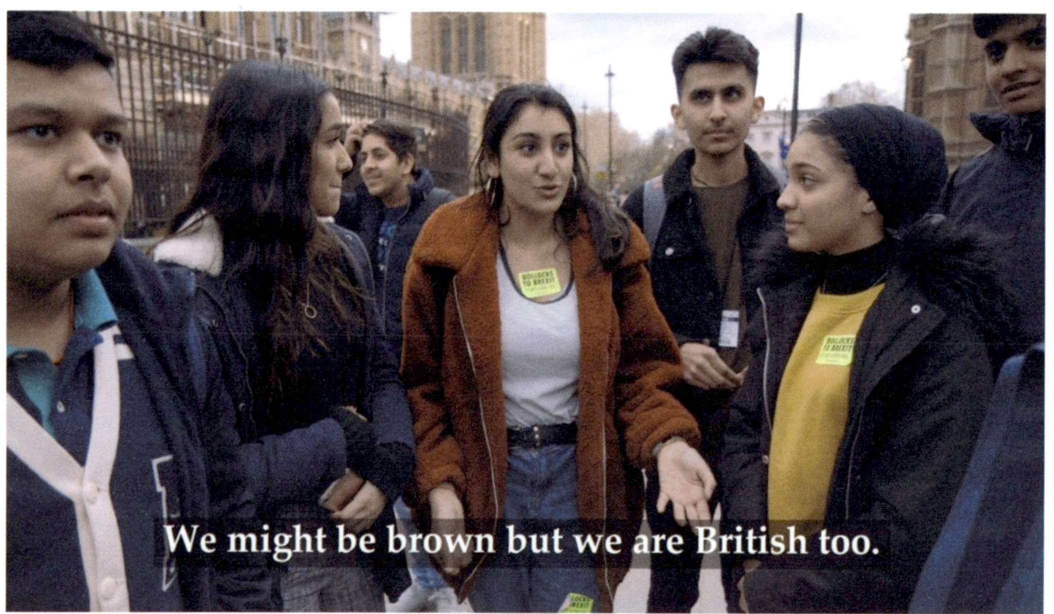

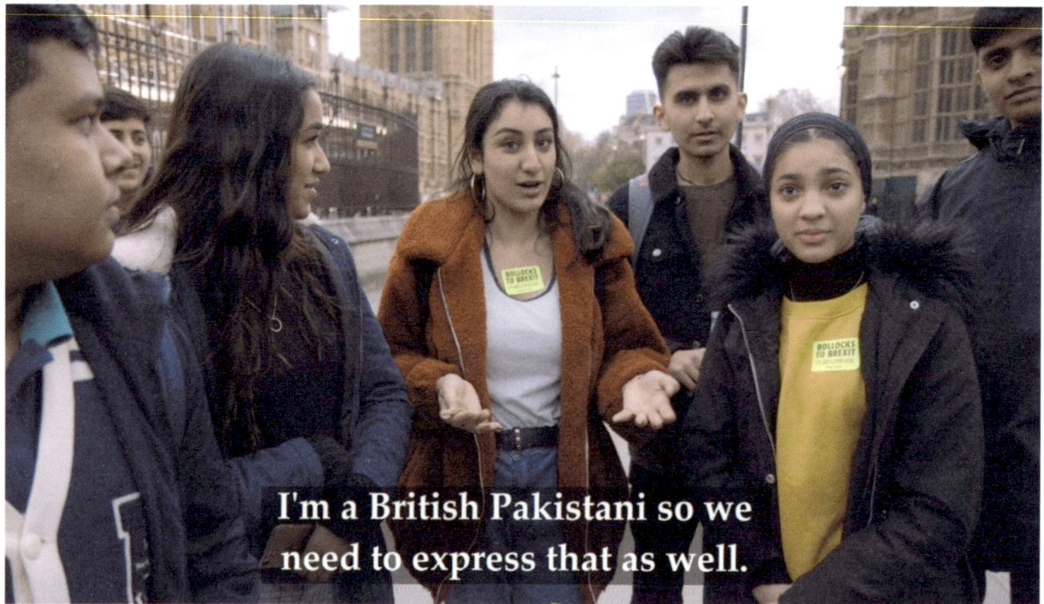

I bumped into this group of young people who had just been racially abused by a Brexit supporter. Despite this, they were hopeful and positive about the future of the UK. 'It's our nation too' were their final words to me. This was in marked contrast to the supporters of Brexit, who, despite their patriotism, seemed very down on Britain despite having achieved their goal of leaving the EU.

attention. I worked by myself some days and on others with Jared Schiller, a friend and filmmaker who is somehow even shorter than me. Together, we comprised a non-threatening presence, which was important as the pro-Brexit supporters were very suspicious of anyone who looked even vaguely official. There was a lot of real-time in-person trolling which I filmed but it was so soul-destroying to watch back. In the end the film does have a few pro-European voices as it would be almost unwatchable otherwise, for people like myself at least.

It helped that the film was being made for an art exhibition, which meant that again we posed no threat. Some people were quite happy to be filmed being overtly antisemitic. This was a real thread running through so many of the conversations; as was the Second World War and the sacrifice of soldiers' lives being squandered. The title I hope is self-explanatory.

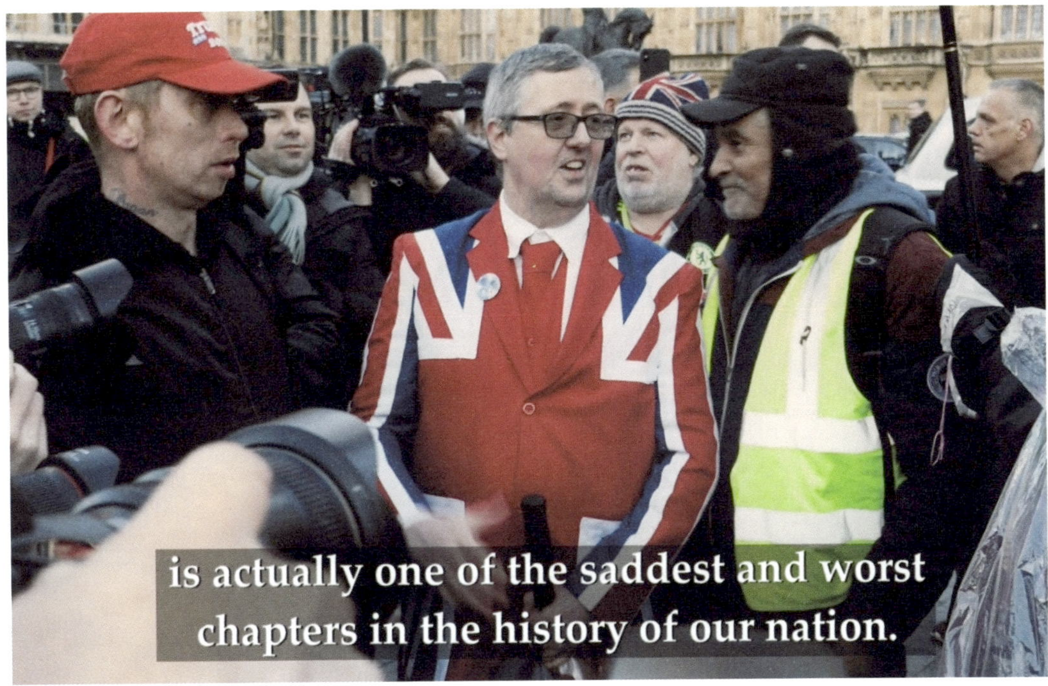

The subtitled words are by Nigel Farage, from a speech he gave in Parliament Square on 29 March 2019. I'm using them against him. This small group of men had a good line in terrorising pro-EU protestors and hogging the limelight. The police basically had to follow them around everywhere. They knew the limits of what they could say in public and were quick to accuse anyone of assault even if they brushed up against them by accident. Some of them later found a new lease of life at anti-vaccination rallies.

I think a lot of people became addicted to being in Parliament Square, much in the same way that some people who visit Jerusalem can't leave and end up dressing in biblical-era garb.

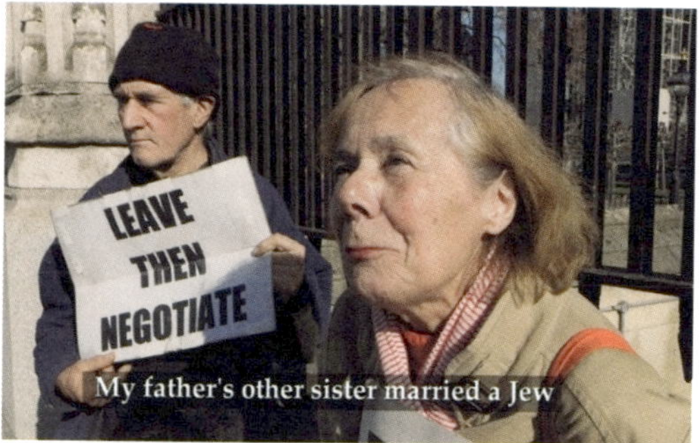

This woman was quite 'famous', and was only too happy to talk. The subtitle refers to a longer story about her two uncles. One was a German who served in the Wehrmacht; the other was Jewish and drove a tank in the British army. No need to ask which one she preferred.

The last time I went to a rally was on 29 March 2019, when conspiracy theorists and far-right groups gathered together in anger and in celebration of their culture. A loyalist pipe band marched around the square, and a large group of football crews took a lap of honour. The atmosphere was both festive and threatening – it was the first time many of these people had been able to meet in person. Not only did it feel like a historic occasion, but it was also possibly the closest we got to a January 6, Capitol-style storming of our seat of government.

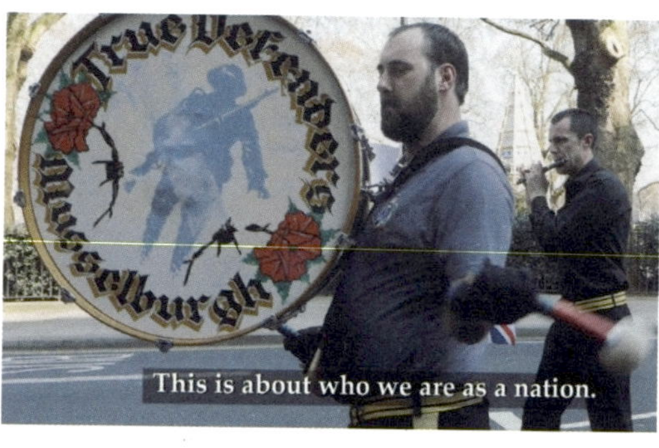

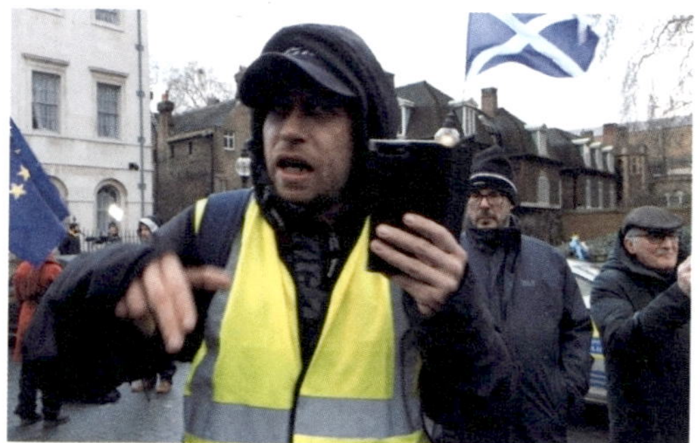

'I'm live on media … the government are not supporting our veterans that are coming back from the war, if they come back. They are homeless as well as not given a pension. The government are failing everyone. Even social services are failing our children. They're taking our children away, forced adoption. And everything like that. It's disgusting what they are doing to our people.'

A regular at the demos livestreams to his followers on Facebook.

An almost sacrilegious moment from the film as 'Get Up, Stand Up' by Bob Marley is played by pro-Brexit supporters who genuinely felt that that song spoke to them and their struggle to get the Brexit they desired. The overwhelming impression for me was that a lot of English people (despite all their displays of patriotism) did not know who they were.

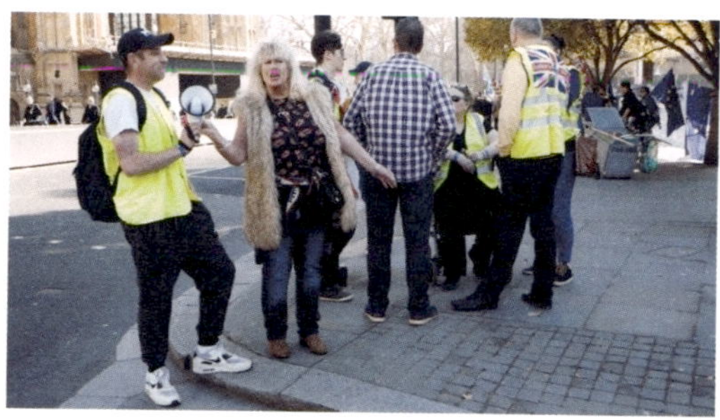

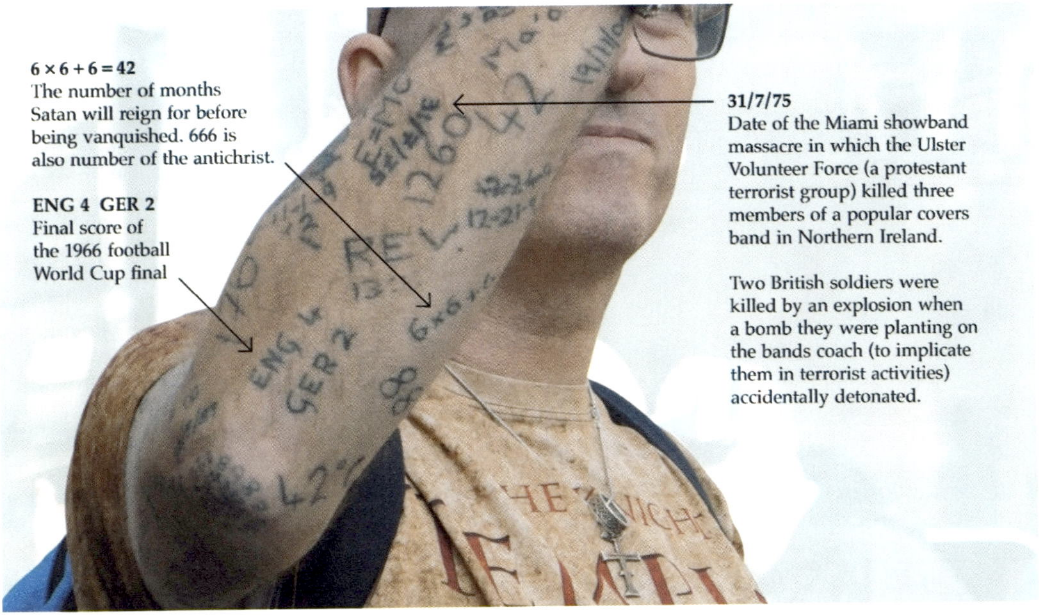

6 × 6 + 6 = 42
The number of months Satan will reign for before being vanquished. 666 is also number of the antichrist.

ENG 4 GER 2
Final score of the 1966 football World Cup final

31/7/75
Date of the Miami showband massacre in which the Ulster Volunteer Force (a protestant terrorist group) killed three members of a popular covers band in Northern Ireland.

Two British soldiers were killed by an explosion when a bomb they were planting on the bands coach (to implicate them in terrorist activities) accidentally detonated.

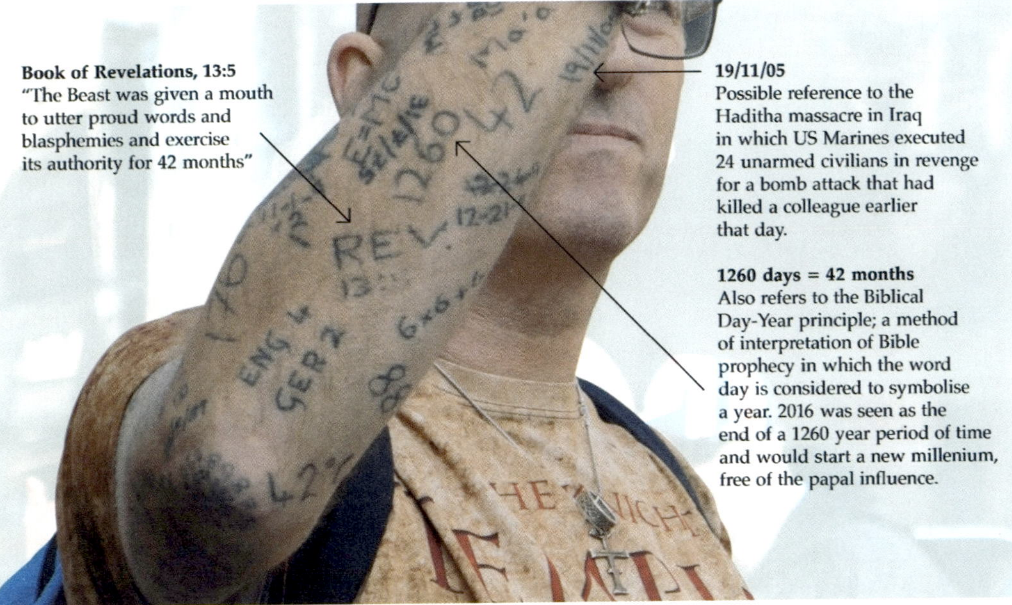

I wish I had had the nerve to talk to this guy, as he was really not shy about his interests in crusades (contemporary and historical), football, apocalyptic biblical passages and Adolf Hitler (note: 88 tattoo = 88 = HH = Heil Hitler). When I filmed him, I knew I would have to take time to decode his body later.

I'm still a bit haunted by some of the people I filmed and interviewed in Parliament Square. It doesn't get any easier to watch this film.

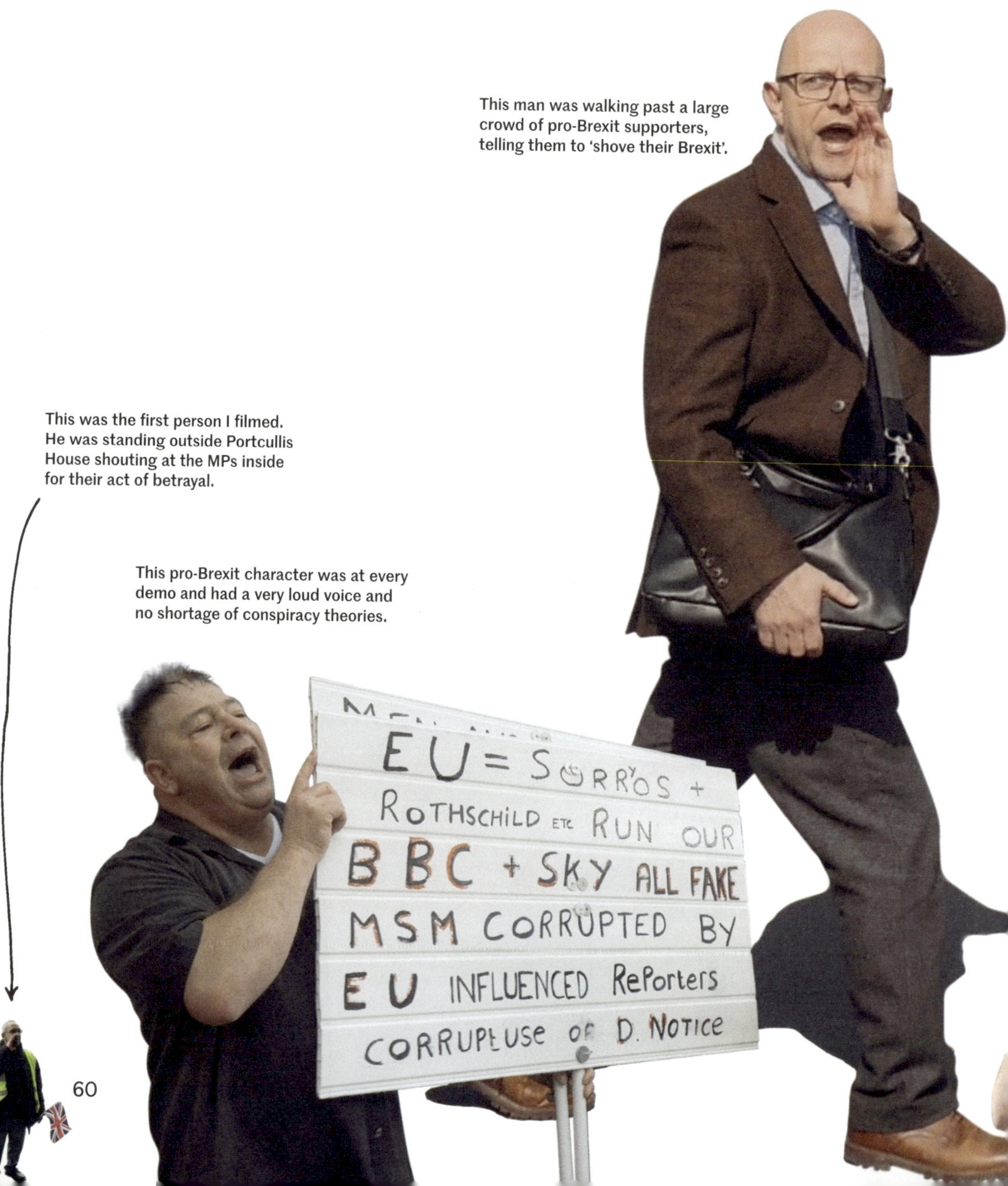

This man was walking past a large crowd of pro-Brexit supporters, telling them to 'shove their Brexit'.

This was the first person I filmed. He was standing outside Portcullis House shouting at the MPs inside for their act of betrayal.

This pro-Brexit character was at every demo and had a very loud voice and no shortage of conspiracy theories.

The angry antisemite.

A Q anon early adopter.

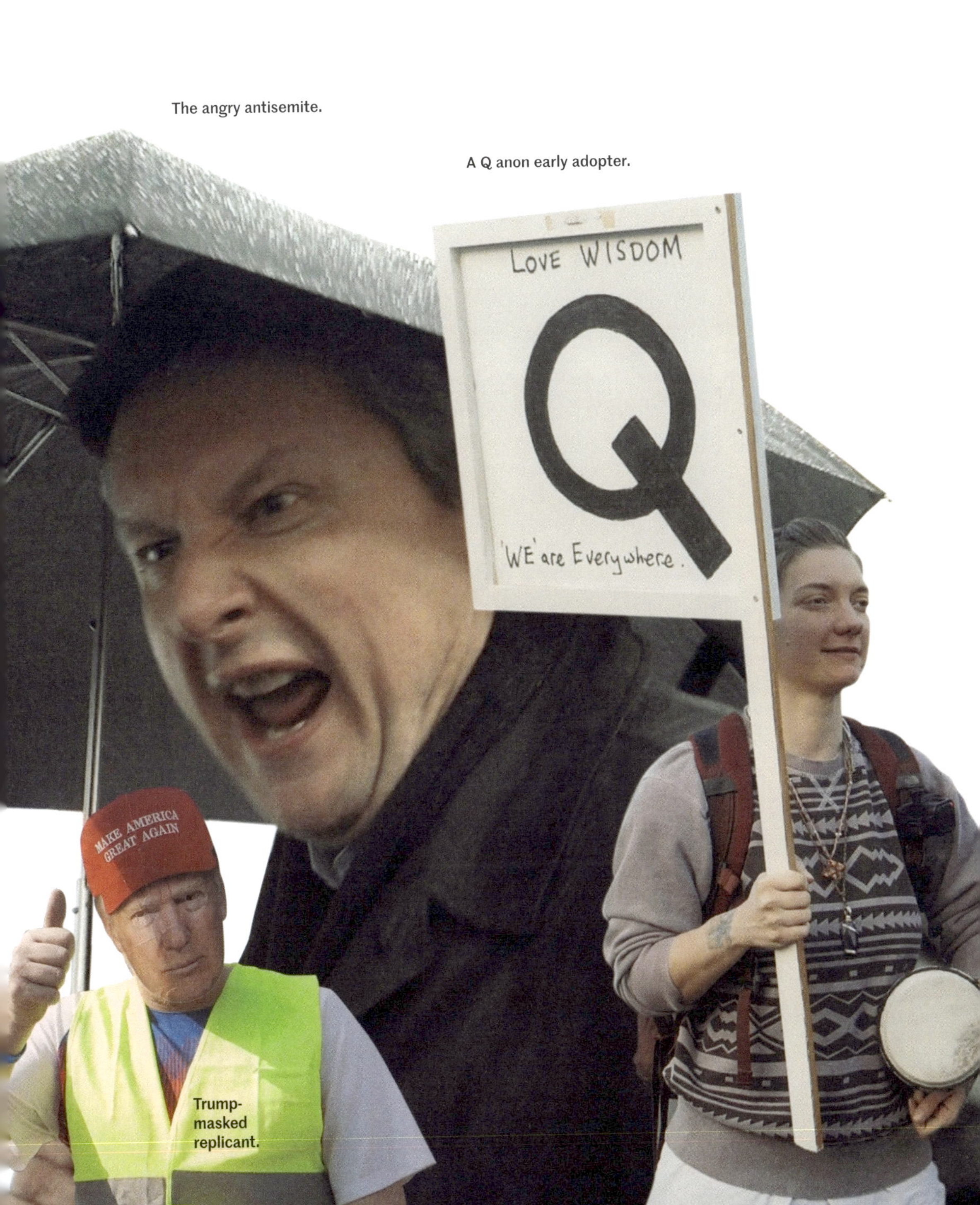

Trump-masked replicant.

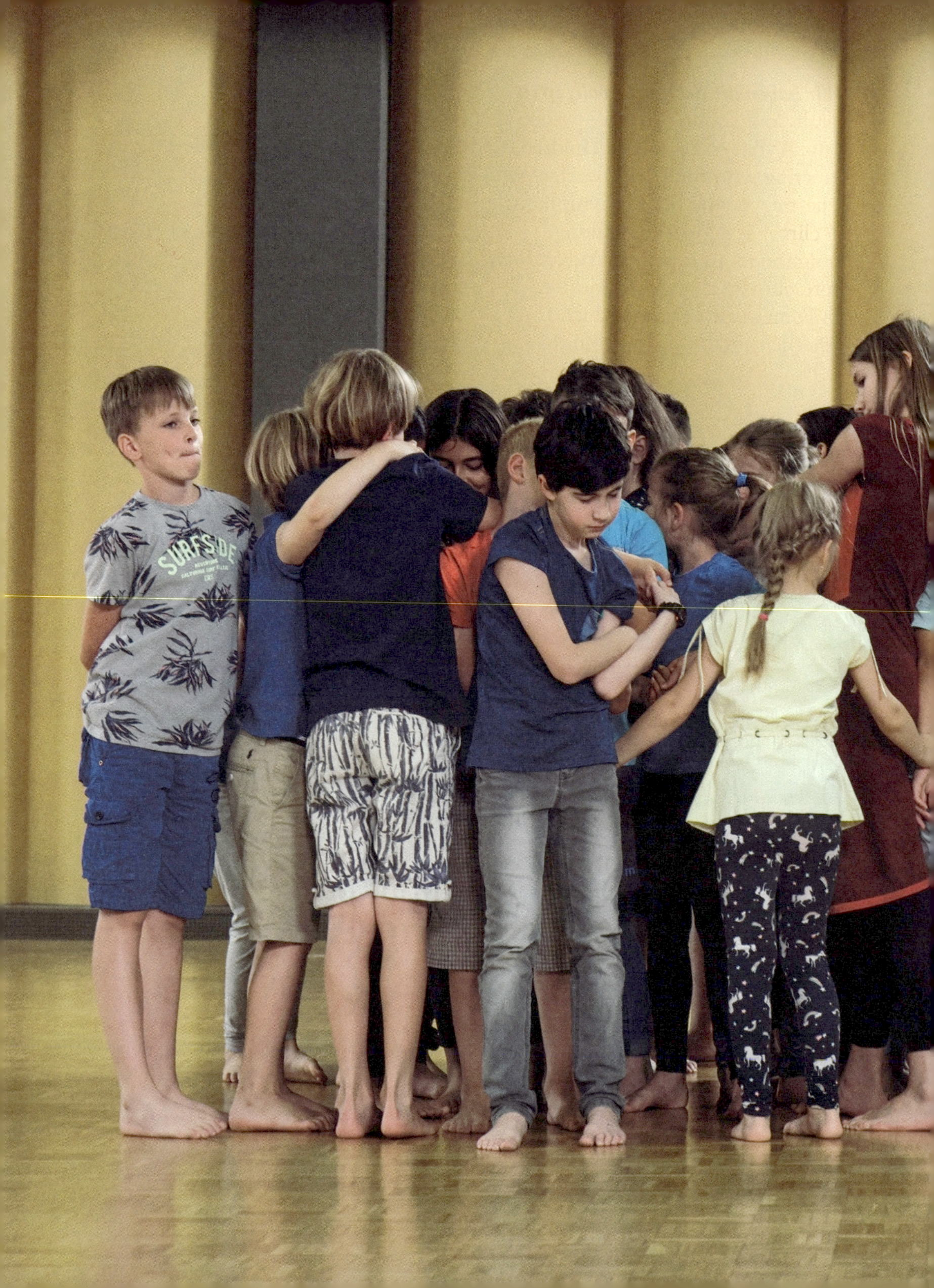
SURFSIDE

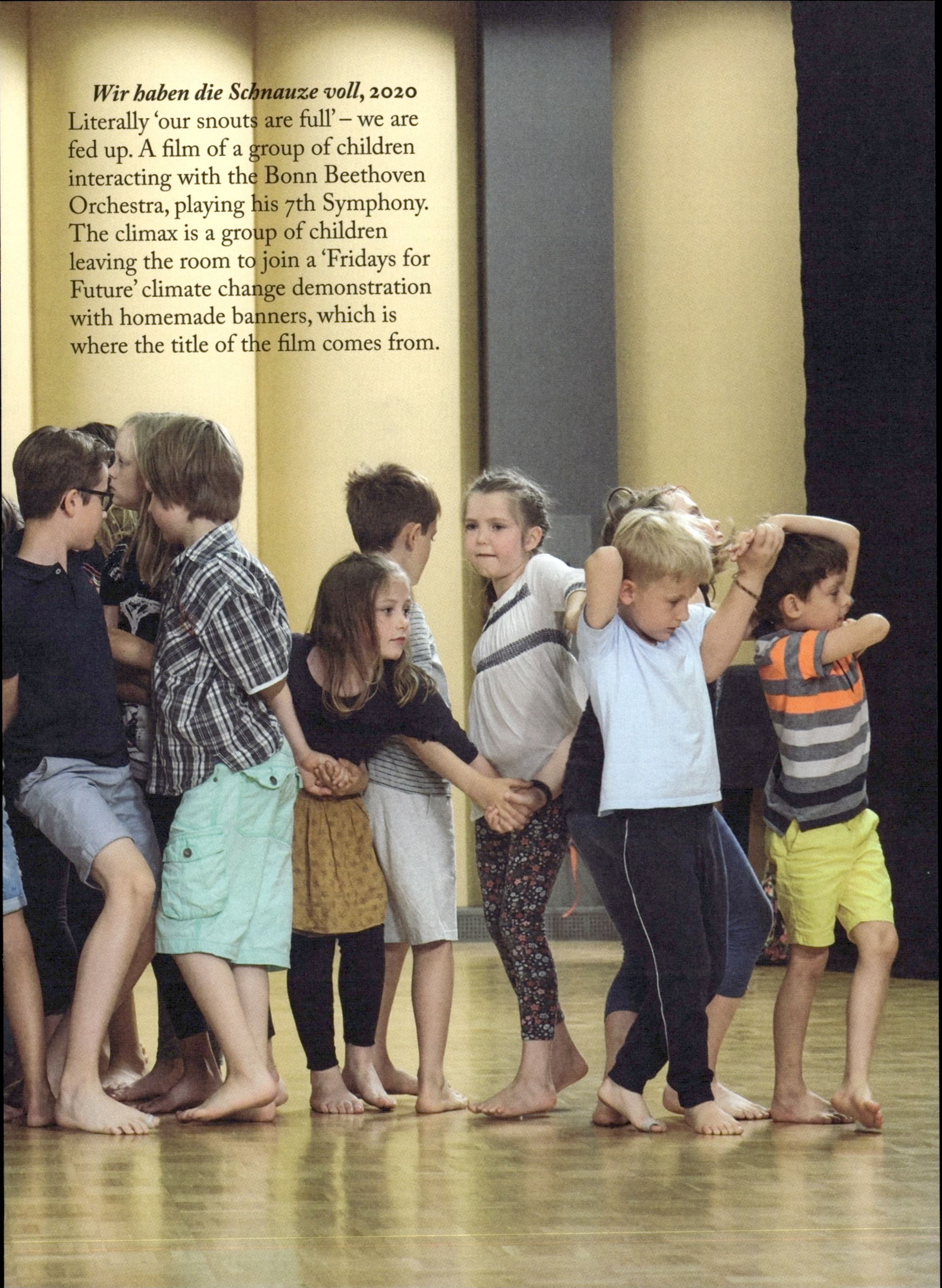

***Wir haben die Schnauze voll*, 2020**
Literally 'our snouts are full' – we are fed up. A film of a group of children interacting with the Bonn Beethoven Orchestra, playing his 7th Symphony. The climax is a group of children leaving the room to join a 'Fridays for Future' climate change demonstration with homemade banners, which is where the title of the film comes from.

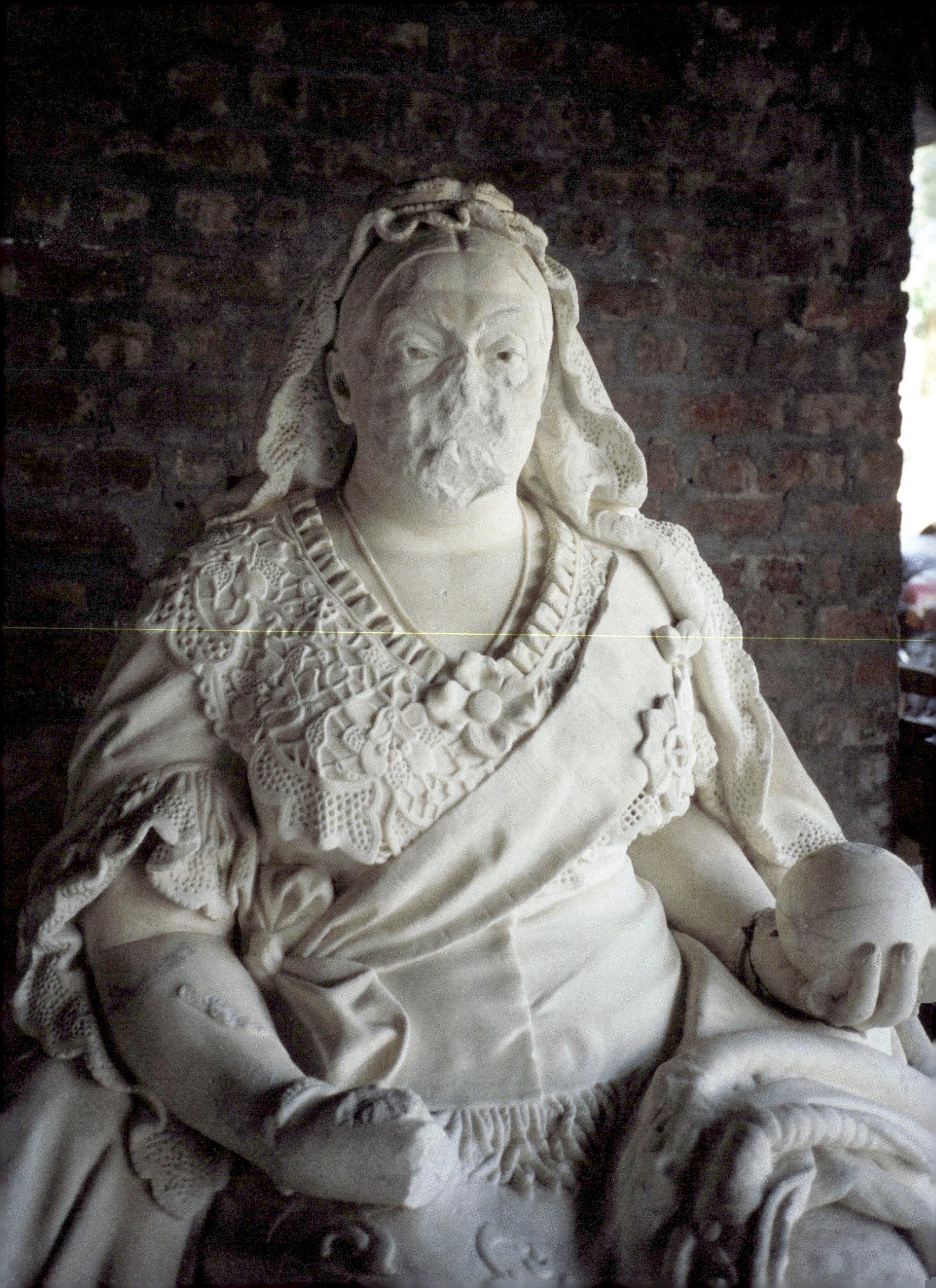

Chapter 5

Queen Victoria with her face smashed in

Jeremy and Mary Beard in conversation about public statuary

A few years ago, I had a discussion with the academic and broadcaster Mary Beard about public art and statues in particular. Below is a transcript with the odd update.

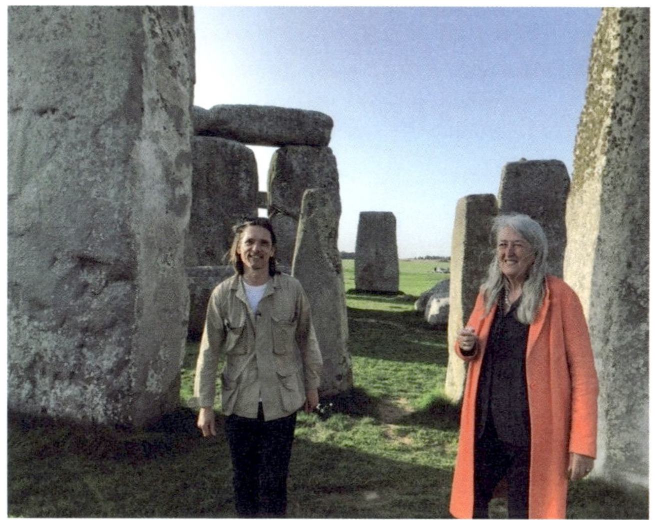

JD and MB at Stonehenge, 2020.

Mary Beard: I want to kick off this discussion by being completely honest and saying that public sculpture came very much into the popular consciousness with what happened to the statue of Colston in Bristol. When I watched his toppling, I have to say that I felt quite excited, I felt something was happening, somebody was taking notice of something going on. I thought it was a good moment, in a funny way. Even though I occasionally masquerade as an art historian, I wonder what you thought about watching that footage.

← A vandalised statue of Queen Victoria around the back of the Indian Museum in Kolkata.

Jeremy Deller: The way it was taken down and then put into the dock literally and metaphorically had a satisfying poetry to it. Now it is being displayed prone with the graffiti still on, which seems appropriate – the opposite of putting someone on a pedestal.

M: What I felt gloomier about was not that moment – which for me was very exciting, a real moment of a work of art in the public domain – but that the discussions about statues that have followed have been much less uplifting. They have been rather crude and have come down to disappointing polarisations between the statue upholders, the statue-philes and the enemies of statues in a way that's got us almost nowhere in thinking about this.

J: Yes, even though it was a political act, it quickly became politicised, probably because the government took an immediate and definite position on it. Shortly after, I went to one of the 'Protect the Statues' events in Parliament Square – not as a participant, I hasten to add. There were about 2,000 people, mainly men, standing around waiting for something to happen. Ironically, the statues of Gandhi and Nelson Mandela were covered up because I think it was felt they were at risk of being vandalised. A lot of these men had experience of street fighting, and it degenerated into a general attack on the police. Or anyone that looked like they supported Black Lives Matter, in the end. I think a lot of the frustration was about not being able to attend football matches during lockdown that year.

M: In some ways, without basic ground rules being established, it does seem to me that apart from a very, very few people who are probably borderline pathological, there isn't anybody who wants all statues to stay up forever. There are very few people who think this lovely statue of Hitler was put up in my local square in 1939 and it

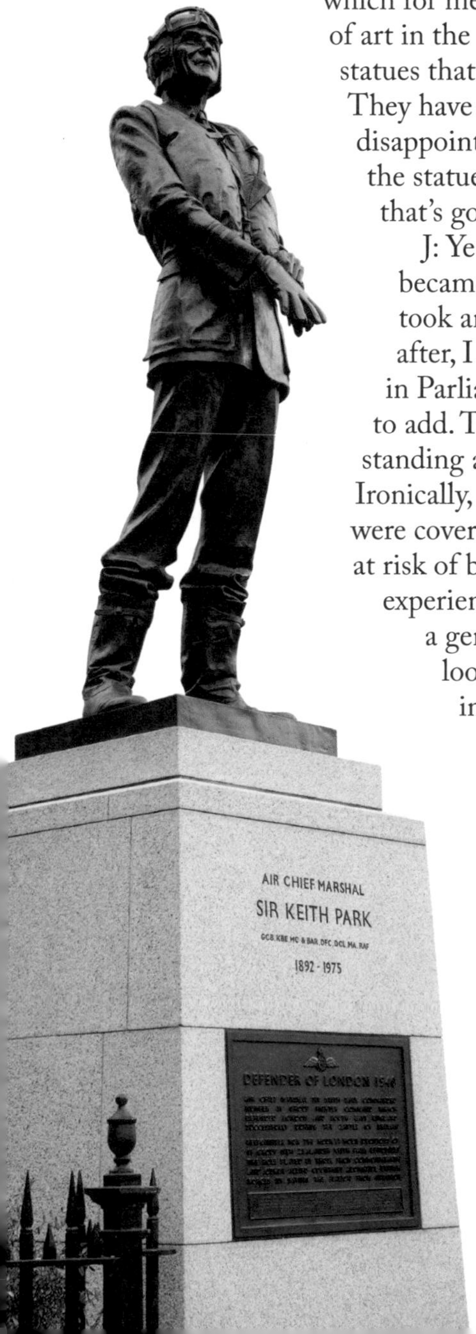

AIR CHIEF MARSHAL
SIR KEITH PARK
1892 - 1975
DEFENDER OF LONDON 1940

The Keith Park statue standing very tall near the Duke of York steps, central London. The problem with statues on plinths is that they are actually quite difficult to see and photograph.

would be a real shame to get rid of it because it would be destroying history. So, we're arguing not about whether public sculpture is inviolable but about where you draw the line and where on the spectrum offence is caused, or whether things should be moved. That's what we're disagreeing about.

J: Yes, what is the shelf life of a statue? Where is the law that once a statue goes up it cannot be touched? If you think about the public realm in Britain, buildings get demolished all the time, buildings are places where people live and experience their lives so why is it that statues should be treated in such a special way? Some statues run out of their life really, don't they? They become meaningless after a while – their point has been made. We have forgotten who these figures are even when their statues are in front of us, so they are clearly not doing their job.

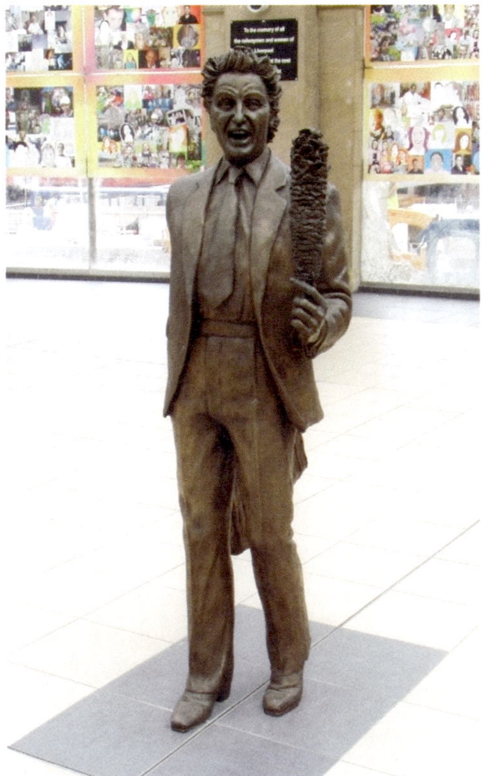

The Ken Dodd statue at Liverpool Lime Street station. Comedians are often displayed at ground-level height as they are folk heroes. People want to be close to them and have their photos taken with them. Their role in society is to prick the pomposity of the establishment. Keith Park and other military heroes are, conversely, rarely displayed at ground level, as they are not future-proofed by history and serve a different purpose. Veneration, not interaction.

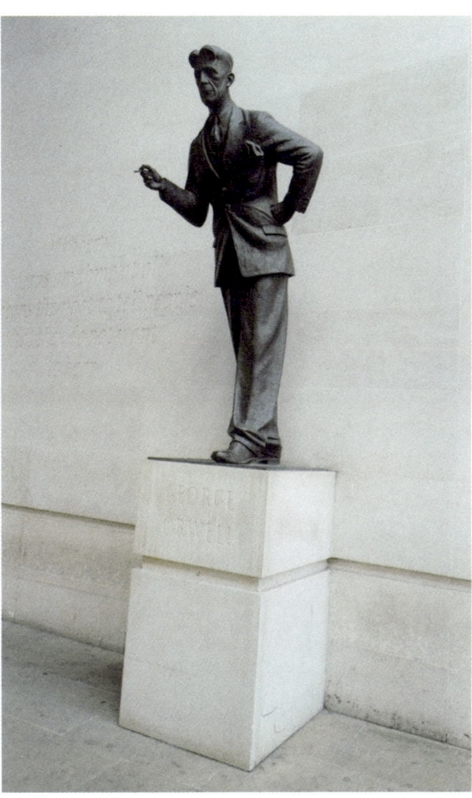

The George Orwell statue outside BBC Broadcasting House, London. As a character, he has more in common with Ken Dodd than Keith Park.

M: The big question for me is what on earth we think these statues or other elements of public sculpture – not necessarily figurative statues – are for? There is a sort of blanket assumption that we put up things to admire in the public realm and I'm not sure we do, honestly, or indeed should.

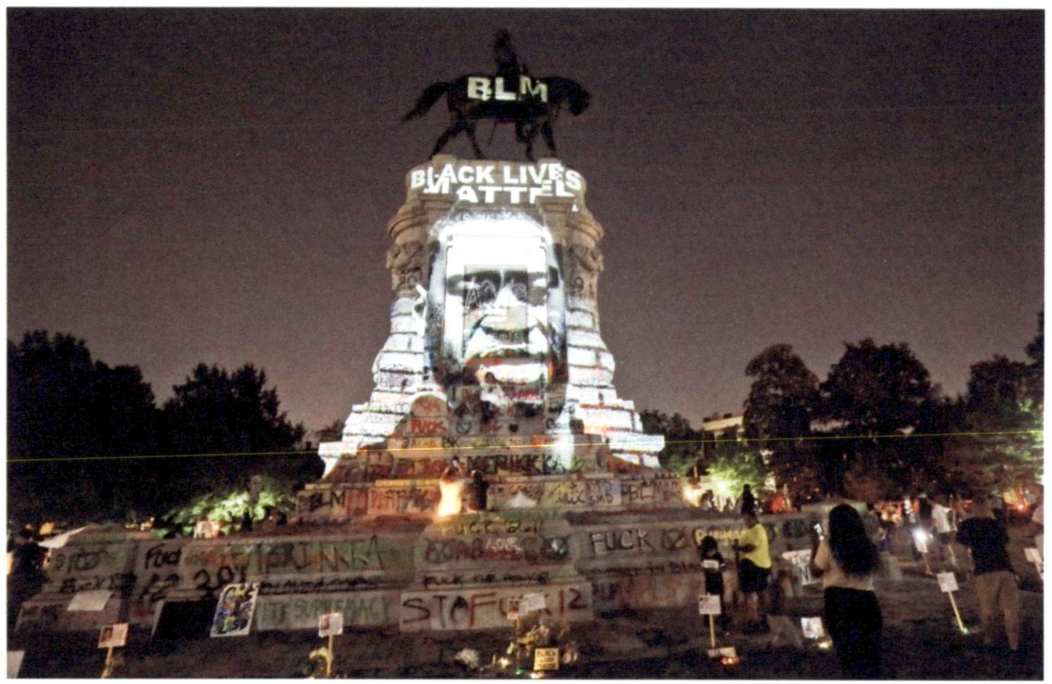

The Robert E. Lee statue in Richmond, Virginia, was adapted and reconfigured before finally being removed in September 2021. The pedestal was dismantled and the statue now resides in the Black History Museum and Cultural Center of Virginia.

J: I have a few theories. One I think, is anxiety, either of forgetting about people or forgetting about moments in history. I think we're just about to come up to a massive moment of anxiety when the last surviving soldier from the Second World War dies, and that whole Captain Tom phenomenon was concerned with this. So, we put up representations of warriors, like of Keith Park and Bomber Harris, in case we forget them: the Second World War was after all a holy war for the English, a sacred moment in our history, never to be repeated for some at least. In the United States, the Confederate statues were put up at times when people felt threatened by social change.

At the opposite end of the spectrum, for me, is the idea that statues should bring happiness into the public realm. Some of my favourite statues are of comedians – Ken Dodd at Liverpool Lime Street station was put up when he was alive. What's interesting is that these are on ground level so you can have your photo taken with them. They are there to animate the space around and make you feel happy. Maybe we need a bit more joy in our public statues, rather than these figures on plinths looking down on us. I think the BBC made a mistake with the George Orwell statue outside Broadcasting House as it was put on a plinth, when he should have been at ground level holding out an ashtray to smokers.

M: But I also think they challenge me, and in a productive way. I walk through central London and see those stuffed-shirt military statues, most of whose names mean nothing to me, and they remind me about where I've come from and where I am now. I go past, and I want to put two fingers up at them and say, 'You didn't think I should have the vote, did you? Well, sorry, got it!' They're part of a way in which I interact with the parts of history that I might choose not to remember.

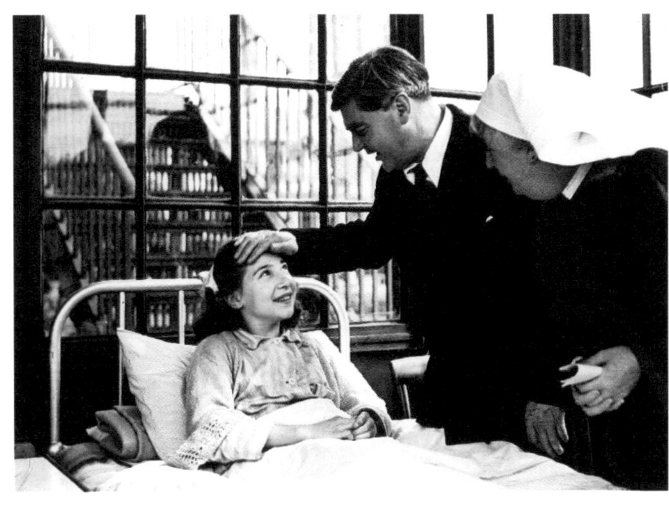

Minister of Health Nye Bevan visits Park Hospital in Davyhulme, Manchester – the 'birthplace of the NHS', on the 5 July 1948. It is difficult not to see this as a religious photograph; all the iconography is there.

Now, it would be easy for me to say 'Up yours' to these stuffed shirts because I'm in a position of power, relatively speaking. They lost, I won. But I am aware I am not a person of colour looking at a statue of a slave trader. However, I also think that the complexity of public memory can't come down solely to seeing people we approve of in our public realm.

J: But I think then you look at how these statues are contextualised in the public space – what surrounds them and how they are interpreted. You can change the meaning of a statue by a text that's critical of that person or questioning their deeds. Look at the reaction to the Robert E. Lee monument in Richmond, Virginia – it was defaced, or appropriated, you could say, so his strength became his weakness. The projections and graffiti in the short term, at least, I felt was a brilliant solution.

M: Also, it is often the case that the higher the plinth, the more contentious the person. I think it's put up so high it is difficult to topple. With further to fall. I think plinths are extremely interesting. If you look at what the British Museum has done with Hans Sloane, he was on a plinth in the Enlightenment gallery and he was never looked at, because, in the British Museum, column plinths are ten a penny. The consequence of moving him out of the background and contextualising him is that he is now noticeable. He is now set within the context of the slave trade, with a lot of text and images, such as plans of the slave ships.

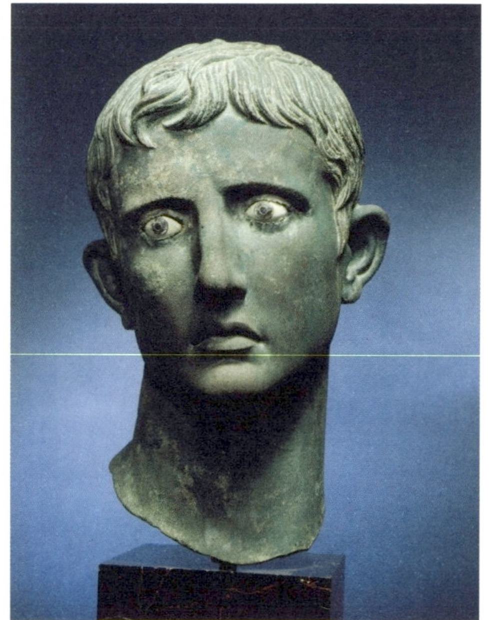

Bust of Emperor Augustus, 27–25 BC

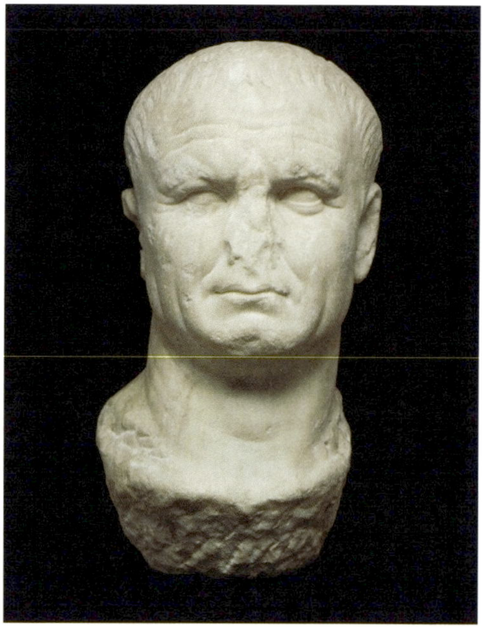

Bust of Emperor Vespasian, AD 70–80

Museums have an important role to play here, and I'm biased because I'm part of the trustees of the British Museum, but I think what they've done is excellent in recontextualising Sloane. I do get more worried, though, when I hear people say, 'What should happen to him?' referring to some guy we no longer want to see, and our answer is, 'Put him in a museum.' It is as if a museum was going to be our 'Get out of jail free' card for not destroying these guys but putting them out of sight. It's like the Richmond statue. I think there are many ways forward here but one of the things that we need to be working on is surely how they can be recontextualised in public. Let's say we put the slave trader in the Museum of Slavery, but I don't imagine that most white supremacists decide of a Sunday afternoon, 'Come on, darling, let's go and see the Museum of Slavery.' So, there is a kind of preaching to the converted that happens when, if the statues stayed out there, we might have a debate involving more people and more shades of opinion.

J: To have that debate, you almost need that statue to have a debate with another statue, I would argue. You must surround it with maybe something contemporary, some other imagery, other sculptures perhaps. It might not just be text; it might have to be something else entirely to change the meaning of it. I think art can help with that. The greatest war memorial for the Second World War is the NHS, so if we can think of an equivalent of a thing rather than a person on a plinth, that would be more suitable or appropriate.

M: It seems to me that statues and sculpture are a tremendously good material for that, because of the physical embodiment. Nobody has got very worked up about the painting of the death of Colston in Bristol and that's partly because he is dying, but it's also because it's a painting. There is something about the physicality, the three-dimensionality, the idea of a body from the past kind of erupting into the public sphere, which makes sculpture much more pressing for us.

J: Well, it almost makes the person immortal, doesn't it, because they are made of this very tough material that could last forever, presumably. Maybe it's also a fear of iconoclasm and the literal madness of that and its connection to extremist ideologies. I'm interested to hear what happened in Roman times with statues of emperors. When they became unpopular, were they toppled?

M: I'm glad you asked that because I think this isn't just our problem. What you do with statues you no longer want has been a cultural issue for hundreds and thousands of years, so we haven't just discovered there's a problem here. Emperor Vespasian came to power at the end of 70 AD after a civil war that had replaced Nero. Nero committed suicide at the end of 68 AD and there were a few short-lived leaders in between before Vespasian came along. There is a statue of him in the British Museum and if we look at it carefully, it wouldn't take us long to see that this sculpture of Vespasian has had a longer history than at first thought. It seems that it has been re-tooled and re-chiselled from a statue of Nero. You start with a statue of Nero. He falls, then – after a brief intermezzo – there is the new guy on the block, Vespasian, and you change the old statue of Nero into a new statue of Vespasian. I think there's all kinds of reasons for this, simple cash being one of those reasons: you've just invested a large amount of money in a marble portrait of Nero, and you don't want it to go to waste so you change it to Vespasian. But I think in some way it is a Colston manoeuvre, an obliteration. You can say, 'I don't want Nero anymore, I want Vespasian now.' More cynically, it is an indication that if you are a Roman, then one emperor is much like another and all you have to do is get your chisel out and you can easily change one emperor into the next. At some level, they're facing our problem of what you do with an apparently time-expired public sculpture.

J: I was in India at a museum in Kolkata and around the back of the building there was a line of imperial monuments that had been taken down. The Queen Victoria statue had had her face smashed in.

M: I do think that more generally we imagine that we're the first generation to face this, but every generation has confronted this. Putting people up in the public sphere is a controversial manoeuvre, whatever. There's a political problem, as it isn't self-evident who are the goodies and who are the baddies.

J: It's risky. It's as if you are performing, where you are powerful yet very vulnerable at the same time. You are opening yourself up to all sorts of potential problems in the future. Are there any other examples from the ancient world?

M: I think this is just a kind of real irony of the politics of public statuary. There's a head in the British Museum which was found in Sudan in excavations in the early twentieth century. It's a statue of Emperor Augustus, once the head of a full-length bronze statue, we assume, which had been captured from Roman Egypt by a successful raid by the Kingdom of Kush. They chopped the head off, took it to the city of Meroe and buried it as a trophy underneath the steps of their temple. And ironically, the only reason that one of the finest statues of the Emperor Augustus to survive anywhere in the world was due to people protesting the imperial regime that this guy represented. It was excavated and taken back originally to Liverpool by a skilled team of imperial British archaeologists, who had found the relics of the Roman empire underneath the steps of the temple. I think it's a nice story of the sort of long-term complexities of damage, of preservation, but also of politics. Which we see in Colston, in fact.

J: It's not a straightforward journey for a lot of these statues. Let's say there was a statue of an emperor in a far-flung part of the Roman empire. When a new emperor took power, would they put the name of the old emperor under the new one?

M: You just put a new label up. Nobody knows what they look like. I think in a way we are a bit too hung up about statues' identity. People in the ancient world, certainly in part, were very happy with changing heads. We have got this idea that, somehow, it's fixed and there forever, but what you do, Jeremy, by including people, is to animate it.

J: In 2014 I was asked to think about the Somme and how to commemorate it. What I didn't want to create was a traditional war memorial, which is basically a place to go to, where you feel sad and then leave. A discrete space if you like. Because so many people died that day, I thought that the idea of bodies was very important. It was a kinetic artwork which travelled through Britain. The participants didn't look like statues. Although they were static some of the time, they were moving around. This was a place that would intervene in your life. You didn't have to go to it because it would come to you. It was unannounced, too. Also, the surroundings change around statues; they went up 200 years ago and the setting today might be unrecognisable to when they were erected. With *We're Here Because We're Here*, these men were wandering around contemporary Britain – it's not an environment anyone in 1916 would have understood. So, there's that kind of visual jolt. But it was only there for one day – it wasn't going to be a permanent memorial, even though it cost as much to make as a permanent memorial. It's a memorial on people's Facebook pages and Twitter and Instagram. It's part of the national memory. But it doesn't exist physically anymore.

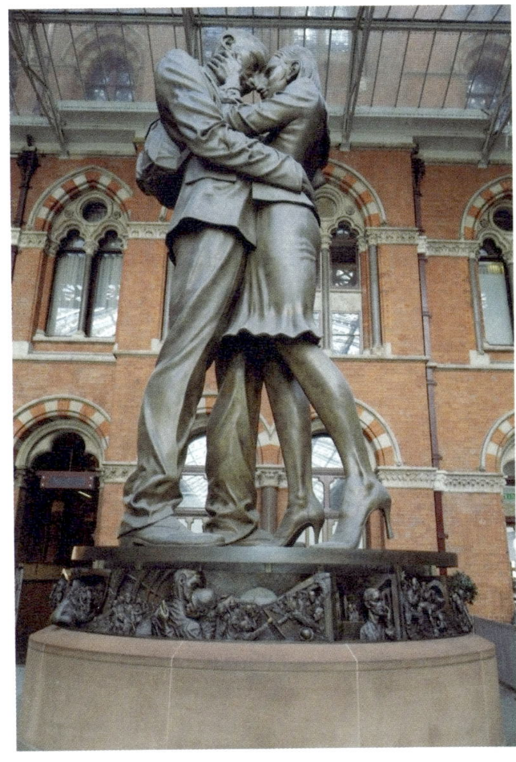

The embracing aliens at St Pancras station, which should be toppled Saddam-style.

M: When you see the stills from it, you do a double take between what might be an inanimate statue and what is a living, human body, so it plays with the reality of the statue quite effectively.

J: The double take you mention is interesting as there was a phenomenon during and after the First World War of people fleetingly seeing dead loved ones in the street. It's related to the rise in interest in spiritualism as a means to contact dead relatives, and its subsequent exploitation of the grief of women, mainly. We know how good a lot of First World War memorials are in terms of their realistic depiction of the soldiers. I had those statues, those memorials, in mind, but I wanted it to move like a virus around Britain.

M: If you think of the relatively traditional framework of a full-length human-sized (or larger than human-sized) figure in bronze or marble in a public place, how good do you think we are at doing that now? We can all think of some truly ghastly examples of this.

J: We both talked about the embracing couple at St Pancras station. That's a national scandal, it's so ugly and totalitarian. It looks like it was made by artificial intelligence, which makes it sound more interesting than it is. I think the bigger the plinth and the more outsize the figure is, it can show a lack of confidence in

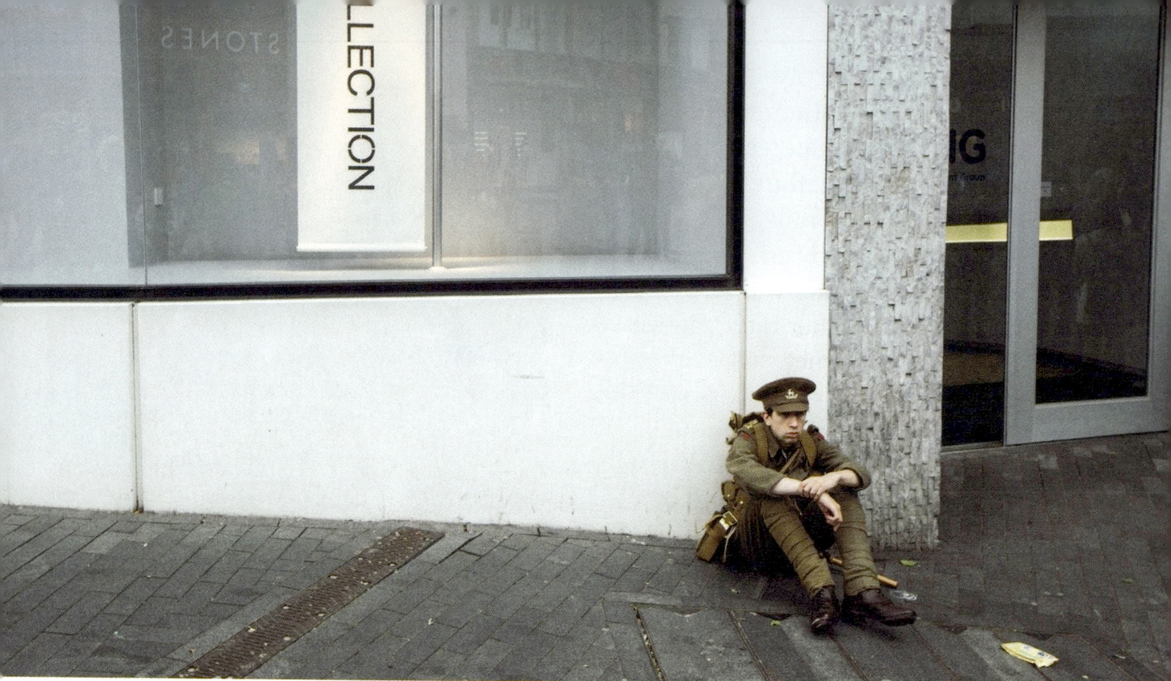

We're Here Because We're Here was an attempt to make a living memorial across the UK for a day. In a sense, it was an anti-statue artwork.

the subject and what you are doing. So, the Keith Park statue that Boris Johnson when mayor wanted on the Fourth Plinth of Trafalgar Square permanently, which didn't happen, but it is now round the corner. He's one and a half times life-size and it's not good because of this. There's a very good one outside the Central Library in Birmingham by Gillian Wearing of a typical family just walking, at ground level. Mark Wallinger's *Ecce Homo* was elegant and life-sized, too.

M: Do you think the Fourth Plinth has been a successful innovation then?

J: I must admit that because I am a member of the liberal elite, I'm on the selection committee for the Fourth Plinth.

M: You've got to say yes!

J: I loved Heather Phillipson's *The End* – the whipped cream with the cherry and the drone. It was put up during lockdown and became the background to demos by anti-vaxxers and conspiracy theorists. I'm sure similar-minded people looked at those images and attached a conspiracy explanation to the sculpture.

M: It's also a justification for art in public rather than even in a museum or gallery, because you find people commenting and discussing the work on the Fourth Plinth in Trafalgar Square as they pass by. If they saw it in a gallery they might say, 'That's a load of rubbish,' but because it's outside, you can respond to it without falling into the stereotypes of how you are going to respond to a work of art.

J: It justifies the idea that not all sculpture should be permanent, and also when sculptures are permanent, they sometimes become invisible. It's a very good model I think, for this, as it gets the conversation going. I couldn't tell you who else is in Trafalgar Square.

M: Can I finish by asking you to do a bit of forward prediction about where you think we're going with this: whether the statue wars will fade because they'll burn out? Or whether there's going to be a change in what we see in public?

J: I hope the statue wars burn out, but I do also hope that the discussion around statues stays. I hope it's still an energetic debate, not a nasty, divisive one. I think public space 'post-Covid' is going to be so important for people to come and almost heal themselves. We need public spaces where we can be around other people, other kinds of people even. It's good that statues and memorials are really being thought about. So, I am trying to be hopeful, but with the current government, it's sometimes difficult, I have to say.

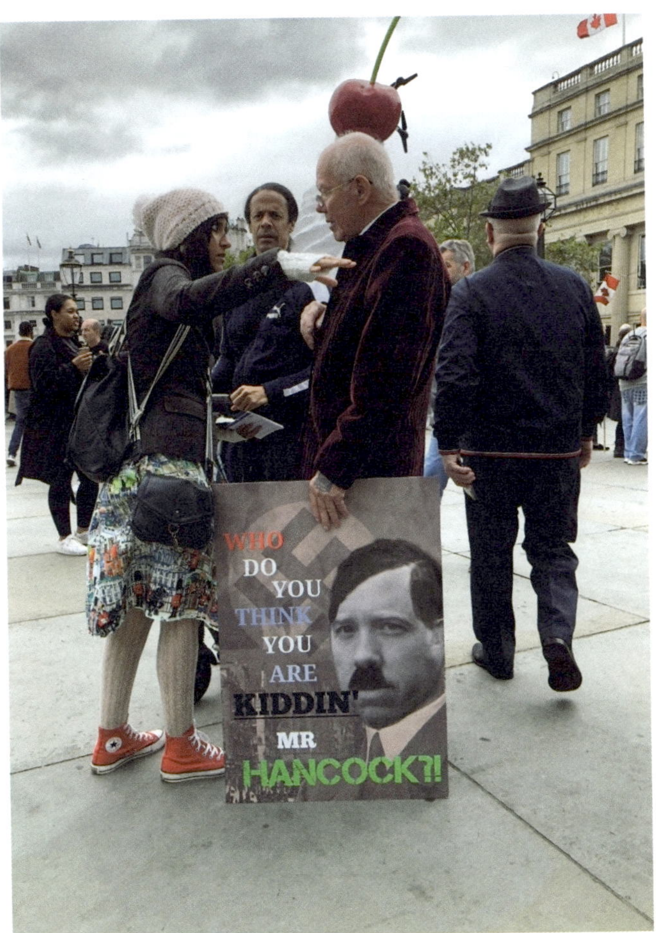

Many anti-lockdown protests took place in Trafalgar Square, with Heather Phillipson's *The End* on the Fourth Plinth (a giant sculpture of a cherry on a cream swirl, with a fly and drone attached) as a background. This sculpture would have appeared in many photographs of the protest, which may have caused havoc in the online conspiracy theory community, as people tried to interpret its 'real meaning'.

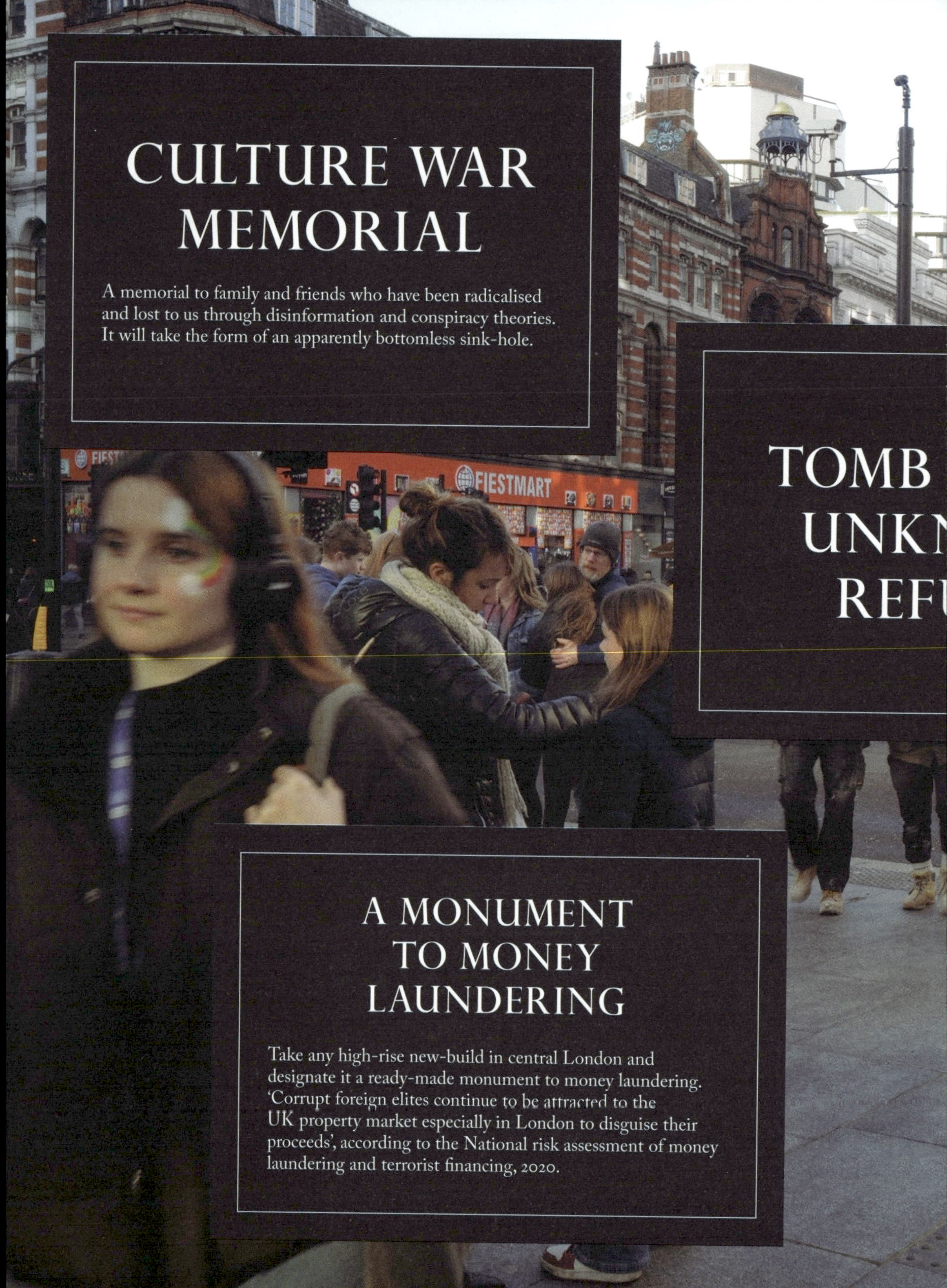

CULTURE WAR MEMORIAL

A memorial to family and friends who have been radicalised and lost to us through disinformation and conspiracy theories. It will take the form of an apparently bottomless sink-hole.

TOMB UNKN REFU

A MONUMENT TO MONEY LAUNDERING

Take any high-rise new-build in central London and designate it a ready-made monument to money laundering. 'Corrupt foreign elites continue to be attracted to the UK property market especially in London to disguise their proceeds', according to the National risk assessment of money laundering and terrorist financing, 2020.

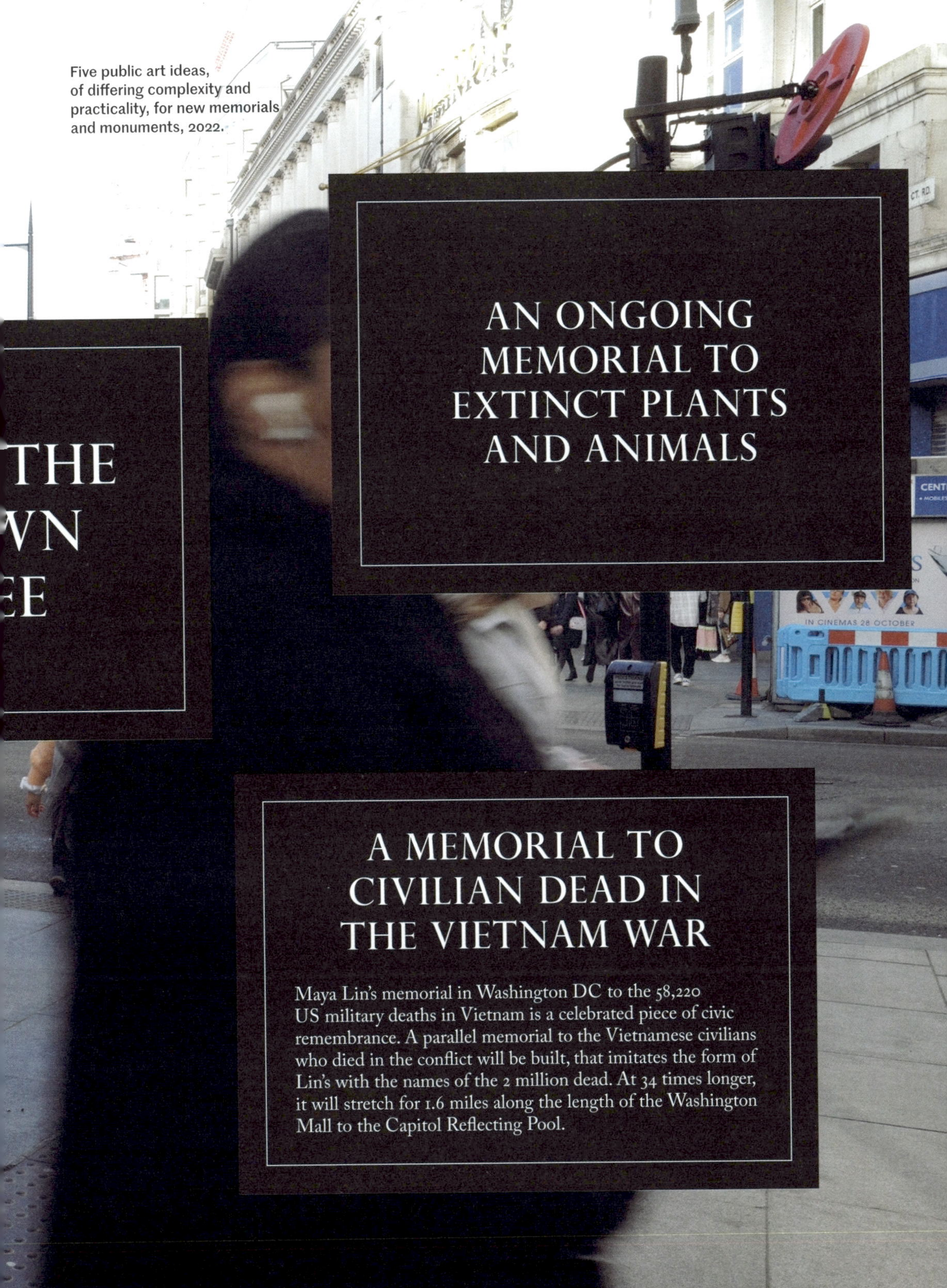

Five public art ideas, of differing complexity and practicality, for new memorials and monuments, 2022.

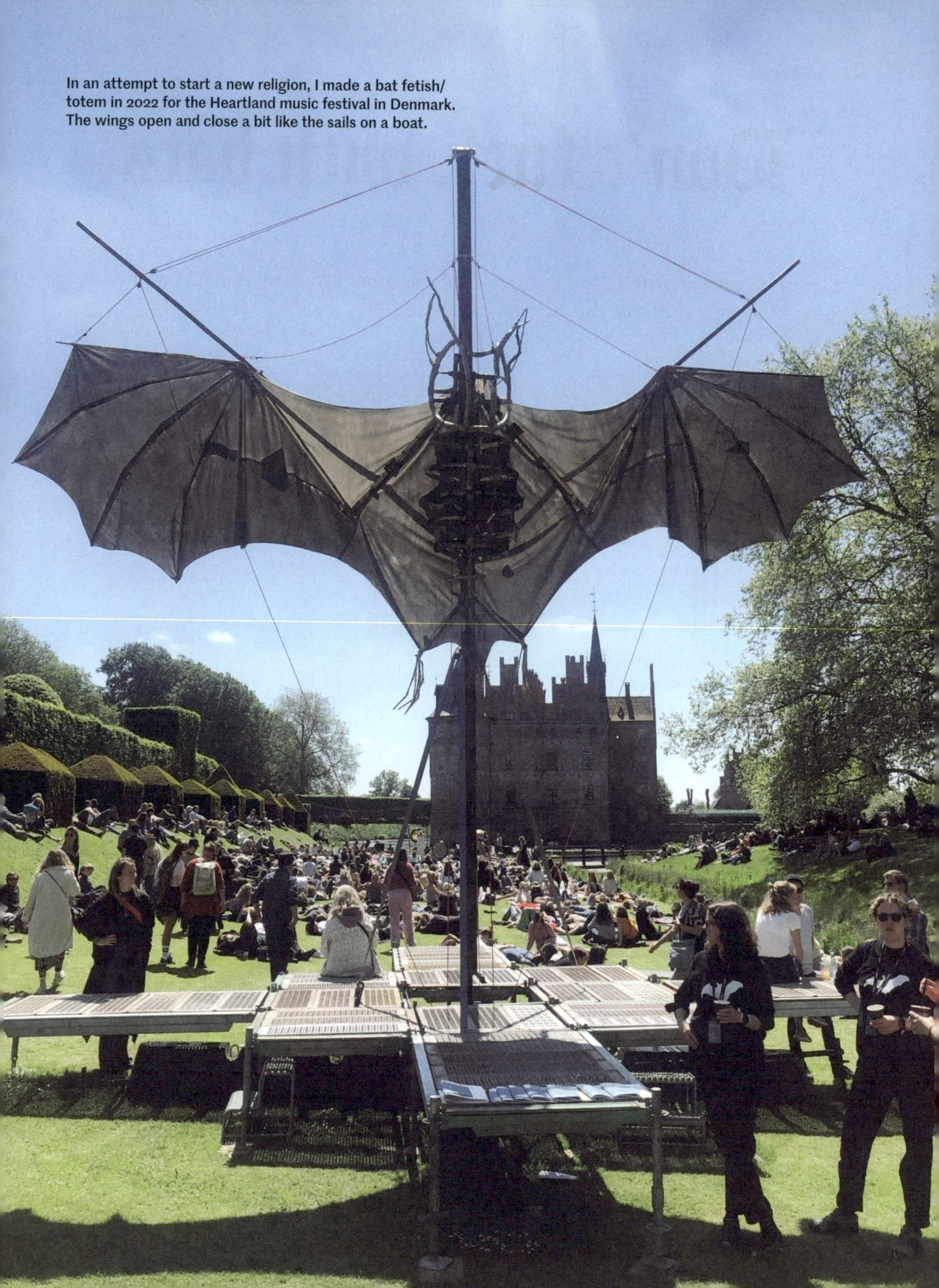
In an attempt to start a new religion, I made a bat fetish/ totem in 2022 for the Heartland music festival in Denmark. The wings open and close a bit like the sails on a boat.

Chapter 6

Don't fuck with bats

The more disappointed I am in humanity the more I look to animals to provide some kind of way out of the current multi mess.

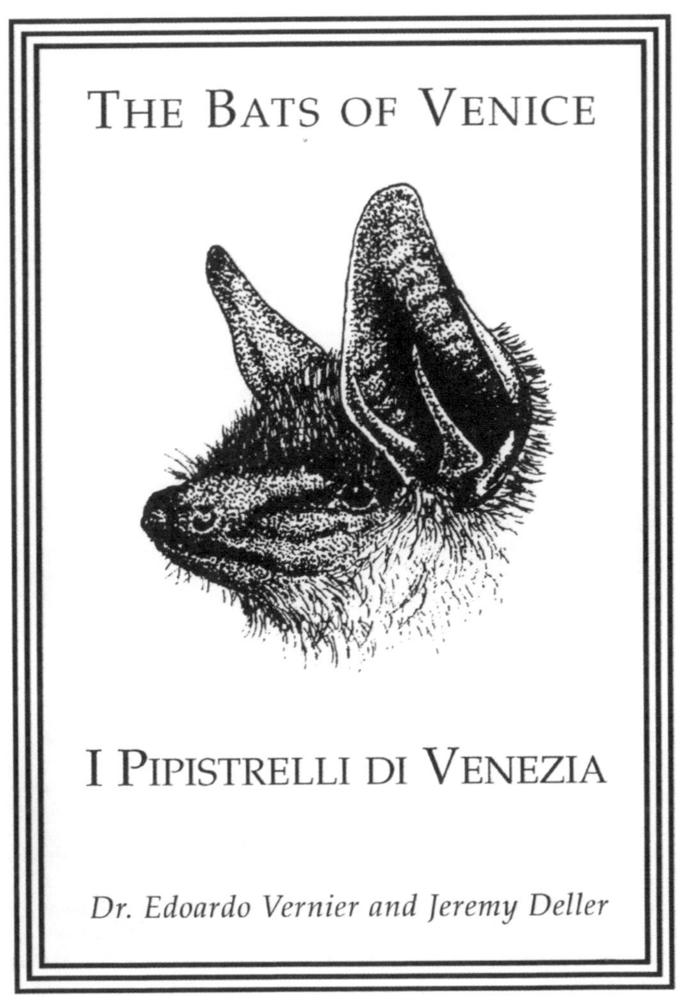

THE BATS OF VENICE

I PIPISTRELLI DI VENEZIA

Dr. Edoardo Vernier and Jeremy Deller

A modest pamphlet produced for bat-lovers visiting Venice for the Biennale in 2003, and beyond.

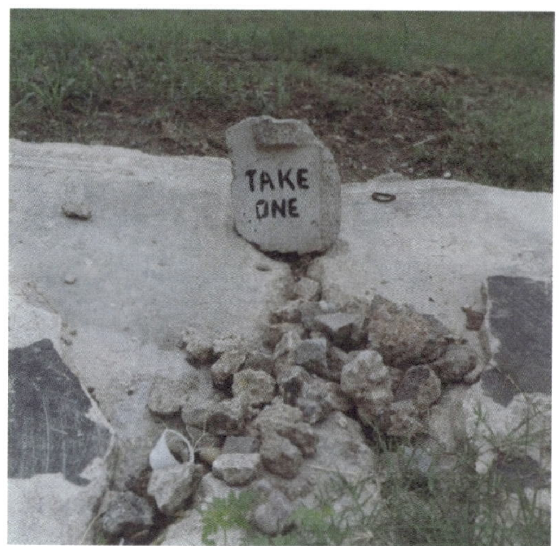

The site of the siege at the Branch Davidian compound is dotted with relics from the ruins of the buildings.

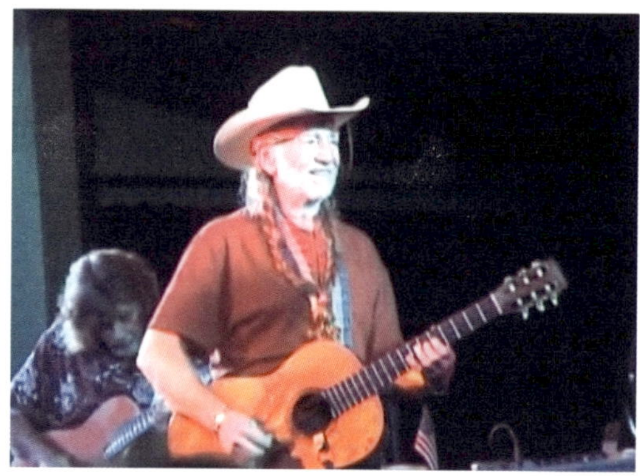

The divine Willie Nelson performing in 2003 at Floore's County Store, Helotes, Texas, a local gig for him. Taken from the film *Memory Bucket*.

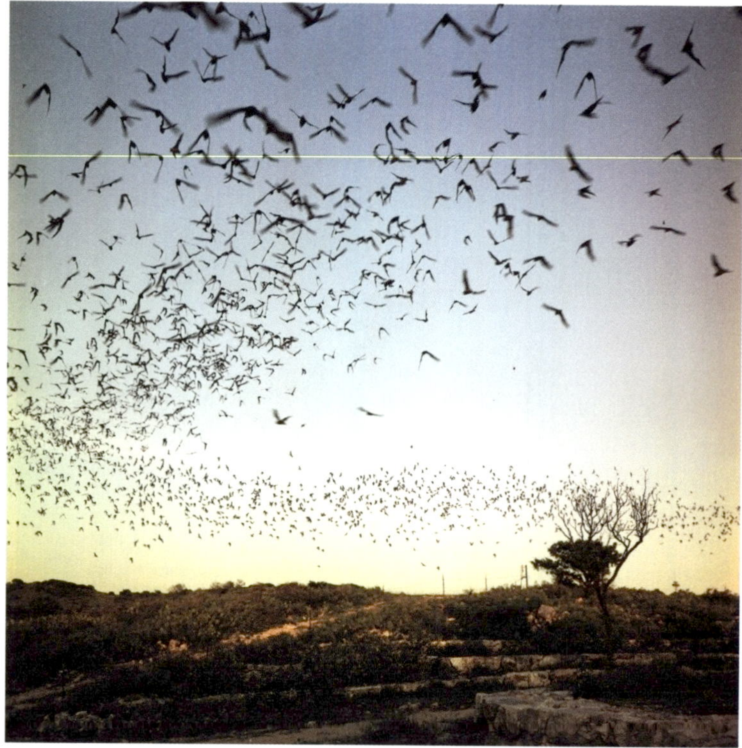

Female Mexican freetailed bats leave the cave at Rio Frio to begin their nightly quest for insects.

Is there anything more captivating and beautiful than a bat? (Answer at the bottom of the page.*) Much as I like dogs and rabbits, there is little mystery to them. Bats, however, are otherworldly and full of magic. There is one that has its eyes situated in its ears. We need to respect or even worship the bat, as they have the power to kill us all.

In 2003, I had a residency with Artpace in San Antonio, Texas, and decided to make a film attempting to document the mood of the state at that time. The film was a 'collage'. It begins at the site of the siege and subsequent massacre at the Branch Davidian ranch in Waco. The Branch Davidians were or maybe still are a Christian sect linked to the Seventh Day Adventists with, at its heart, a predictable belief in the impending apocalypse. Following allegations of child sexual abuse and weapons stockpiling, law enforcement officers attempted to enter the compound, leading to a siege, which resulted in seventy-six people being burnt alive, including the movement's leader, David Koresh.

The site is still owned by the sect and is effectively part visitor centre and part pilgrimage site, so much so that the local tourist information centre has produced a map to the land. Among the relics are burnt remains of toys of children killed in the siege. At the time of my visit, the museum was run by Ron, a survivor. His daughter was killed during the assault on the compound, and he had spent years in prison for his involvement. He remained loyal to Koresh, living in a caravan on the site, dutifully spreading the word about their beliefs.

Close to the Branch Davidian land is the town of Crawford, where George W. Bush, the then president, had a ranch. The town had been turned into a patriotic tourist centre selling 'war on terror'-based souvenirs. I went to a Willie Nelson concert as some sort of cleanse. But despite his presence, it wasn't exactly an uplifting film. Much of it was so unsettling about Texas and its culture that

A painting by Ron Goins of the attack on the compound, on a brick recovered from the ruins.

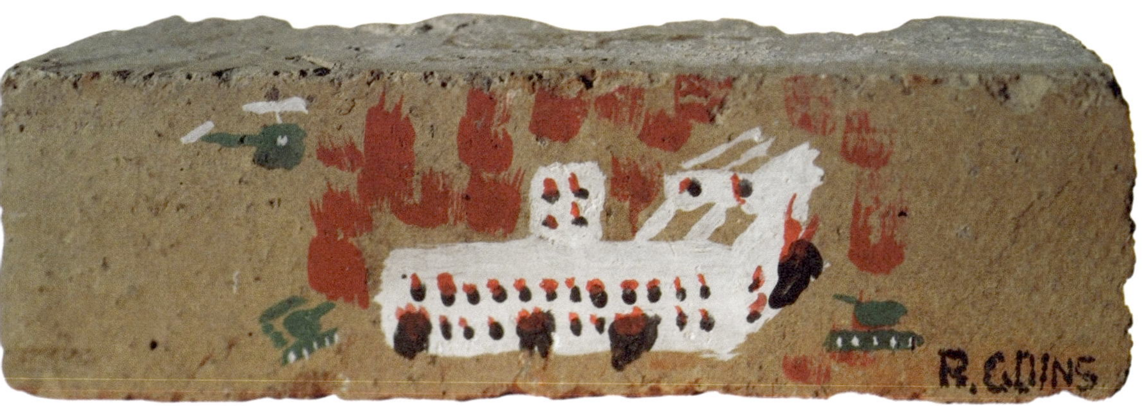

* No.

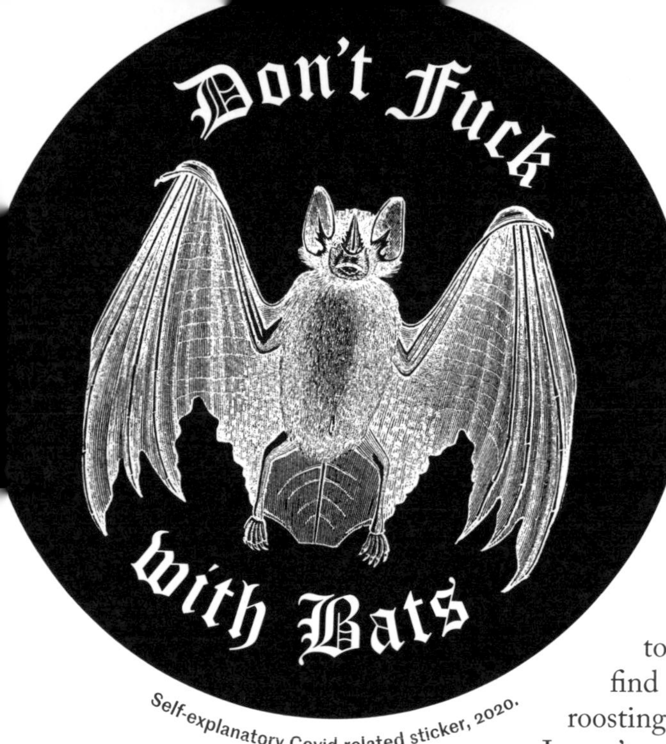

Self-explanatory Covid-related sticker, 2020.

I really couldn't end it that way, Willie or no Willie. I thought bats might help give it an alternative ending, taking it somewhere entirely different. The bats were filmed at the Rio Frio caves in West Texas, where millions roost. When they leave the caves, the female bats fly up to the thermal air currents and feed on up to a thousand insects each on a single run. They then return to the cave and, impressively, can find their young among the millions roosting there and feed them.

I wasn't prepared for this experience: it is simply impossible to anticipate the visual and sensory impact of millions of bats flying a few feet above your head. As a spectacle, it put all the stupid human behaviour in the film in perspective, the bats having no interest in us as they go off to hunt. It was in the best tradition of Romantic art, conveying the force of nature as something both awe-inspiring and frightening – the ultimate nightmare for some people, a sublime experience for me.

I returned to the cave eight years later to make a 3D film and, on this occasion, intended to go right inside it. Even in the short period between my two visits, drought had caused the roost to decline. The heart of the cave is one of the most toxic environments on the planet, on account of the bat guano and airborne rabies. There are also fungi there that, if disturbed and inhaled, can calcify your eyes and lungs, as happened to a National Geographic film crew a few months earlier. Guano is an incredibly versatile material as it serves as both a very effective fertiliser and a key component in explosives. Productive and destructive, rather like bats themselves.

To enter, I had to wear a hazmat outfit and a breathing contraption like a gas mask. The temperature was over 100 degrees Fahrenheit outside and even hotter deep in the cave. As I was having everything fitted and the breathing apparatus fixed up, I felt like I was being slowly suffocated. I could barely breathe, and this was before I had moved a muscle. I thought it better that I had a freakout there rather than deep in the cave.

I did have an idea for a free jazz band to play along with the bats' hunting echolocation sounds. I think this could work with a bit more technical know-how and might still happen at some stage, as long as the bats can't hear the music. In the meantime, I used some of the recordings from the cave to make a dub reggae track, 'Freetail Dub', with Adrian Sherwood, complete with luminous record sleeve.

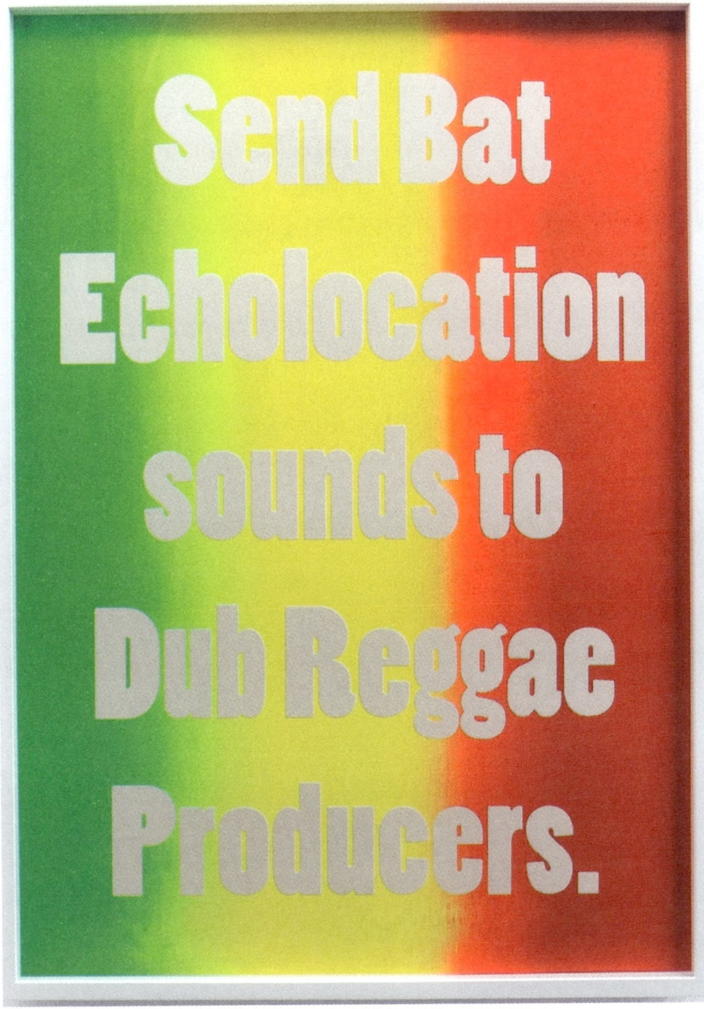

I made a print of this idea to serve as a reminder to myself a few years before I managed to make a record.

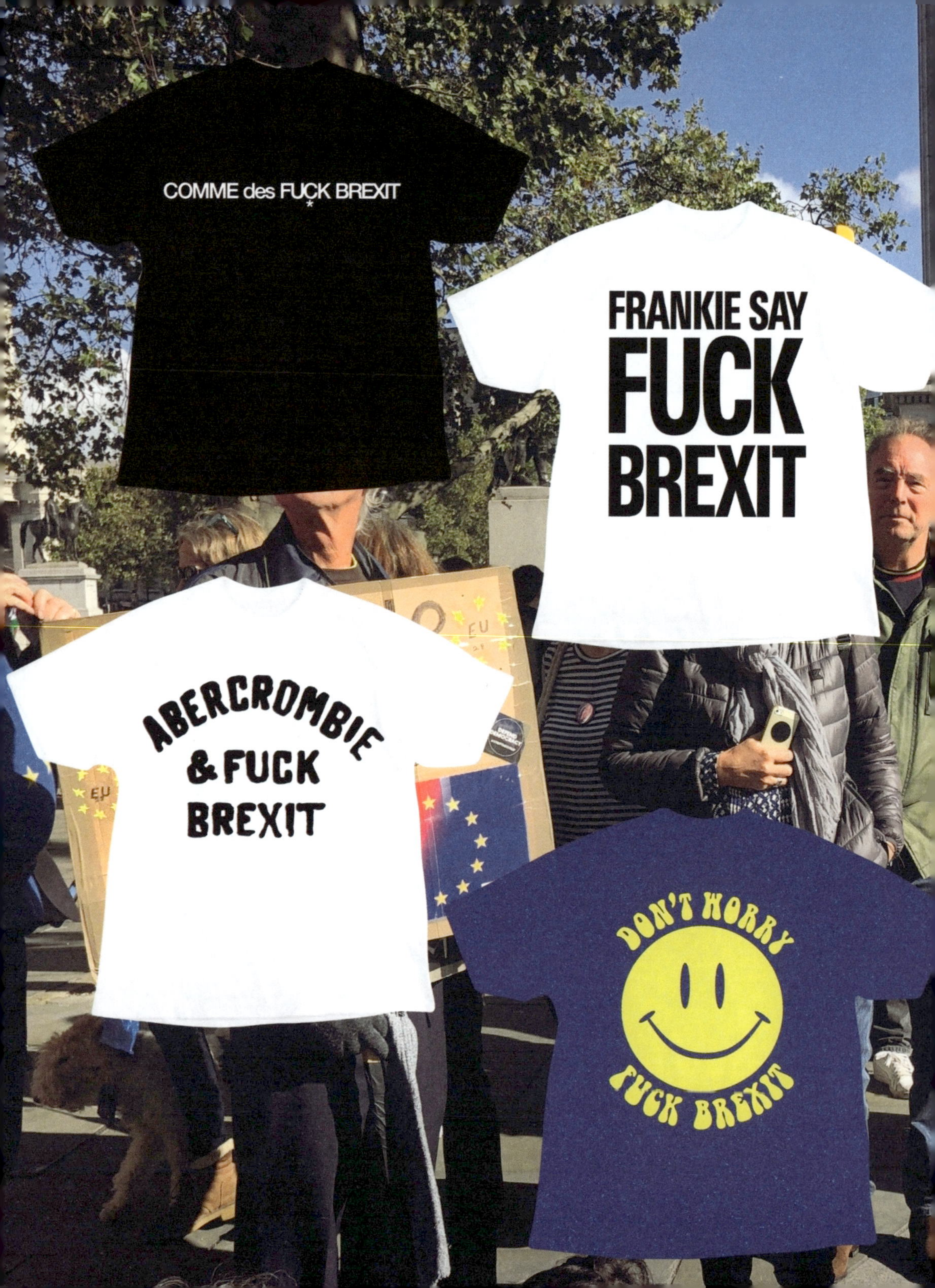
COMME des FUCK BREXIT
FRANKIE SAY FUCK BREXIT
ABERCROMBIE & FUCK BREXIT
DON'T WORRY
FUCK BREXIT

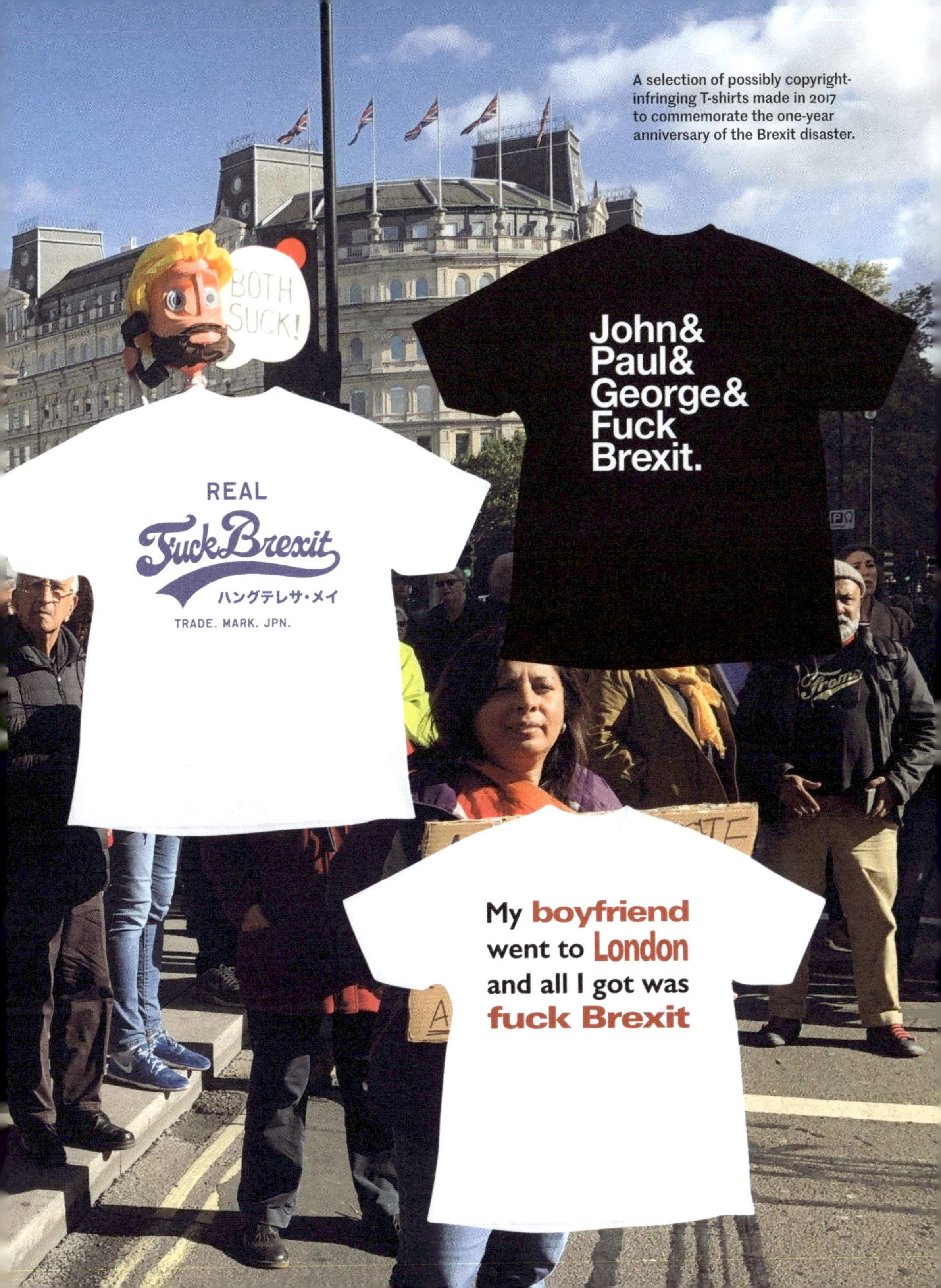

A selection of possibly copyright-infringing T-shirts made in 2017 to commemorate the one-year anniversary of the Brexit disaster.

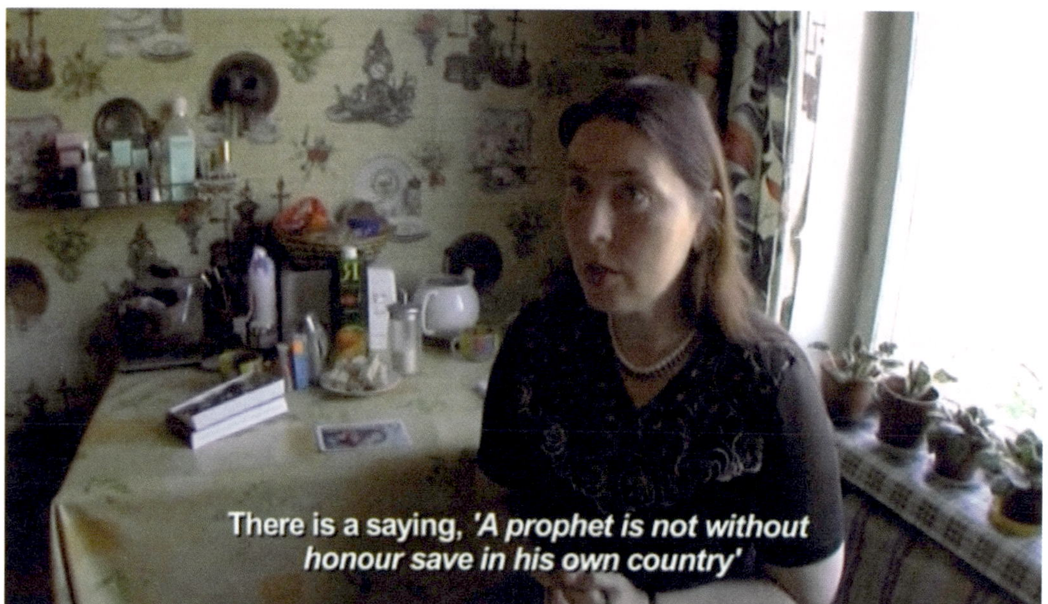

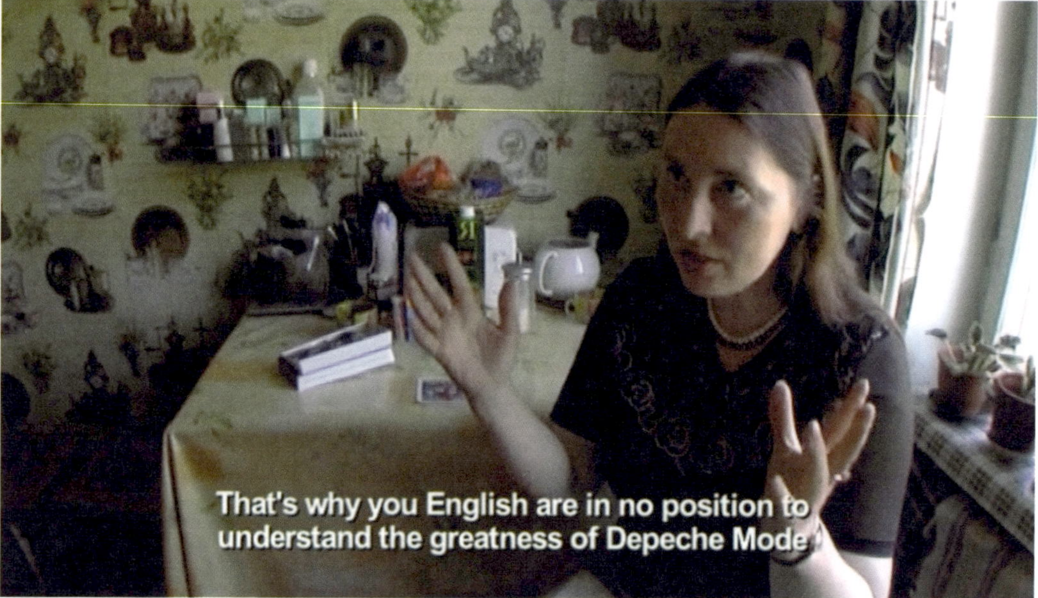

Stills from *Our Hobby is Depeche Mode*, 2006, where Francisca, an academic in Moscow, tells us off for not liking Depeche Mode enough. She had written her PhD on Martin Gore's poetry/lyrics, so she would know.

Chapter 7

'I see your intricate subtlety Martin'

Depeche Mode and their fans

Being a fan of a band or musician can be an almost religious experience. I have myself flirted with this state, so have a lot of sympathy with people who find themselves in this position.

In 2005, my mate Nick Abrahams, a filmmaker, had heard that Mute Records wanted to make a film about Depeche Mode to form part of a twenty-fifth anniversary 'greatest hits' campaign. I had known Nick for about ten years, from when I worked in the Sign of the Times shop in Covent Garden, where he would often film their parties. We had worked together on a video for the Manic Street Preachers' single 'Found That Soul' in 2001. My favourite part of which was during the guitar solo, when we filmed a pile of books being revealed one by one. 'A book solo', of sorts. Nick and I thought it might be interesting to make a film about Depeche Mode's fans. We had heard about the mythic,

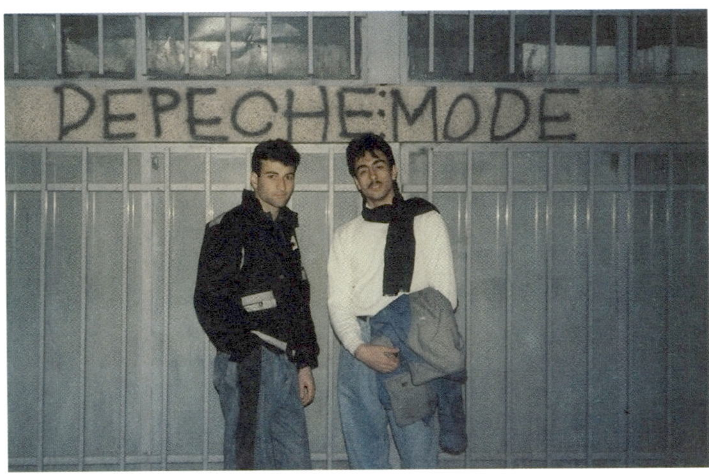

Peyman (right) and friend in Tehran, around 1994. Peyman now lives in Canada and was interviewed in the film. In a sense, his experience of being a fan of the band under a disapproving authoritarian regime was very similar to that of young people in Russia and the Eastern Bloc countries in the 1980s.

obsessive following the band had in Eastern Europe and Russia, but it was hard to grasp the true extent of it. When we dug more into this, it turned out that the fans in these countries were absolutely what we were looking for, countries where the liberating effect of the music was akin to what the UK and United States had experienced with the Beatles in the early 1960s. The band had inadvertently embedded itself in the social and geopolitical history of these times of change. One of those brilliant cultural accidents that makes the world of culture go round.

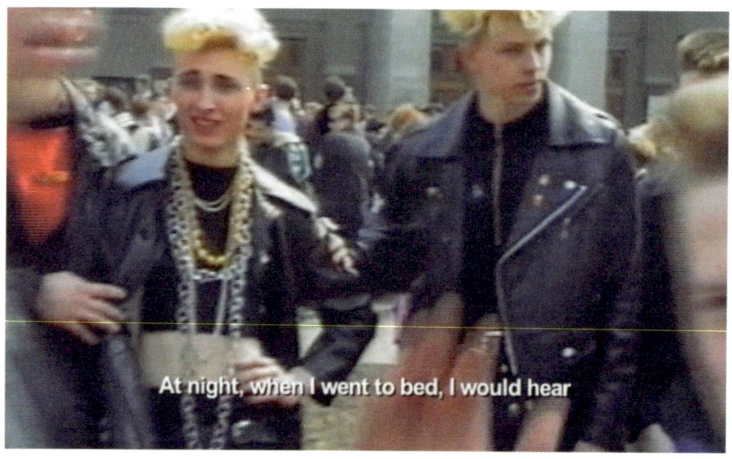

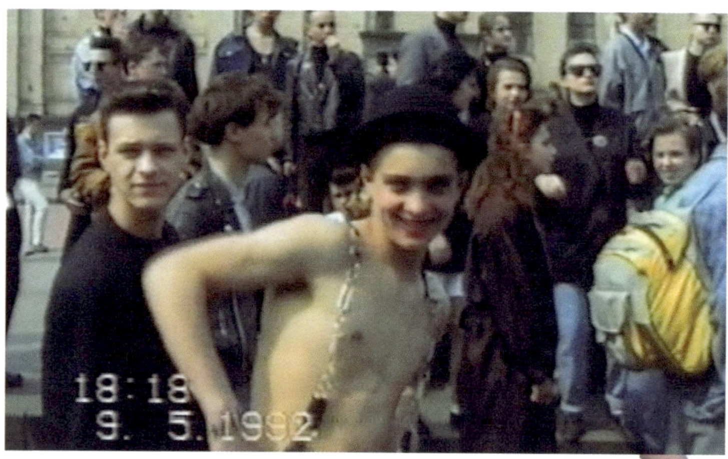

May 9th is lead singer Dave Gahan's birthday and Victory Day in Russia, when fans take to the streets to celebrate his life and the defeat of fascism. Here are two stills from remarkable footage of the day in 1992. As fans congregate in Mayakovsky Square, it seems like a few mums had their wardrobes liberated by their sons to get the Martin Gore look. Needless to say, we used this archive extensively in our documentary.

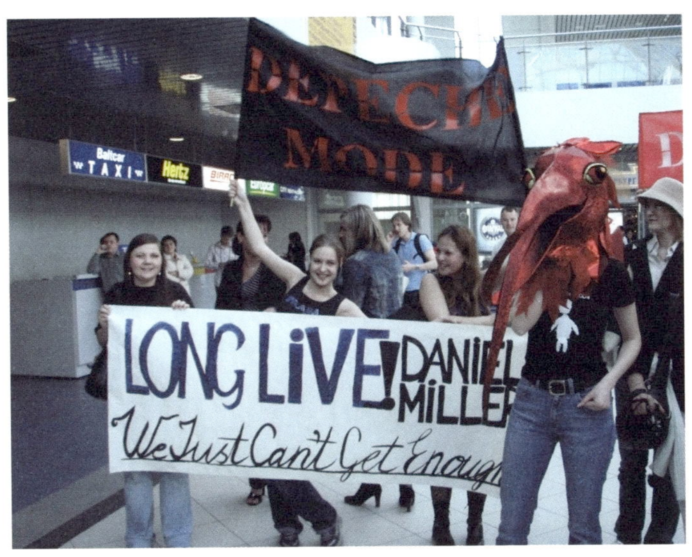

Low-key welcome to St Petersburg after more or less a day of flying from Mexico. This set the tone for the following forty-eight hours, as we were basically kidnapped, in a good way, by a group of fans.

We were never sure if anybody else even pitched their ideas for the film, but I think a key reason we got the commission was because it didn't require the band to be in it. The fans were also much more enthusiastic about the music, and possibly more into the band, than the band themselves. We contacted fans via the most obvious route: the band's website, which was our first near-disaster. We received way over 5,000 emails, all of which we had to reply to, without really knowing who the senders were or whether they would be at all helpful for the film.

To be honest, we were flying a bit blind for much of the film, turning up in countries we barely knew, meeting people we didn't know, desperate to find interesting material with little clue as to how we might do this. Our standard schedule was to spend three days in each country, which doesn't give you much room for error. It was when we arrived in Russia that we knew the idea was going to work. The fans were totally devoted to the band. In a sense, it was quite an old fashioned, Soviet-style approach, even in 2006.

One of these homemade works was an elaborate comic book which tells the story of a girl and her friends, each of whom marry a member of the band and live together in the same house. The women

The origin of the title of this chapter – again, from the St Petersburg airport welcoming party.

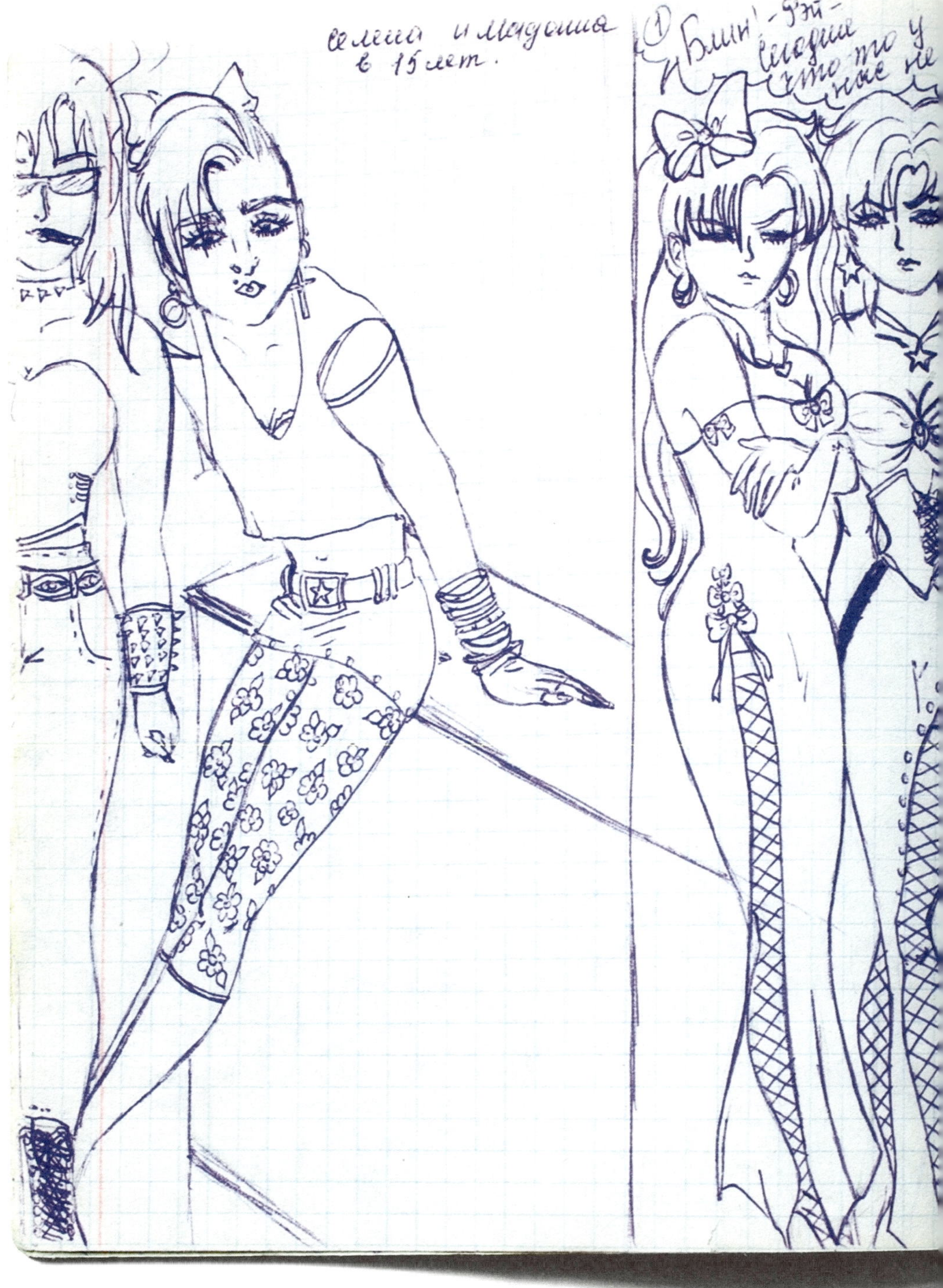
Селена и Мадонна
в 15 лет.
①
Блин! - Рэй -
сегодня
что-то у
ное не

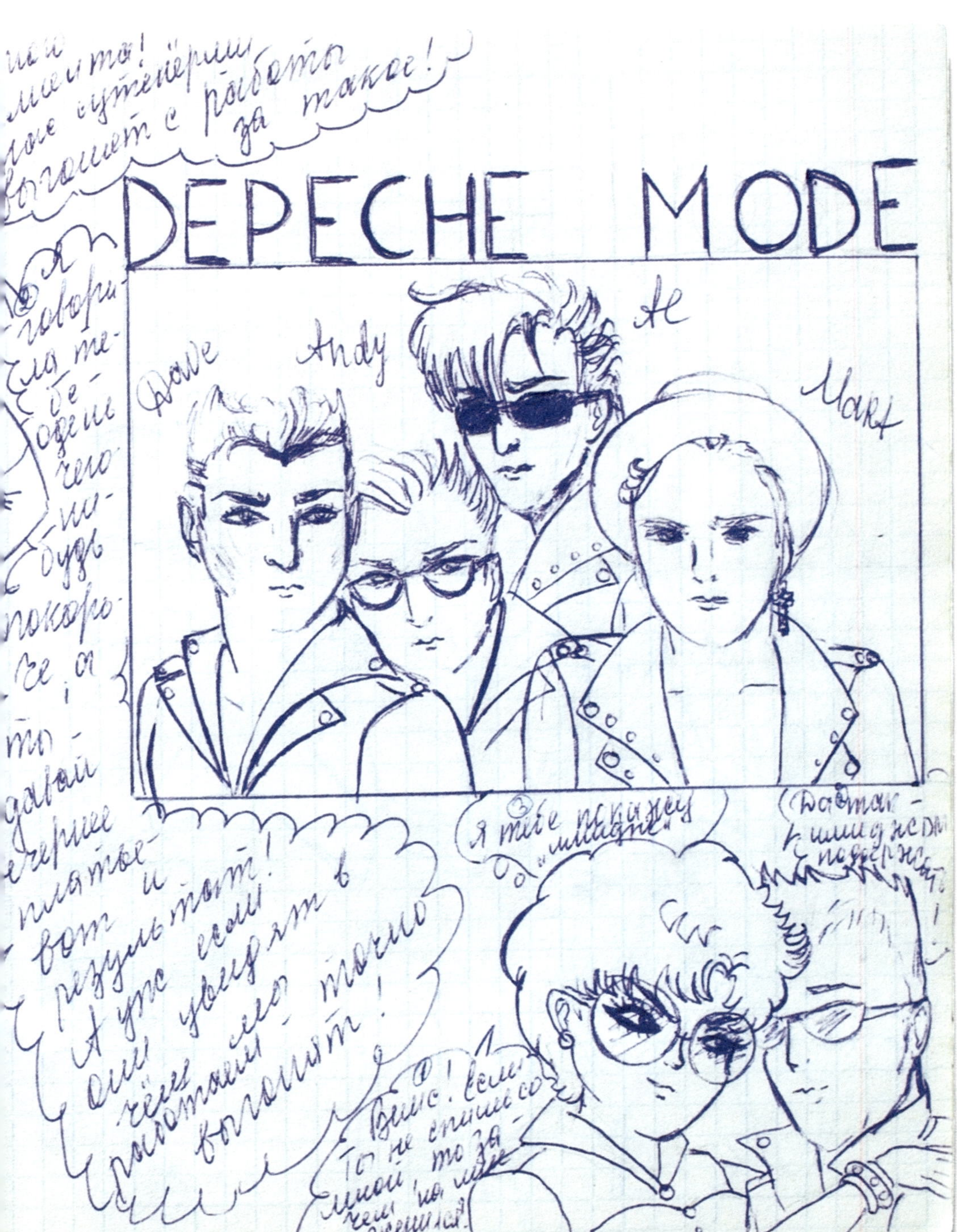

Masha's incredible folk art masterpiece graphic novel of her and her mates' escapades with the band. Weirdly, Madonna is never mentioned in the book or our interview with her.

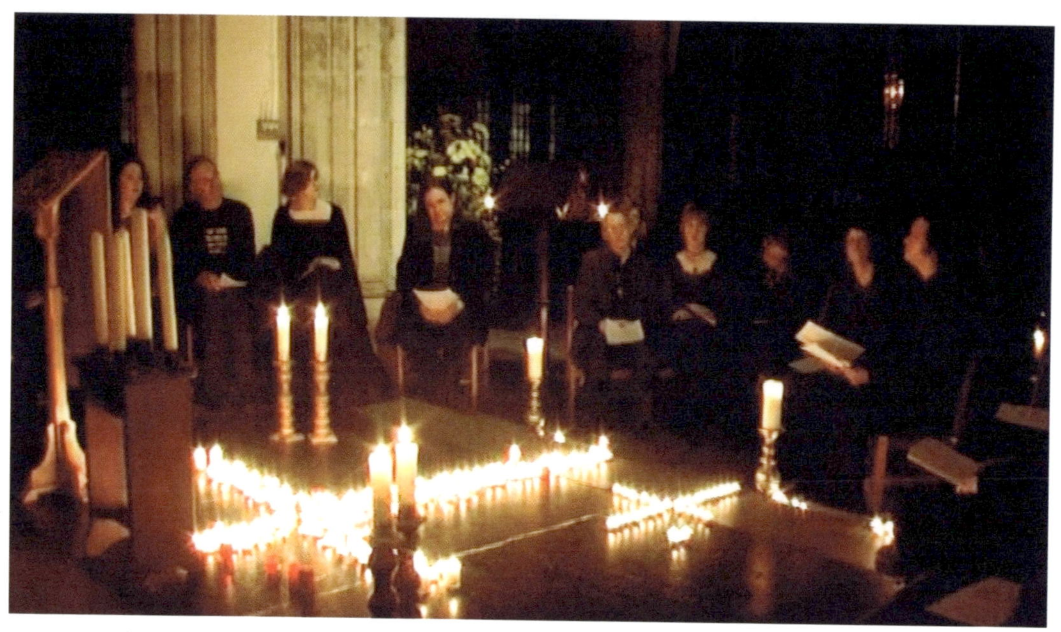

The Goth Eucharist service at St Edward King and Martyr church in Cambridge. Something of a contrast to the exuberant Depeche-partying of Russian fans.

create perfumes, which work as aphrodisiacs to get the band excited and fall in love with them. While they are portrayed as being sassy and sexy, the band turn out to be drunks and totally incapable. May 9th is Dave Gahan's birthday, but is also a national holiday celebrating victory against fascism in the Second World War. Fans traditionally have gathered on this day to discuss and celebrate the band. In the early 1990s, thousands would meet as word of mouth was the only way to find out about the music.

We went to a Depeche-themed club night playing only their music, culminating in strippers recreating videos, cheered on by the mainly female fans. This sequence didn't make it into the film. In contrast, in the UK we filmed in St Edward King and Martyr church in Cambridge at a service for goths. 'Gothic music', for want of a better term, was incorporated into a sombre communion service, including some slower Depeche songs – a total contrast to the scenes of abandon in Russia. We ended up with 100 hours of footage, which was something of a challenge to edit down to the required hour. When it was finally ready, we sent the film to Mute with a great sense of relief, unaware that some classic record-company politics were going on behind the scenes. Quite understandably, our film was not anything of a priority for them.

It's unclear to this day whether the band ever saw the film. The guy who ran the website apparently told them that it was the worst film ever made, which probably didn't help. I think he was a bit miffed because we didn't put him in it.

There was an online petition to remove footage of a former East German family from the film. The family are obsessive Depeche fans, who dress up in different looks from the band's videos. We loved their fanaticism and humour, but some German fan groups felt that this was verging on sacrilegious. When you are dealing with fans of a band like Depeche Mode, you have to be aware you are entering a bear pit when trying to navigate it. The film's title – *Our Hobby Is Depeche Mode* – came from the mother of that family. The film does get screened but in an appropriately underground Soviet style in case the Depeche police find out.

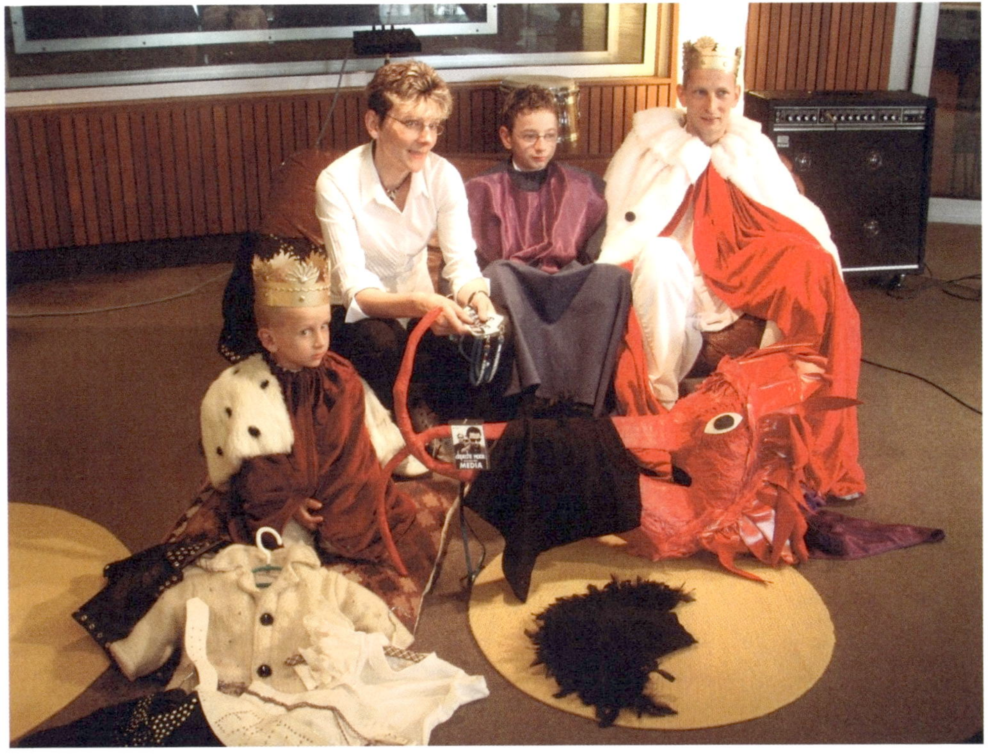

The Granzow family at Hansa Studios in Berlin. Claudia runs a fancy dress and carnival shop and, in her spare time, dresses family members up as characters from Depeche Mode videos and films them, much to the annoyance of other German fans. Their teenage son David was more into Eminem, he told us.

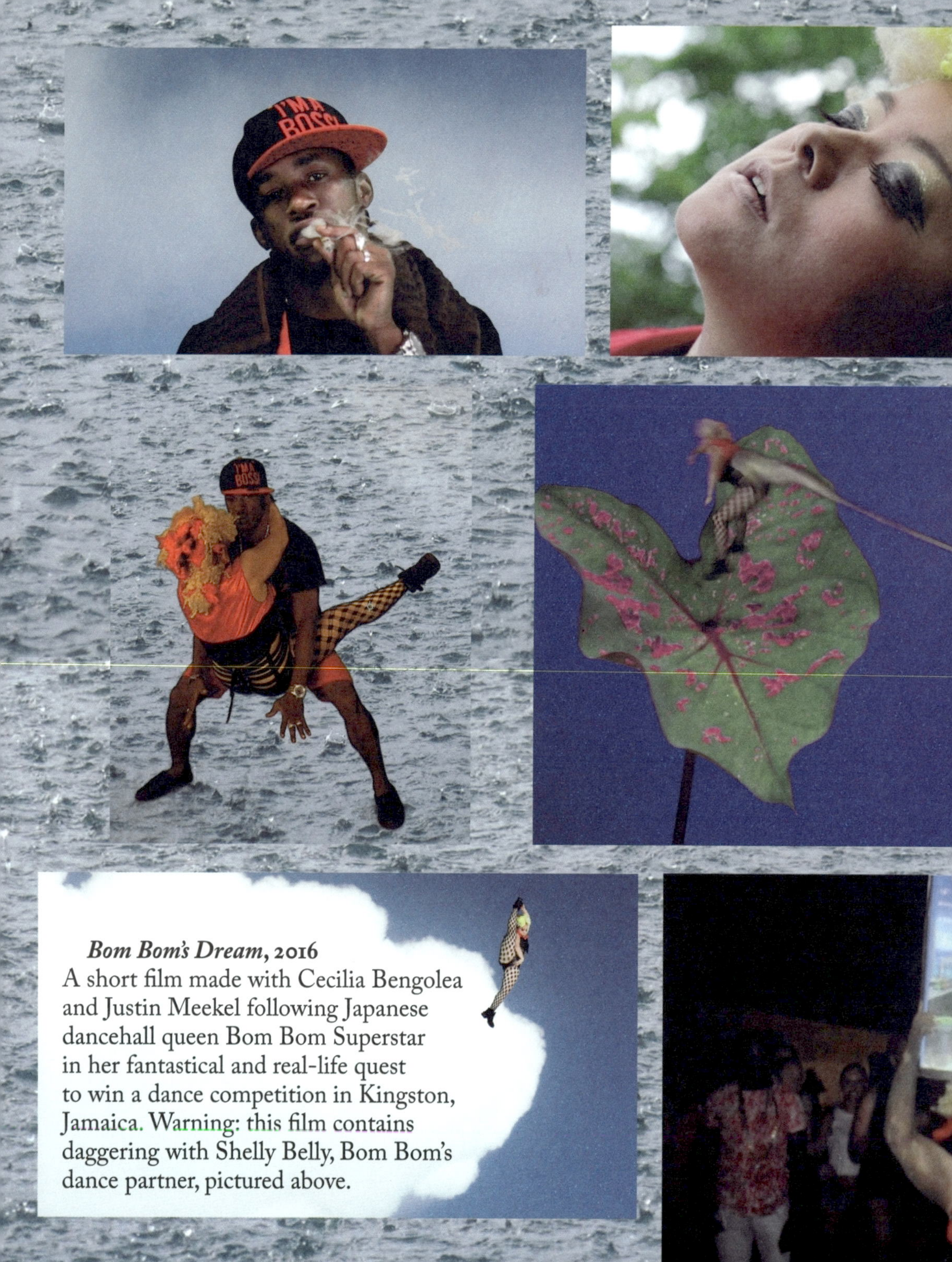

***Bom Bom's Dream*, 2016**
A short film made with Cecilia Bengolea and Justin Meekel following Japanese dancehall queen Bom Bom Superstar in her fantastical and real-life quest to win a dance competition in Kingston, Jamaica. Warning: this film contains daggering with Shelly Belly, Bom Bom's dance partner, pictured above.

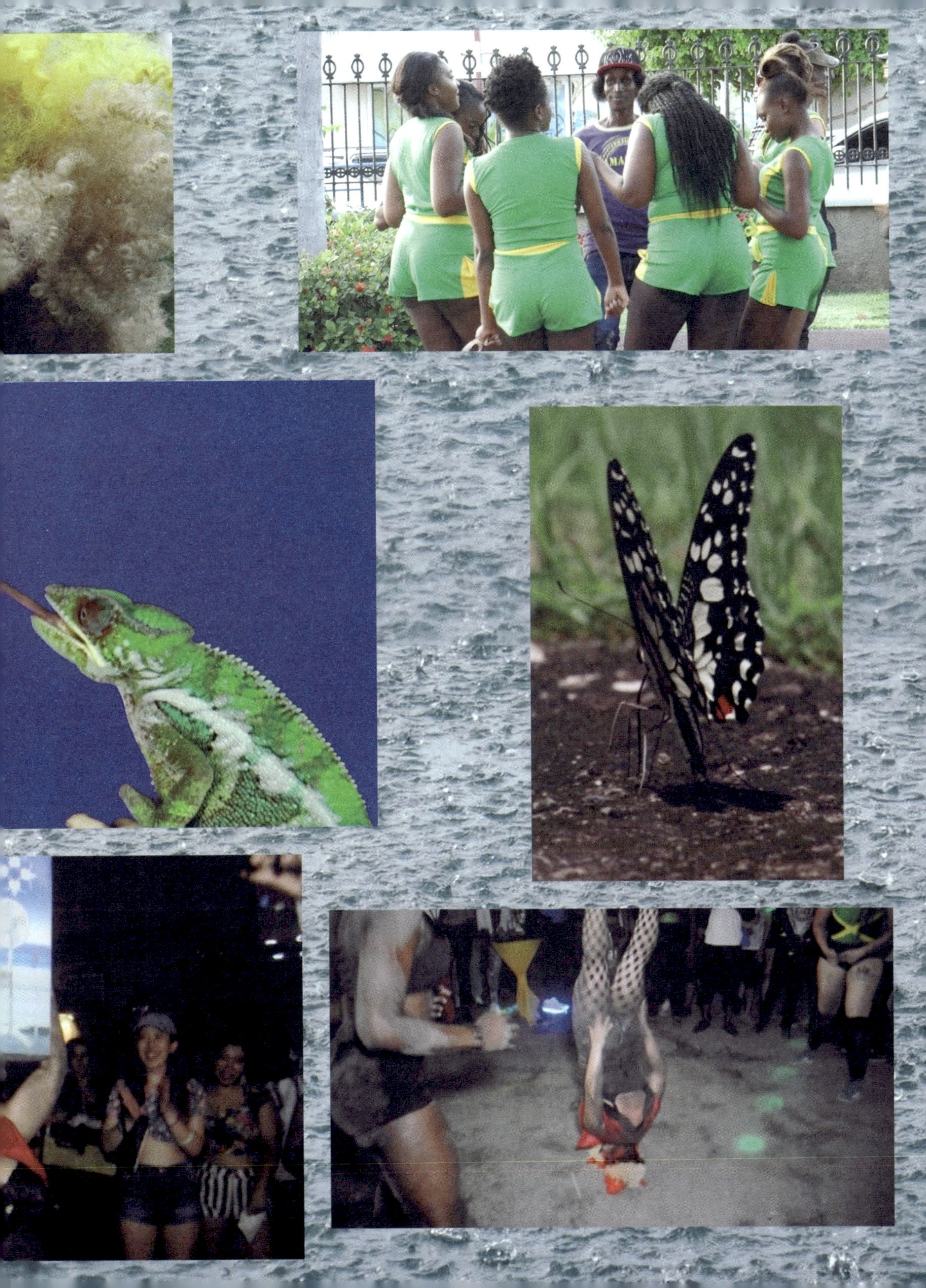

YACHT IDENTIFICATION GUIDE

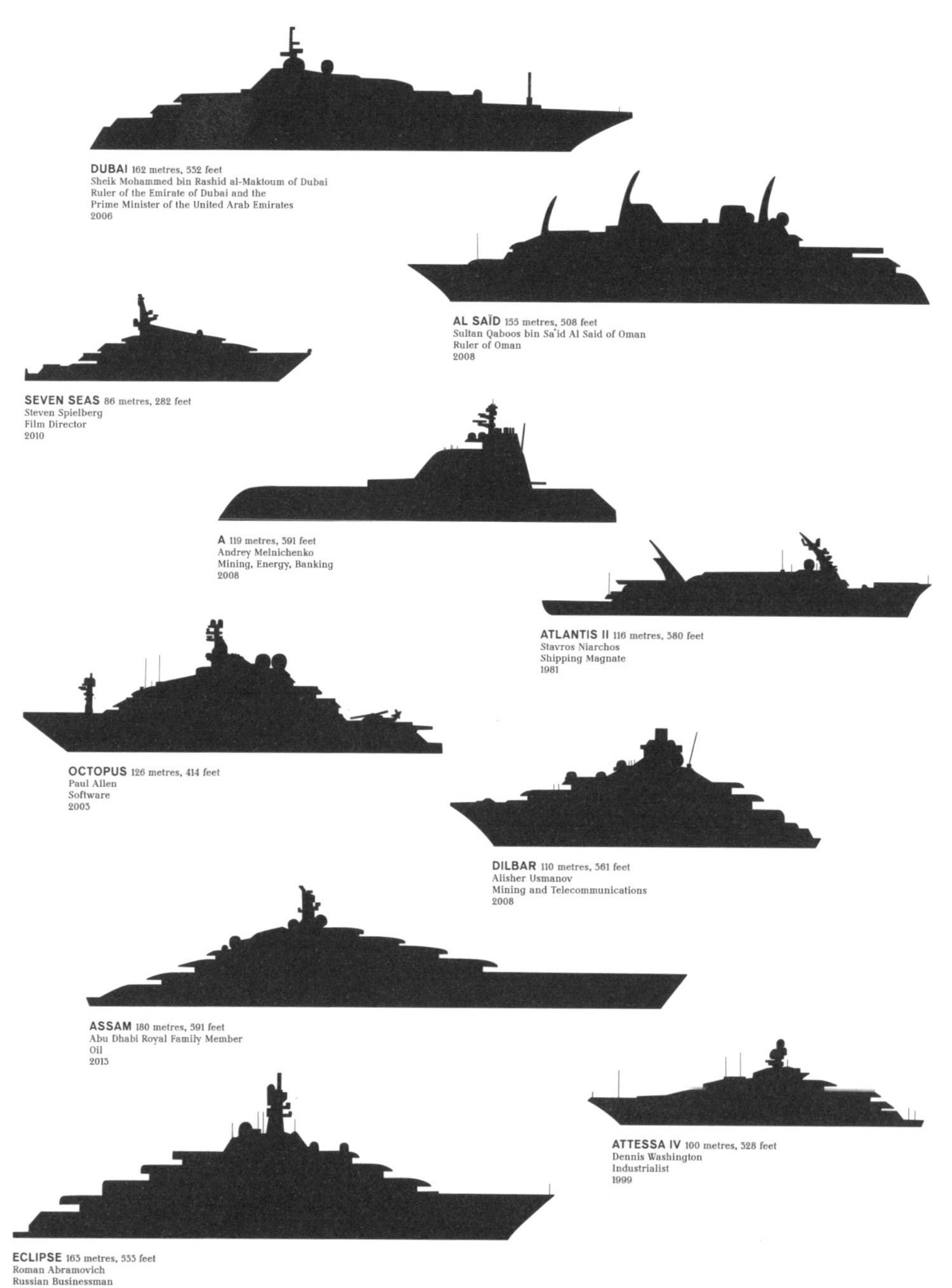

Chapter 8

Warning! Graphic Content

A picture essay

For the past ten years I have worked closely with the designer Fraser Muggeridge and his studio. The relationship goes a bit beyond 'can you make that a bit bigger'. Here are some personal favourites of our work together.

Self-explanatory poster, somewhere in London, 2021. In the UK the word corruption is so rarely used in a domestic context – it's what other people do, we give ourselves an easy ride with the word cronyism, which is a little more cosy.

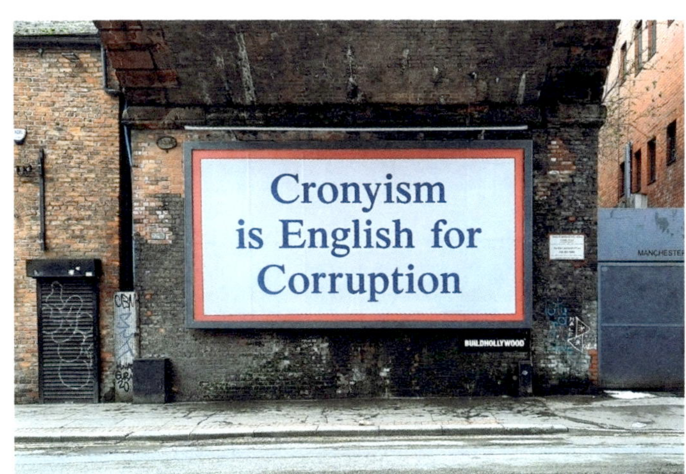

← Possibly my favourite work in the book, handy when at the opening week of the Venice Biennale, 2013.

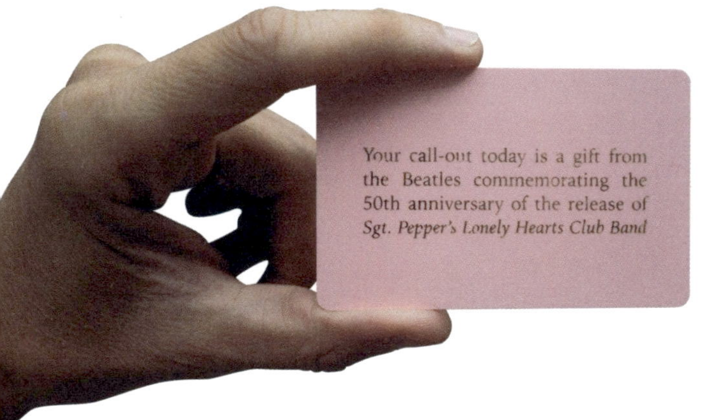

In 2017, to celebrate the 50th anniversary of the release of *Sgt. Pepper's Lonely Hearts Club Band*, I was asked to make a work based on the song 'With a Little Help from My Friends'. I had the idea for a handyman to go to emergency call-outs in Liverpool and then not charge for the work. The wording in retrospect is a bit misleading, as it was not strictly paid for by the Beatles but was in their honour.

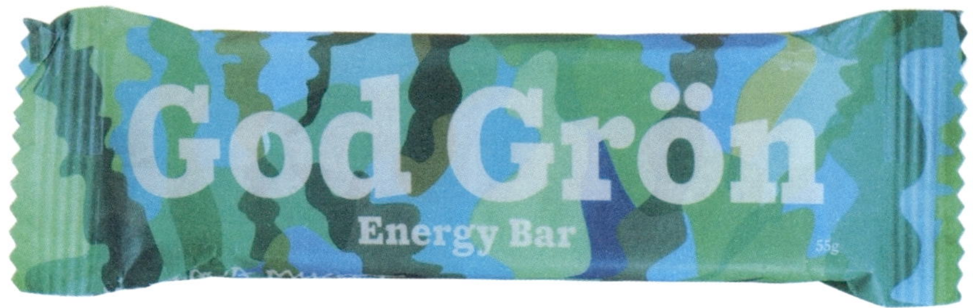

In Stockholm for one day only in June 2022 I made and launched *God Grön*, a kelp energy bar. I also changed the school dinners for 5,000 students that day by incorporating kelp and insect protein into the menu, much to some of their disgust.

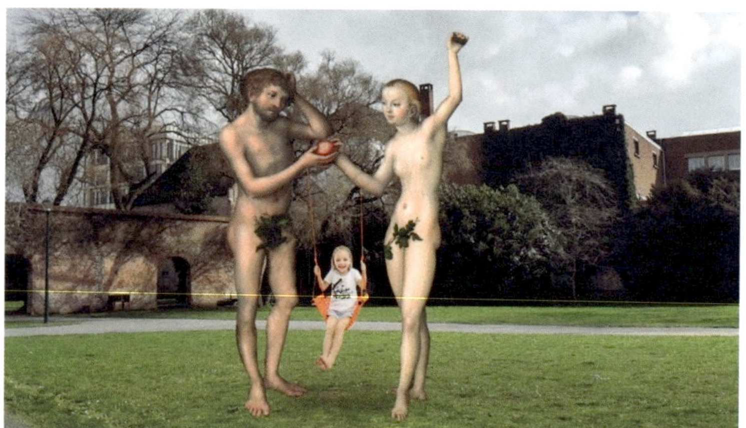

Mum and Dad, Adam and Eve swing mock-up, 2021. This idea did see the light of day but unfortunately it didn't look like this. It goes without saying, but it's easier to make a Photoshop image than it is to paint a sculpture to the quality of a Lucas Cranach masterpiece. Kind of obvious if you think about it, but the mock-up was so persuasive.

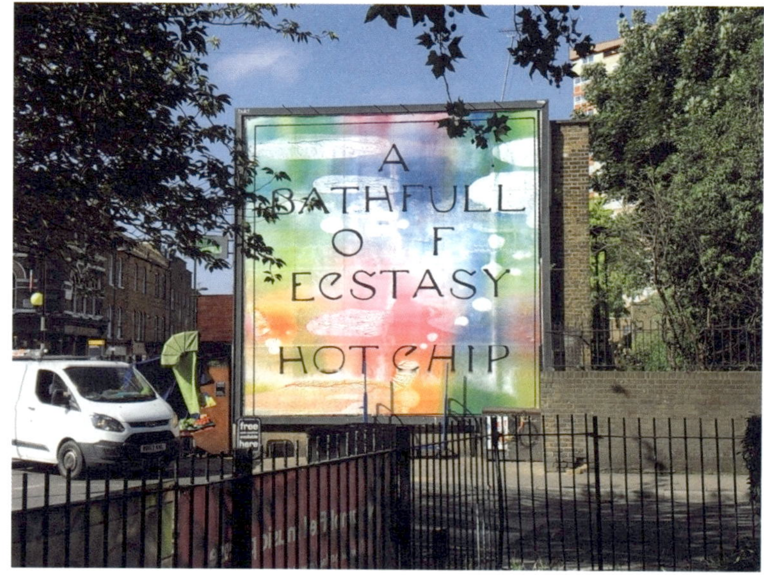

Hot Chip album cover and campaign, 2019. I just wanted something that looked aesthetic – decadent even – that was not made on a computer. Fraser had been making some pure analogue colour prints and I knew this approach was perfect.

Thank God

For

Immigrants

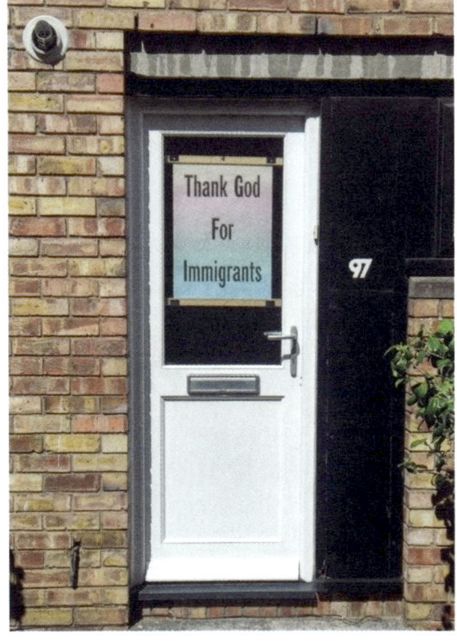

A lockdown fundraiser poster made and sent out by Fraser and myself in April 2020, specifically made to be displayed in a window. The idea partially came from the people I had hung around while making *Putin's Happy* (see page 55), who had anti-immigrant views and whose lives because of Covid were possibly being saved by immigrant healthcare staff. Does someone's opinion about immigration change when an immigrant saves their life?

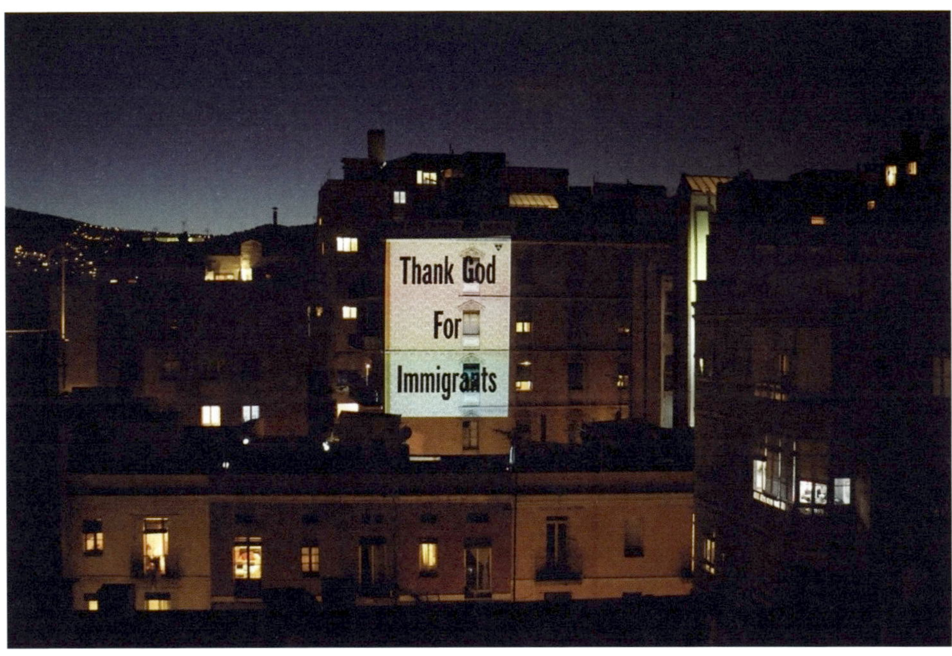

Projection in Barcelona initiated by Raúl Goñi in 2020.

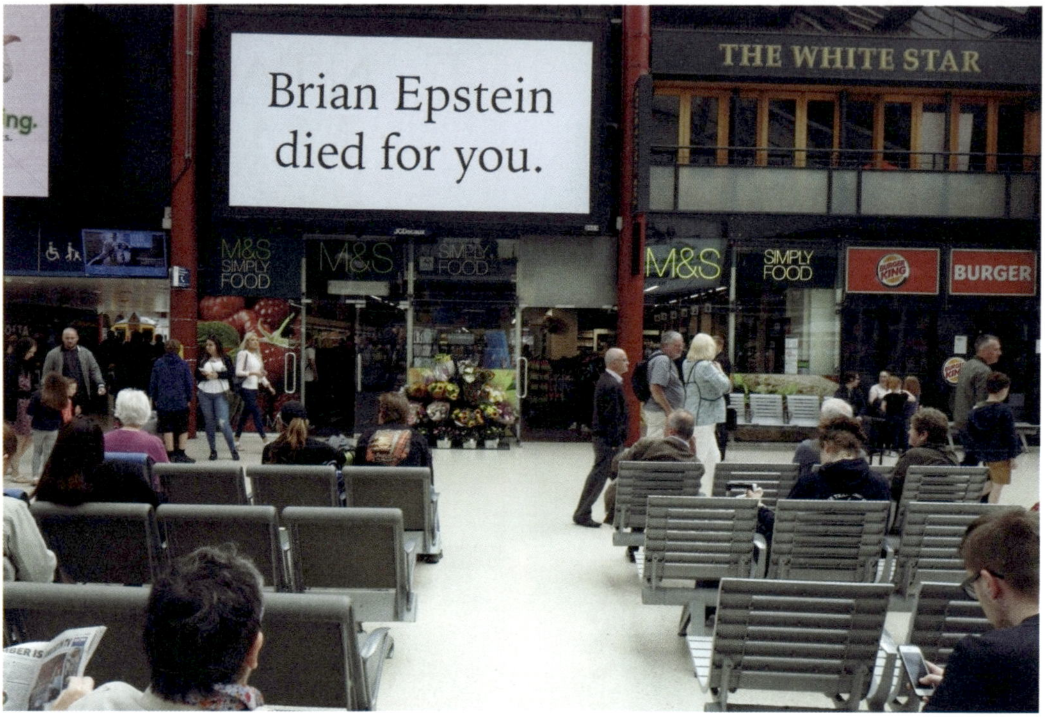

Brian Epstein died for you., Liverpool, 2017. Part of the *Sgt. Pepper* project which covered the town with the message. Without Epstein, God knows where we would be – it doesn't bear thinking about. He died for pop music.

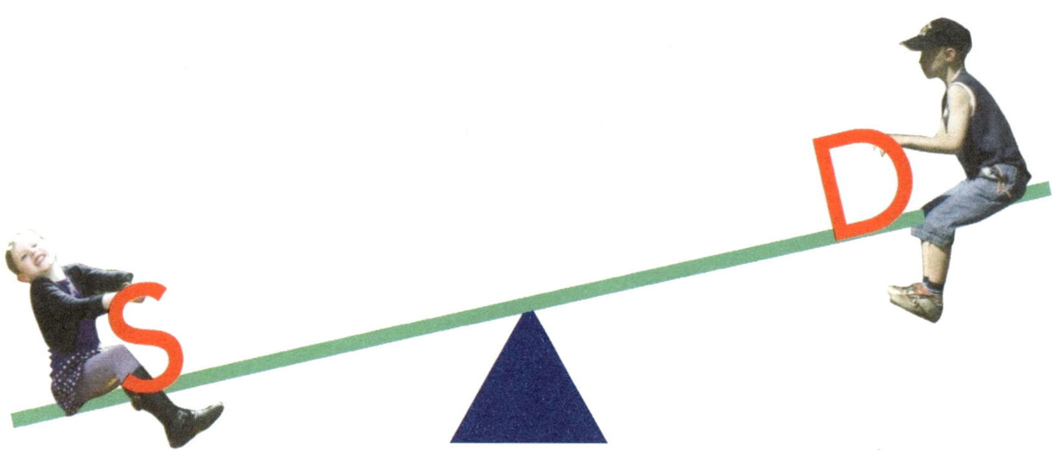

In 2013, I was asked to pitch an idea for a public sculpture in the grounds of the European Central Bank in Frankfurt. I suggested a children's playground where the features illustrated economic principles or at least used economic imagery, hence the supply-and-demand seesaw, the global wealth climbing frame and the euro rocker. I suspect the judges and the bank thought this was a not serious proposal but it was, it just didn't look it.

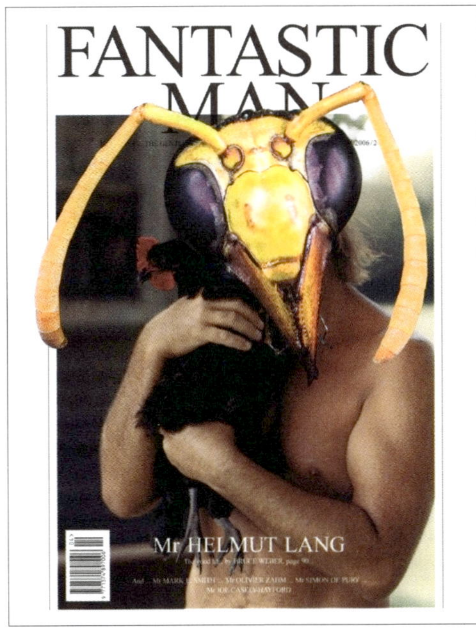

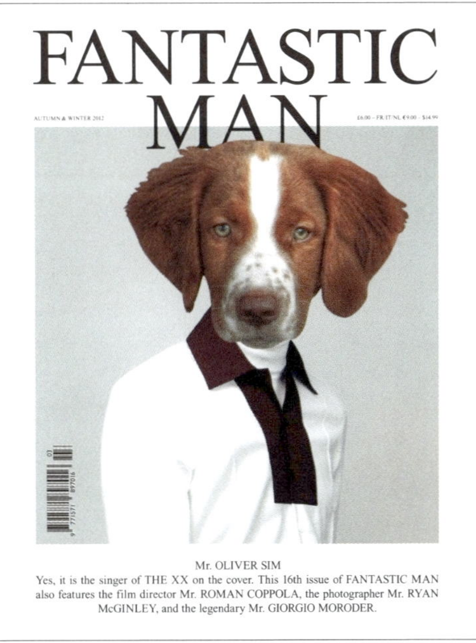

Special edition adapted covers to celebrate *Fantastic Man*'s tenth anniversary in 2015. Didn't get any feedback on these so I presume it was okay.

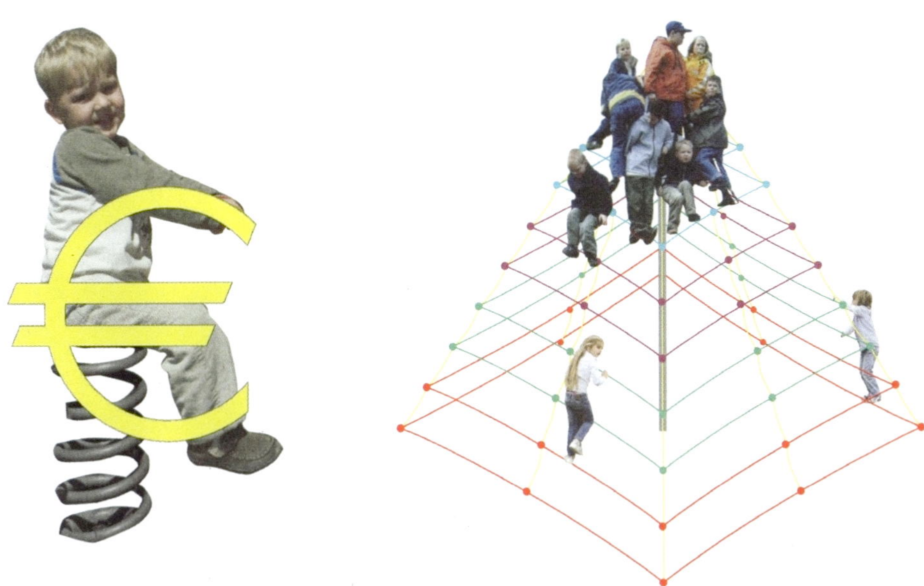

Overleaf: An evergreen work, originally made as an insert for the *Art Newspaper* in 2019. I wanted it to look like something you could buy in Camden Market. Ideally it would have been on a big advertising site at Heathrow arrivals. Little did we know that this was just the beginning.

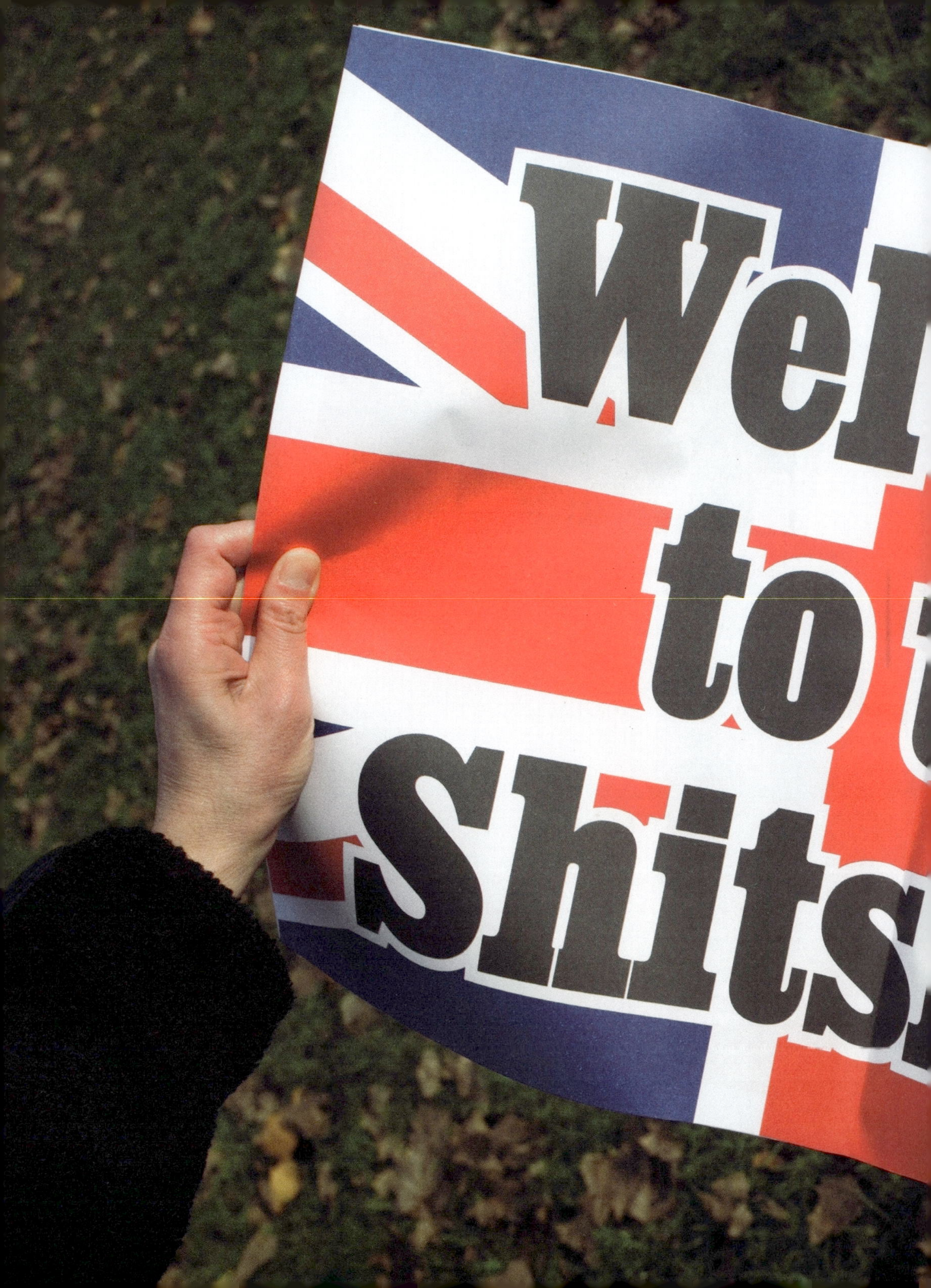
We
to
Shits

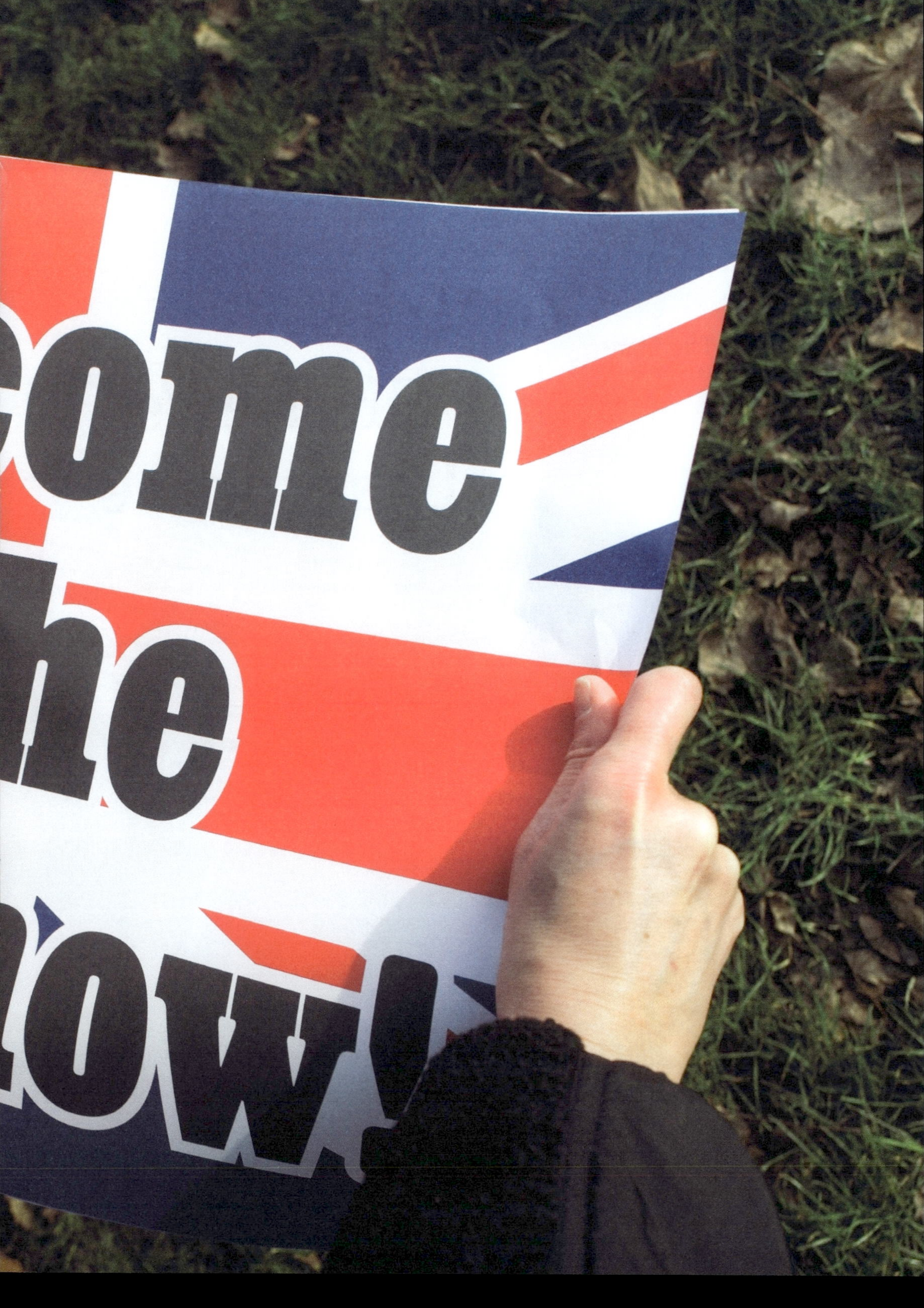

Freedom

Technology

The State

A Venn diagram animated for the film *Everybody in the Place*, 2018, which eventually forms one self-destructive circle. As much a comment on now as on then.

Shelley's Laserdome

I loved the idea of club names being big on a TV or film screen for the film *Everybody in the Place*. They were such special sites. Cities and towns in this era were defined by the clubs there. Shelley's Laserdome, in Stoke-on-Trent, was mythic.

Come See My Peaks, Edale, Derbyshire, 2019. Bit of a difficult one to explain. In my mind there is a connection between the fetishism of rambling gear and the outdoors with that of bondage wear and the 'indoors'. These cards, imitating the kind of sex worker cards that would be pinned up all over London in the 1980s and 1990s, were made for a phonebox in the Peak District as part of a project with Jarvis Cocker (who also supplied the voice on the recorded message and who I will blame if the morality police get in touch) and the National Trust. →

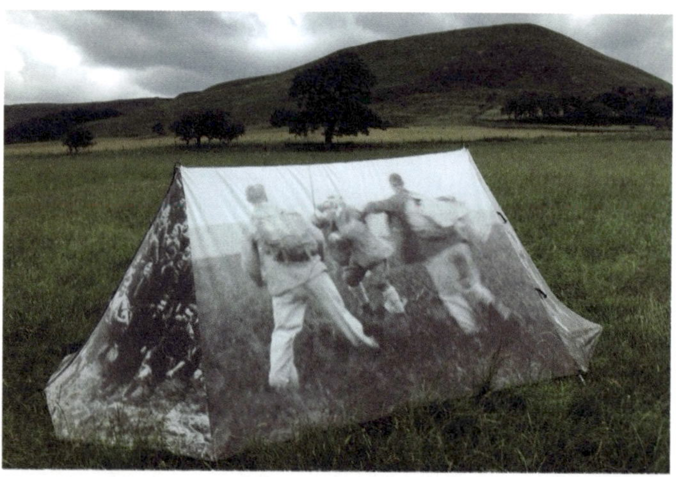

As part of the project with the National Trust, we installed a couple of tents with images from the Kinder Scout Mass Trespass. On this side of the tent, a gamekeeper thumps a few ramblers.

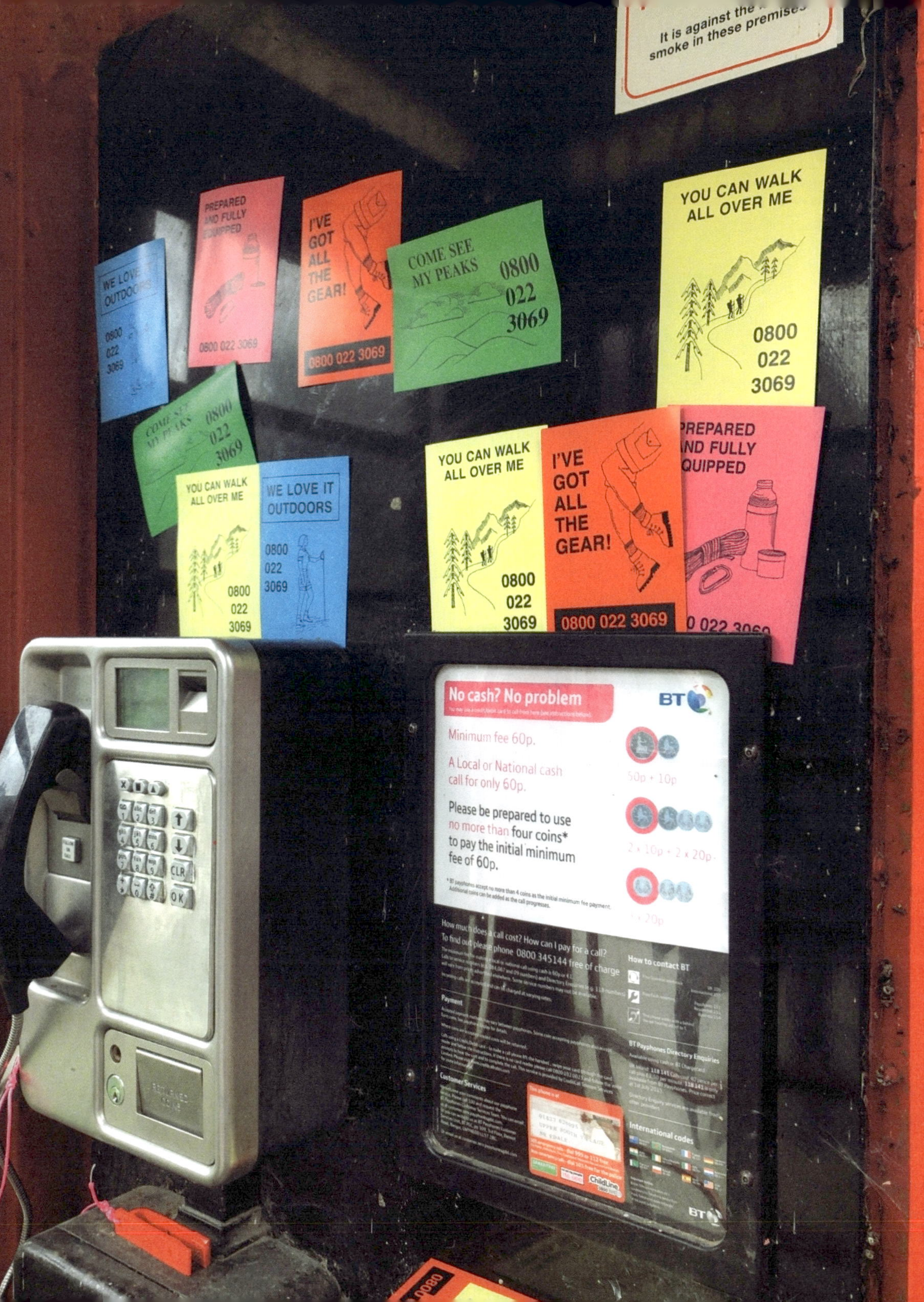

It is against the
smoke in these premises
PREPARED AND FULLY EQUIPPED
0800 022 3069
I'VE GOT ALL THE GEAR!
0800 022 3069
COME SEE MY PEAKS
0800 022 3069
YOU CAN WALK ALL OVER ME
0800 022 3069
WE LOVE IT OUTDOORS
0800 022 3069
No cash? No problem
BT
Minimum fee 60p.
A Local or National cash call for only 60p.
Please be prepared to use no more than four coins* to pay the initial minimum fee of 60p.
50p + 10p
2 x 10p + 2 x 20p
* BT payphones accept no more than 4 coins as the initial minimum fee payment. Additional coins can be added as the call progresses.
How much does a call cost? How can I pay for a call?
To find out please phone 0800 345144 free of charge
How to contact BT
Payment
BT Payphones Directory Enquiries
Customer Services
International codes
ChildLine
CLR
OK

Wiltshire Before Christ at 180 Studios in 2019 was an exhibition about neolithic culture and its continued relevance and relationship to the present. It was made in collaboration with the photographer David Sims and the clothing company Aries Arise. It had all sorts in it, from a fashion shoot at Stonehenge to archaeological artefacts from digs around the site, and much in between.

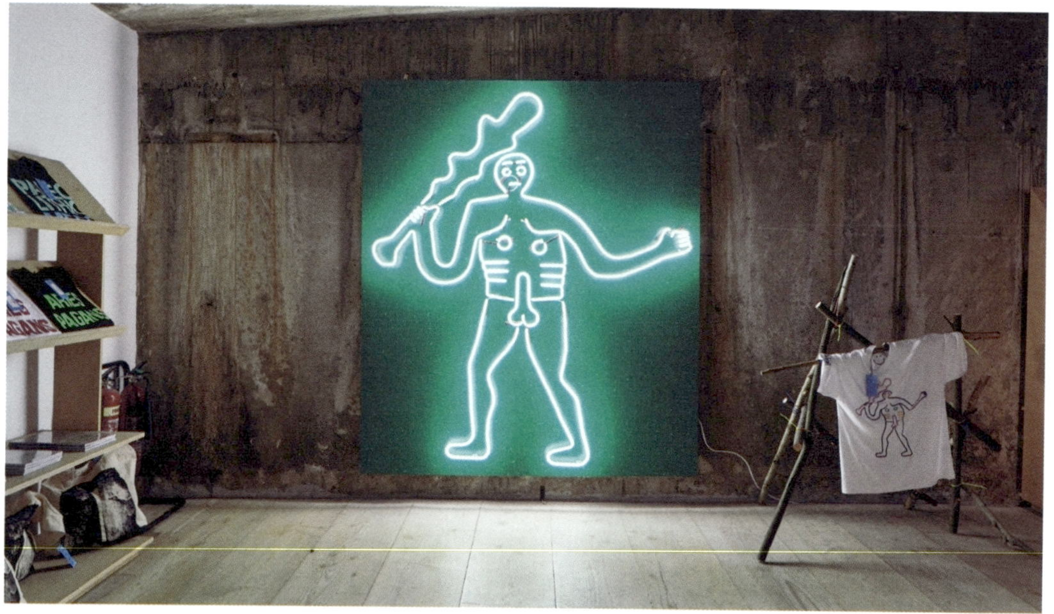

Neon Cerne Abbas Giant in the shop area of the exhibition.

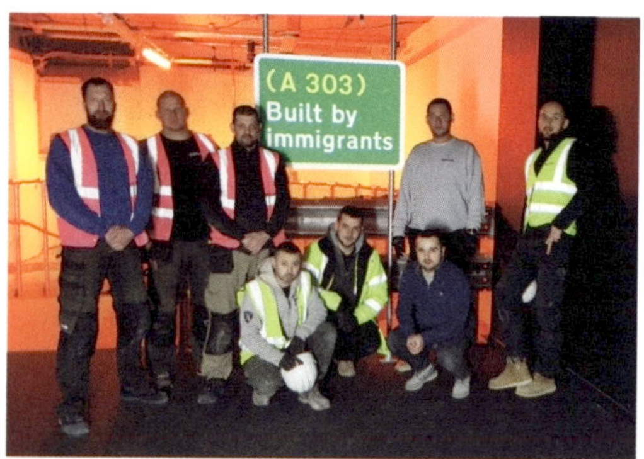

Installation crew of the exhibition, posing with road sign.

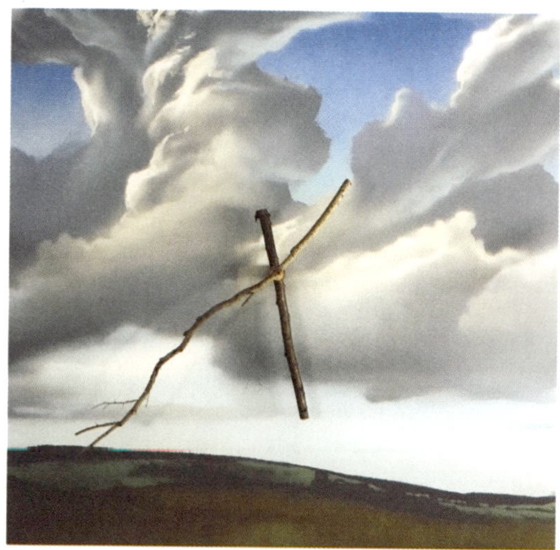

Working clock made out of two branches. The wall painting by Tommy Joffe was on all four walls and served as a twenty-four-hour landscape from day to night to day.

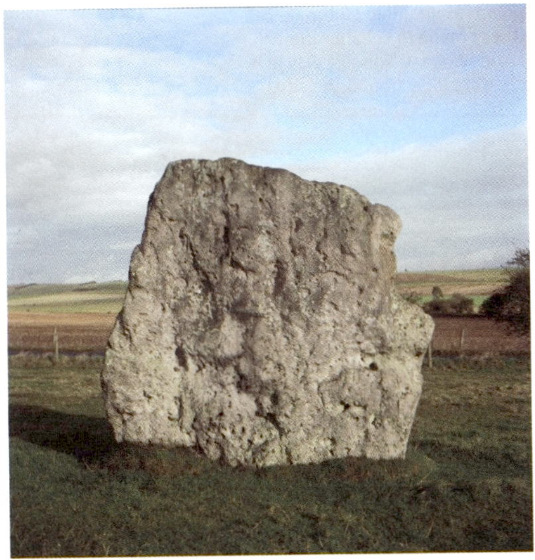

Profile of William Morris detected in a standing stone at Avebury, 2013. As a child Morris would walk to Avebury from Marlborough and write about the stones in his diary.

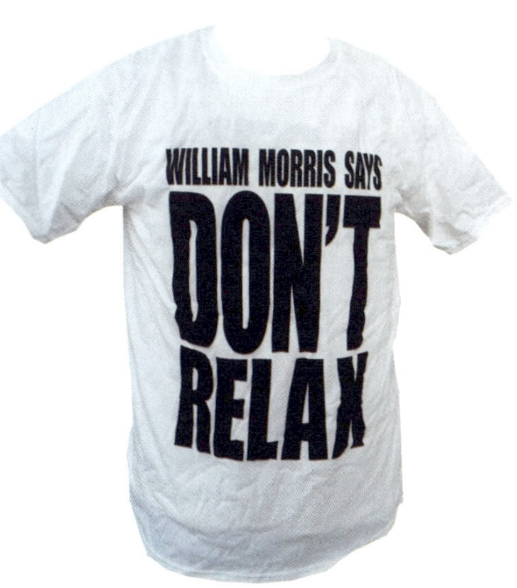

Slightly niche and creased T-shirt that I am very fond of, 2014.

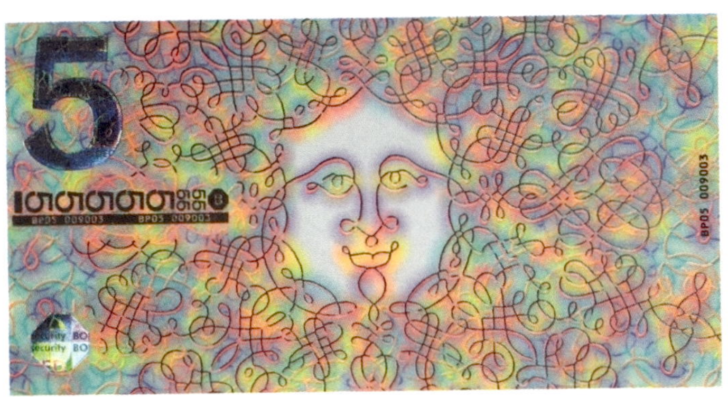

For a while Brixton experimented with its own currency – this £5 note made in 2014, was legal tender in certain shops and businesses. We designed a mystical medieval sun figure on one side and a quote by Marx (Karl) on the other about the occult power of money. I wanted the Marx side to look as though it had barely been designed at all in contrast to the excess of the sun side.

Capital is money, capital is commodities… By virtue of it being value, it has acquired the occult ability to add value to itself. It brings forth living offspring, or, at the least, lays golden eggs.

Karl Marx, *Capital*

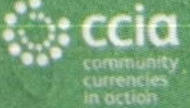

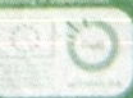

5

Overleaf: Strangely unreal-looking Human Rights Day poster at the epic site on the end of Broadway Market, East London, 2020. Part of a series marking the ongoing relevance of World Human Rights Day in some of the shittest places on earth.

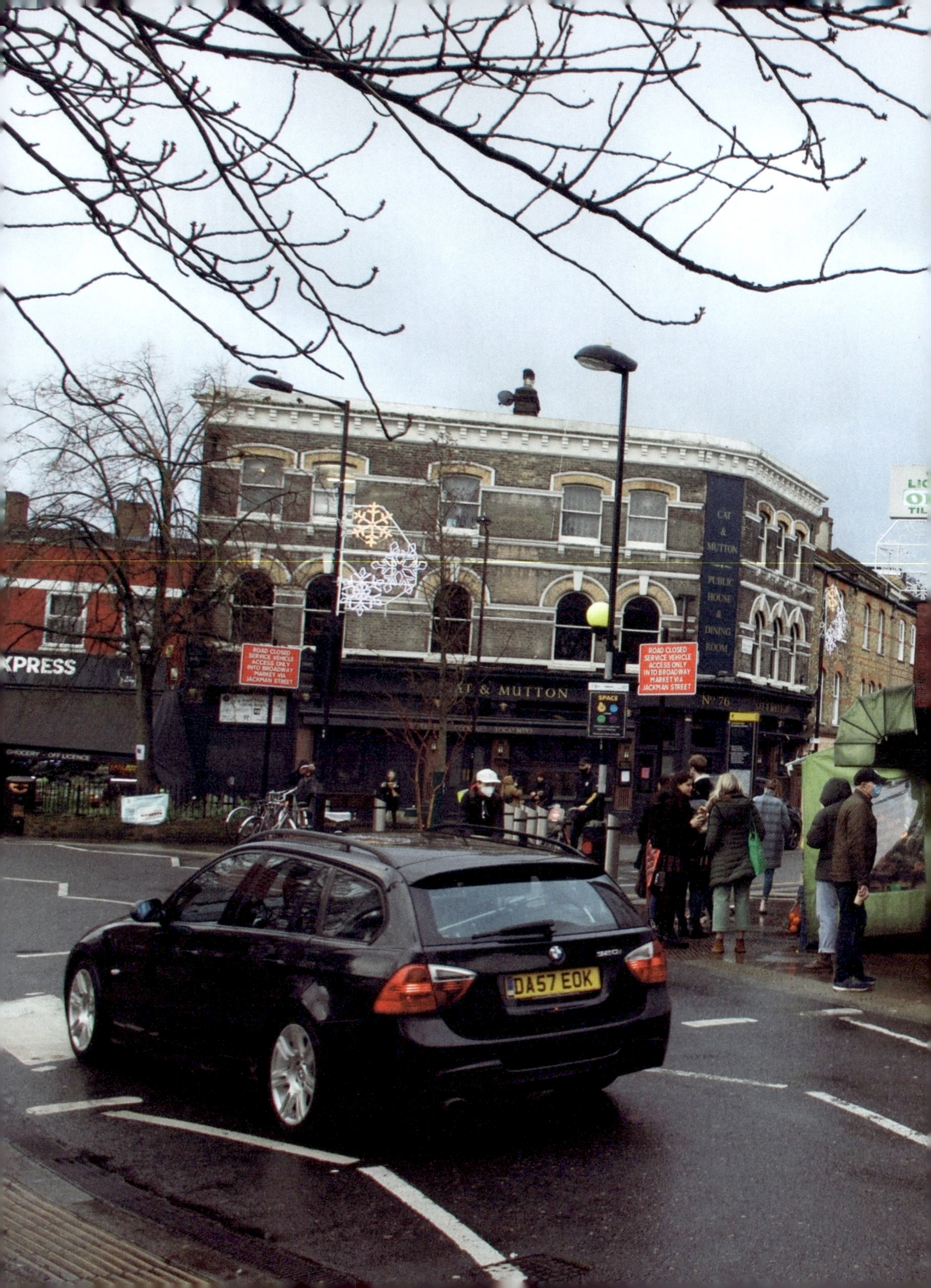
CAT
&
MUTTON
PUBLIC
HOUSE
&
DINING
ROOM
ROAD CLOSED
SERVICE VEHICLE
ACCESS ONLY
INTO BROADWAY
MARKET VIA
JACKMAN STREET
ROAD CLOSED
SERVICE VEHICLE
ACCESS ONLY
INTO BROADWAY
MARKET VIA
JACKMAN STREET
XPRESS
AT & MUTTON
SPACE
Nº 76
DA57 EOK

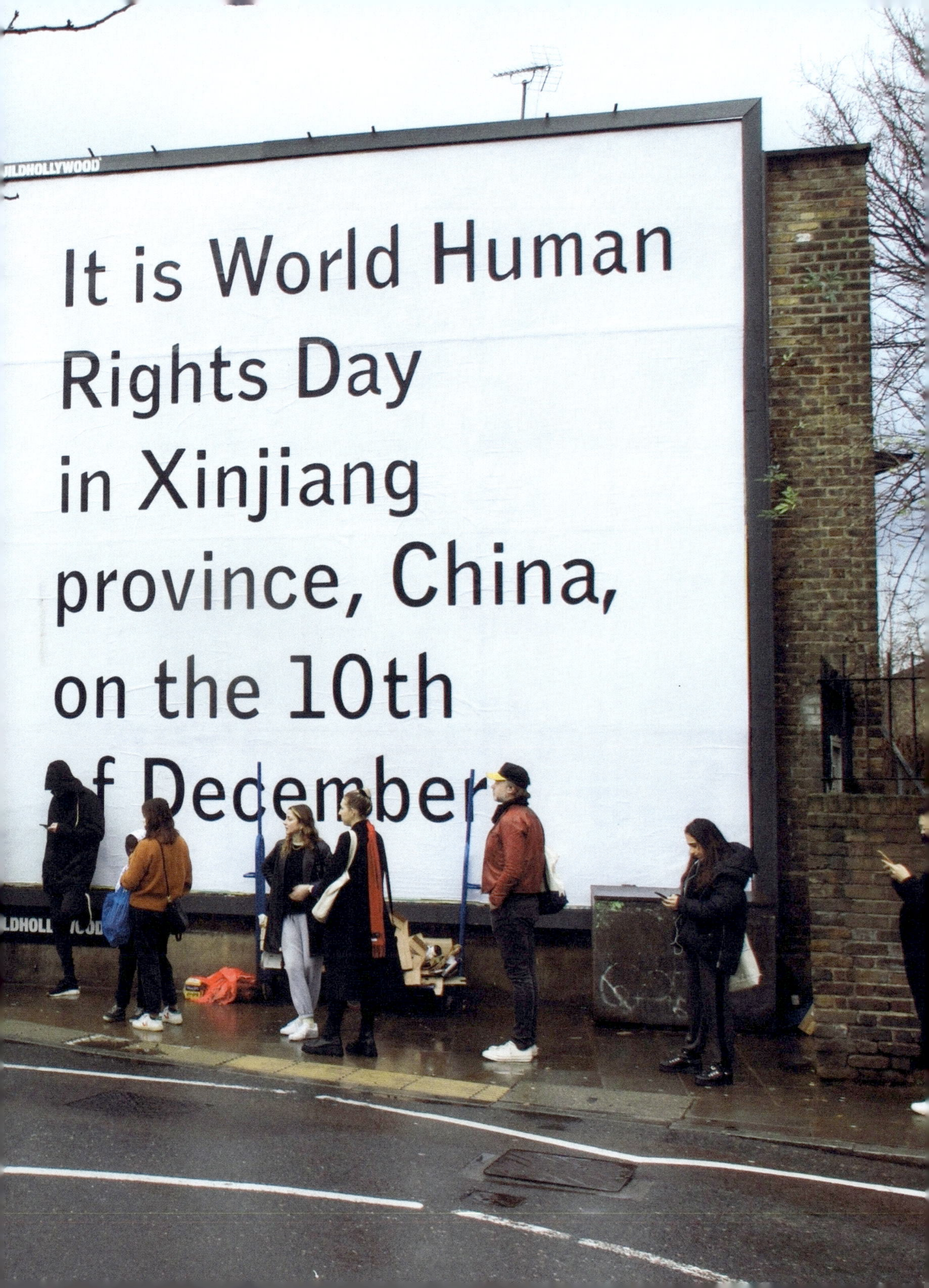
It is World Human
Rights Day
in Xinjiang
province, China,
on the 10th
f December

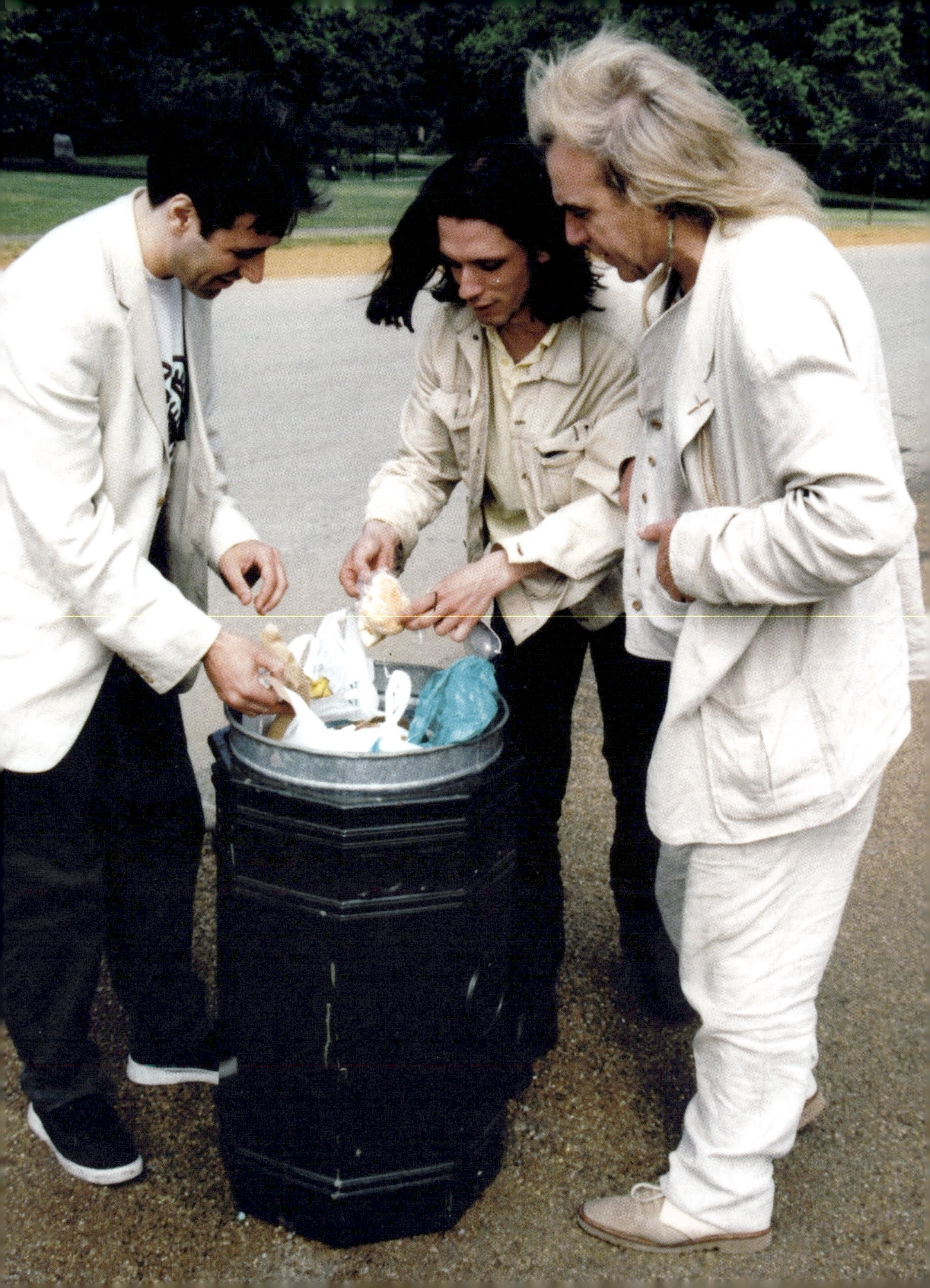

Chapter 9

How to make a critic cry

A conversation with Alan Kane about *Folk Archive* and other bits and bobs

Alan Kane is an old mate of mine and for a time we were partners in crime having fun in the art world. I am beyond fond of the work we made together so I thought it would be good to talk to him.

Daniel Scott: How do you two know each other?

Jeremy Deller: I remember first meeting Alan in Spitalfields, around 1992 or 1993. He was there with Simon Periton. In those days, there were a lot of artists'

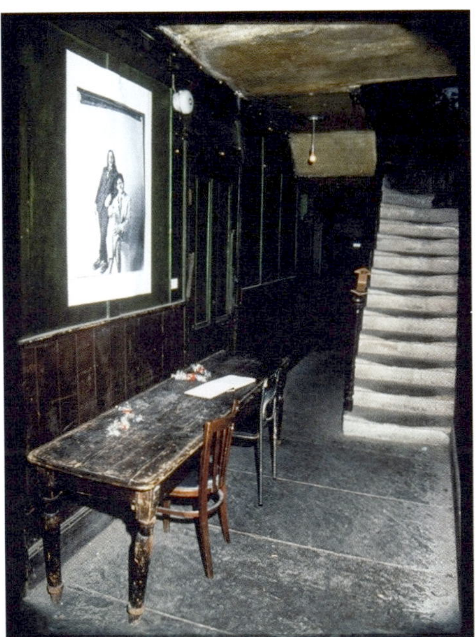

Installation shot of Alan Kane and Simon Periton's *Gild the Lily* exhibition in the suitably Dickensian Princelet Street Synagogue, 1993.

← Peter Stringfellow (ask your parents if you don't know who he is – though be warned that they might struggle to explain him) wisely keeps his hands in his pockets as Alan and I look for food to feed the ducks with in Hyde Park, 1995. None of us conferred on outfits that day, but we are more or less dressed the same – weirdly.

studios around Shoreditch and Spitalfields. I had seen Alan and Simon around at private views and I noticed that we were the only people at these things who seemed to be smiling and laughing. Maybe you also saw the absurdity of the art world as it was then.

Alan Kane: Funnily enough I was just thinking about this, and I thought that you probably didn't want to hang around with people who didn't make you laugh, which is why we drifted together.

J: Then you did that show in the derelict synagogue in Princelet Street.

A: Ah, so you saw my work before I saw yours. Simon and I played around in a photographic studio for an afternoon with some props and three rolls of black-and-white film. We only had the beautiful synagogue space for

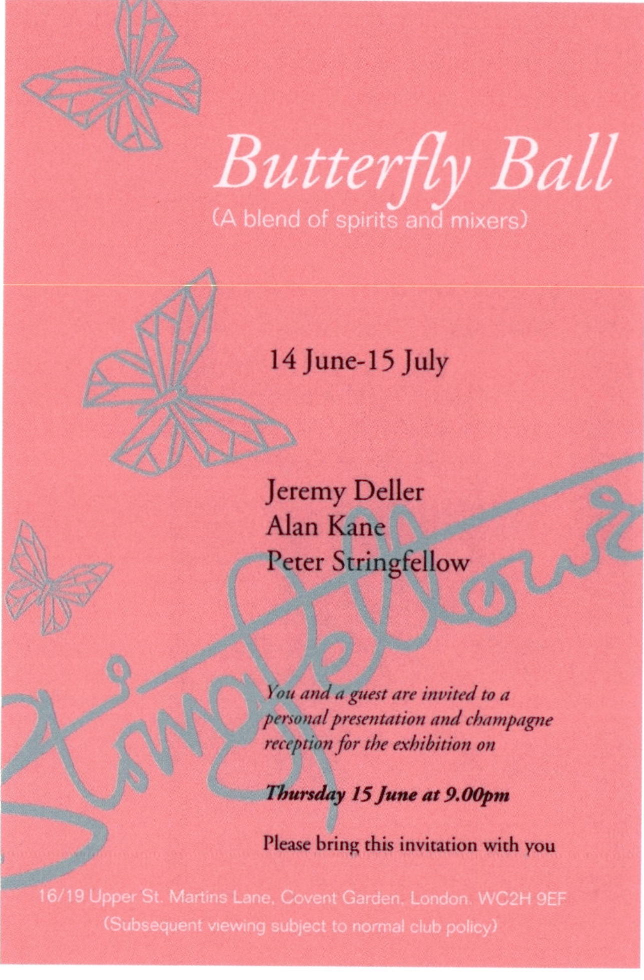

Appropriately oversize A4 invite to the exhibition at Stringfellows, 1995. A place where everything was larger than life.

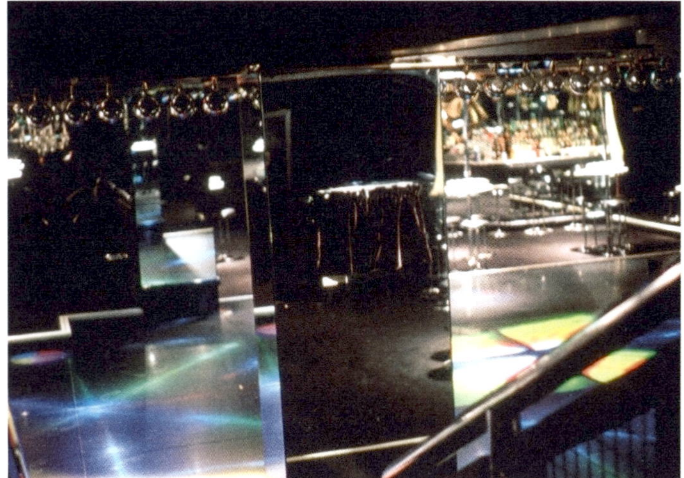

A confusing installation shot at Stringfellows of a photograph hidden behind a black velvet curtain on a mirrored column. The autofocus on my camera clearly had no idea what to do.

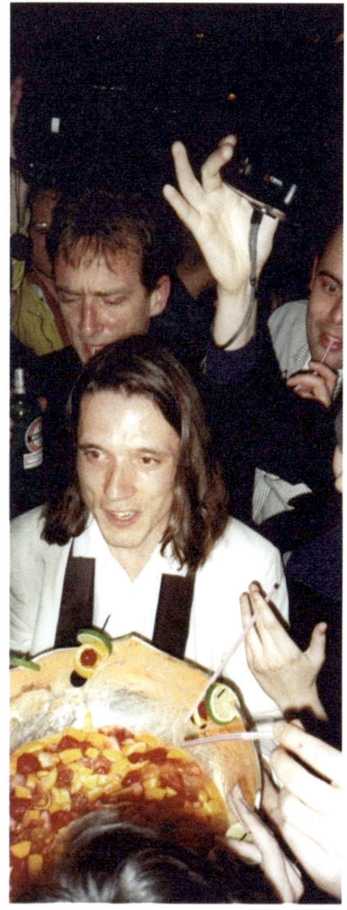

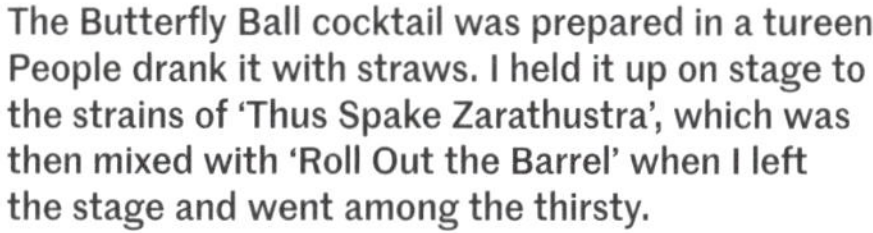

The Butterfly Ball cocktail was prepared in a tureen. People drank it with straws. I held it up on stage to the strains of 'Thus Spake Zarathustra', which was then mixed with 'Roll Out the Barrel' when I left the stage and went among the thirsty.

one evening, so we thought we would do a show of posters, cheaply produced, on sale for £10 each, simply laid on the ground so they were best seen from the balcony running around the synagogue. The show was called *Gild the Lily*. The posters were jokey homages and parodies of art history and culture more generally, Gilbert and George, *The Fast Show*, all sorts of things. We did quite well commercially with that. Did you buy anything?

J: No, I had no money.

A: We also realised we were local to each other, with me in Brixton, Jeremy in Dulwich. We made each other laugh. We just kept talking about ideas we quite fancied pursuing.

J: Pub ideas really, mainly in the Coach & Horses in Soho and after openings.

A: Maybe we were drawn to each other because neither of us was confident that being an artist was a virtuous thing to do.

J: The whole Young British Artists (YBA) thing came out of art schools, which we didn't go to, so to pretend to be part of that phenomenon would have been stupid and a bit desperate.

A: Also, it didn't look very interesting.

J: The hype around it seemed a bit silly and we just couldn't take it seriously. I guess we were exploring what you might be able to call art. We staged a three-man show with Peter Stringfellow, which was quite an experience. It comprised an exhibition and opening in his club in Covent Garden of a bunch of material the three of us had produced. We even produced a fake art Becks bottle, as they were the ultimate accompaniment to many openings.

Stringfellows was an amazing space, all black and mirrored, the opposite of an art gallery and something of a 1970s-time warp, not least in how the female staff had to dress. We had a great day out with Peter around London, with Simon taking the pictures which were essentially the exhibition, which we called *The Butterfly Ball* (the name of the most expensive cocktail in the world at that time apparently, which was served in the club).

There are photos of us rowing on the Serpentine, looking in a bin, looking at art, eating oysters. The show was photos of our day out but covered up by little curtains, so they didn't interfere with the club aesthetic. Each picture was named after a famous club – the Blitz, Taboo, Shoom – with Stringfellows continuing that legacy. Peter was just not taken seriously in cultural terms. In many ways, everything about him was confusing and wrong. He was one of the few public figures in the UK who talked about sex in a positive, guilt-free way yet was also a supporter of Margaret Thatcher. He was the least likely person you would do an artwork with, which was the big appeal.

A: Though everyone knew his name, he never appeared in the broadsheet papers, just the tabloids.

D: I remember seeing him walking into his local newsagents in Soho, chatting with the staff, flicking through *Hello* magazine and putting it back on the shelf when he realised he wasn't in it that week.

J: He turned up at the opening having just come from the Oxford Union, where he had given a talk. He walked in and couldn't believe there were 300 youngish people in his club on a Wednesday evening at 9 o'clock.

A: My favourite thing about it was getting an advert for the exhibition in *Frieze* – which Peter paid for.

J: But do you remember we didn't put the date of the exhibition on it? One attraction of the night was the 'public distribution' of the most expensive cocktail in the world. It cost £250! I had wanted to spike it with MDMA.

A: You would probably have gone to prison. Most of the people went because they knew they couldn't go into Stringfellows in any other context. Making that exhibition did make a number of people quite cross, which was brilliant. It really brought out some people's self-loathing: I was told by one artist how terrible it was that he had had to come to this club to see art, and drink free beer. We felt that many of our contemporaries were working in quite a narrow field of art production and delivery whereas we had a whole world *plus* art to visit – not that we did really push the envelope very far.

J: We discussed the forthcoming Millennium Dome and what we would like to see in it, which we thought stood no chance of being represented, objects made by hand, for instance. We thought we would assemble our version of the Dome and tour it round Britain in a tent, which obviously we didn't do.

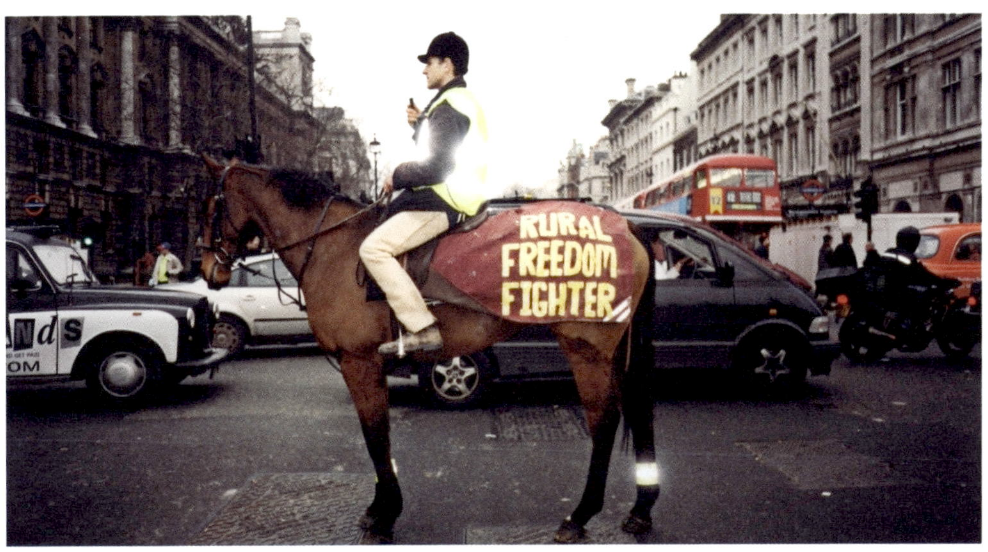

Countryside Alliance protestor in Parliament square, 2000. We received some criticism for including ostensibly right-wing protest imagery like this in the show. But for us the country/city tension in the UK is itself a feature of much of the discussion around folk art and its interpretation.

A: We were coming from a position of disappointment about something which had not yet happened. We were responding to the awful Cool Britannia bollocks, looking for an antidote to that. It didn't represent what we thought was exciting about our culture. We started with a few things we both liked, which were the foundation of *Folk Archive*. I had bought a sculpture of a couple kissing from a junk shop in Brixton, which was kind of the beginning.

J: Crop circles were an early important example of something we liked, as they represented something contemporary but deeply linked to the past and ritual. A friend of ours, Rod Dickinson, was making them and the process was fascinating to us. He didn't document them himself, but simply used other people's photos and newspaper reports, so he could remain anonymous.

A: Like us, he enjoyed that space between what you understand and what you don't. So already we were seeing how broad the range of work could be in the show, which was both exciting and a challenge.

J: The Tate asked us to be in a group show it was doing in 2000, so we thought this was the perfect opportunity to get the project rolling.

A: We assumed we would put out a call via this exhibition and we could sit back, and people would send us great things. The room in the Tate show was called *An Introduction to Folk Archive*, so we produced cards giving details about it and asking people to send in what they had seen and the things they had made. Almost nothing came in (only about three people got in touch), so we realised we would have to go out and find things ourselves. This was in the earliest days of the internet; ten years later there would have been no point in doing an exhibition at all, as it is basically something the internet and almost everyone on it now does very well.

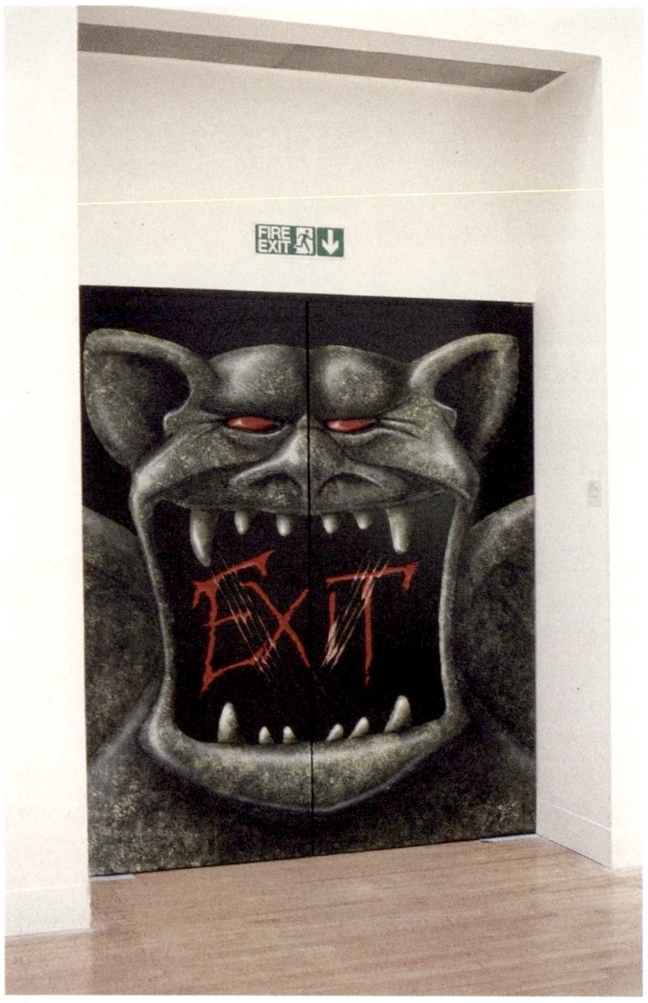

Exit door at Tate Britain from the *Folk Archive* room.

J: Ours was the final room in the show, so we had a set of double doors that looked like they were from a ghost train mounted as the exit from the exhibition. It was a bit of a joke, pushing open the doors to hell as you went out into the rest of the Tate. The doors were beautifully made by someone who made work for fairgrounds. There were maybe thirty objects in the show, along with film footage and about forty photographs. We were picking up objects as we went around the country in a very unmethodical way, bumping into things.

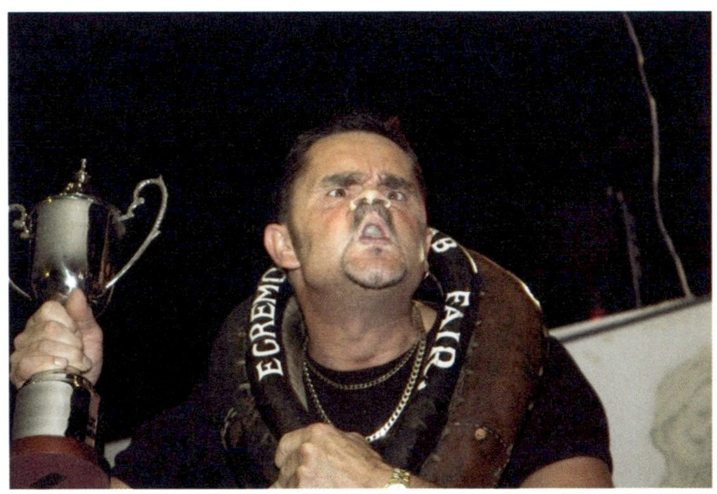

Here is champion Gurner Tommy Mattinson, winning the 2003 World Gurning Championship in Egremont, Cumbria (gurning is the art of making yourself look as ugly and grotesque as possible by pulling a face). This event was one of the most intense experiences of our lives.

A: We would have a loose plan to go in some sort of direction, then end up going off at a tangent. We were updating the idea of folk art to include performance and sound and other things contemporary art had adopted. I have always been drawn to the relationship between what goes on in art galleries and what goes on outside them, and how contemporary art draws on – or milks – folk art. We would discuss what folk art might have become since it was last looked at in this way. While some of the focus was on traditional events like the Mari Lwyd and the Egremont Crab Fair in Cumbria, we were keen to update the notion of what folk art might be and see where it had migrated to since the turn of the twentieth century. The people making the work were not naïve, they were simply looking beyond art museums for inspiration. Having said that, it was very easy to draw parallels with contemporary art practices.

Folk Archive was conceived as a temporary exhibition with the bulk of the work as documentation or on loan. We saw the whole project as a suggestion on how to do your own looking, as we didn't really want to take ownership of it.

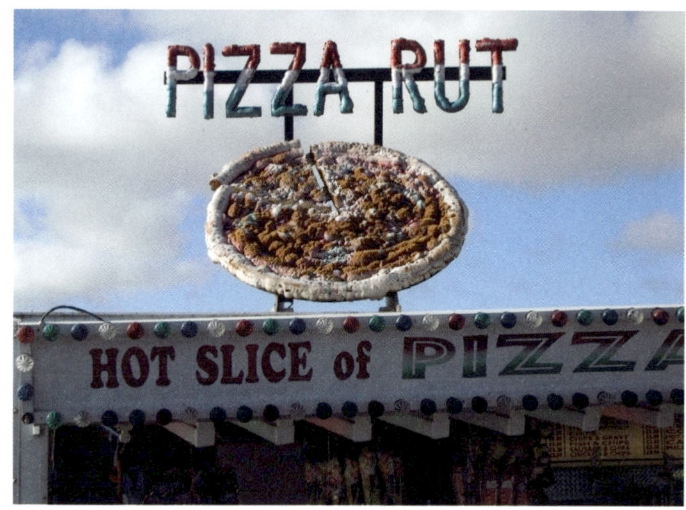

Blackpool, a town where reality is inverted, is full of bad taste – like this counter-intuitive handmade sign on the south pier, 2000.

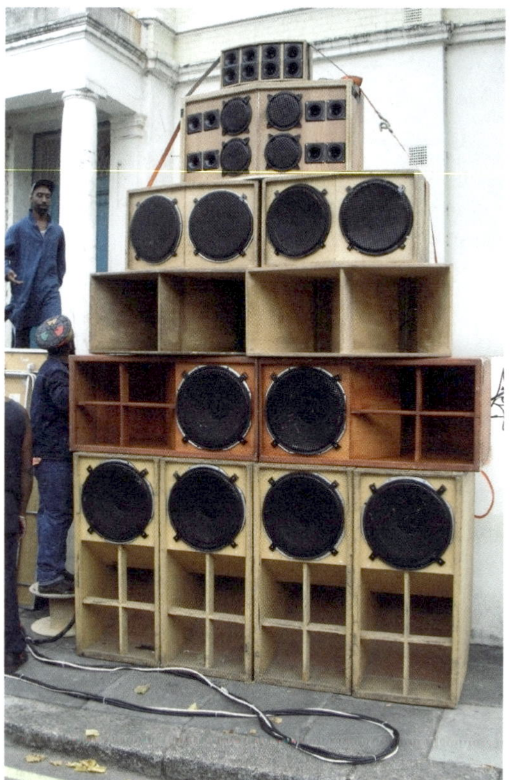

Speaker stacks at Notting Hill Carnival, 2001. An undeniable physical and aural presence.

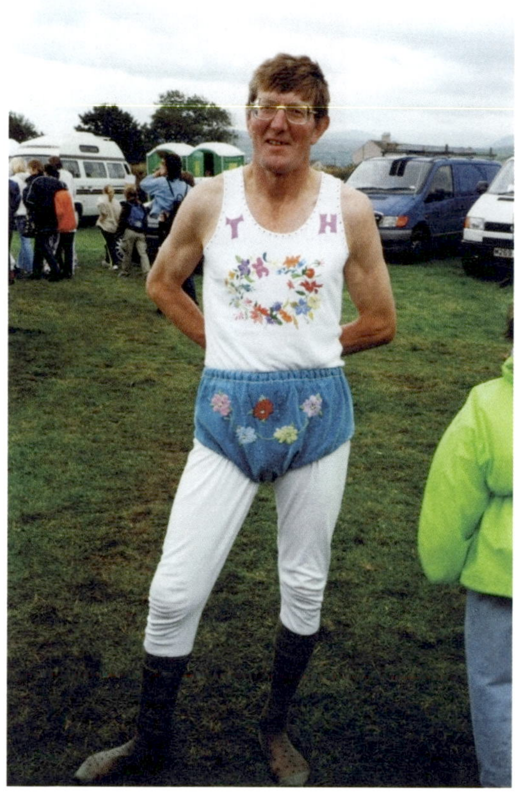

Champion wrestler Tom Harrington at the Crab Fair, Egremont in 2000, wearing an embroidered Westmoreland wrestling outfit. An admirable combination of violence and craft, wrestlers are judged on their outfits as well as physical prowess. One wrestler had a tractor embroidered on his vest.

The procession before Hare Pie and Bottle-kicking, Hallaton, 2004. Like a game of no-rules rugby between over 100 predominantly drunk men from opposing villages, this was a very watchable scene from a distance, but my idea of hell close up. The women's roles were to taunt the other team and egg the men from their villages on, and also to occasionally pull unconscious lightweights from the scrum.

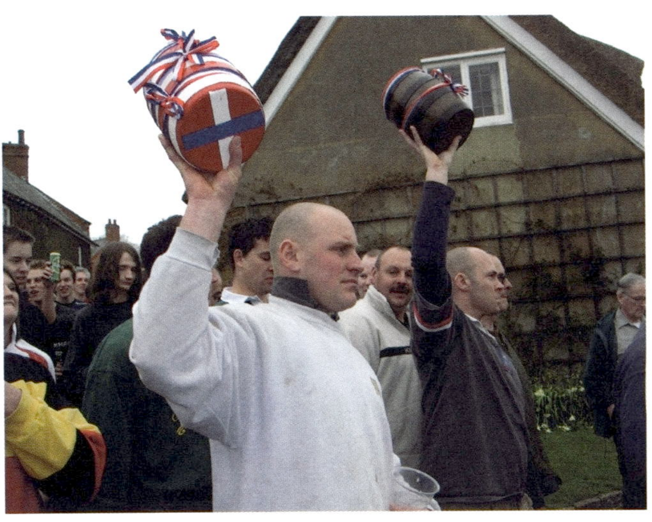

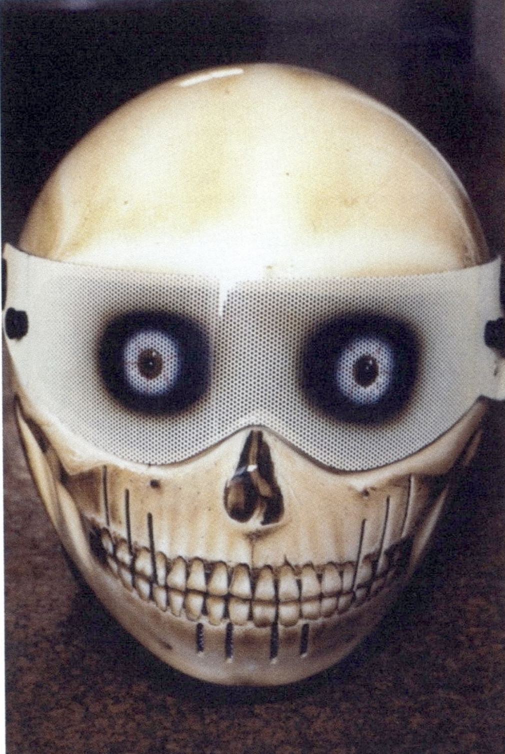

Crash helmet made for a neurosurgery technician. Ironically, many of his patients were motorbike crash victims. Painted by Stuart Hughes in 2001, who is something of a genius with the airbrush and whose work you will see elsewhere in this book (on page 182).

This wall hanging in a Lancashire church hall had it all: tech, craft and religion, 2002.

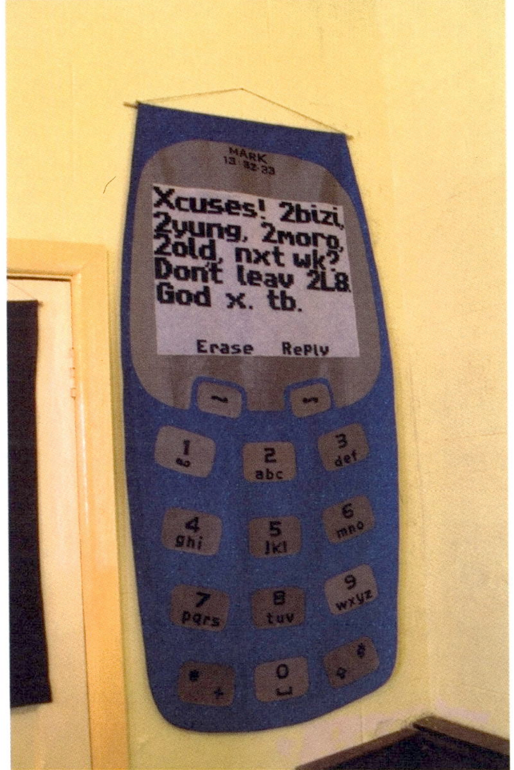

While the subject really engaged us very naturally, we were both keen to avoid being always seen as 'the folk guys'. After the Barbican, it went to five other venues around the country.

J: It then went to a museum in Basel, Switzerland. It was taken really seriously, with a big opening with long speeches. There were some funny moments. In the collection there is a model of Coronation Street and I saw a Swiss man pointing out the back-to-back terraced housing to his son, saying, 'Look! This is how English people live,' which they both found very amusing. It even toured India after the British Council bought it. To show that English culture is not just the Royal Family and stately homes felt like a good thing.

D: Was the response it got in London different to the responses it received elsewhere?

J: The Barbican show had the most fervent, violent reviews of any show I've been involved in before or since. Absolute stinkers. The *Daily Telegraph* reviewer said he was disgusted he had even been asked to review it. At the press view, a journalist came up to us crying, saying we had deprived real artists of a space to have a proper exhibition. I suspect there was a lot of class anxiety around the work.

D: I guess any presentation of what you see as folk art runs the risk of being seen as patronising.

A: From my point of view, I aligned myself as closely with the people featured in this show as the art world generally. I even brought in items made by members of my family, so it came right up to my own front door. I felt a very strong affinity with people who were dressing up for a night out as a creative endeavour.

D: Did you curate the show?

A: We cheated that really. To some extent we were researchers of the subject but as artists making an exhibition or a work, we also gave ourselves the licence to do whatever we needed to get our point across.

J: We didn't curate it. We selected it but it was also meant to be chaotic and boisterous – a bit like real life.

A: Jeremy's chaotic, I'm boisterous. At the heart of it is the fact that most people are creative to some degree, yet the art world makes out that creativity is the sole exclusive territory of 'real' artists. We ended up with a lot of material – display cases, framed work, things we had bought – and we were both living in small flats so had a bit of headache looming when the tour finished. When the British Council asked to borrow *Folk Archive*, I cheekily suggested that if it had a few thousand pounds, it could buy the lot and, essentially, pay off our debts from the exhibition.

D: Were the people whose work you borrowed aware of what the show was attempting to do?

A: Anyone we were talking to for more ambitious loans or bigger elements of the show we discussed the idea for the show with and they all understood the proposition, I think. My overriding experience was that the people whose work we borrowed were excited to have it in an exhibition. If you are asking about the exploitation angle, you must recall that pretty much all the work was made for public display before we found it – the only thing we did was relocate where it was displayed. A lot of artists also enjoyed this project because they (like us) enjoy visual culture in the world outside.

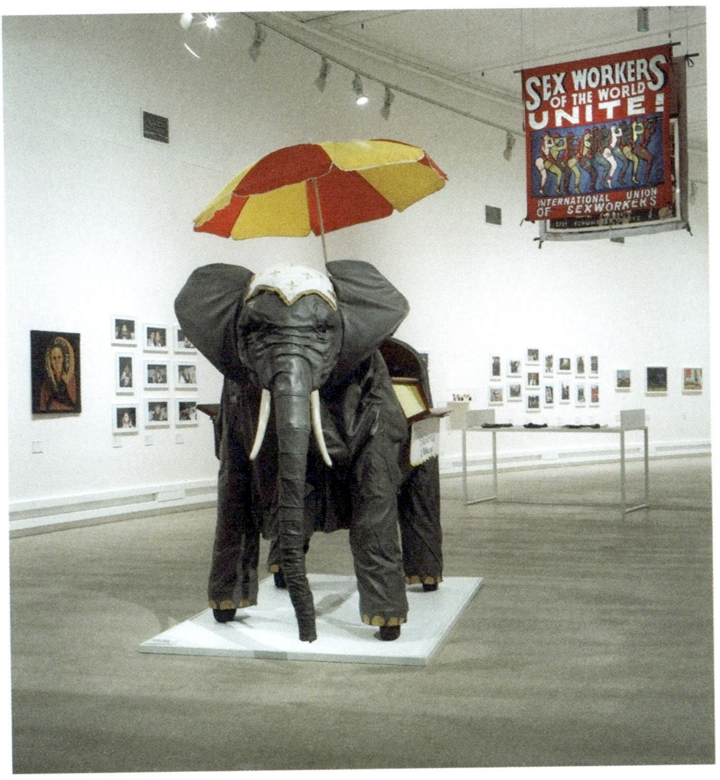

Folk Archive installation shot at the Barbican with Peter Clare's incredible mechanical elephant, *Snowdrop*, taking deserved pride of place, 2005. When we saw this in Egremont we nearly cried with happiness. Also note the Ed Hall sex worker banner above.

J: There is a Warhol quote that pop art is about liking things and I said folk art is about loving things. That's copyright, by the way. Think that still holds up.

A: We decided to make an exhibition of other people's work because it was more interesting to us at that moment in time than our own work.

J: If you were to do a Venn diagram of what Alan and I thought *Folk Archive* should be, there would be about 5 per cent where we didn't agree.

A: We only disagreed about a few things. I didn't want anything royal in it and he didn't want my parents' things in it as he felt it was nepotism!

J: However, when I saw the toy cooker his dad made, I got it. I am very proud of the work. We did it pretty much as we wanted.

A: The prison art is a bit of an anomaly and ended up in our possession through a rather complicated chain of events, but it was so good we just couldn't leave it out.

J: Since *Folk Archive*, we made the *Greasy Pole* in Egremont in 2008, the first work of public sculpture for both of us. Every year during the annual crab fair in Egremont, they erect a thirty-foot greasy pole which people would climb up. An excellent tradition.

A: Public liability insurance was not available for a temporary structure, so we made a permanent structure which acts as a sculpture 364 days a year, when you can't climb up it, and one day of the year when you are encouraged to. Still super-dangerous, but there are risk assessments, crash mats and other more boring things to make everything safer.

J: If you succeed in climbing the pole, you win prize money and a lump of meat which is kept in a basket on the top of the pole. In the first year it was won by a roofer who was wearing a wetsuit, which I think was cheating. We tried to make a beautiful thing; it was created by a mast maker in Essex, so it is completely sturdy. I learnt so much from Alan about how things should be made. He brings intellectual rigour and perfectionism to these projects.

A: Having said that, you rarely fuck it up on your own.

J: For another work we made together, we bought £10,000 worth of prison art to be displayed around the Home Office, almost as a reminder of the people who are their clients/targets.

A: Jeremy impressed me on this project when we had what was going to be a thorny meeting at the Home Office about one of the pictures called *Lovely Bum*. A senior civil servant from the Home Office was anxious about this loving depiction of a woman's backside and was just about to stress his concern about the work being unsuitable for a workspace. Before he had time to say anything, Jeremy blurted out, 'It's great, isn't it? It's like a Leonardo. Art history is full of images like this.' Jeremy completely took the wind out of his sails – I don't suppose he has that happen often. Wonder if it is still there.

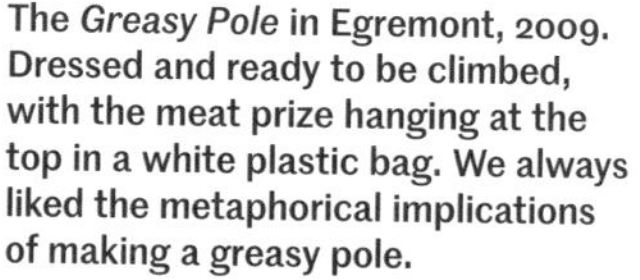

The *Greasy Pole* in Egremont, 2009. Dressed and ready to be climbed, with the meat prize hanging at the top in a white plastic bag. We always liked the metaphorical implications of making a greasy pole. →

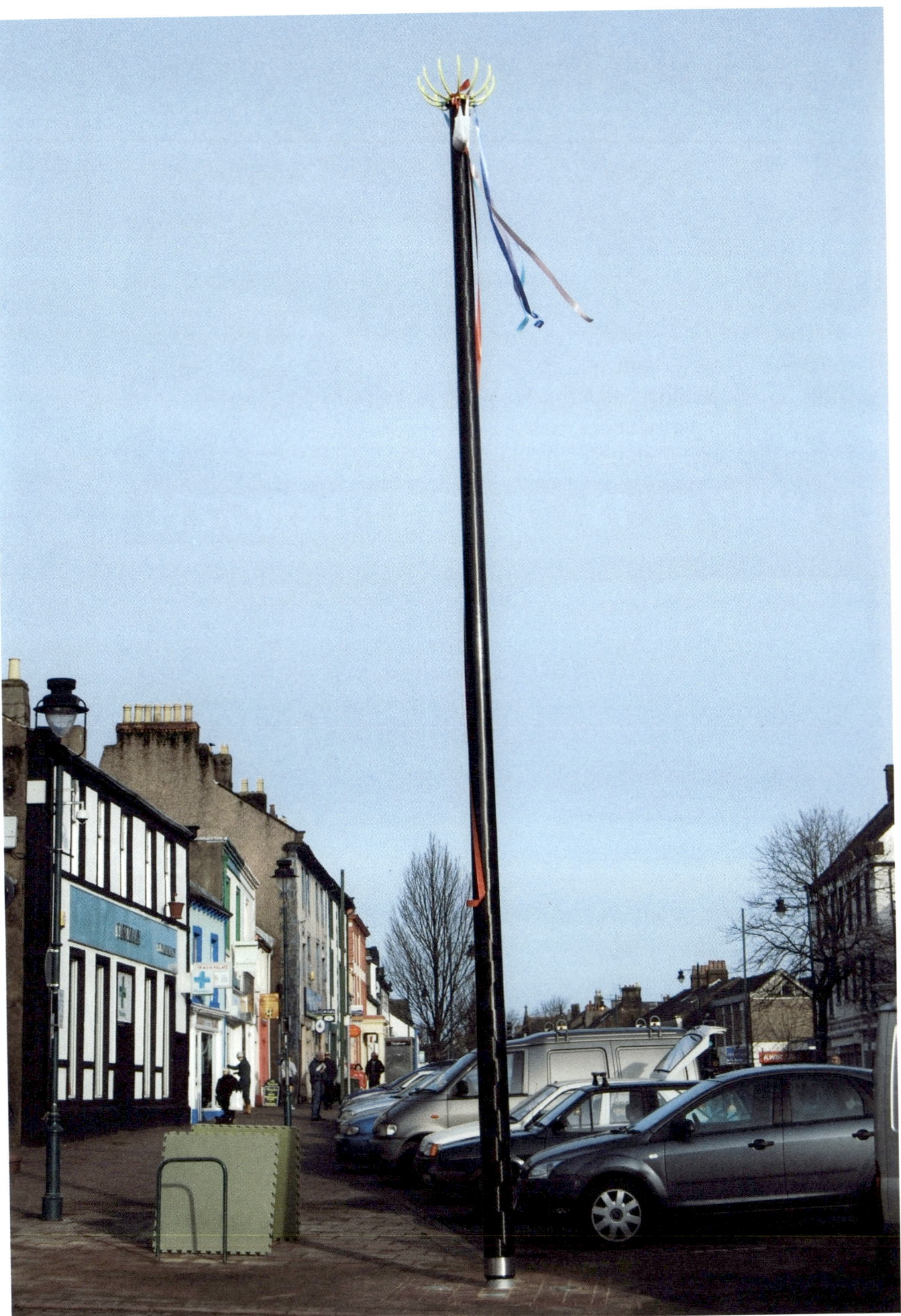

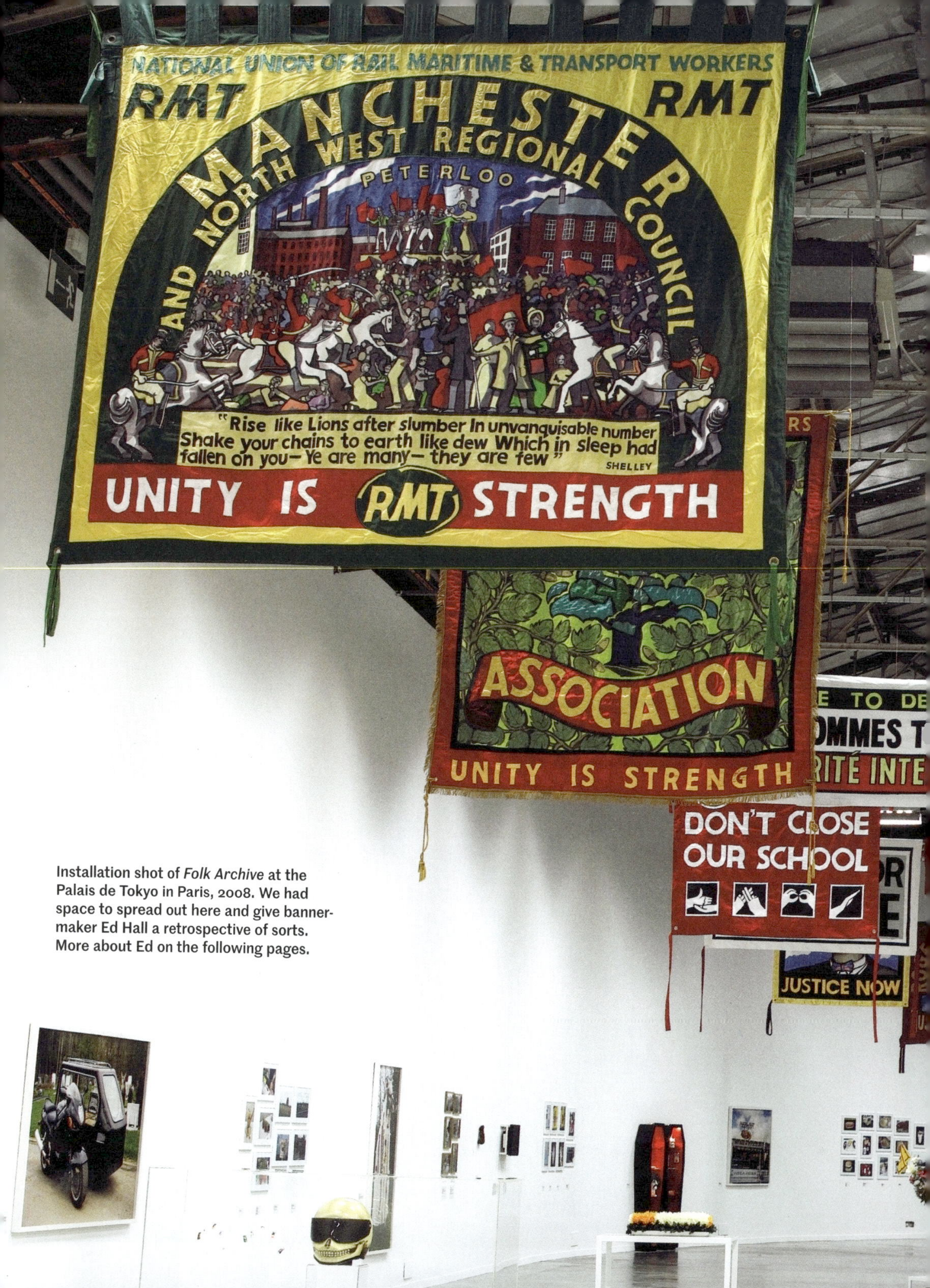

Installation shot of *Folk Archive* at the Palais de Tokyo in Paris, 2008. We had space to spread out here and give banner-maker Ed Hall a retrospective of sorts. More about Ed on the following pages.

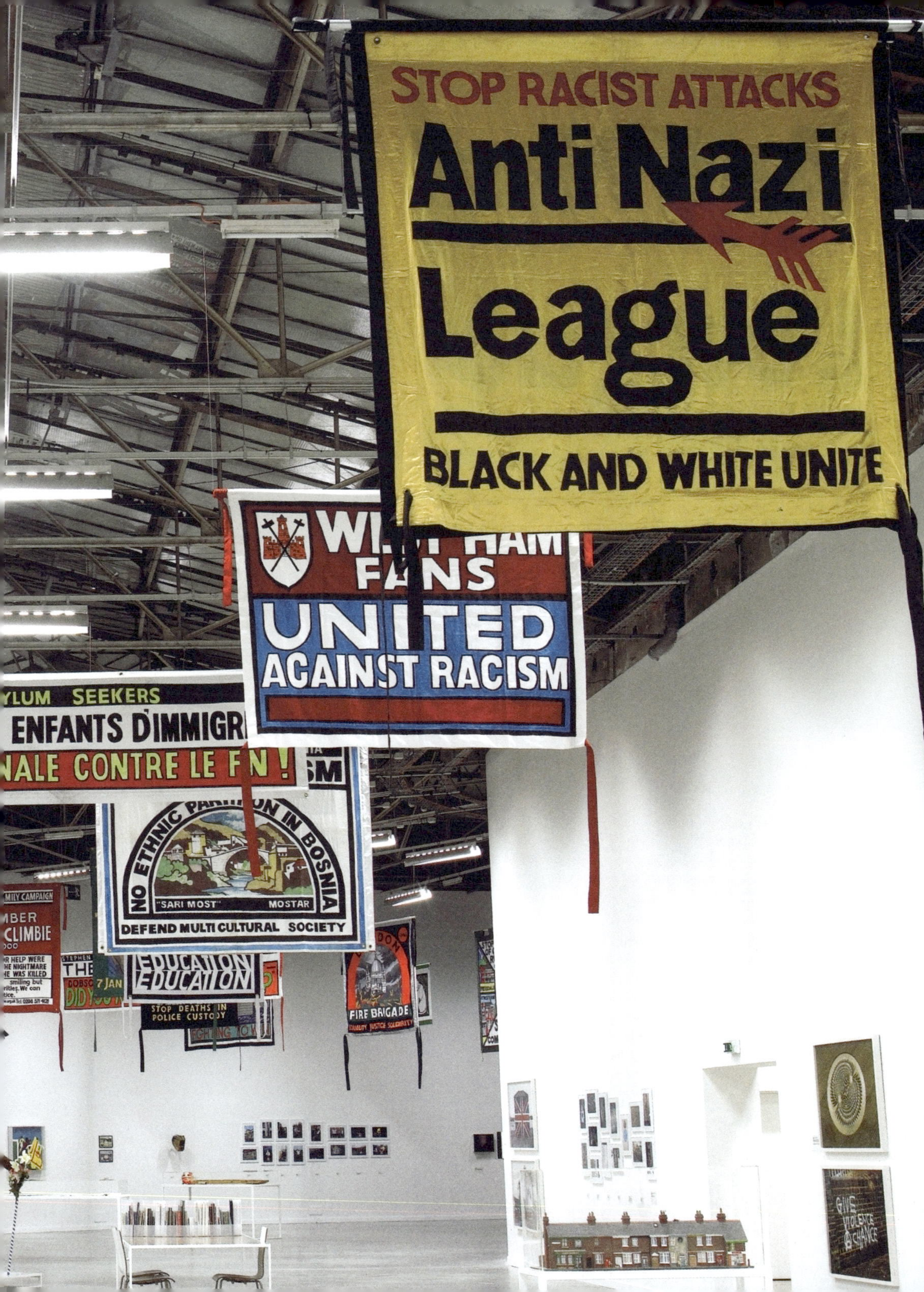
STOP RACIST ATTACKS
Anti Nazi
League
BLACK AND WHITE UNITE
FANS
UNITED
AGAINST RACISM
SEEKERS
CONTRE LE
"SARI MOST"
MOSTAR
DEFEND MULTI CULTURAL SOCIETY
EDUCATION
EDUCATION
STOP DEATHS IN
POLICE CUSTODY
FIRE BRIGADE

I ♥ Ed Hall

Ed Hall is a, if not *the* banner maker in the UK. He has produced thousands for unions, charities, myself and any organisation he feels in sympathy with. His banners are works of beauty in an often ugly world, so truly inhabiting the spirit of William Morris. When I first met him in 1999, he showed me a big folder of his work and I felt like I had discovered a folk art Holy Grail. Since then we have had a number of artistic adventures together, not least recently working with his beloved Arsenal Football Club.

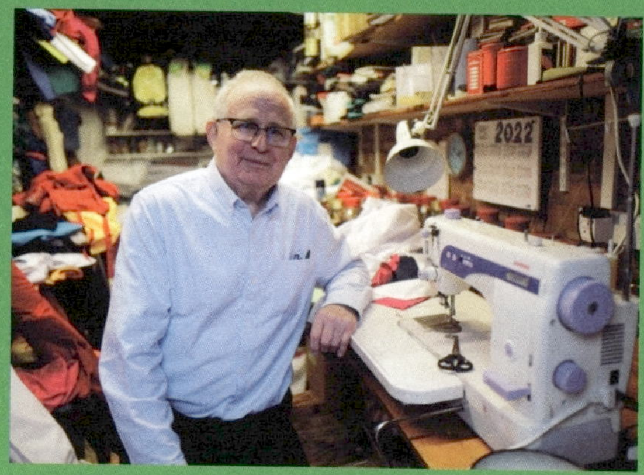

The lovely Ed in his studio in South London, 2022.

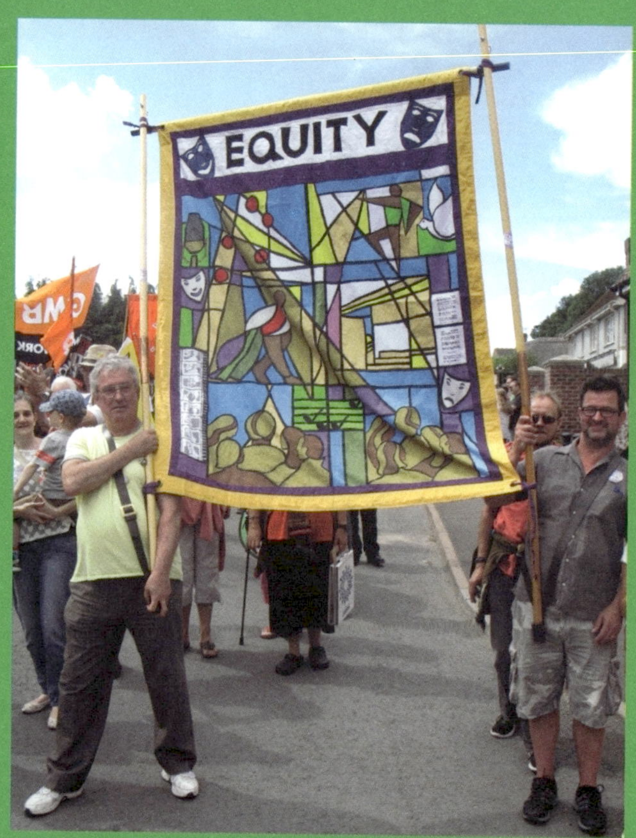

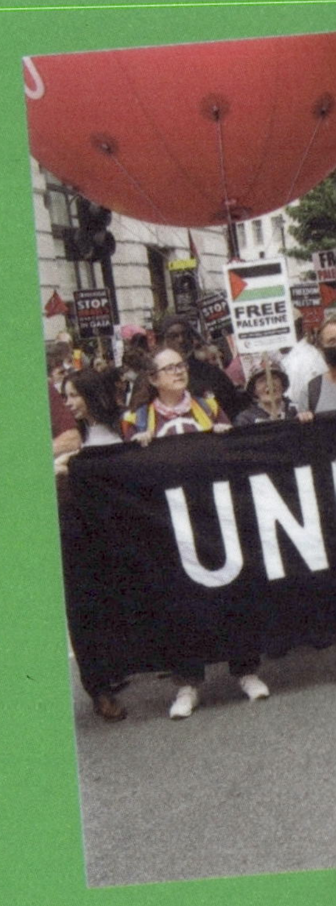

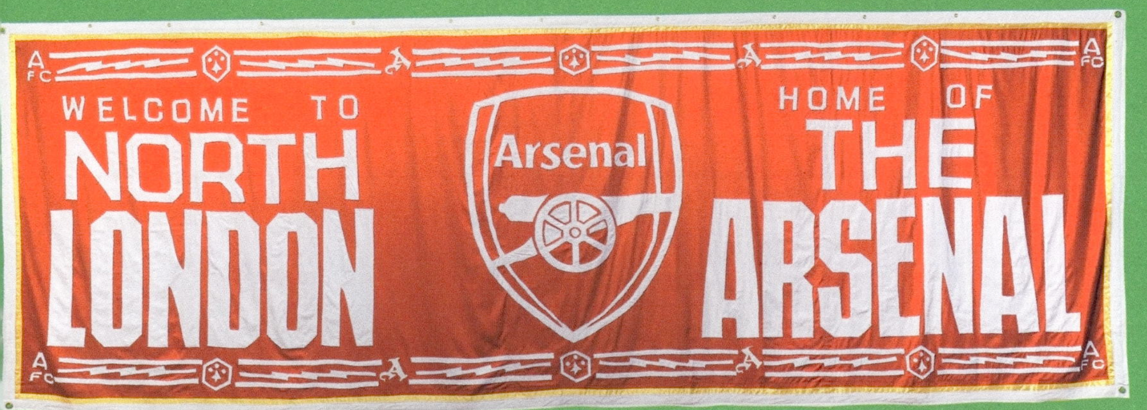
WELCOME TO
NORTH
LONDON
Arsenal
HOME OF
THE
ARSENAL

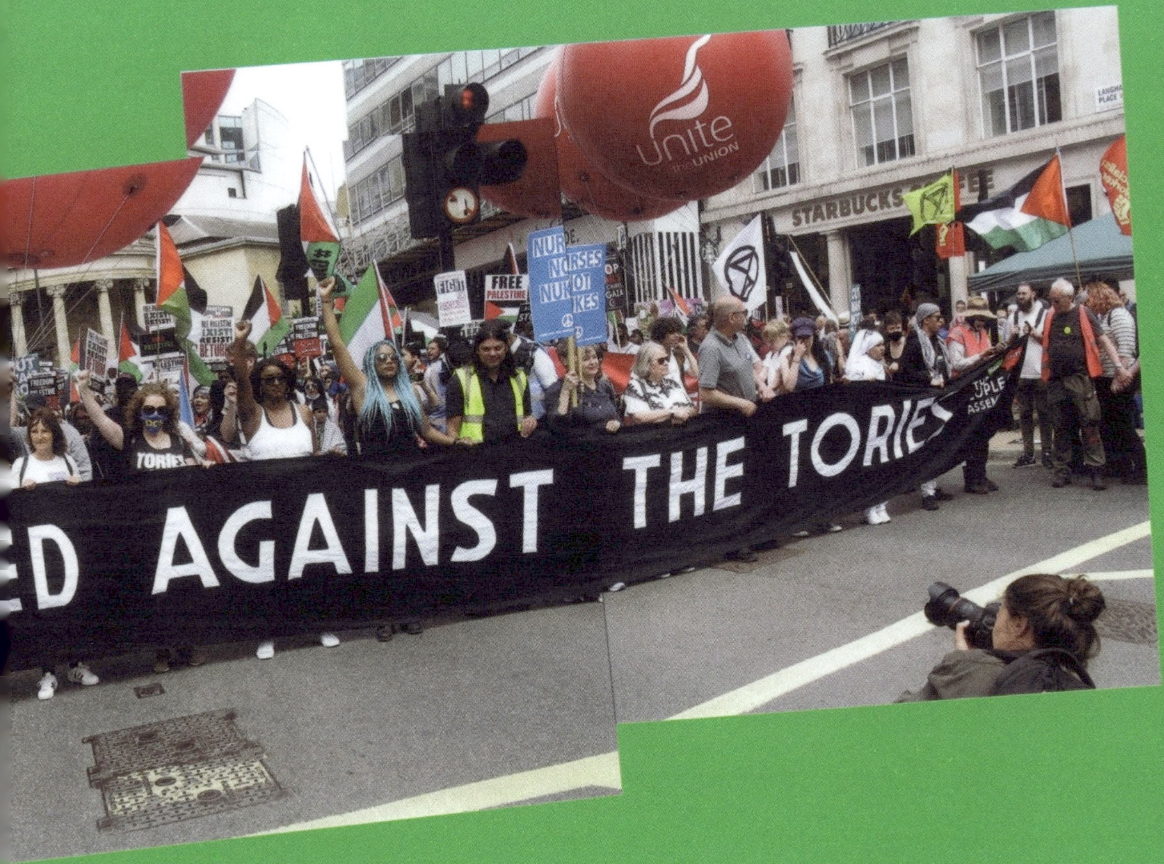

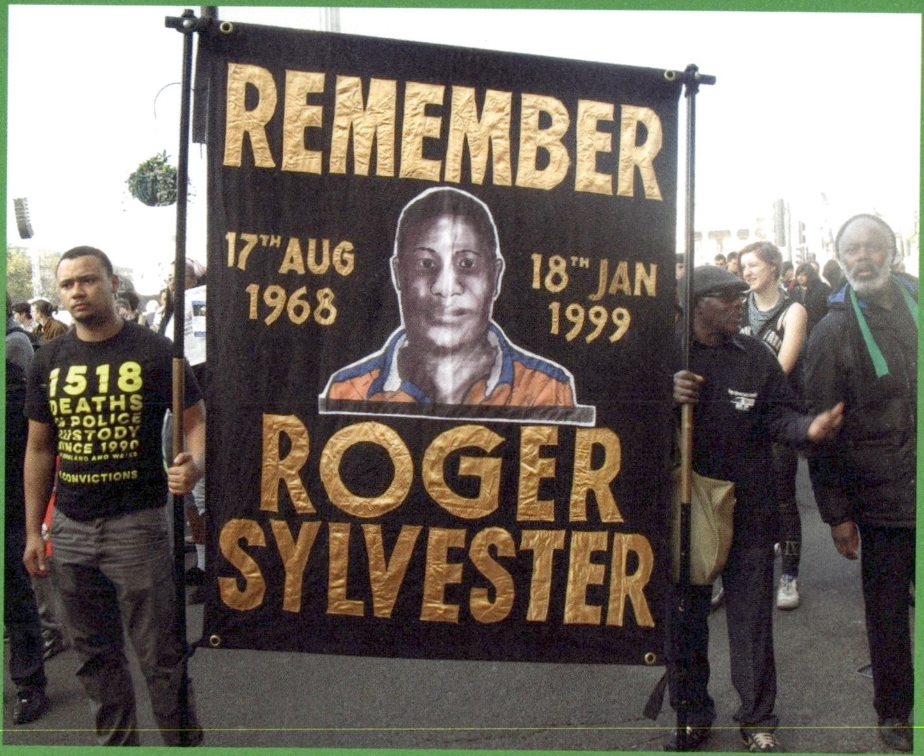

REMEMBER
17TH AUG 1968
18TH JAN 1999
ROGER SYLVESTER
1518 DEATHS
SINCE 1990
CONVICTIONS

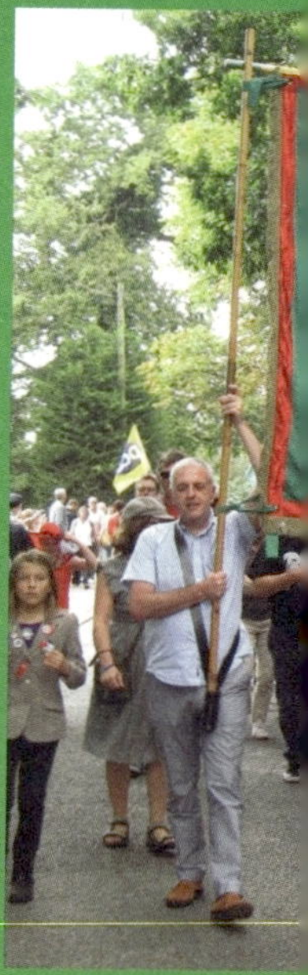

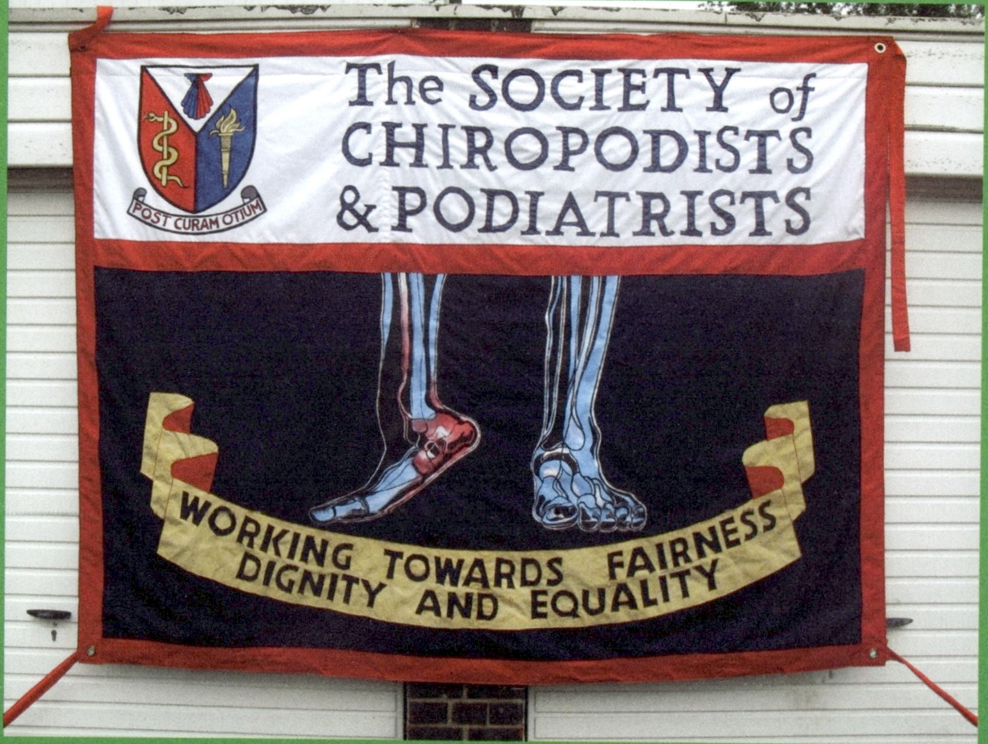

The SOCIETY of CHIROPODISTS & PODIATRISTS
POST CURAM OTIUM
WORKING TOWARDS FAIRNESS DIGNITY AND EQUALITY

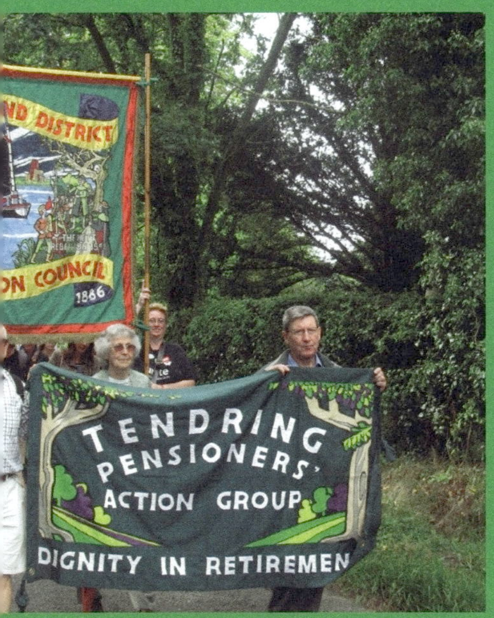

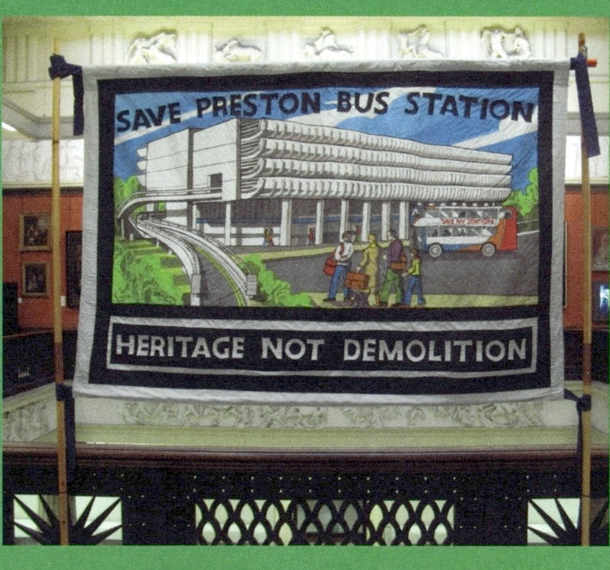

'Come
friendly
bombs
and
fall on
Eton'

With apologies to John Betjeman, 2018.

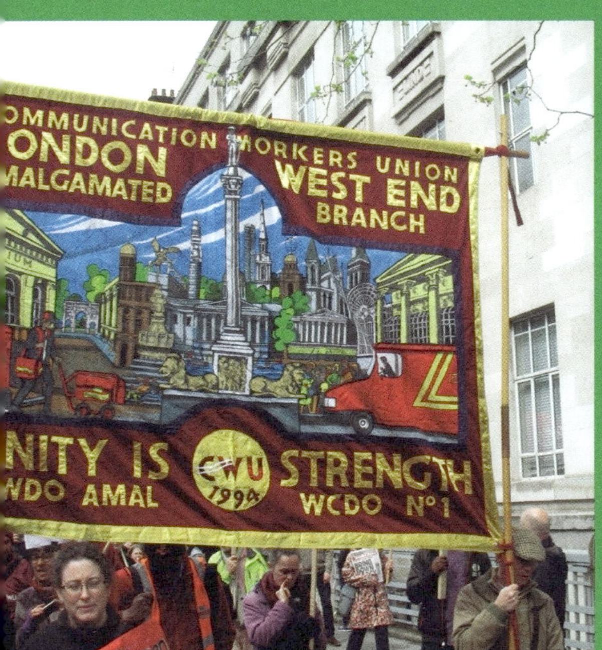

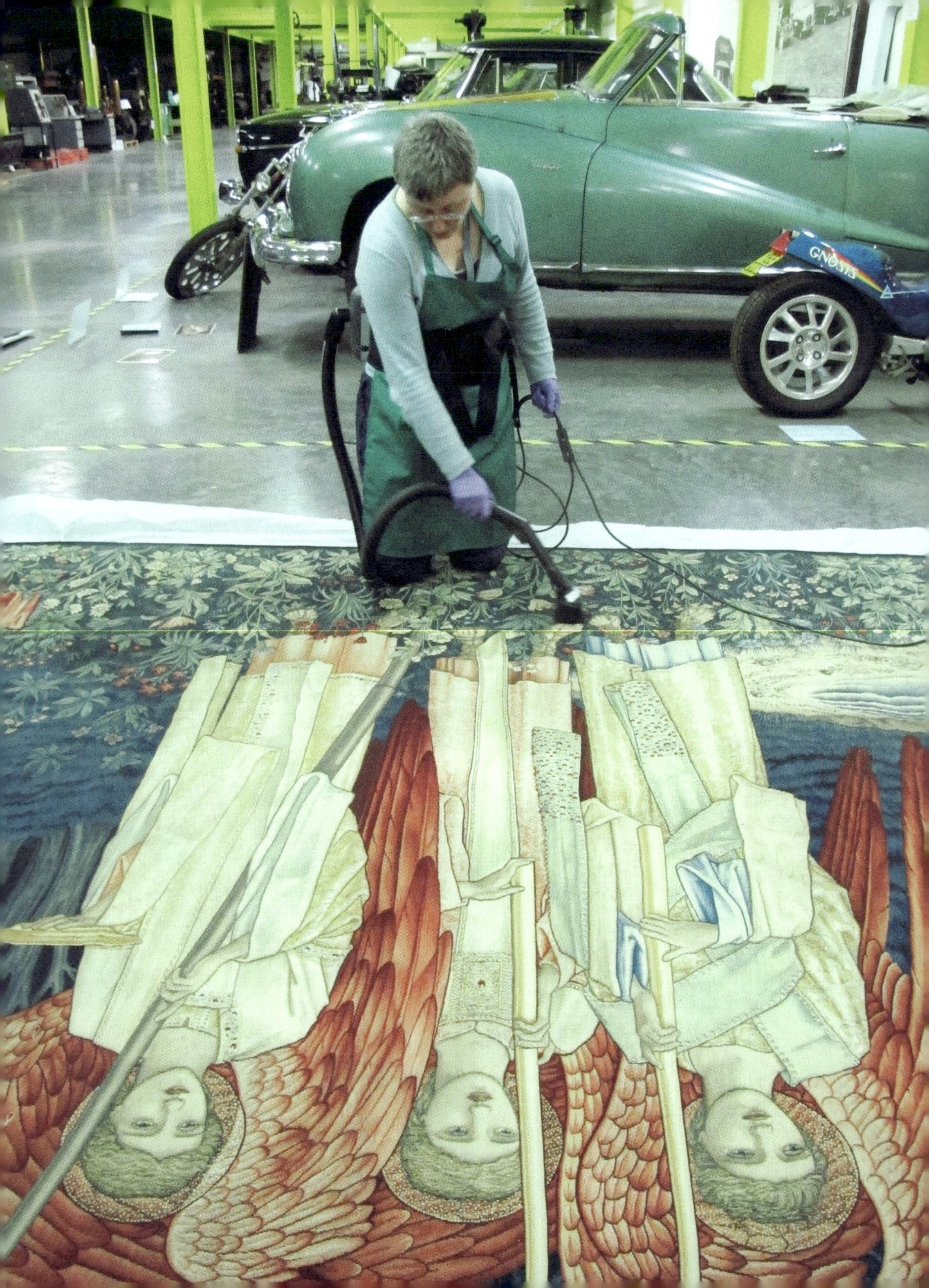
GNOSIS

Chapter 10

A pub called The Curator

There is a pub at Heathrow Airport called The Curator, which I reckon is there to brighten up the day by enabling the social media posts of real-life curators as they catch early-morning flights to Venice or Istanbul, or wherever. I'm more of a selector than a curator, choosing objects to go alongside each other in a museum to create some kind of vibration or tension.

Unconvention, 1999

I have had a long-held desire to put on an art show in a village hall for just one day, but with Andy Warhol's and Willem de Kooning's works rather than the work you might expect to see by local artists. Of course, this is totally impossible – no estate or institution would loan a work under these circumstances.

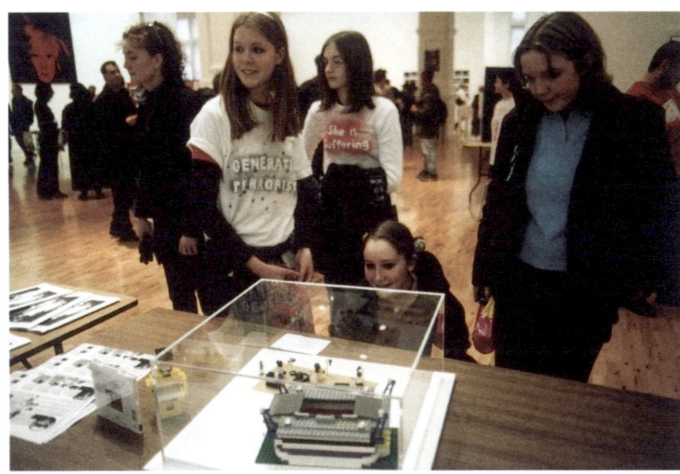

Fans in homemade T-shirts at the opening weekend of *Unconvention* admiring a Lego model of the Manic Street Preachers playing at the Cardiff Millennium Stadium. Note Warhol in the top left keeping watch.

← One of my favourite things is to go backstage at museums. Here at the Birmingham Museum's store (which in this photograph looks like an underground car park) the *Holy Grail* tapestry, the Arts and Crafts masterpiece by Edward Burne-Jones and William Morris, is cleaned before being lent to Modern Art Oxford for *Love Is Enough: An Exhibition about Andy Warhol and William Morris*, 2014.

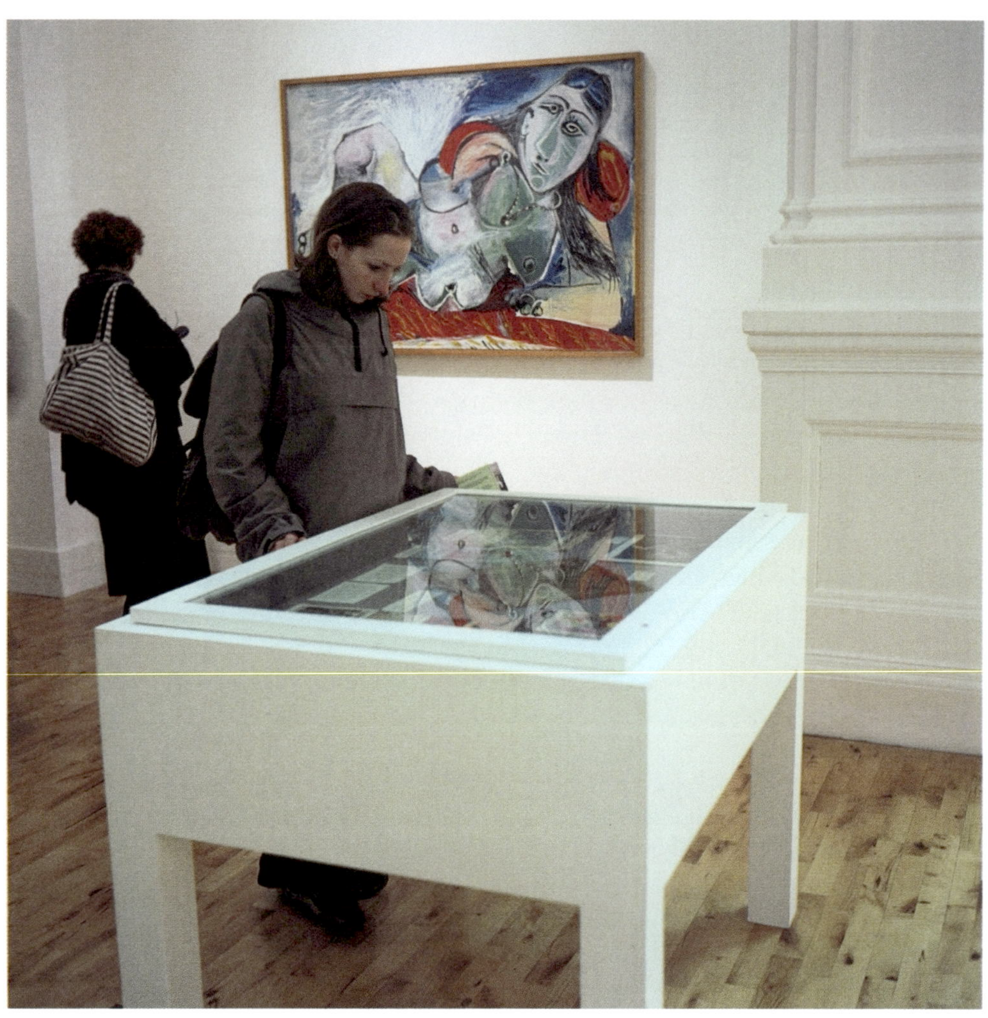

Installation shots without the public can be a bit sad, I think. Sometimes you need people in them to complete the picture. Here, a woman looks at a vitrine with funeral cards of Welsh miners who, as members of the International Brigades, were killed in Spain in the civil war, overlooked by an epic late-Picasso nude that we managed somehow to get from the Tate. When the painting arrived, the loading bay hadn't been opened. So the artwork (which was in an open travel crate) could be seen on the streets of Cardiff being carried into the building. I've always wanted to make a 'parade of paintings'. Here I did so by accident.

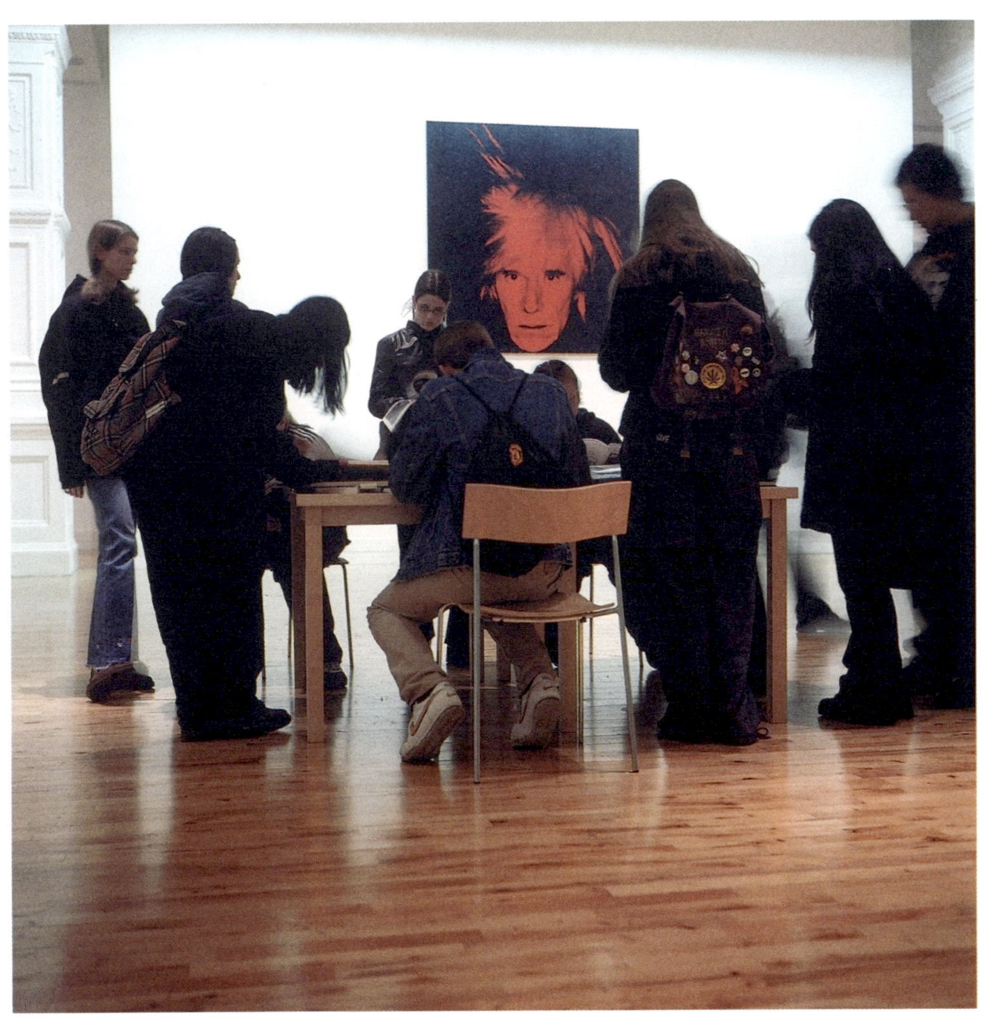

Andy Warhol looks benevolently over a group of young people at the book table, which proved just as popular as the art. Art will always be a meeting point for like-minded people.

Unconvention came out of this daydream. Originally planned as weekend of events, it ended up being a much more elaborate affair which took place at the Centre of Visual Arts in Cardiff. The plan was to bring together works which the band Manic Street Preachers had referenced over the years in their lyrics, record sleeves and interviews. Alongside curator Bruce Haines, we drew up a hit list of works which we would like to show, which included Picasso, Warhol, Francis Bacon, Jackson Pollock, Edvard Munch, Jenny Saville, Martin Kippenberger and de Kooning, as well as photography from the Vietnam War and the Spanish Civil War. Amazingly, we pretty much got what we wanted, something which has never happened since, in any show I have worked on, so it must have been either pure beginner's luck, or Bruce was in possession of some incredible kompromat on the curators at the Tate.

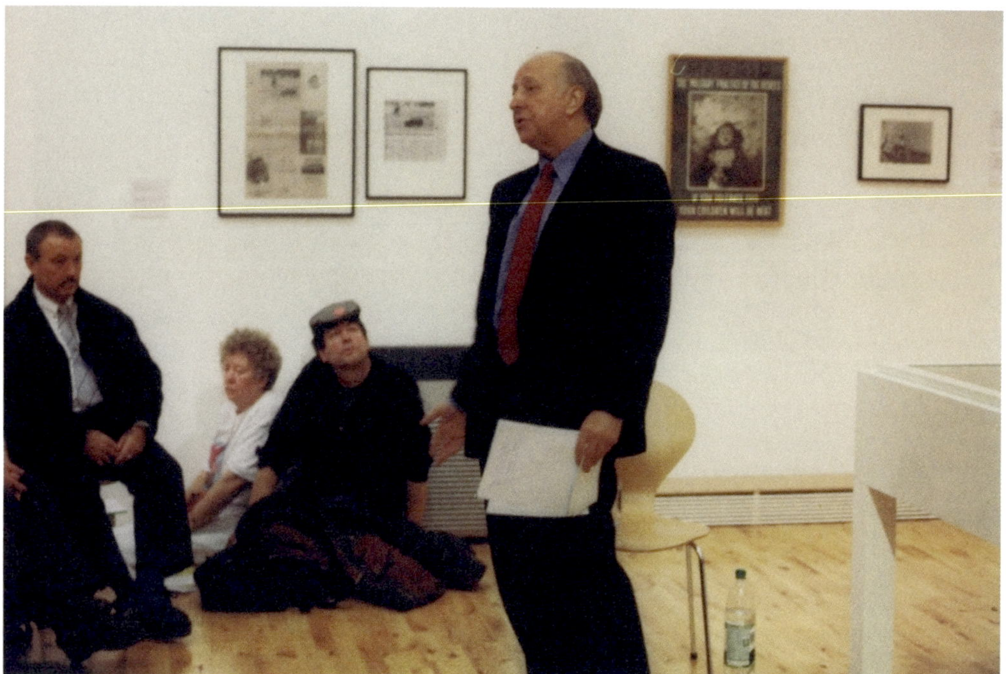

Arthur Scargill (former leader of the National Union of Mine Workers) made a rare public appearance during the opening weekend of *Unconvention* to speak about the relationship between art and politics. He did so in the section of the show examining Welsh miners' role as part of the International Brigades in the Spanish Civil War.

We were attempting to make a portrait of the band drawing on these influences. It was, I suspected and hoped, their teenage bedroom walls come to life, but with the real works of art rather than posters and images cut out of books and magazines. It was essentially an exhibition about the transformative power of art on young minds.

The heart of the show – and what was closest to my original village hall plan – was a weekend where local organisations (independent publishers, human rights charities, etc.) came along, set up a trestle table, and showed the public what they did in the Cardiff area, while being overlooked by these great works of art. Arthur Scargill, the former National Union of Mineworkers leader, gave a talk on art and politics. The show was centred around a large late-Warhol self-portrait, very much a painting as meeting point: just as the 1960s Factory was a home for waifs and strays, so bands like the Manics play a similar role.

***All That Is Solid Melts Into Air*, 2014**

… was an exhibition that examined the influence of the Industrial Revolution on late twentieth-century life; most notably its influence on the world of work, and the rise of rock music as a means to redefine the country. In some ways, it was a traditional-looking show with exhibits borrowed from industrial museums interspersed with contemporary material. The strict rules which governed behaviour in a Preston cotton mill in 1830 were juxtaposed with the body-worn devices used now by warehouse staff in fulfilment centres that track your every move.

In a way this exhibition was based on the cliché that musicians from industrial areas make music that in some sense replicates the sounds of the factory. On the whole I think there is some truth to this, with caveats and subtleties concerning the specific industries in question. In Manchester, for instance, the machinery in the cotton mills made a very different, almost polyrhythmic, dance sound, compared to the metallic sound of a steel works.

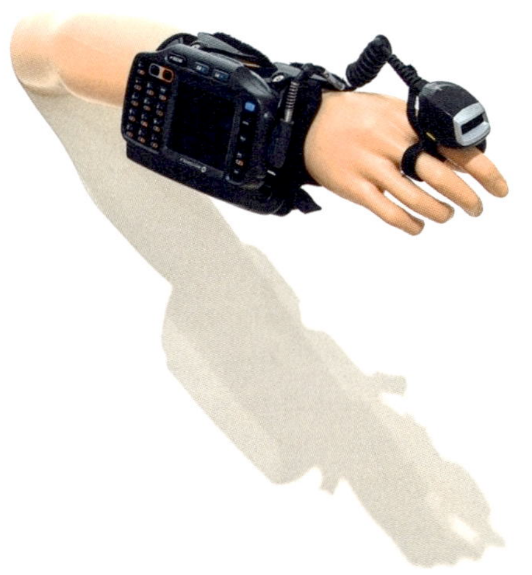

Installation shot of the Motorola WT4000 wearable terminal. A device worn in warehouses that gives instructions, and monitors the work rate and location of the employee. If said employee is not hitting their productivity target, it automatically ~~electrocutes them~~ sends a message to warn of this situation.

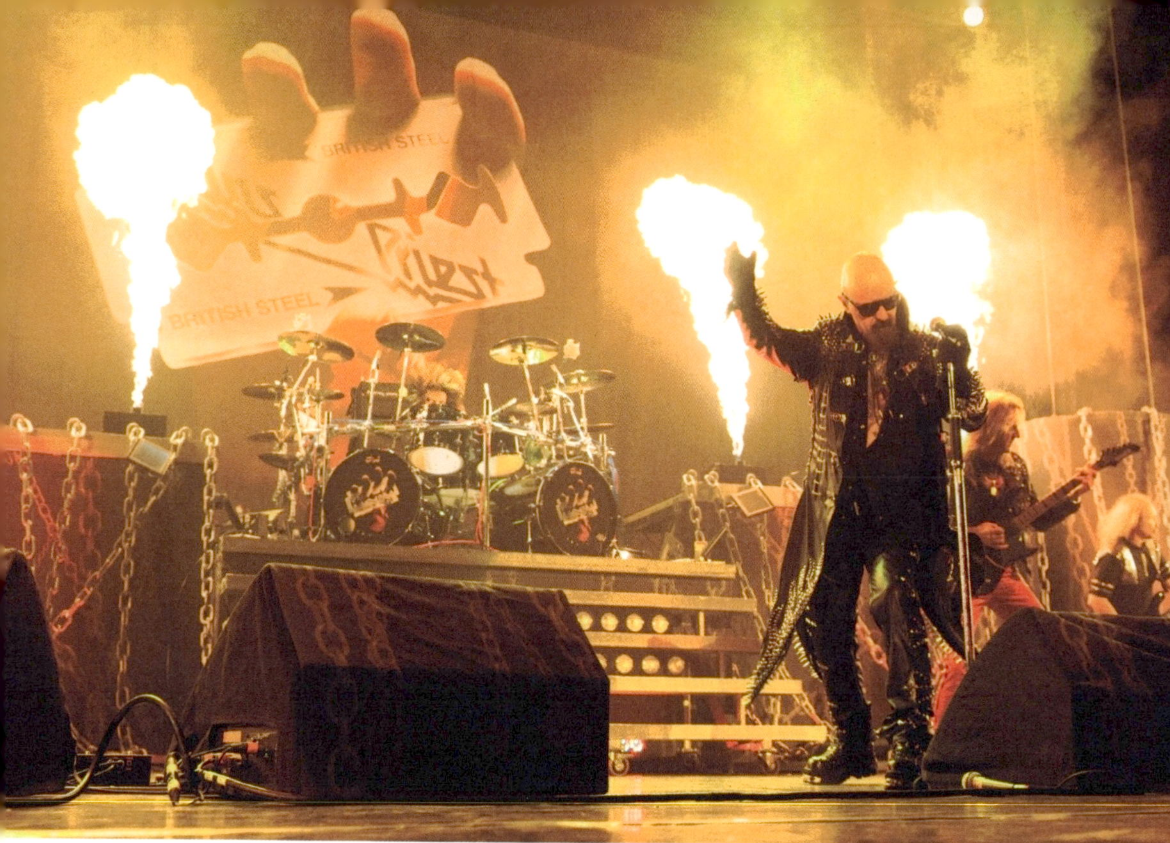

Heavy metal in the 1970s and 1980s was a ritualistic re-creation of heavy industry – an artistic if not operatic depiction of dangerous factory life, replaying the sights and sounds of the workplace. A metal gig was noisy, full of light and fire, with hyper-macho men working really hard at their job. This was taking place at exactly that moment in history when these jobs and the culture itself were disappearing and were no longer a certainty for life. Perhaps the closest the teenage audience would get to a factory (maybe like the one their dad or older brother worked in) would be at a concert.

We managed to borrow an A-list Old Master painting by John Martin: *The Destruction of Sodom and Gomorrah*. In it, Martin depicts the chaos and impending implosion of Victorian cities as an Old Testament story. Unusually, Martin was also an accomplished engineer, obsessed with how to deal with noxious fumes and the sewage enveloping and bubbling in London and other cities. His warnings about the cholera and typhoid emanating from all the shit in the Thames and its tributaries, and the possible ways to deal with it, were raised in Parliament in 1834. Even though the capital was destroying itself with disease, his plans for a sewage system were met with ridicule. Twenty-five years later, a similar plan by Joseph Bazalgette was adopted for London.

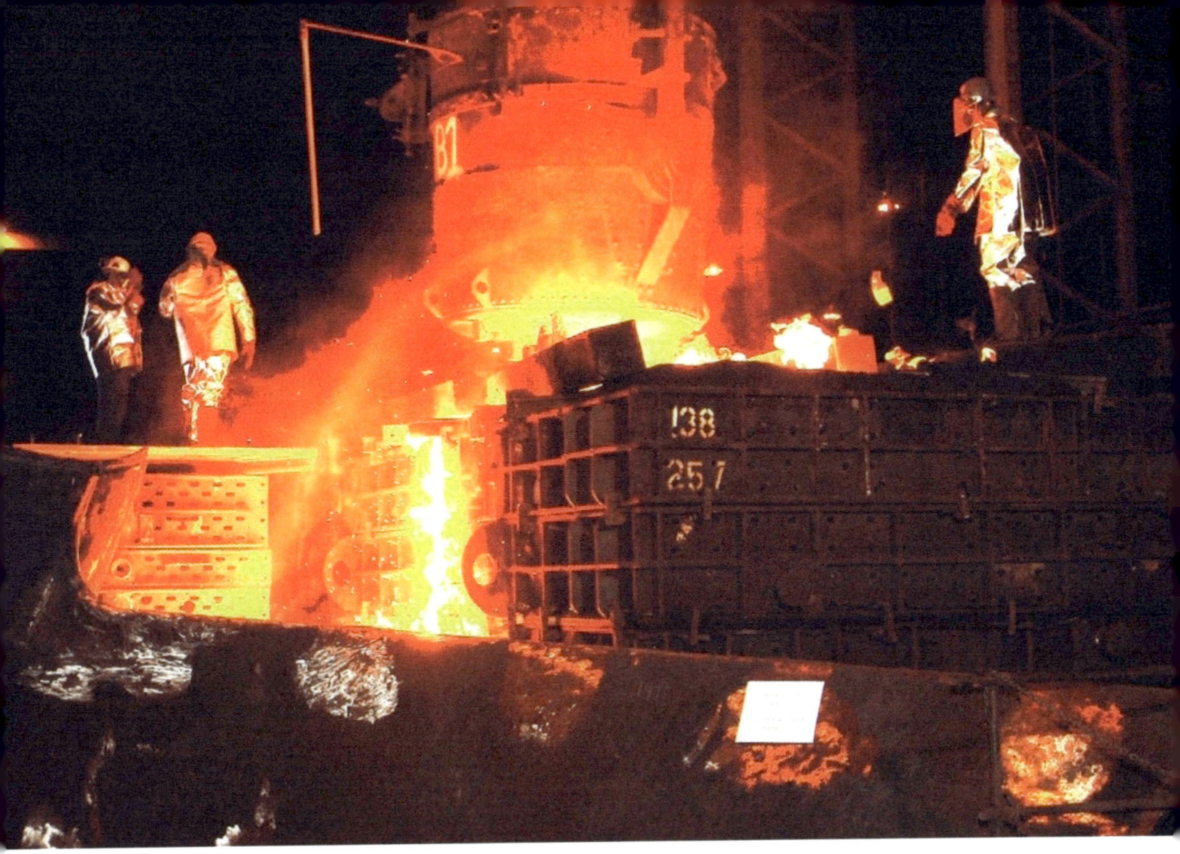

Judas Priest (left) and a steelworks (right) both in full throttle. The visual and aural similarities between heavy metal and the metal industries themselves are almost too obvious at times. Heavy metal is a requiem mass for a dying way of life.

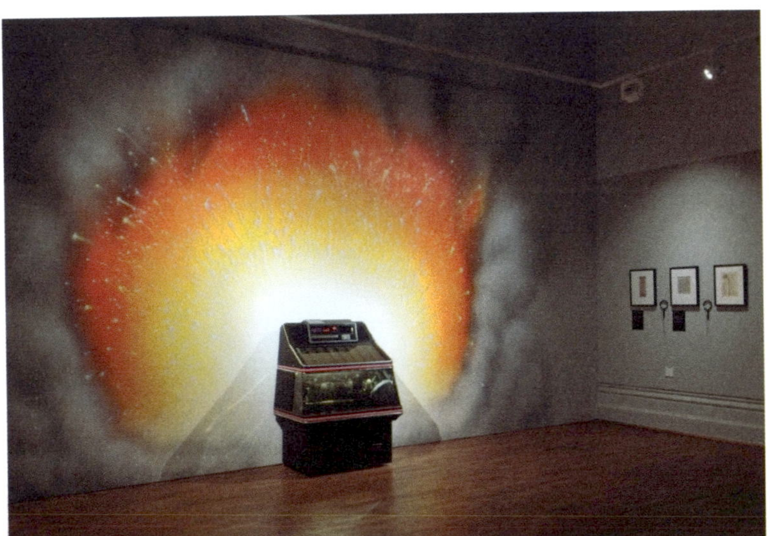

Factory Records, a jukebox in the exhibition, played sounds from industries around the UK, mostly recorded in the 1970s and 1980s as they were closing.

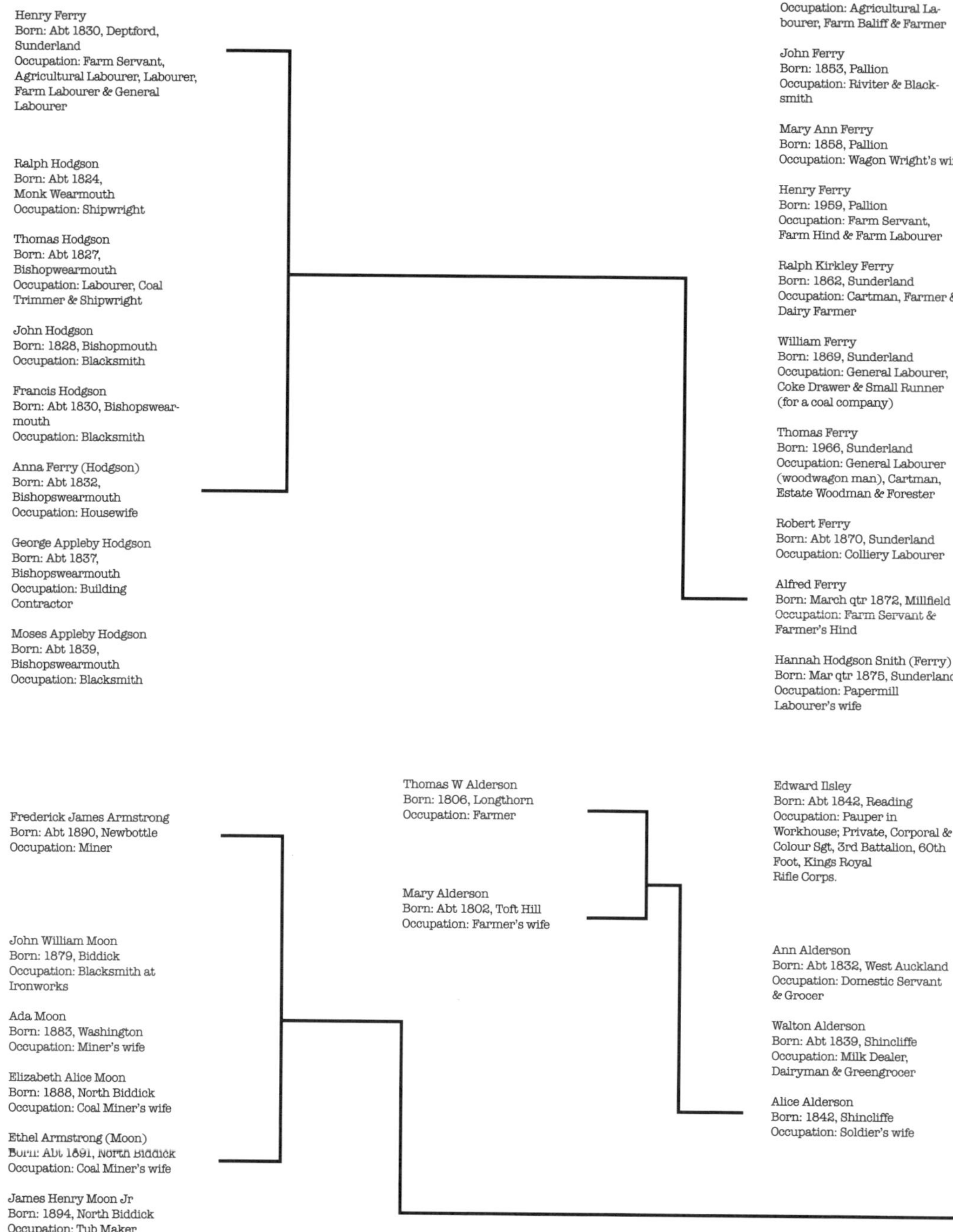
Henry Ferry
Born: Abt 1830, Deptford, Sunderland
Occupation: Farm Servant, Agricultural Labourer, Labourer, Farm Labourer & General Labourer
Ralph Hodgson
Born: Abt 1824, Monk Wearmouth
Occupation: Shipwright
Thomas Hodgson
Born: Abt 1827, Bishopwearmouth
Occupation: Labourer, Coal Trimmer & Shipwright
John Hodgson
Born: 1828, Bishopmouth
Occupation: Blacksmith
Francis Hodgson
Born: Abt 1830, Bishopswear-mouth
Occupation: Blacksmith
Anna Ferry (Hodgson)
Born: Abt 1832, Bishopswearmouth
Occupation: Housewife
George Appleby Hodgson
Born: Abt 1837, Bishopswearmouth
Occupation: Building Contractor
Moses Appleby Hodgson
Born: Abt 1839, Bishopswearmouth
Occupation: Blacksmith
Richard Ferry
Born: Abt 1853, Pallion
Occupation: Agricultural La-bourer, Farm Baliff & Farmer
John Ferry
Born: 1853, Pallion
Occupation: Riviter & Black-smith
Mary Ann Ferry
Born: 1858, Pallion
Occupation: Wagon Wright's wife
Henry Ferry
Born: 1959, Pallion
Occupation: Farm Servant, Farm Hind & Farm Labourer
Ralph Kirkley Ferry
Born: 1862, Sunderland
Occupation: Cartman, Farmer & Dairy Farmer
William Ferry
Born: 1869, Sunderland
Occupation: General Labourer, Coke Drawer & Small Runner (for a coal company)
Thomas Ferry
Born: 1966, Sunderland
Occupation: General Labourer (woodwagon man), Cartman, Estate Woodman & Forester
Robert Ferry
Born: Abt 1870, Sunderland
Occupation: Colliery Labourer
Alfred Ferry
Born: March qtr 1872, Millfield
Occupation: Farm Servant & Farmer's Hind
Hannah Hodgson Snith (Ferry)
Born: Mar qtr 1875, Sunderland
Occupation: Papermill Labourer's wife
Frederick James Armstrong
Born: Abt 1890, Newbottle
Occupation: Miner
John William Moon
Born: 1879, Biddick
Occupation: Blacksmith at Ironworks
Ada Moon
Born: 1883, Washington
Occupation: Miner's wife
Elizabeth Alice Moon
Born: 1888, North Biddick
Occupation: Coal Miner's wife
Ethel Armstrong (Moon)
Born: Abt 1891, North Biddick
Occupation: Coal Miner's wife
James Henry Moon Jr
Born: 1894, North Biddick
Occupation: Tub Maker
Olive Mary Moon
Born: 1896, North Biddick
Occupation: Soldier's wife
Thomas W Alderson
Born: 1806, Longthorn
Occupation: Farmer
Mary Alderson
Born: Abt 1802, Toft Hill
Occupation: Farmer's wife
Edward Ilsley
Born: Abt 1842, Reading
Occupation: Pauper in Workhouse; Private, Corporal & Colour Sgt, 3rd Battalion, 60th Foot, Kings Royal Rifle Corps.
Ann Alderson
Born: Abt 1832, West Auckland
Occupation: Domestic Servant & Grocer
Walton Alderson
Born: Abt 1839, Shincliffe
Occupation: Milk Dealer, Dairyman & Greengrocer
Alice Alderson
Born: 1842, Shincliffe
Occupation: Soldier's wife

Detail of *Another Time, Another Place*. Bryan Ferry's family tree. In the exhibition, the clearest way to illustrate the relationship between the entertainment industry and heavy industry was to show the family trees of three musicians from different parts of the industrial heartlands of the UK. I chose: i) Shaun Ryder of the Happy Mondays to represent Manchester and the North West; ii) Noddy Holder of Slade to represent the metal industries of the Midlands; and iii) Bryan Ferry of Roxy Music to represent the coal mining and shipbuilding industries of the North East (pictured here). You don't have to go back far, or at all for that matter, to see that they were all from profoundly working-class industrial dynasties. For Ferry, especially, his life and subsequent class journey would have been inconceivable to his ancestors. Designed by Scott King.

Thomas Walton Ilsley
Born: 1859, Sunderland
Occupation: Soldier's son

Edward Ilsley
Born: Abt 1867
Occupation: Labourer

Arabella Eveline Ferry (Ilsley)
Born: Abt 1869, Madras, India
Occupation: Domestic Servant & Housewife

Frederick Charles Ilsley
Born: Abt 1871, Bellary, India
Occupation: Coal Dealer & Cart-man (own account)

Alice Eva Lovett (Ferry)
Born: 1891, West Herrington
Occupation: Hind's wife

Hannah H Ferry
Born: 1893, Middle Herrington

Alfred Ferry
Born: 1896, Middle Herrington
Occupation: Farm Servant

Ethel Murray (Ferry)
Born: 1898, Middle Herrington
Occupation: Miner's wife

Mary Ellen Ferry
Born: 1901, Old Penshaw

Ada Ferry
Born: 1902, Old Penshaw

Evelyn May Laws (Ferry)
Born: 1906, Old Penshaw
Occupation: Engineer's wife

Frederick Charles Ferry
Born: 1908, Old Penshaw
Occupation: Farmer, Pity Pony Handler & Gardener

Mary Ann Ferry (Armstrong)
Born: 1909, North Biddick
Occupation: Teacher

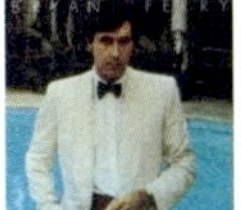

Bryan Ferry
Born: 1945, Washington
Occupation: Singer

***Love Is Enough*, 2014**

… was an exhibition at Modern Art Oxford in 2014 comparing the careers of William Morris and Andy Warhol. It wasn't even my idea to pair these two but as soon as Sally Shaw at the gallery suggested it, I could see how it could work. To my mind, they had so much in common: an interest in commerce, and both were famed printmakers interested in repetition. The more I looked, the more the connections seemed uncanny. Both artists had sprawling, almost ungovernable careers that set few boundaries for themselves and for art in general. They were ambitious and prolific image makers, populists in the best sense of the word, understanding the power of art and its necessity in everyday life. They were also prophetic figures. Warhol was the first internet artist, despite working in a pre-internet era, and his hunger for information, his need to connect and document his daily life, reflects so much of the social media landscape today. Morris was a key figure in the Modernist movement before it had even been named, and his writings on art and its importance in society remain influential today.

The exhibition was arranged thematically, opening with myths. As children, both Warhol and Morris retreated into fantasy worlds due to ill health. The brave men and beautiful women of medieval literature (Morris) and mythic Hollywood (Warhol) respectively provided great comfort to them in childhood and endured as lifelong obsessions. A section on their working practices showed how these were intimately connected to how they saw the world and how the world of work could be different. Morris wanted to bring dignity and craft back into labour in the face of the dehumanising work of the factory. Warhol's Factory in the 1960s, with its blurring of social life and work, has since become the blueprint for any creative office environment. Warhol documented the US empire at its height. And his most celebrated works, certainly the most highly valued now, are his death, disaster and race riot images, the opposite of his glamorous portraits. Morris's politics are well documented, with Marx and Chaucer his guides. He was one of the earliest public figures in Victorian England to criticise the British empire for its destruction of the domestic cotton industry in India.

Both artists had access to and were feted by the powerful but remained disdainful of them, expressing the frustrations of working for the often tasteless rich. They wanted to cover the world with their work, seeing beauty as a very powerful weapon. My only regret was that in the flower room I allowed myself to have captions with each work, when in fact it should have been a room with no text in it: simply the work of two visionaries.

Warhol or Morris?

If you are sceptical of the similarities between these two artists, here are some quotes by William Morris and Andy Warhol – but who said what? Answers at the bottom of the page.

1. I had thought civilisation meant the attainment of peace and order and freedom and goodwill between man and man, not more stuffed chairs and more cushions.

2. I think having land and not ruining it is the most beautiful art that anybody could ever want to own.

3. Whenever people in civilisations get degenerate and materialistic they always point to their outward beauty and riches.

4. I think it's desirable that the artist and what is technically called the designer should practically be one.

5. My country is really beautiful, but it would be more beautiful if everyone had enough money to live.

6. Make it mechanical with a vengeance.

7. I believe in work.

8. Machines – I have boundless faith in their capacity.

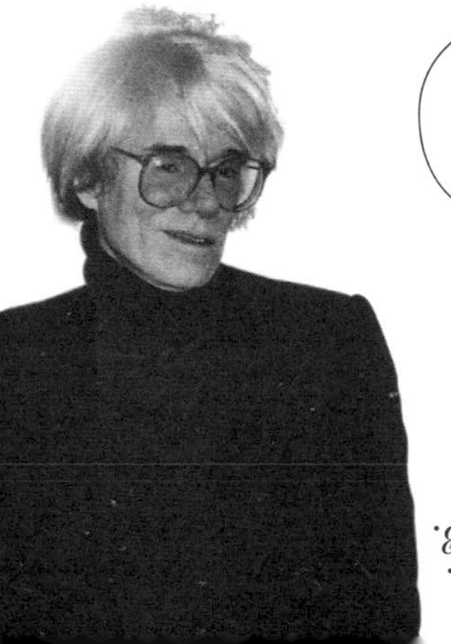

2. 3. 5.

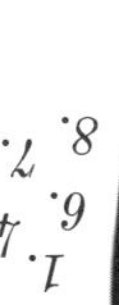

1. 4. 6. 7. 8.

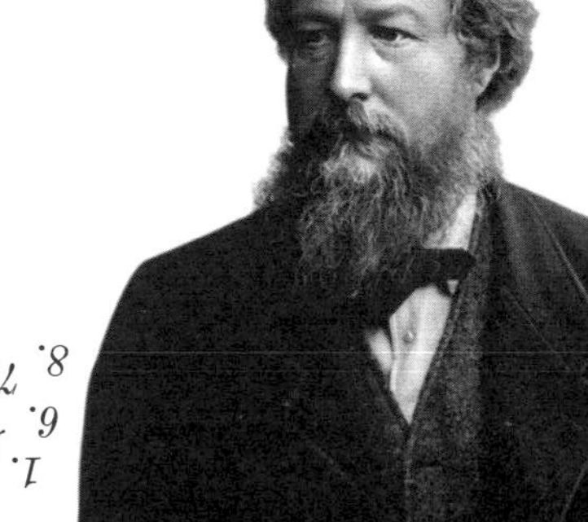

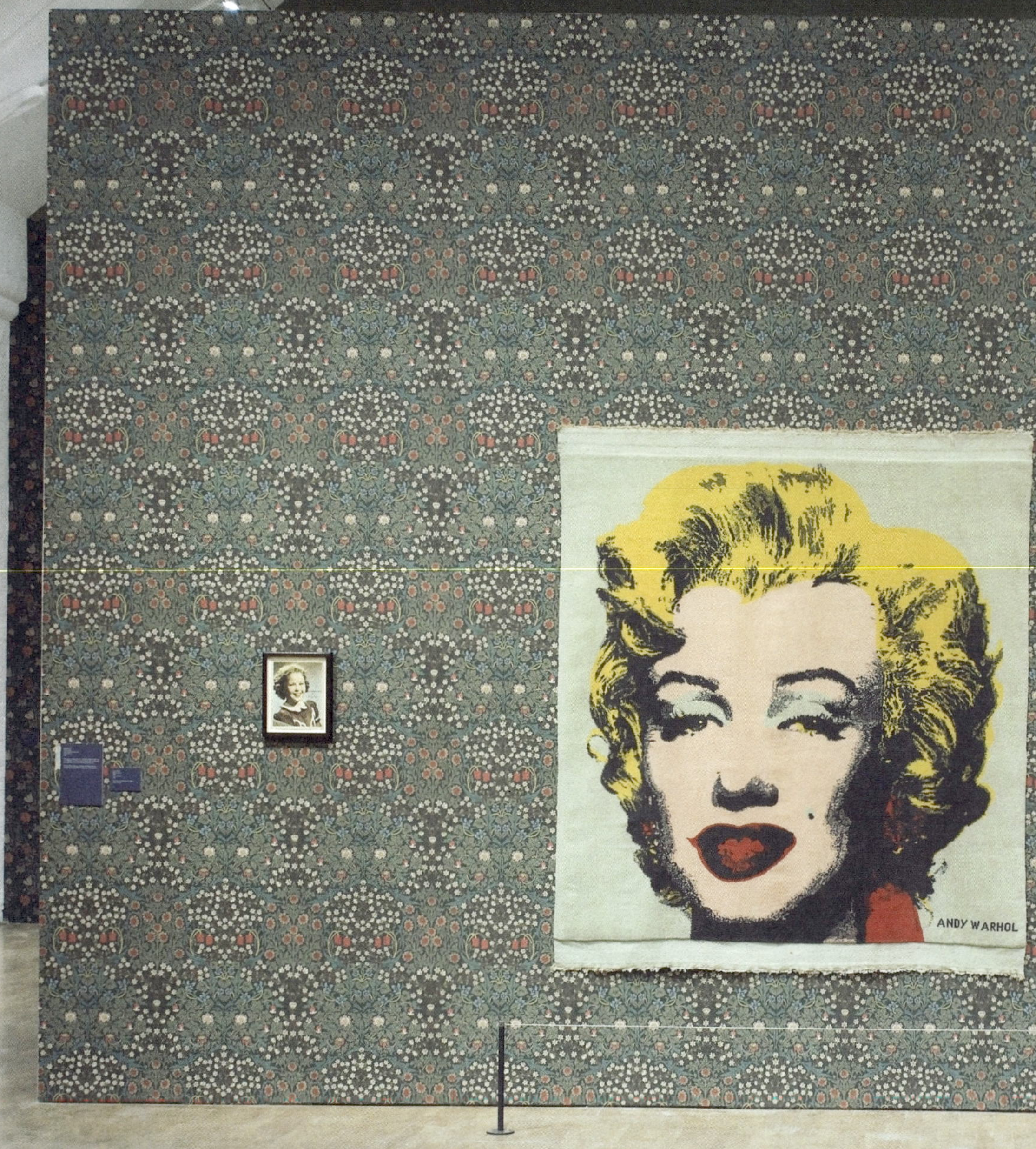

In this installation shot, a tapestry of Warhol's *Marilyn* was hung next to his signed photo of Shirley Temple. This vivid hand-coloured image of the child star was surely a huge influence on the young Warhol, who wrote to her from his sickbed in Pittsburgh. On the right are portraits of Jackie and Bobby Kennedy, characters from a modern Camelot.

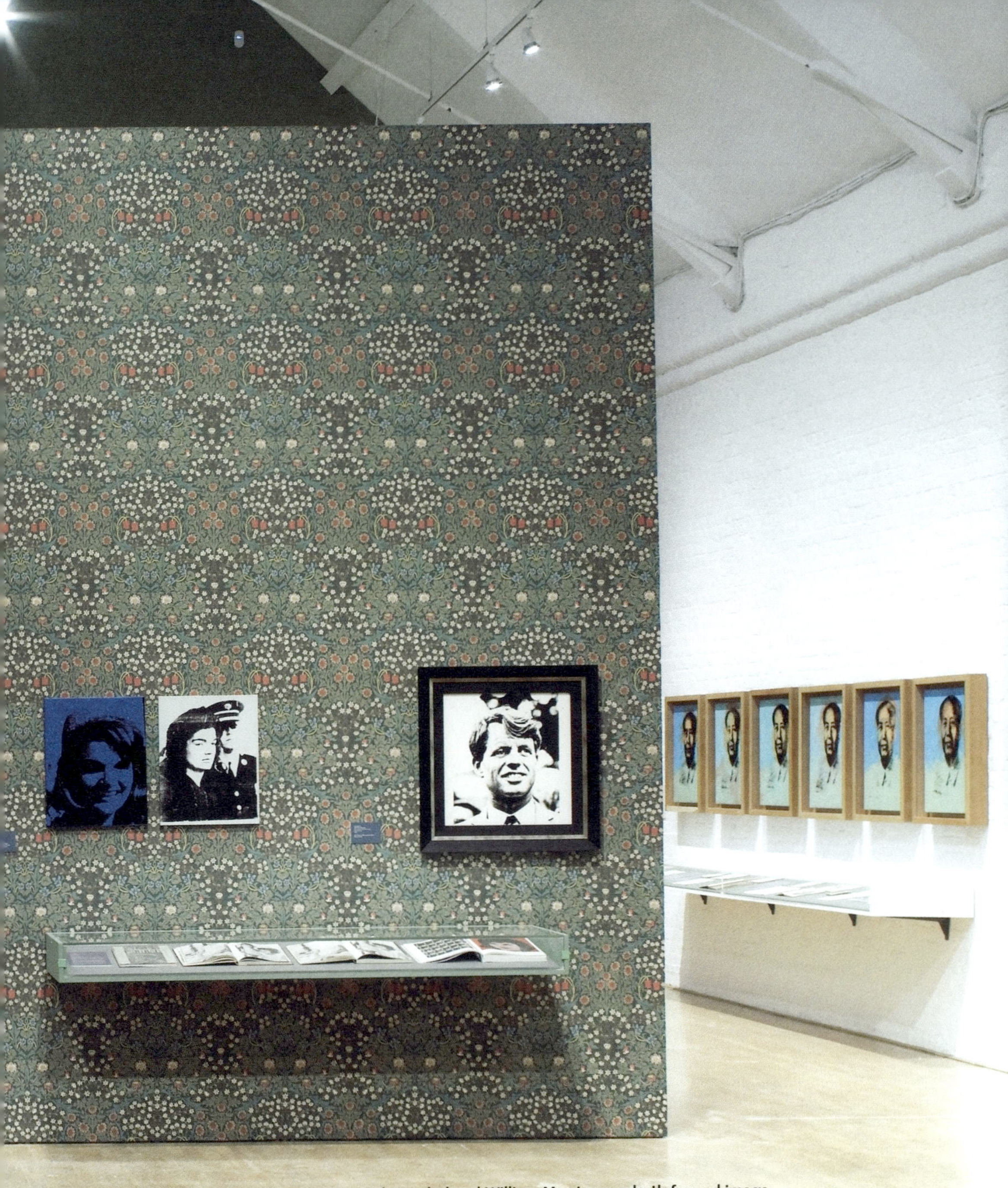

Overleaf: The Flower Power room. Andy Warhol and William Morris were both fecund image makers: promiscuously fertile, even. Here, Warhol's *Camo* painting quadtych was hung on Morris's *Acanthus* wallpaper. In the vitrine was the forty-two-stage print layout of the *Acanthus* wallpaper from base colour to completed design; at the midpoint it looks a bit like camouflage, which is after all vegetation. Surely this is beauty as a weapon against the ugliness of the industrial world. Morris's freehand drawings of these textile designs are on a par with any landscape by Turner or Constable.

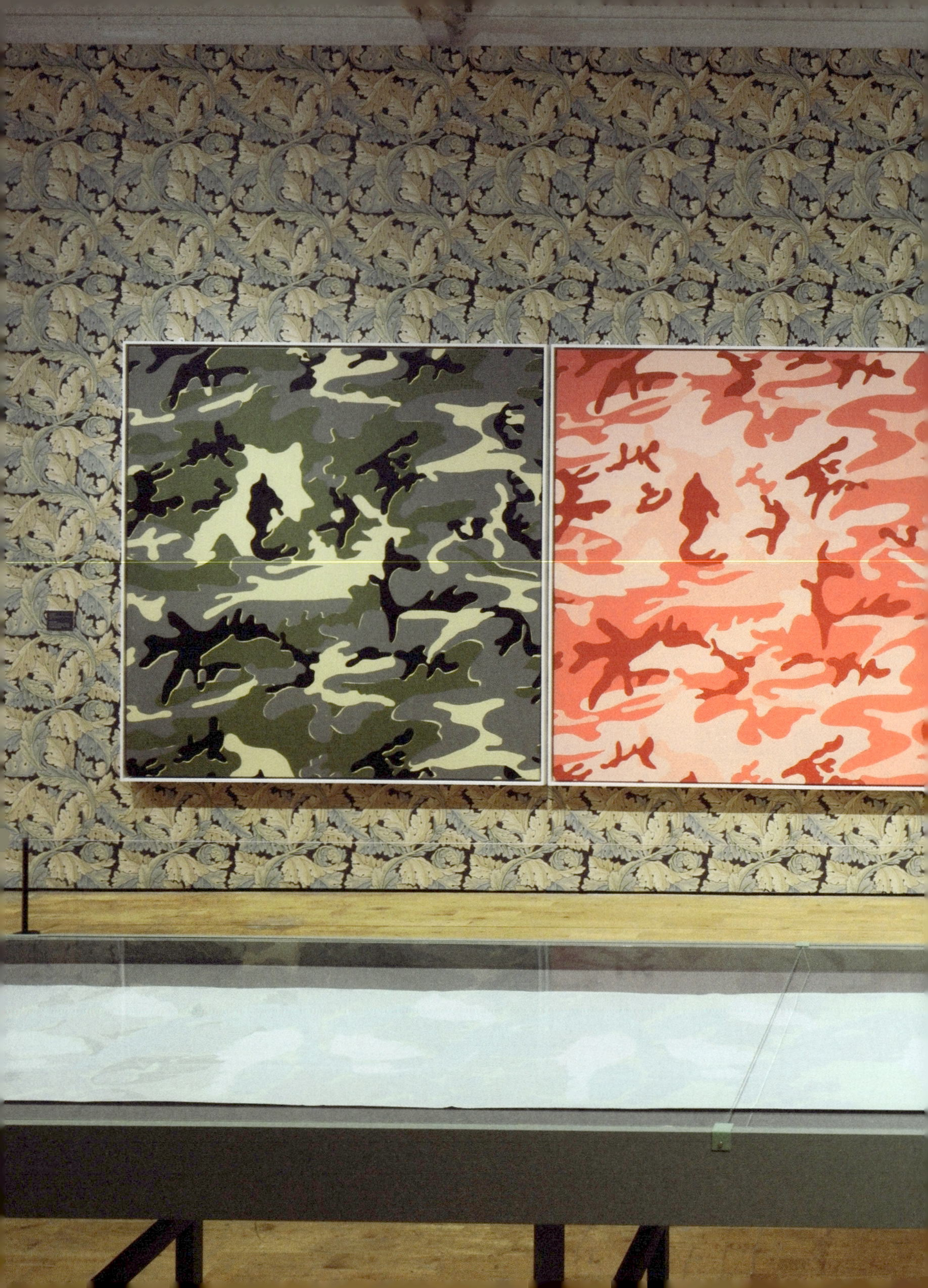

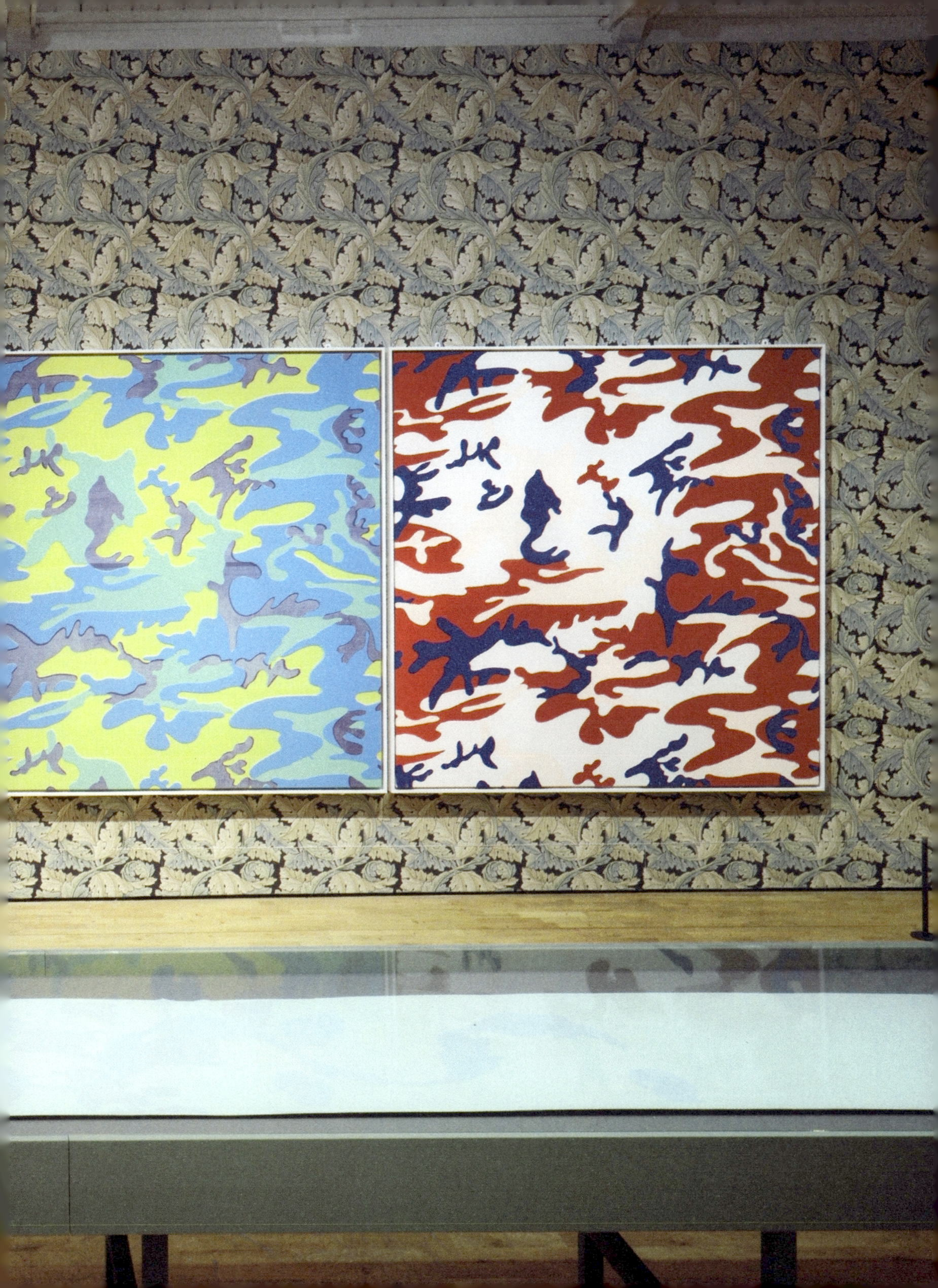

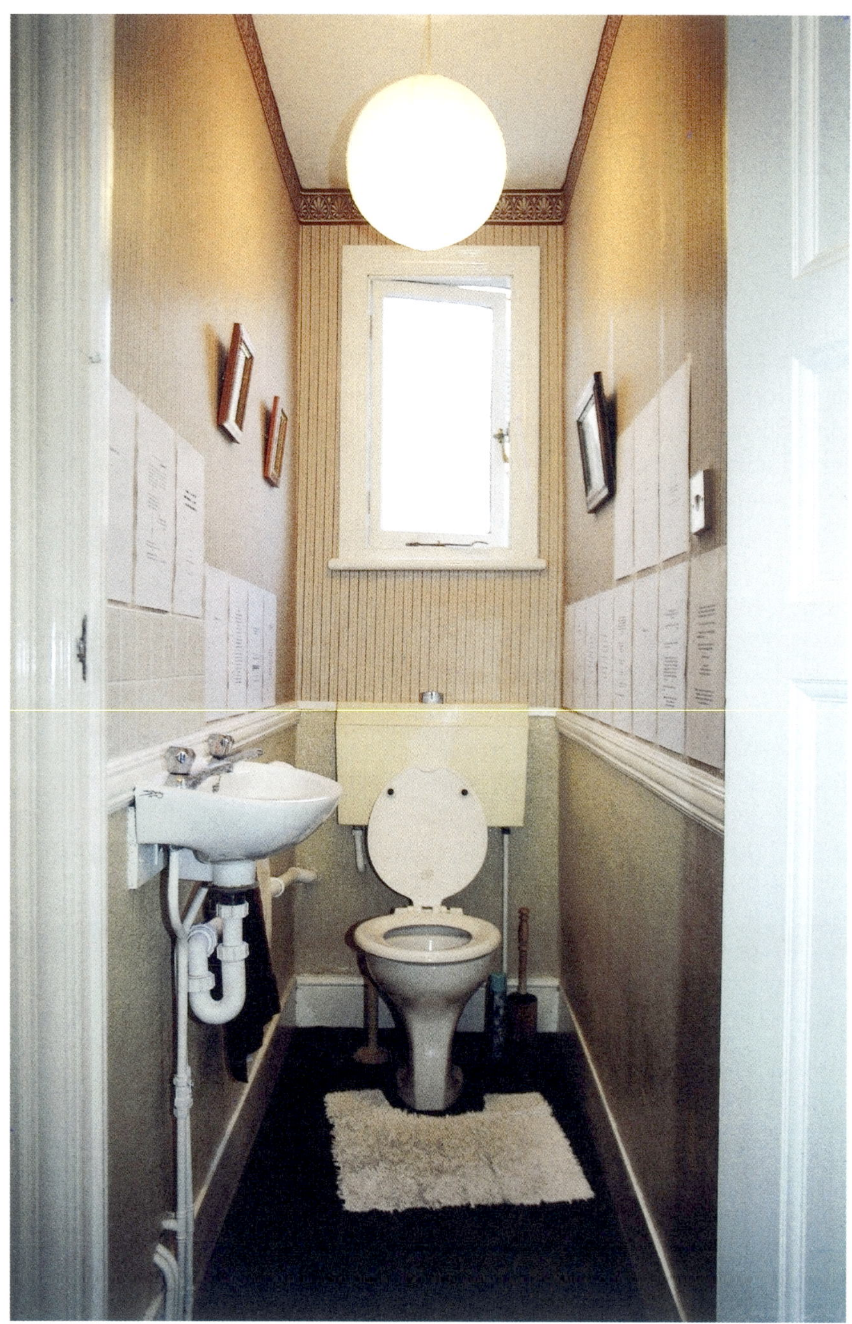

In 1993 I put on *Open Bedroom*, a show in the family home when my parents went on holiday. Here in the loo is an installation of *Pensées*, a zine of annotations of graffiti from the men's toilets at the British Library. The content is a mixture of academic one-upmanship and filth. Reading some of these texts would mean you would have to cancel yourself.

Chapter 11

The Reactionary Ravers

An interview with Daniel Scott

Below is an attempt by Daniel, my editor, to really get to the heart of the matter, and me evading this.

Daniel Scott: Why do you do this?

Jeremy Deller: *[Nervous laughter]*. You mean make art? It's been a process of elimination, in that having studied art history, I soon realised that it was a world I wasn't equipped to be in. The museum world is very conservative, or at least was in those days. I don't think I am good at working in institutions long term – I am better suited to participating for a short time and then leaving.

D: But surely you didn't have that perspective when you were a student?

J: I loved being around art but working around it in an institution was an entirely different thing. I worked in a commercial print gallery as a technician and, as I wasn't a very technical person, it was a constant minefield. I burnt a David Hockney print on my first morning at the gallery. The job was to remove an auction house label stuck on the back of its frame. I was given this thing which looked like a hairdryer but is actually used to strip paint and wallpaper. I did a very thorough job of removing the label but when I turned the frame round, I realised I had also done a very thorough job of burning the print and had caused condensation on the inside of the frame too. It was a portrait of one of David's friends (can't remember who), but now with an additional big black sooty mark. I had a look at it and quickly slipped it back into the storage racks. Not the best start to a job.

D: In years to come, you could have made it out to be a collaborative thing like a Warhol/Basquiat, a Hockney/Deller.

J: More like when Rauschenberg rubbed out a de Kooning drawing but, in my case, without anybody's permission. I think it was ultimately sold without anybody being aware of what had happened… I was rightfully sacked for all-round incompetence – it was clearly not the job for me – and then I was in the wilderness for a while.

Looking back, the timescale gets very mushed up. It lacks coherent lines. I was just doing one thing, then another. Some things worked, some things didn't. Between 1990 and 1996, I couldn't tell you what year things happened.

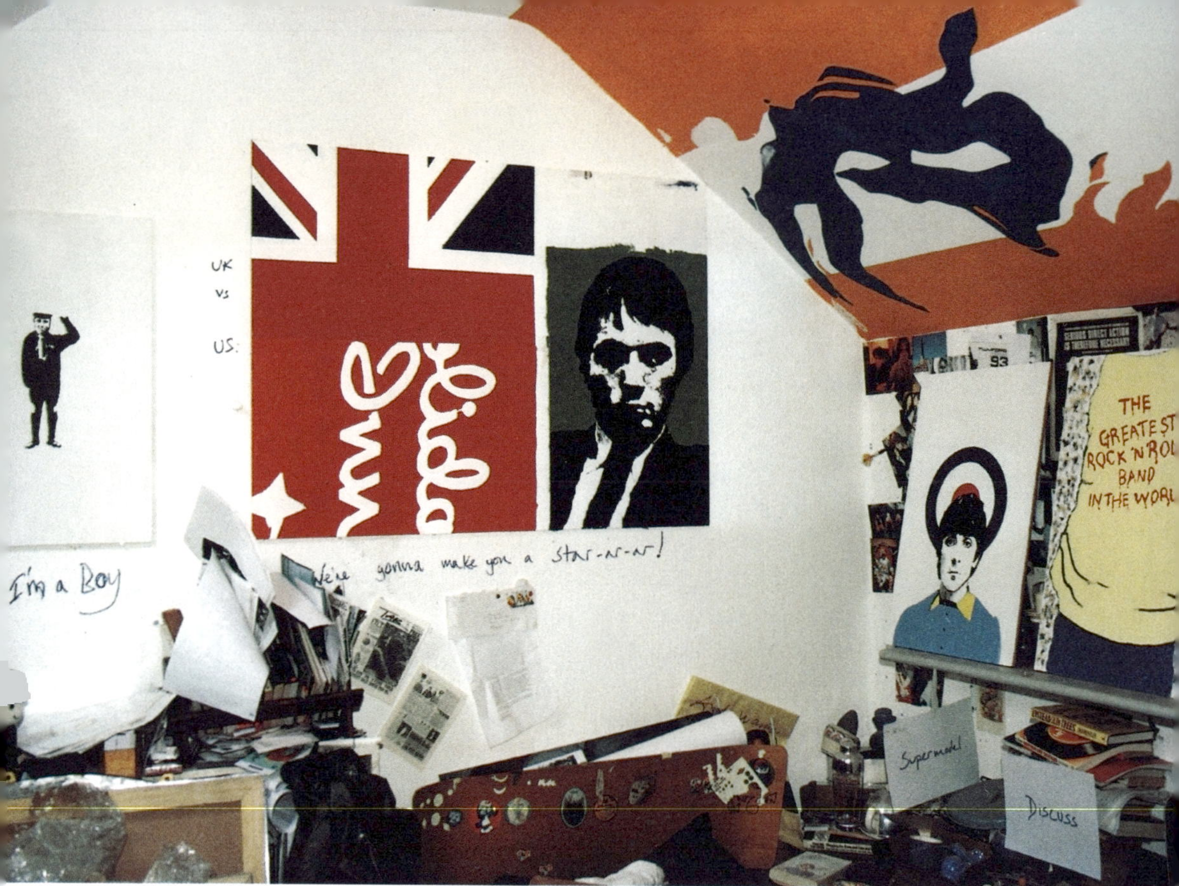

As part of *Open Bedroom*, I also exhibited a series of paintings on the life of Keith Moon in my messy bedroom. A sort of 'Stations of the Mod'.

You and I were hanging around together but it's hard to recall what happened when.

D: What about the Zelda Cheatle exhibition? That was pretty early.

J: Yes – 1990. Zelda had a photography gallery in Cecil Court in London, and I was in a group show there. I was really interested in photography from an early age. I went on a school trip to Wales when I was nine and had been lent a camera to take along with me. When the pictures came back, my parents thought they had been mixed up with somebody else's pictures because they were not terrible. Her gallery was a place where you could meet all these fascinating senior documentary photographers like George Rodger, Grace Robertson and Bert Hardy – photographers who did so much to document the social history of the UK. Within a few minutes of meeting George Rodger, he told me about being at the liberation of Bergen-Belsen concentration camp in 1945. He clearly had to tell this terrible story to everyone he came across to try to make some sort of sense of it. Bert Hardy was like a character from one of his pictures – a jolly

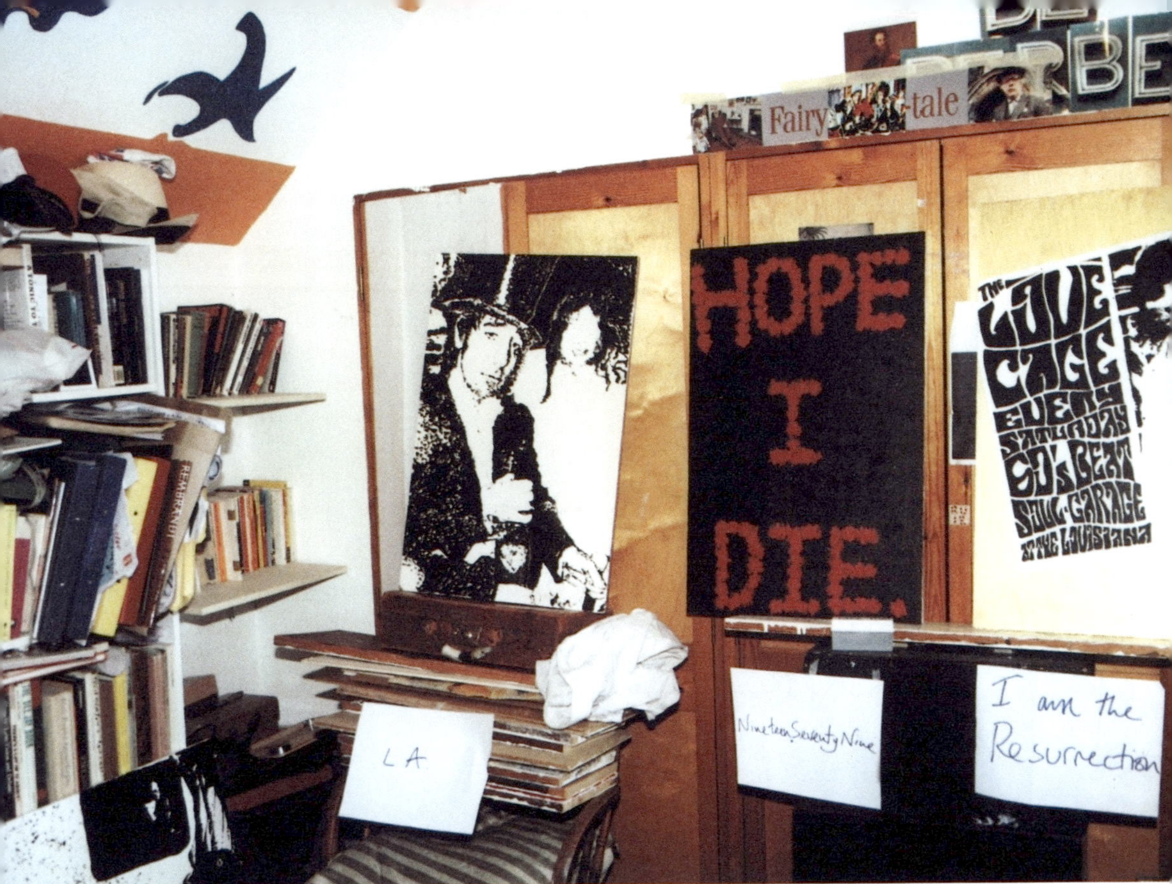

cockney boozer with a red nose. Grace Robertson was tall and distinguished. They were proper grown-ups with interesting lives.

D: Can you identify a point where a seed was sown from which you can plot what happened subsequently?

J: Yes, I think that might have been when I put on the show in my parents' house in 1993 – *Open Bedroom*. It was quite a private thing with a small number of people, as I was worried about the house getting wrecked. It just felt right to do a show in the house, with different works spread around the place. In the loo, I pinned up pages of a book I had made of graffiti from the men's toilets at the British Library, which was both highly academic and filthy.

D: You work within institutions and organisations. How do you negotiate this?

J: I have never made myself to be outside of the art world, whatever that is. Institutions are difficult to avoid in any walk of life and can be frustrating by design.

D: Was one of the attractions of acid house… the freedom it promised?

J: Yes, though I was just as interested in what it meant for the country.

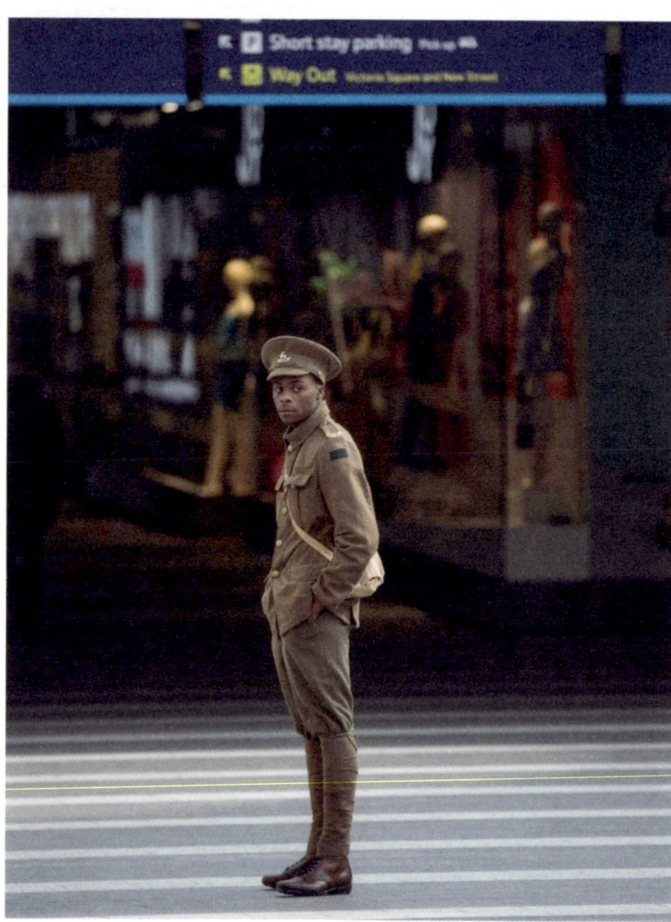

We're Here Because We're Here, 2016. A soldier appears in Birmingham New Street station.

I am not a joiner-inner, despite often looking to collaborate with people, so I was very much on the margins of the rave scene… but its historical significance was clear to me. So, in the film *Everybody in the Place*, I am presenting a subject a lot of people experienced firsthand in a more profound way than I did. It seemed to touch a nerve, though perhaps it offered a fresh route through a well-trodden area. Having said that, I received some quite amusing criticism from 'reactionary ravers', as I will call them.

D: You claim to run away from emotions, yet works such as *We're Here Because We're Here*, a nationwide event on the centenary of the first day of the Battle of the Somme, were intensely moving.

J: It had no emotional effect on me. I had been working on it for two years, so when it finally took place, I thought, 'My work here is done.' If I had become emotionally connected to it, it would have destroyed me.

D: You must, however, have been aware of the impact it had on those people participating?

J: True, but I can disengage emotionally, in the same way an anthropologist or a doctor probably does. That said, I hoped it would be unsettling and even frightening. I wrote in a notebook, 'I want to make children cry,' which goes against everything held dear in contemporary culture.

As a teenager, some things which really affected me – the paintings of Francis Bacon and the film *Tommy*, for example – also disturbed me, which can be a good thing. I wanted to create a bit of that.

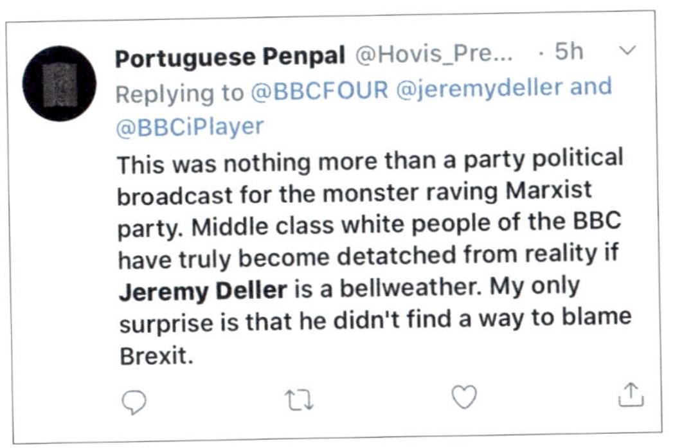

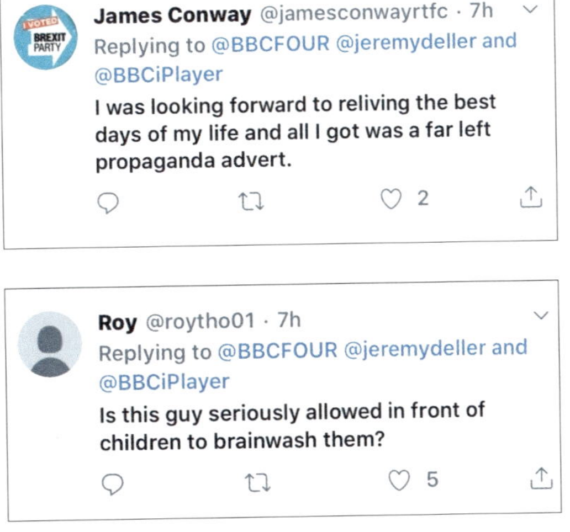

Brilliant angry tweets critical of my film *Everybody in the Place*. It was based around me giving a class on dance music and politics to A-Level students, hence the fury.

D: I think, with some of your work, you want people to be disturbed rather than horrified, which is more complicated. I think a lot of the emotional heft of your work has been through other people. If you look at the response to *Father and Son*, the burning of two life-size wax figures of Rupert and Lachlan Murdoch, there was a real outpouring of anger from the viewers of the work, as people were given an opportunity to watch something really vicious.

J: It was meant to be nasty, personal, grotesque and beautiful. But it had to have, for me at least, a spiritual dimension, containing within it the violence and transcendence which a lot of religious art has. It was also an unequivocal attack on two people. I put my cards clearly on the table so there was nothing between me and the work. There are very few alternative interpretations of that work, although it would be interesting to hear one. It was also one of those 'why not?' moments in that you would only get this made through the medium of art. Like the inflatable Stonehenge, it was an artwork, or idea for one at least, floating around that I managed to grab first. I wasn't even in Melbourne to see it and didn't watch much of the burning figures online. In retrospect, I can't believe I was allowed to do such a thing.

D: You produce a lot of work – posters, stickers, etc. – for free. Do you think you are driven to do that as a counterpoint to the complexity of seeing your work bought on occasion by people whose views you don't share?

J: There are several reasons I do things for free. I like people having my work as a gift because it goes against a prevailing idea that art is expensive and exclusive. Of course, it can be a bit self-sabotaging. The only people who earn anything from my free stuff are those who try to sell it later. I did include a curse on the back of my last poster handout threatening a horrible end to anyone who then sells the work on.

D: It's not a radical opinion but I think you would make more money if you didn't give anything away.

J: That's a basic economic fact.

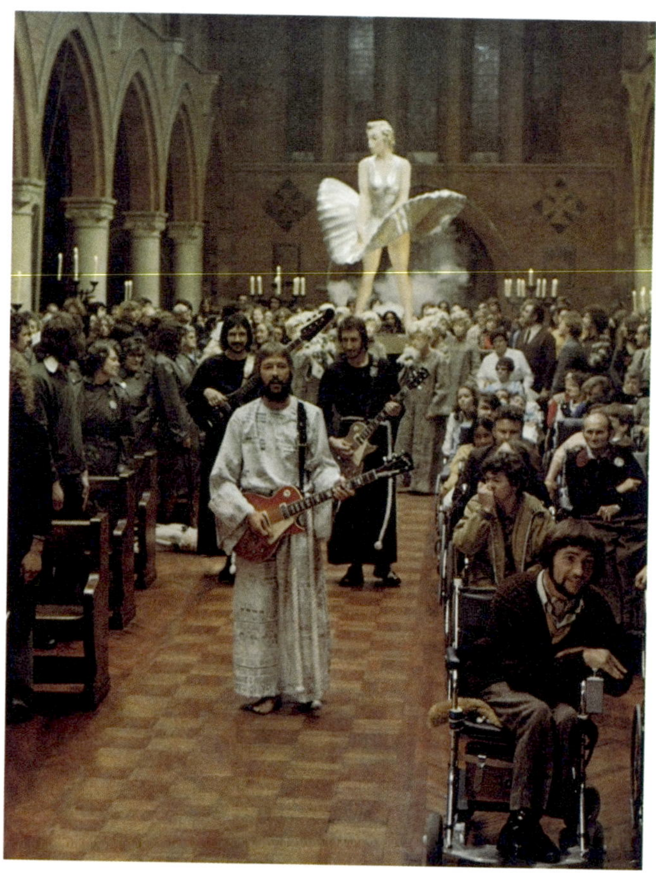

Eric Clapton with The Who in the most impactful scene from the most impactful artistic experience of my life: watching *Tommy* on a big screen in my school gym, mind forever blown.

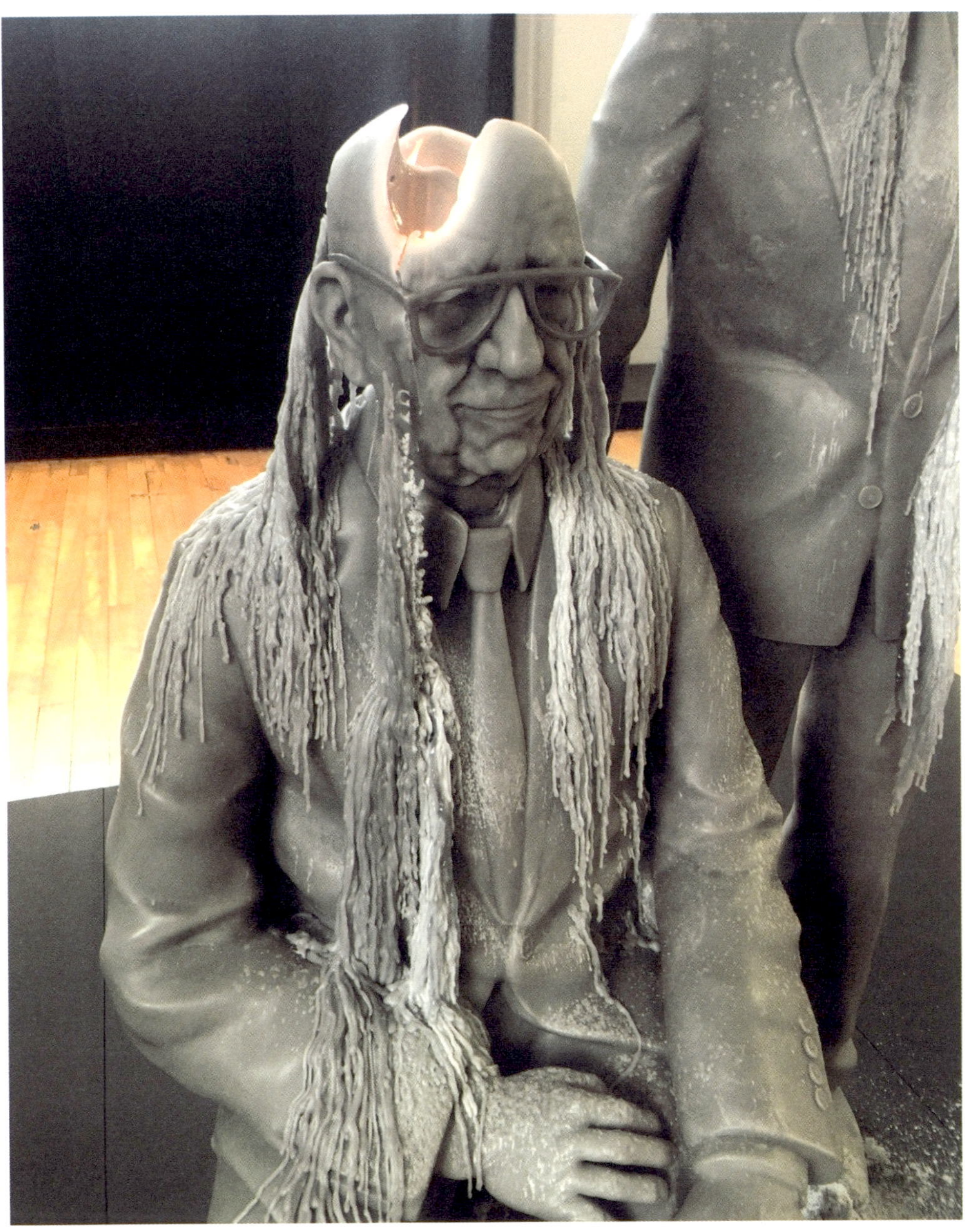

Father and Son, Melbourne, 2021. By the looks of it, this photo of the wax effigies of Rupert and Lachlan Murdoch was taken about five hours into the burn.

Overleaf: *The Deliverers*, 2022. A short film that charts the journey of the Lindisfarne Gospels from London to the Laing Art Gallery in Newcastle, so a homecoming of sorts. It's a fantastical odyssey through time and space, not least because there were security restrictions on filming the treasure. In my version the Gospels descend from space, landing in a Newcastle nightclub.

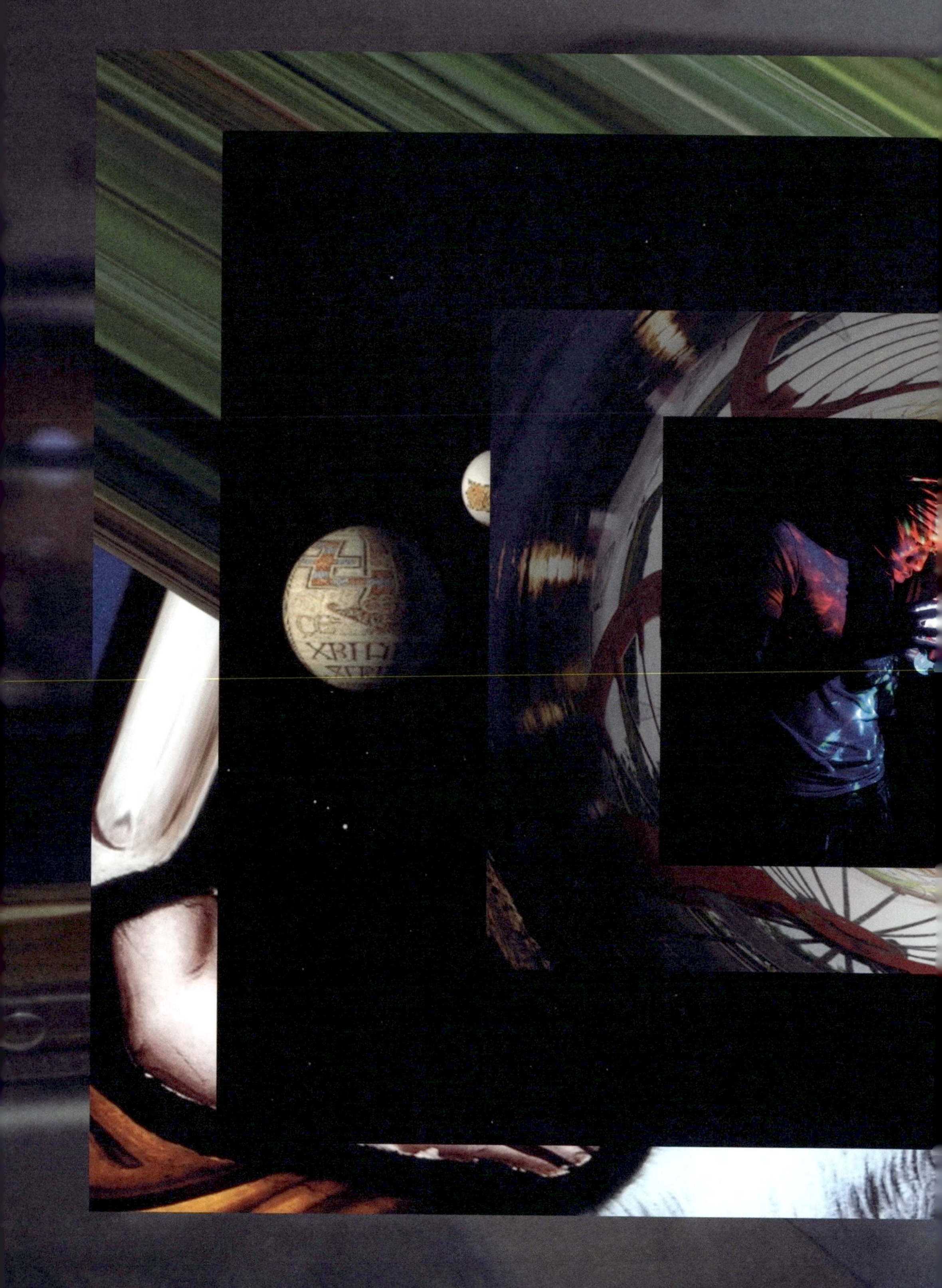

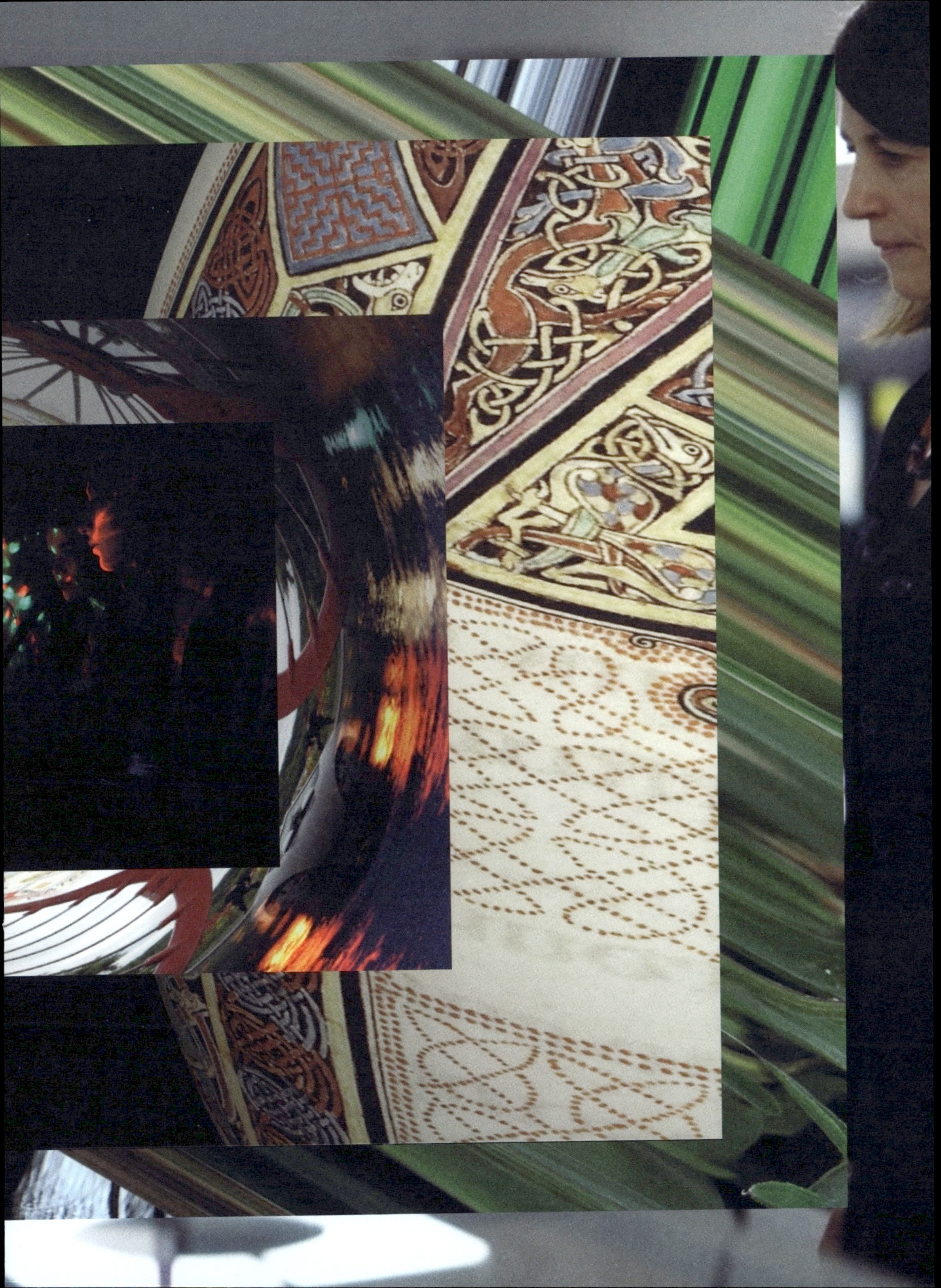

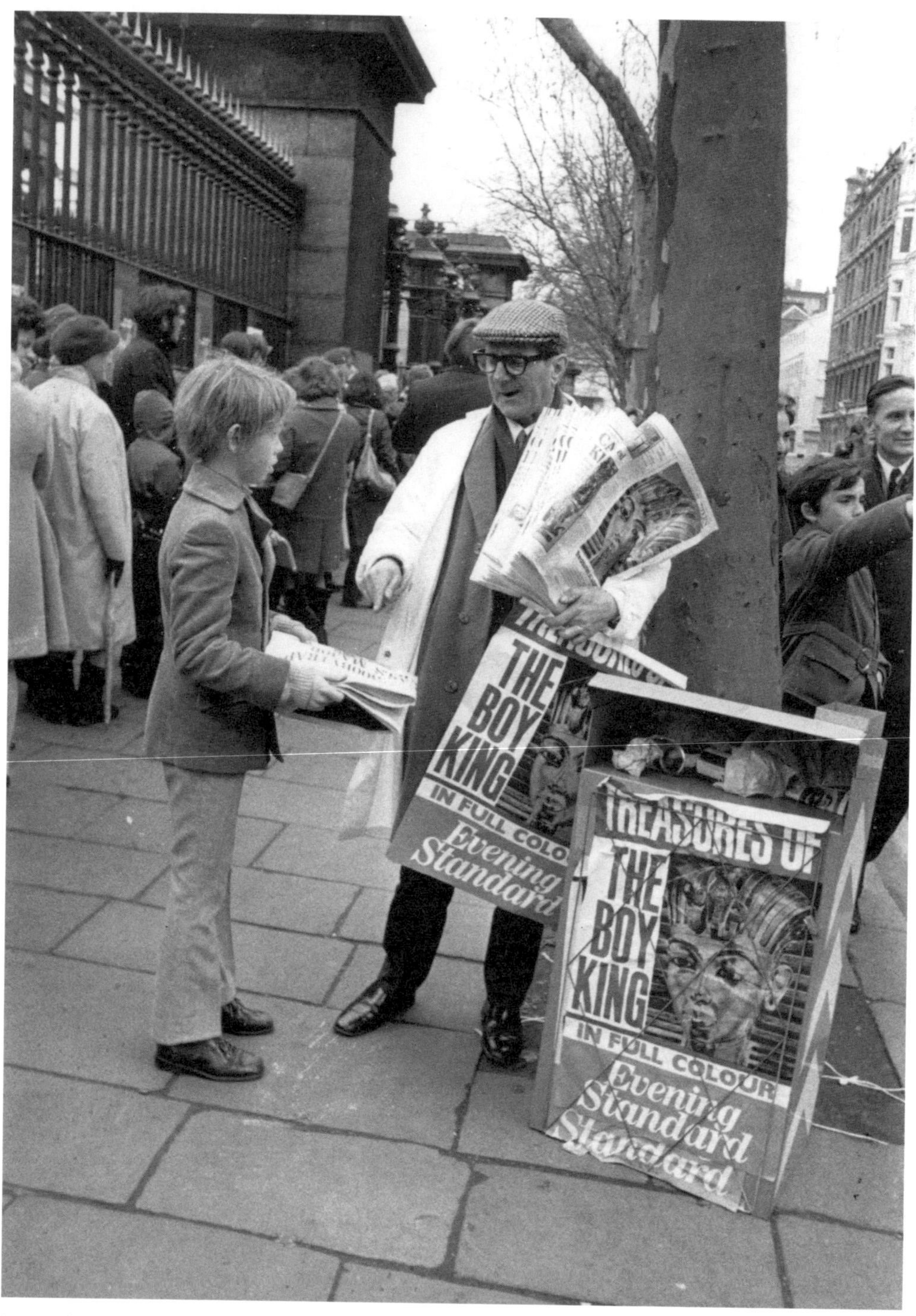

Not me, but it could have been. One of my earliest memories is queueing up to see the Tutankhamun exhibition at the British Museum in 1972. The next time I queued for hours like this was to buy tickets to see Prince.

Chapter 12

VALHALLA IN W12

Glam, Adrian Street and William Blake

Societies often have sacred sites where the gods reside, such as Mount Olympus or Valhalla. For me it was Shepherd's Bush, home of the *Top of the Pops* – my weekly appointment with the gods. The word 'gods' might seem a bit of an exaggeration, but pop music taught me about not only the world, but also the spiritual in popular culture. Glam rock demanded my attention as a child. The music and its appearance were indivisible: I became totally invested in it and was buying more records then than at any time since.

I suspect my and the general population's interest in glam was stimulated by the Tutankhamun exhibition at the British Museum in 1972 (held on the fiftieth anniversary of the excavation of his tomb). It was a sensation and over a million people (myself included) queued to see it. For months, you could not avoid the image of the boy king's gold burial mask – not that I wanted to.

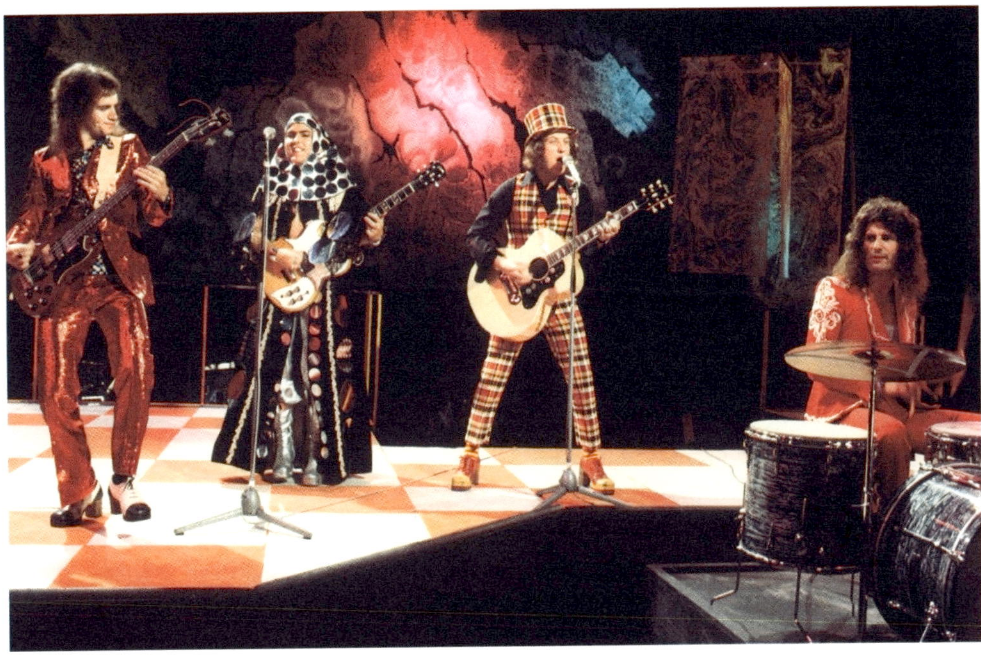

Slade ruling Top of the Pops in 1973. Unbeknown to them and me, they were soon to be deposed.

An early example for me of archaeology's relationship to popular culture, the past encroaching on the future. Pop music also taught me about death and capitalism, which in this case were intertwined. In 1976, the glam rock bands I had worshipped a few years before were effectively redundant. It was a brutal lesson in mortality for me – and for them as well, I imagine. I even felt sorry and embarrassed for them when they would occasionally resurface on television. I was starting to understand, via the medium of pop music, how cruel the world could be, and that death has many faces, sometimes even in full make-up. The market was a death space if you were not successful: you would not be on *Top of the Pops* anymore, it was as simple as that. A hyper-capitalist pantheon. I distinctly remember watching a documentary about The Sweet – still on tour, but no longer having hits. Even at the age of ten, I felt sad for them. The hit parade is brutal, literally a merciless reminder of your standing.

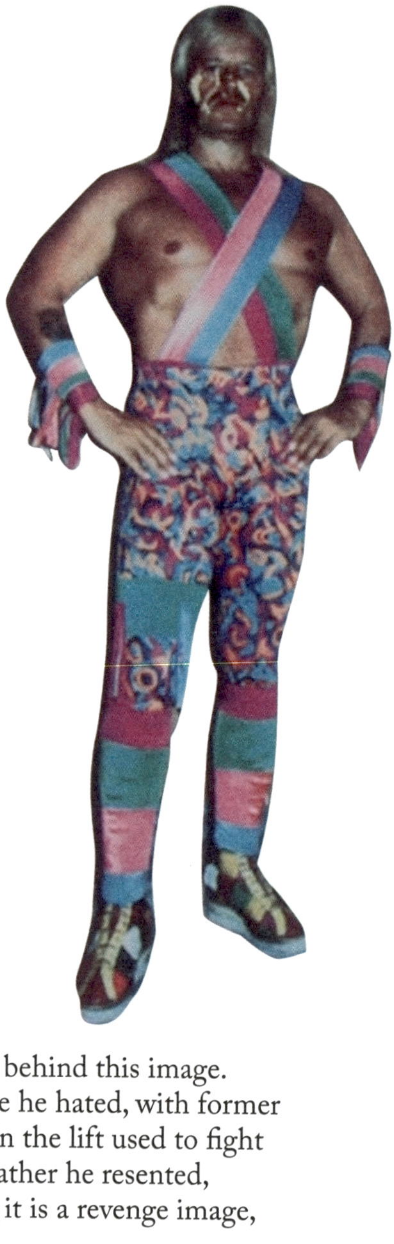

Maybe the image of Adrian Street and his father fascinates me so much because it is shockingly full of both life and death; death being present in the industry and its culture, which were not long for this world. It shows Adrian, the champion wrestler, posing with his middleweight title belt in 1974, alongside his bemused father at the pithead of the Brynmawr colliery in South Wales where Adrian had worked as a teenager. I needed to find out the story behind this image. Adrian purposefully chose to be photographed in a place he hated, with former work colleagues he couldn't stand (he told me the men in the lift used to fight him in the mine because his hair was too long), with a father he resented, to show them what he had made of himself. Essentially, it is a revenge image, as profound as any biblical or Shakespearean story.

Aside from the image's Old Master look, what appealed to me was its articulation of the transformation of the UK after the Second World War: the shift from an industrial to a service economy. It is a change that Adrian literally embodies himself through sheer willpower and self-belief.

Overleaf: Adrian Street and father at the Brynmawr colliery pithead, 1974. A dream of a photo for art historians and cultural theorists alike. Since I made the film he has returned like an unrepentant prodigal son to Wales from Florida.

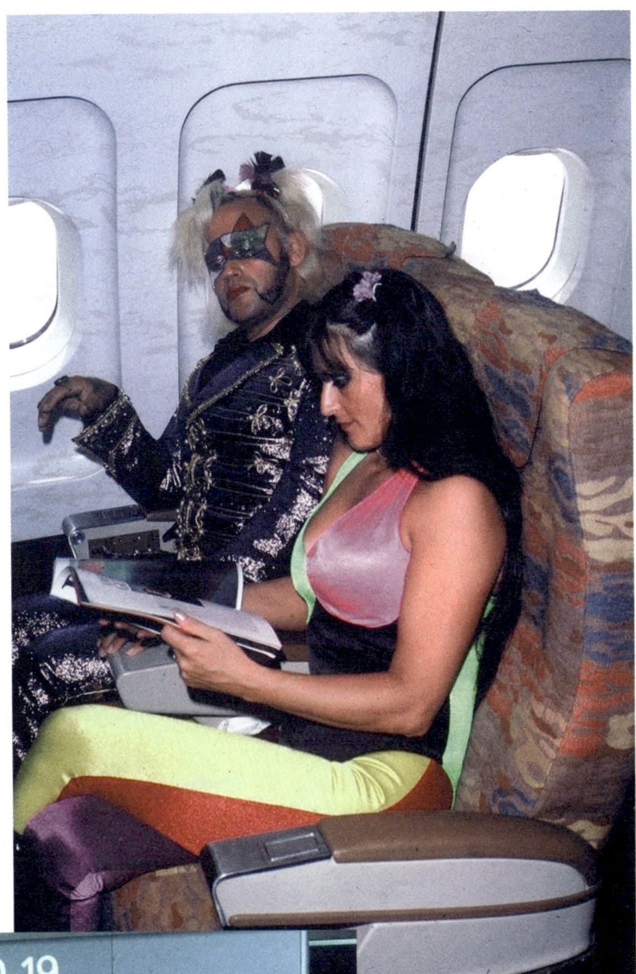

Adrian has remained in character throughout his career. Here he is in the US with Miss Linda, his valet and wife, who also wrestled.

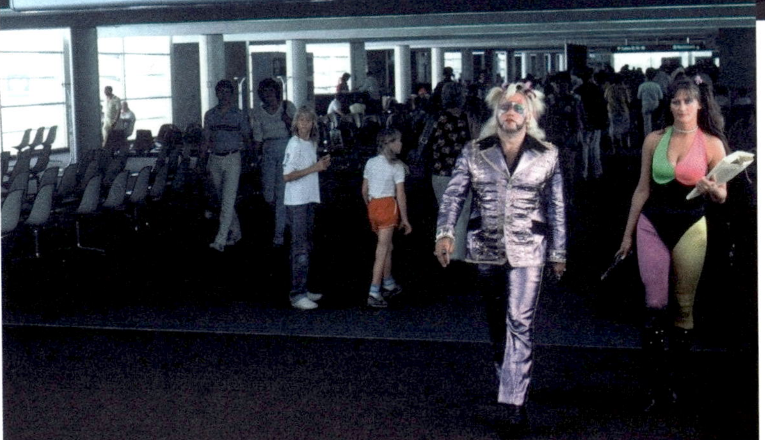

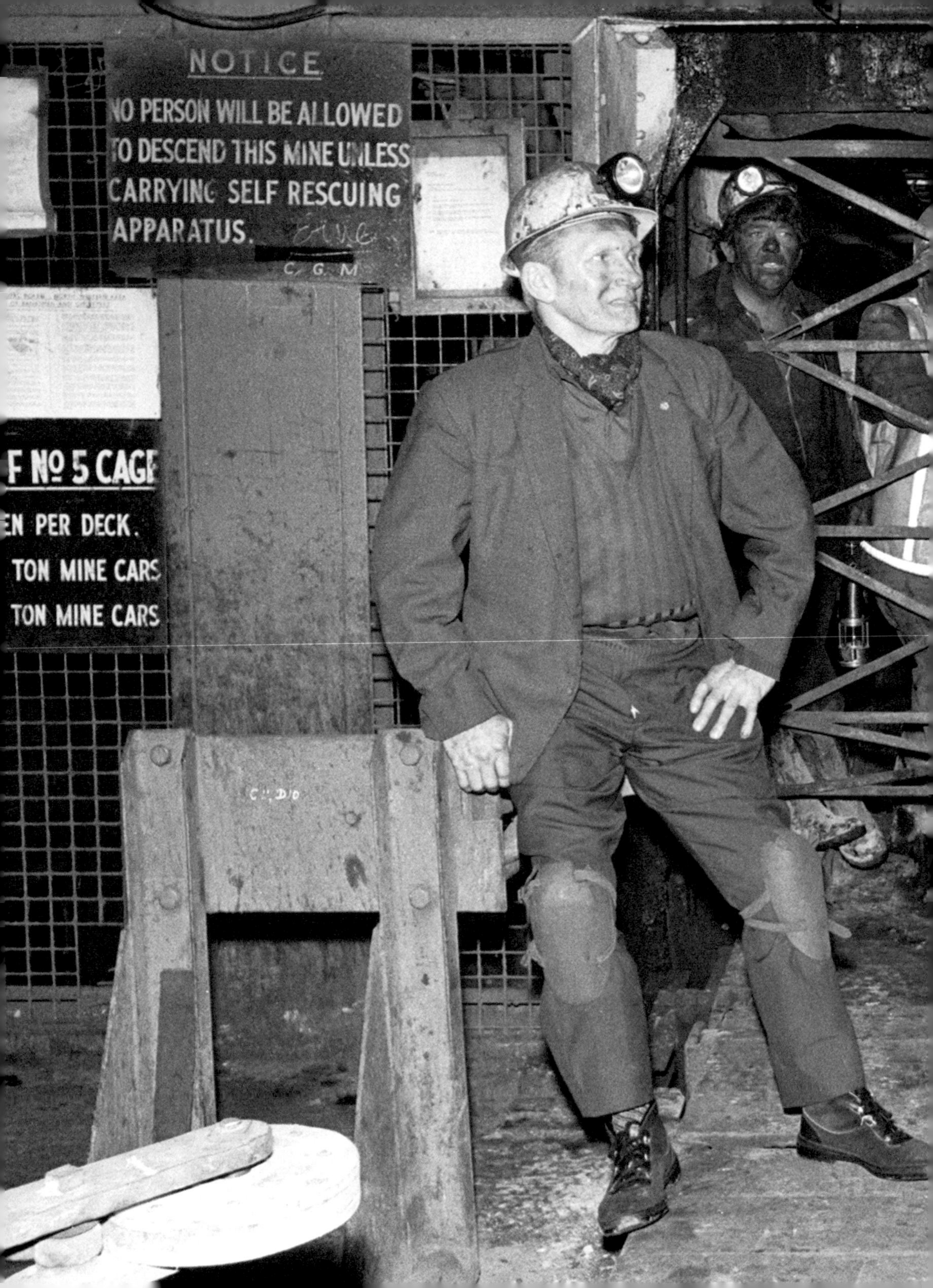
NOTICE
NO PERSON WILL BE ALLOWED
TO DESCEND THIS MINE UNLESS
CARRYING SELF RESCUING
APPARATUS.
C.G.M
F No 5 CAGE
EN PER DECK.
TON MINE CARS
TON MINE CARS

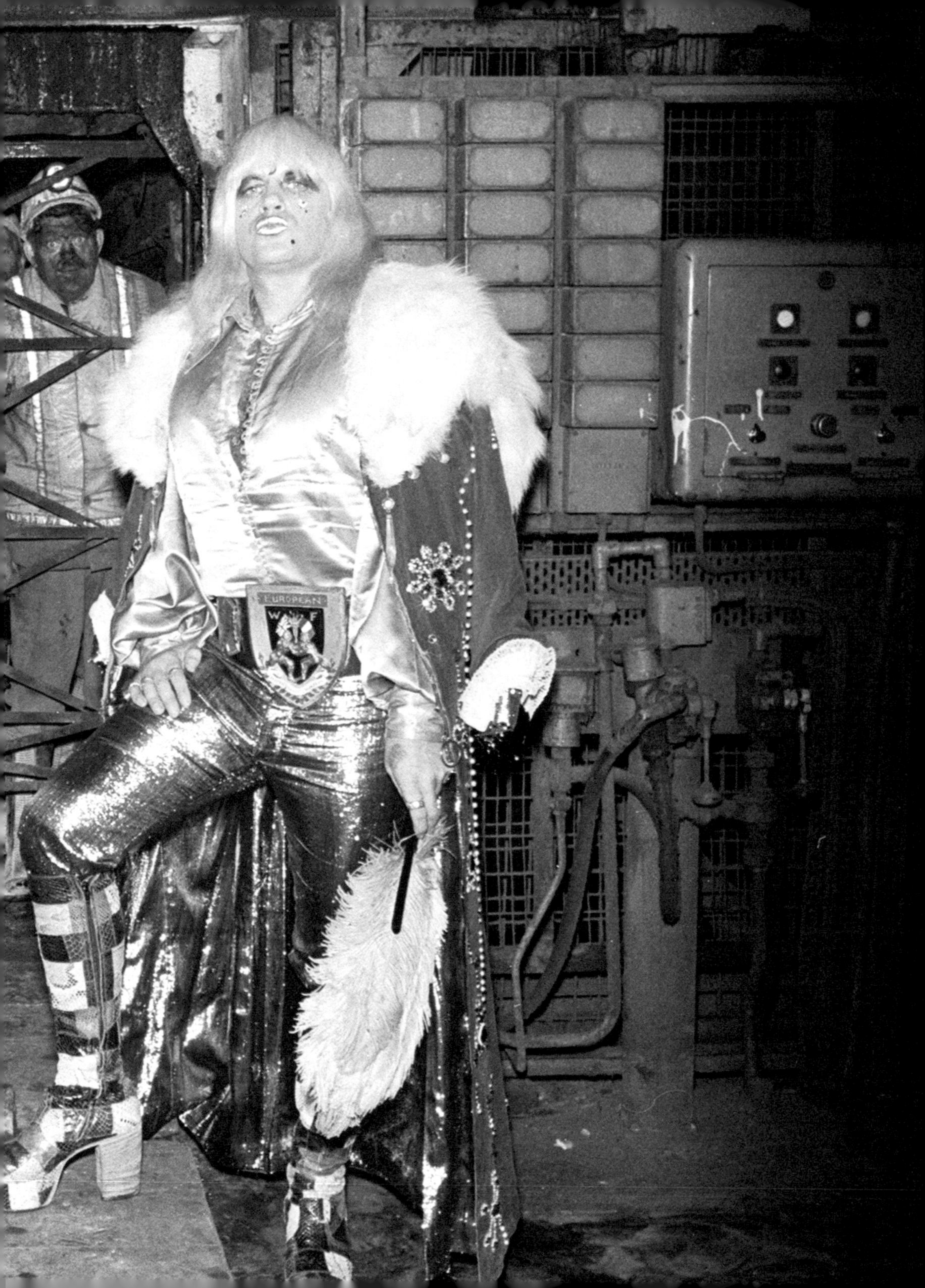
EUROPEAN
W F

Adrian looks like a visitor or prophet from the future which, in some respects, he is. It's a future that will have little time or space for the dirty, dark, industrial culture his father inhabits. Adrian plays a similar role to Christ in the William Blake poem 'Jerusalem', who lands in England in his chariot of fire at the time of the Industrial Revolution determined to build a new society.

I don't think I have looked at another image so much in my life, scrutinising it in a way that I would normally only look at a painting. I got in touch with Adrian in 2009, and he was thrilled at the idea of having a film made all about him. He liked the film but thought it wasn't long enough.

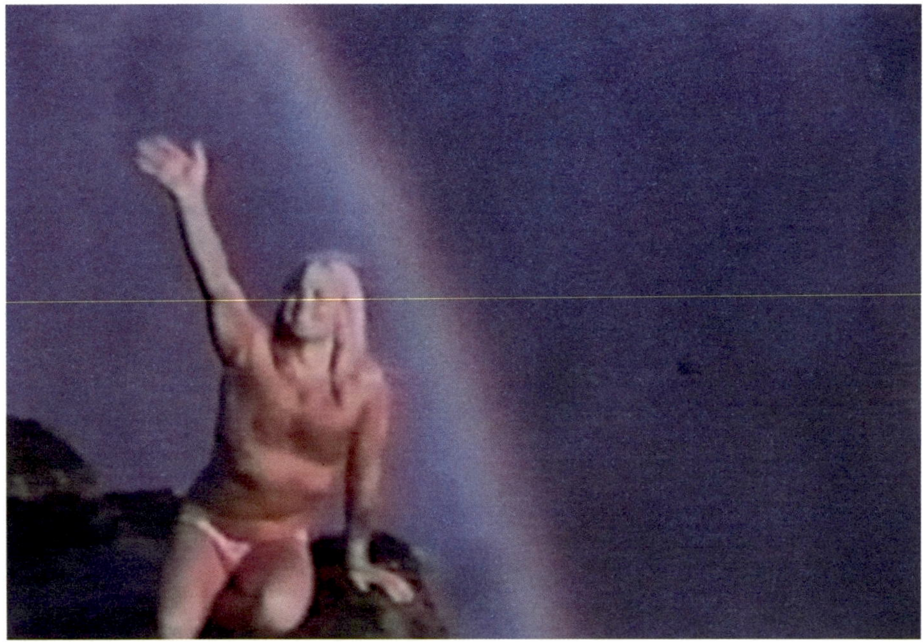

Adrian at Victoria Falls. A still from a holiday film of a visit to Africa that he made in 1975. His boyhood obsession with Tarzan took him there a number of times.

Adrian was a relatively famous figure in the UK in the late 1960s and 1970s, but, if anything, his story chimes with the Dickensian era. After a tough childhood at the hands of a disciplinarian father and a stint in the mines, he left Wales for London at the age of sixteen. There he found fame and fortune, first as a male model and unknowing gay icon, then as a professional wrestler. His persona was a contradictory mix of effeminate and violent, probably picked up from hanging around gangsters and the underground gay scene in Soho.

When fighting, he would kiss opponents as he wrestled them and even applied lipstick and eyeliner to their faces. He was a baddie, or 'heel', as they are known, which made him more of a draw, as people would pay well to see a heel get beaten up. With wrestling disappearing from television in the UK, he moved to the US where his persona became increasingly outrageous if not bizarre. His exploitation of US homophobia made him a big star for a time. During one fight in Alabama, he kissed a black fighter on the lips, resulting in a riot. Adrian lived his life in character during these times in the public eye, and still does to an extent. This was a gift for the film – he had constantly documented his life and activities over the previous thirty years, showing an admirable level of self-obsession. The film ends with a sequence of Adrian on a treadmill striding towards a giant TV that plays a revolving slideshow of his life to a soundtrack of 'Mr. Vain' by Culture Beat (his record of choice, not mine). A great piece of performance art by a modern-day Narcissus.

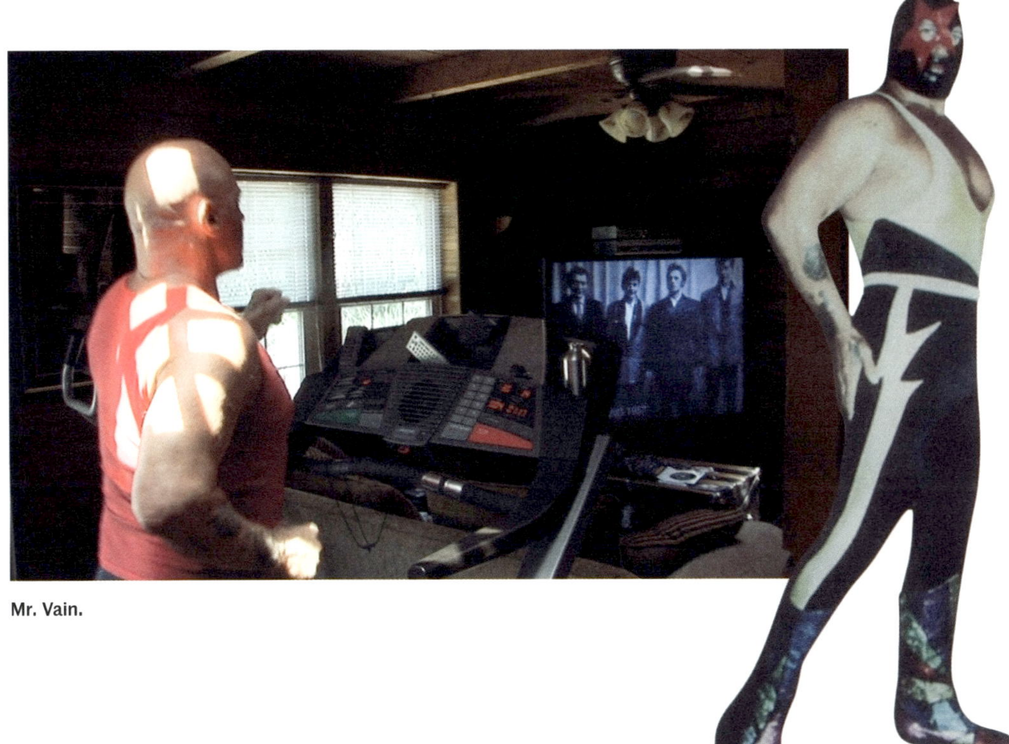

Mr. Vain.

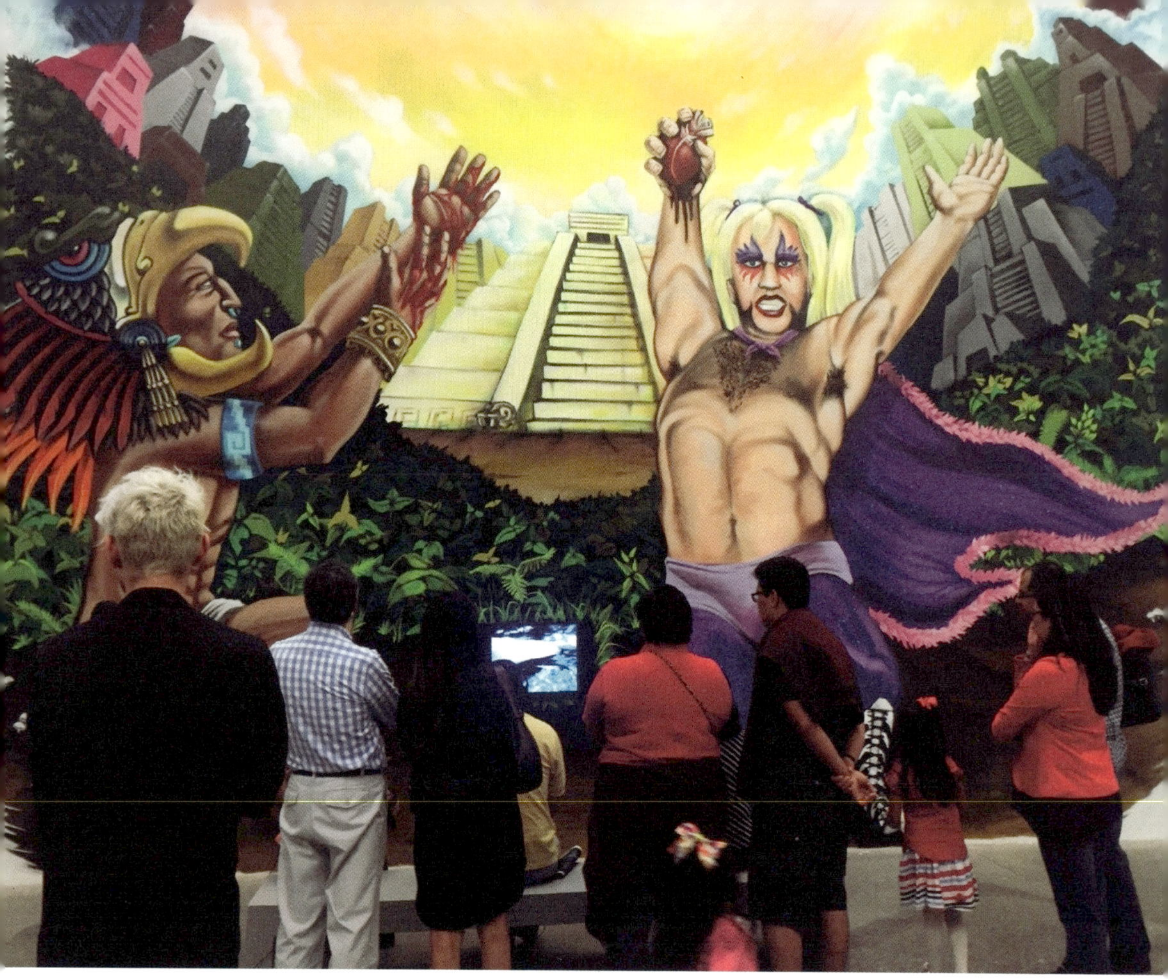

Whenever the film *So Many Ways to Hurt You* is shown in a museum or gallery, a local mural artist is commissioned to interpret it on the wall around the TV. Adrian's epic and fantastical life is operatic and can't be contained by a mere screen. Left: presentation in MUAC Mexico city, 2015; right: CA2M Madrid, 2015.

In the 1980s, Adrian started making spandex costumes for himself and other wrestlers. He produced all the outfits for Mickey Rourke in the 2008 film *The Wrestler*.

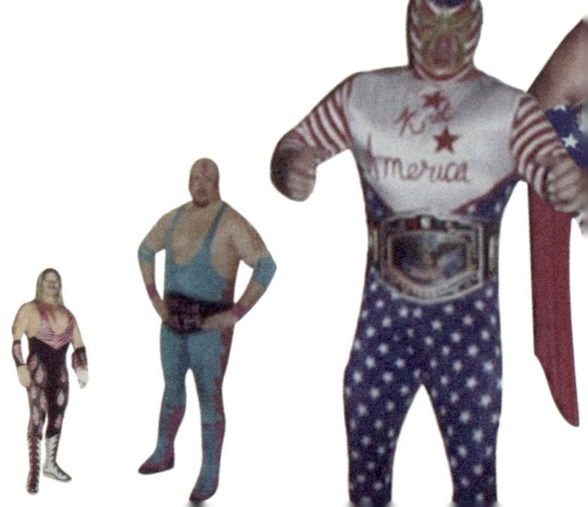

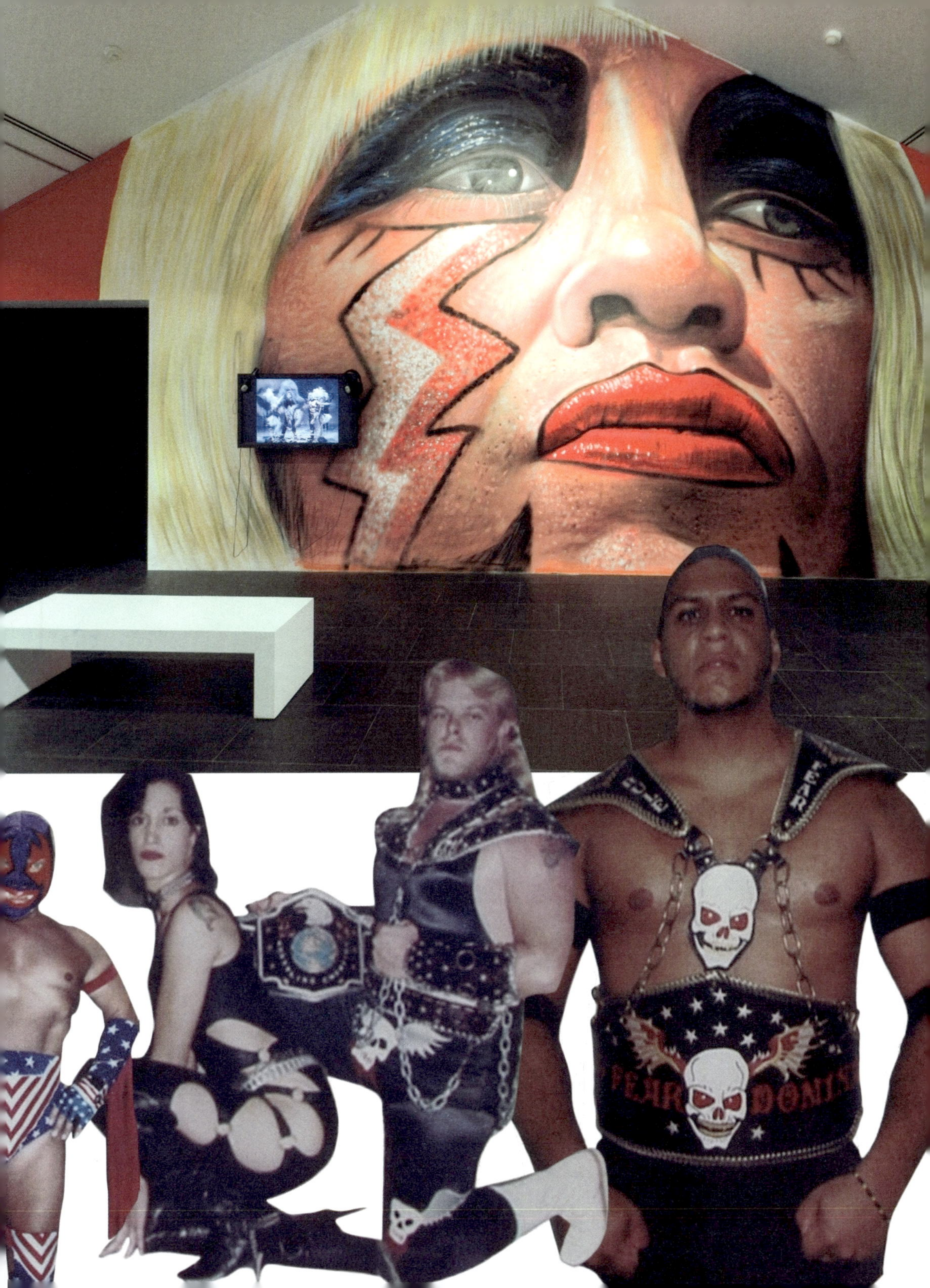
FEAR
FEAR

Ten Years in Eden: Speak to the Earth and It Will Tell You

Between 2007 and 2017 I worked with the forty-one garden societies of Münster to create decade-long diaries of the social and natural lives of their environments. They were kept in large family-Bible-style books which at the end of the ten years were displayed together and made available to read in a garden hut. It will always be one of my favourite projects, hanging around in these idyllic spaces. The books are now in the archives of the Stadtmuseum in Münster.

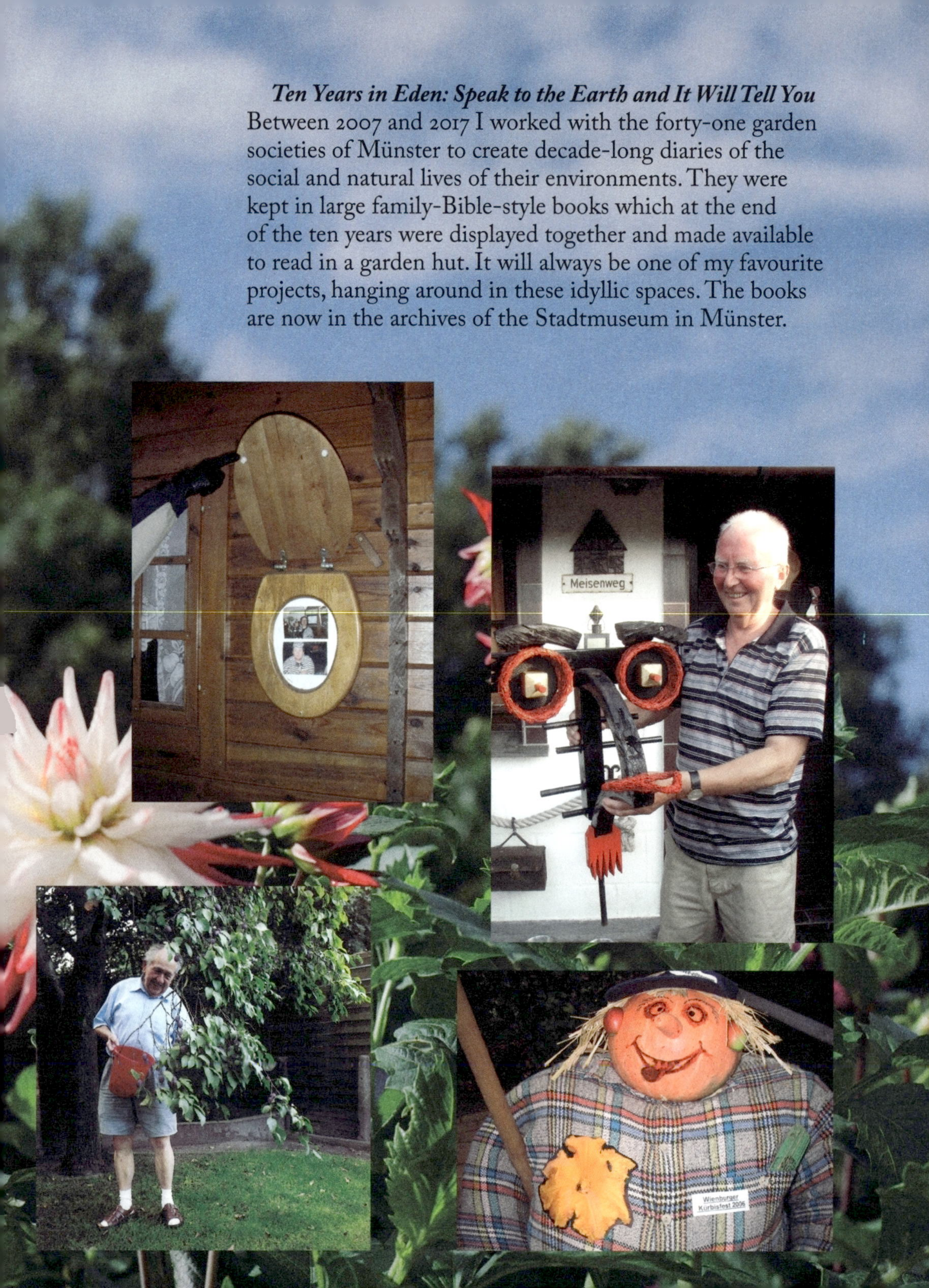

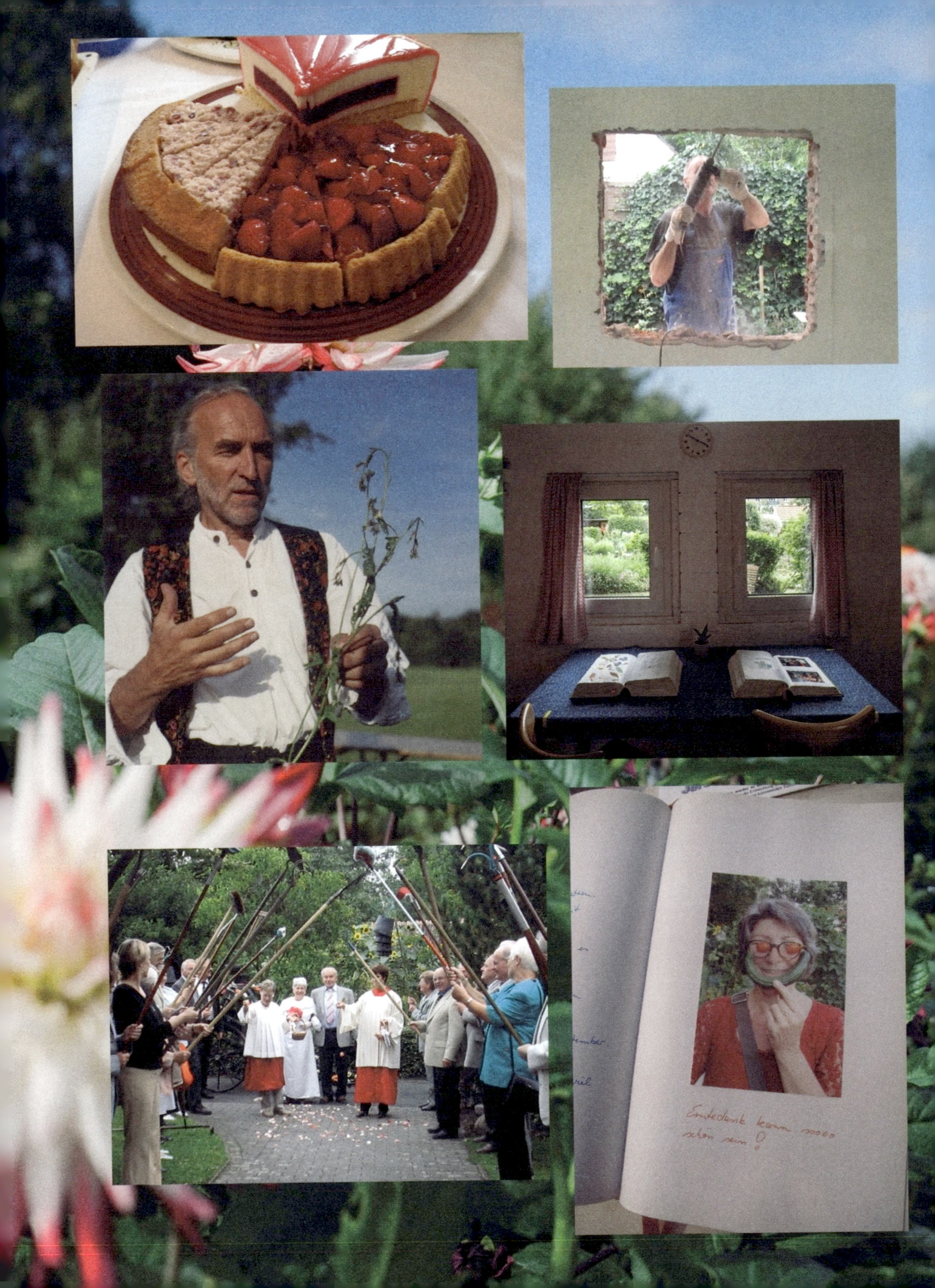
Entdeckend kann soooo
schön sein!

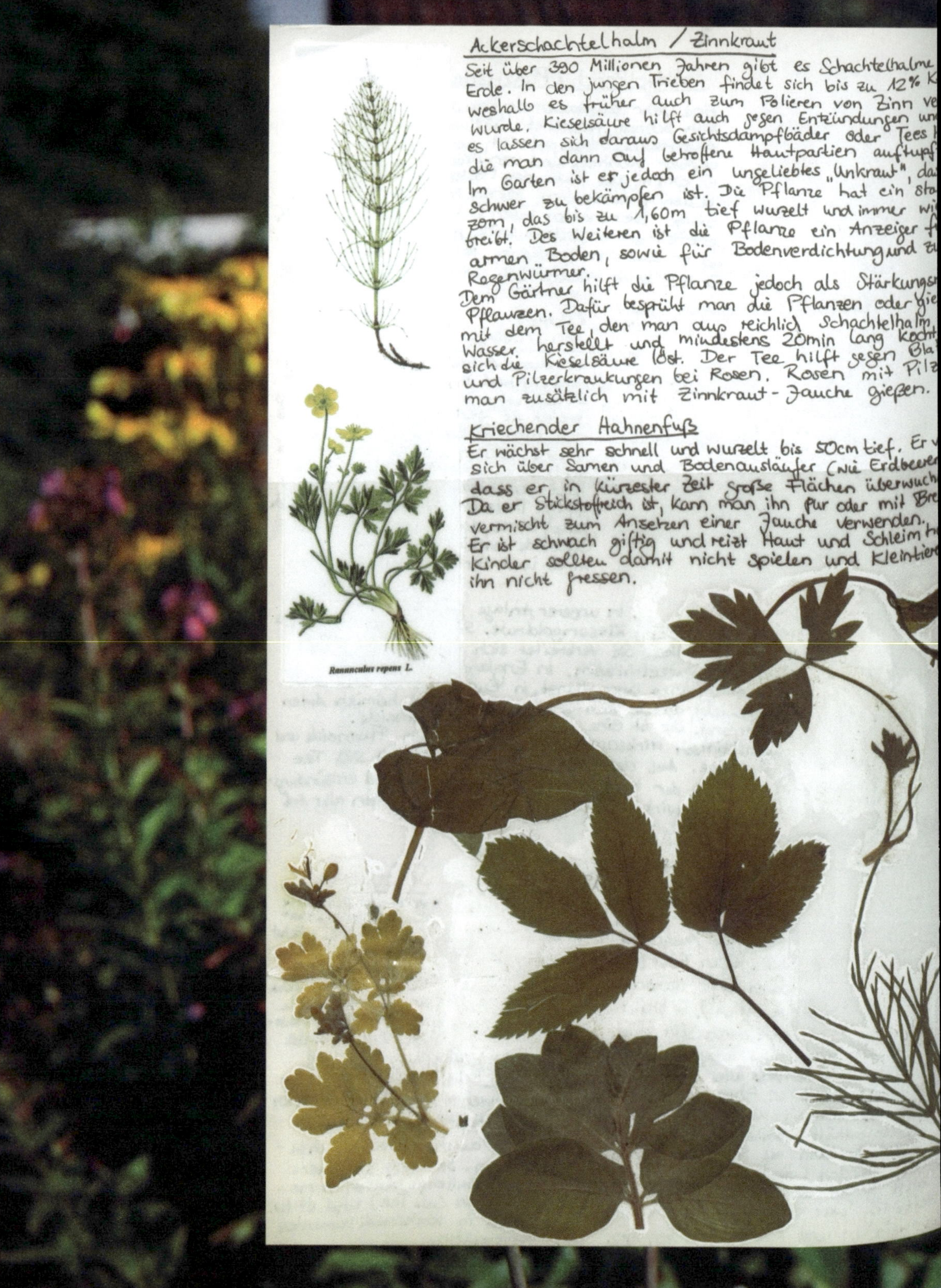
Ackerschachtelhalm / Zinnkraut
Seit über 390 Millionen Jahren gibt es
Erde. In den jungen Trieben findet sich bis zu 12%
weshalb es früher auch zum Polieren von Zinn
wurde. Kieselsäure hilft auch gegen Entzündungen
es lassen sich daraus Gesichtsdampfbäder oder Tees
die man dann auf betroffene Hautpartien
Im Garten ist er jedoch ein ungeliebtes „Unkraut",
schwer zu bekämpfen ist. Die Pflanze hat ein
zom, das bis zu 1,60m tief wurzelt und immer
treibt. Des Weiteren ist die Pflanze ein Anzeiger
armen Boden, sowie für Bodenverdichtung und
Regenwürmer.
Dem Gärtner hilft die Pflanze jedoch als
Pflanzen. Dafür besprüht man die Pflanzen oder
mit dem Tee, den man aus reichlich
Wasser herstellt und mindestens 20min lang
sich die Kieselsäure löst. Der Tee hilft gegen
und Pilzerkrankungen bei Rosen. Rosen mit
man zusätzlich mit Zinnkraut-Jauche gießen.
Kriechender Hahnenfuß
Er wächst sehr schnell und wurzelt bis 50cm tief.
sich über Samen und Bodenausläufer (wie
dass er in kürzester Zeit große Flächen
Da er stickstoffreich ist, kann man ihn pur oder mit
vermischt zum Ansetzen einer Jauche verwenden.
Er ist schwach giftig und reizt Haut und
Kinder sollten damit nicht spielen und
ihn nicht fressen.
Ranunculus repens L.

King of Pop ist tot

Die ganze Welt trauert / In den Herzen seiner Fans lebt er weiter

Er war so erfolgreich, aber dennoch unglücklich: Michael Jackson ist tot. Er starb am vergangenen Donnerstag (14.26 Uhr Ortszeit) in seiner Villa. Eine Obduktion soll klären was wirklich geschah.

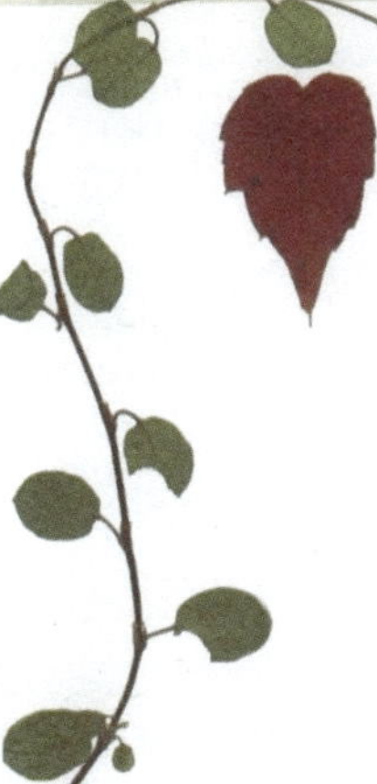

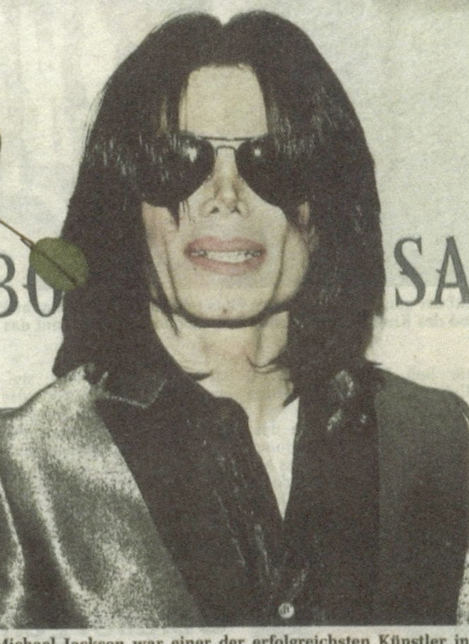

Michael Jackson war einer der erfolgreichsten Künstler in der Geschichte der Popmusik. Foto: AP

Two pages from the diaries: on the left Grüner Krug, on the right Münster-Ost.

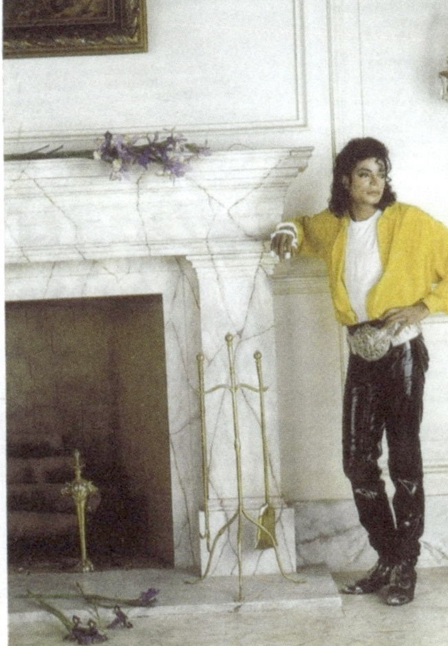

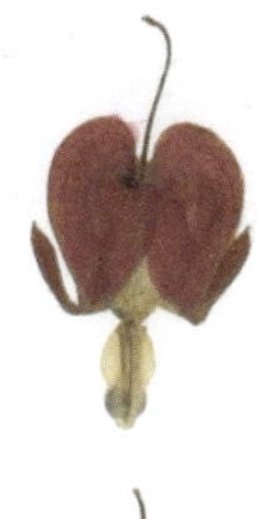

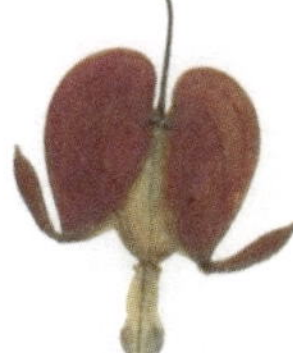

Tränendes Herz

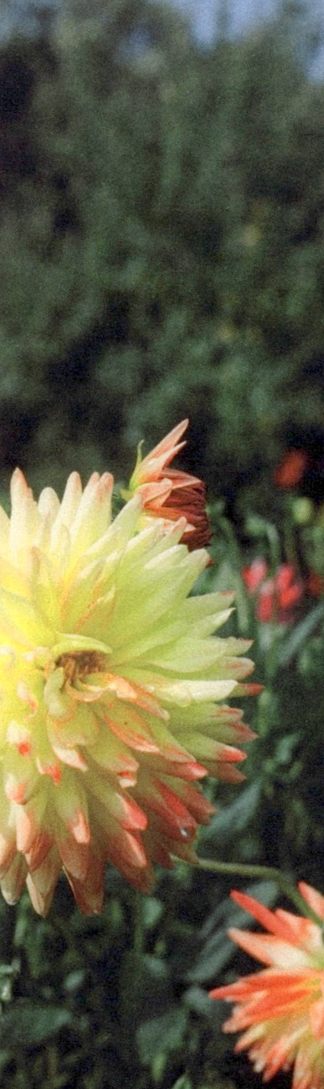

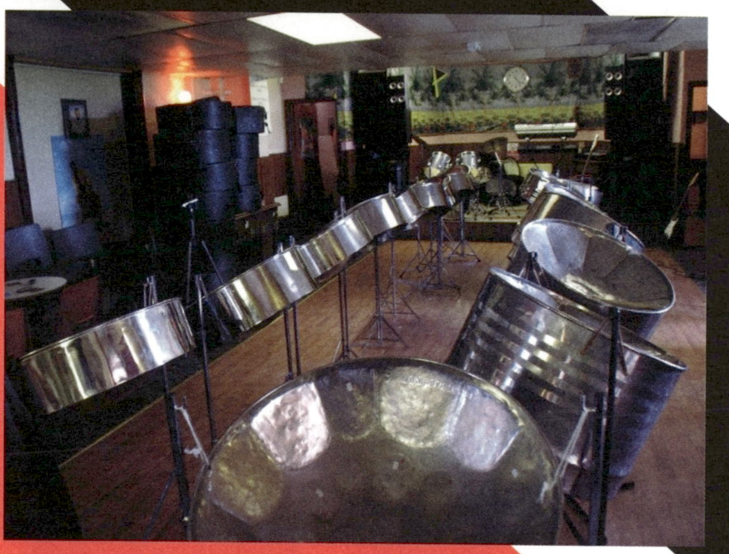

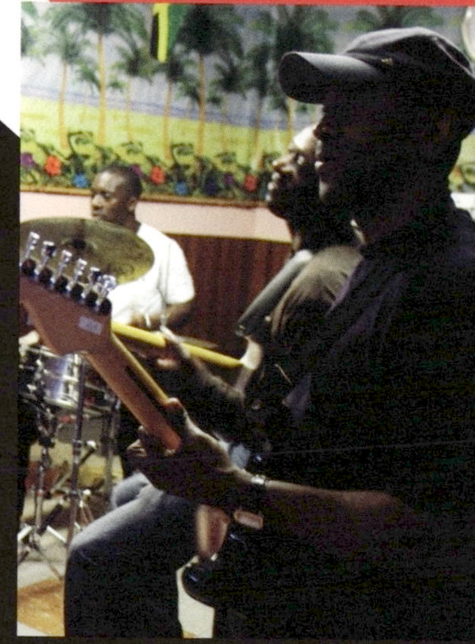

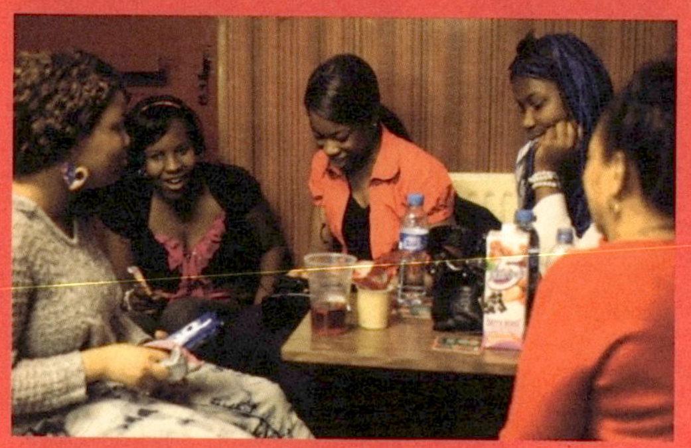

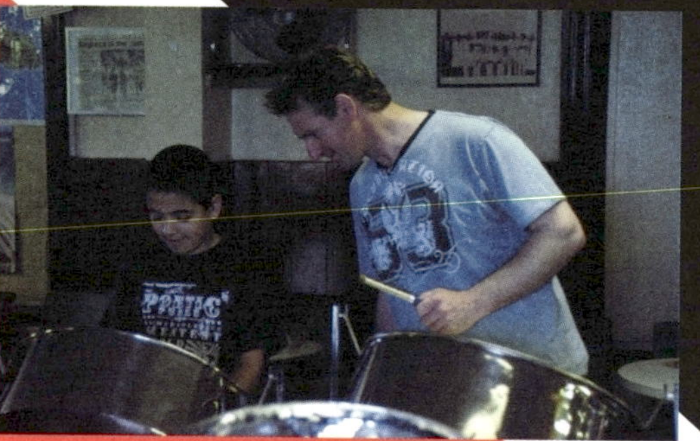

Happiness is a steel band

The experience of mass/group music-making is something of a human ideal for me. It shows that what we are capable of achieving through cooperation is far greater than any individual effort. I think my favourite moments as an artist have been when hanging around steel bands in their rehearsal spaces and at concerts. It's one of the few places where I don't feel the need to look at my phone for news updates. They are often intergenerational family affairs, which gives them an incredible intimacy.

Here are some photos of the two bands I have worked with through the years: Steel Harmony (on this page) led by Andy Gorton (pictured above with his son), and the Melodians Steel Orchestra (on the opposite page) led by Terry Noel.

Overleaf: Steel Harmony performing a cover of 'Transmission' by Joy Division at Procession, a parade I conceived for the Manchester International Festival in 2009.

For Art Night in 2018, the Melodians performed a cover of 'Ghost Town' by the Specials almost continually over a six-hour period. It was in the shell of a soon-to-be-opened Tesco in the newly built mess of the Battersea Power Station development.

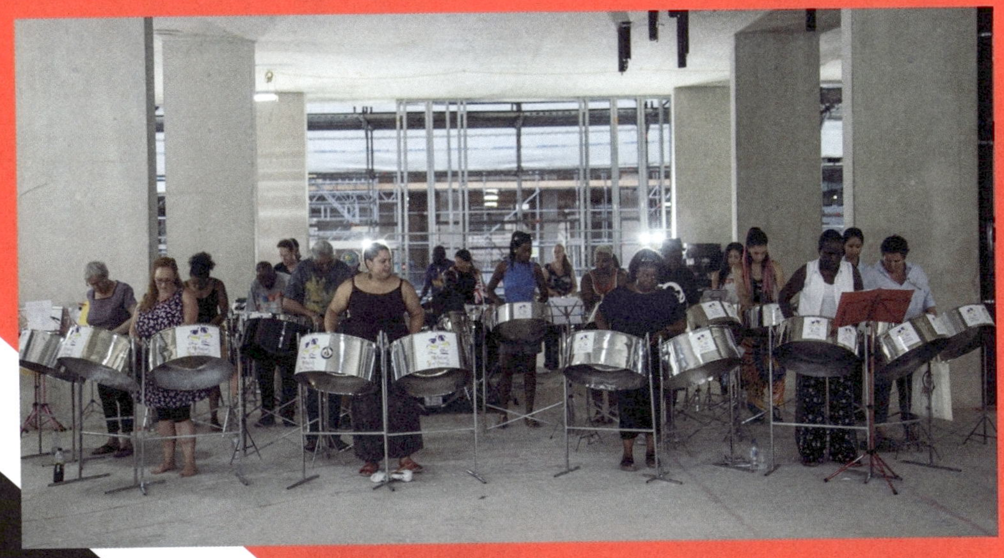

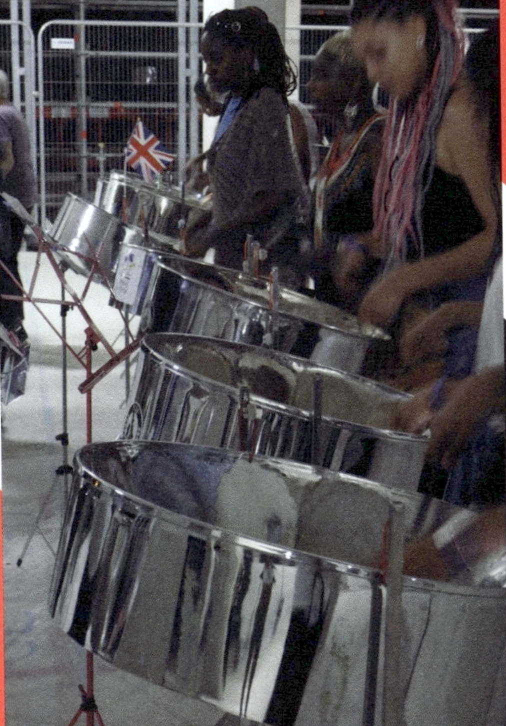

Jerry Dammers (the composer of 'Ghost Town') meets the Melodians.

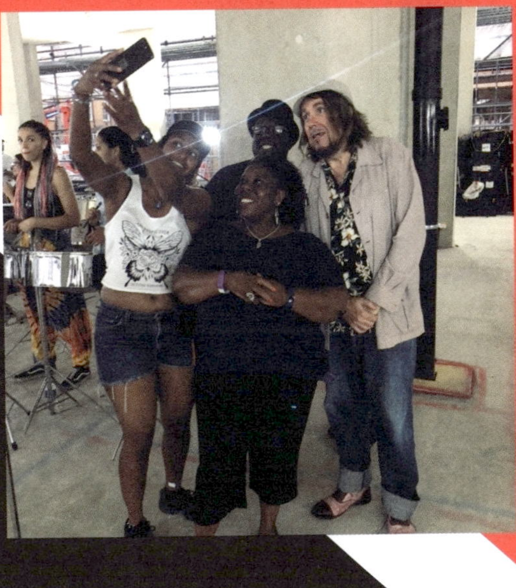

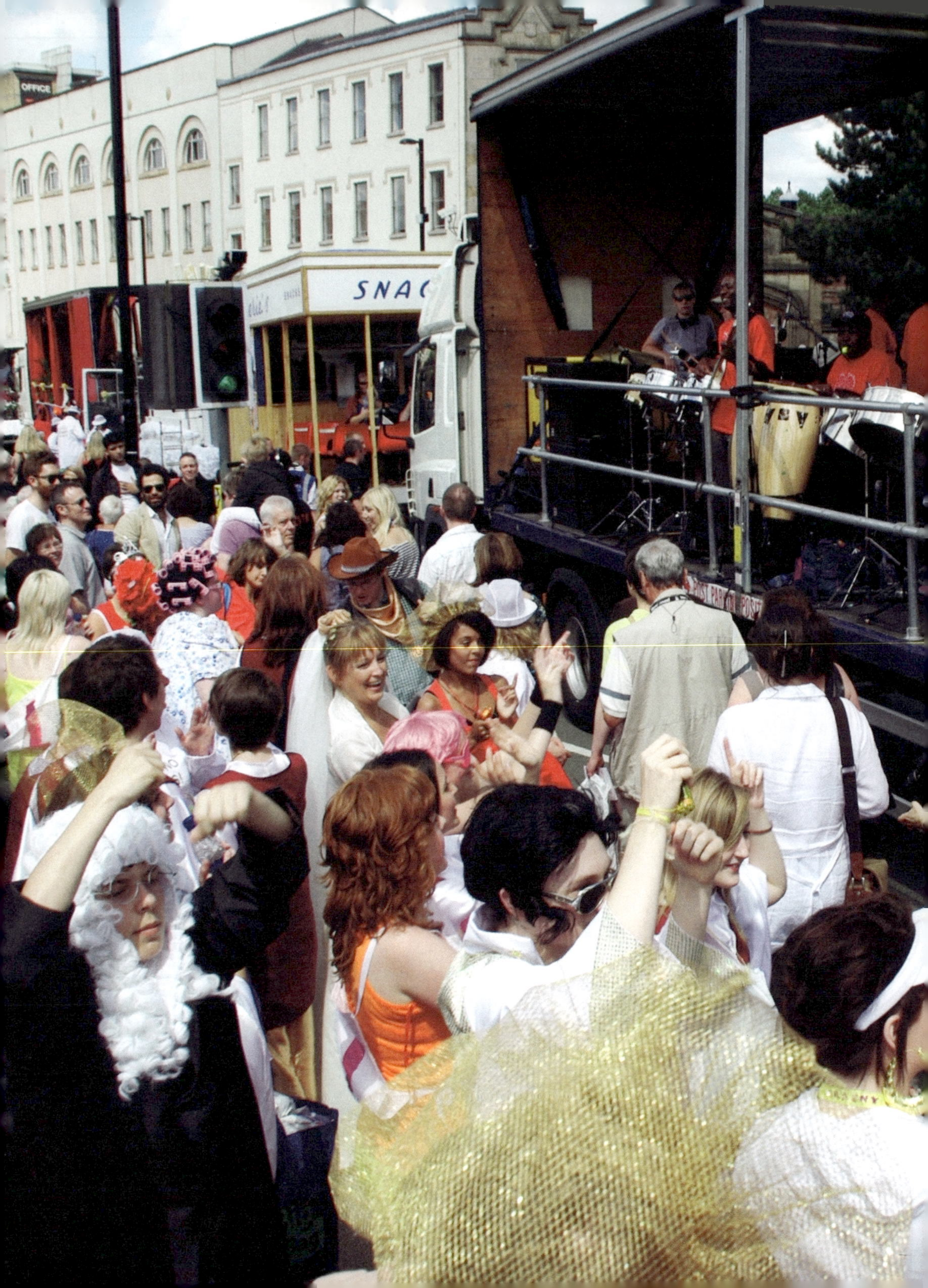

OFFICE
SNAC

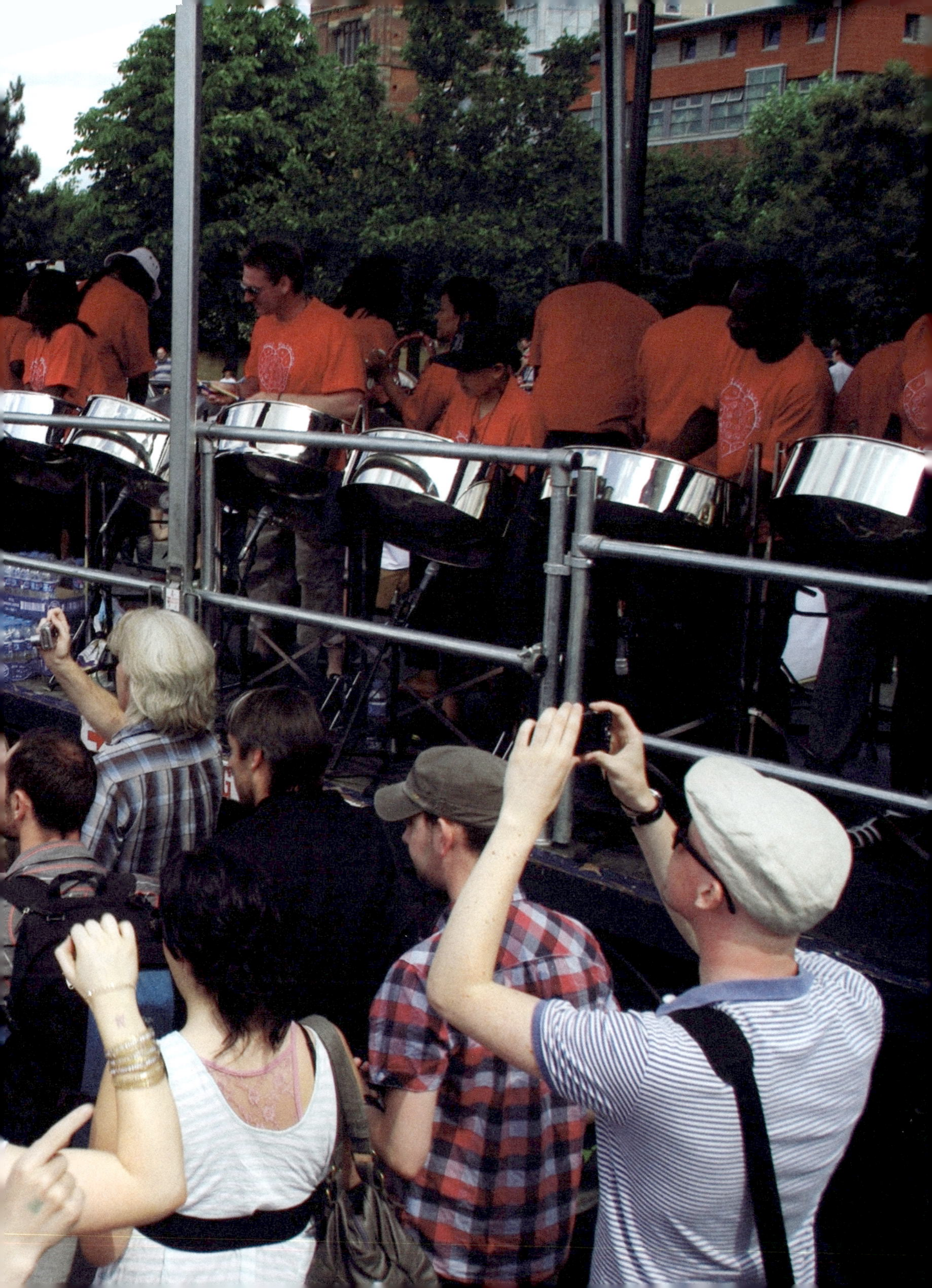

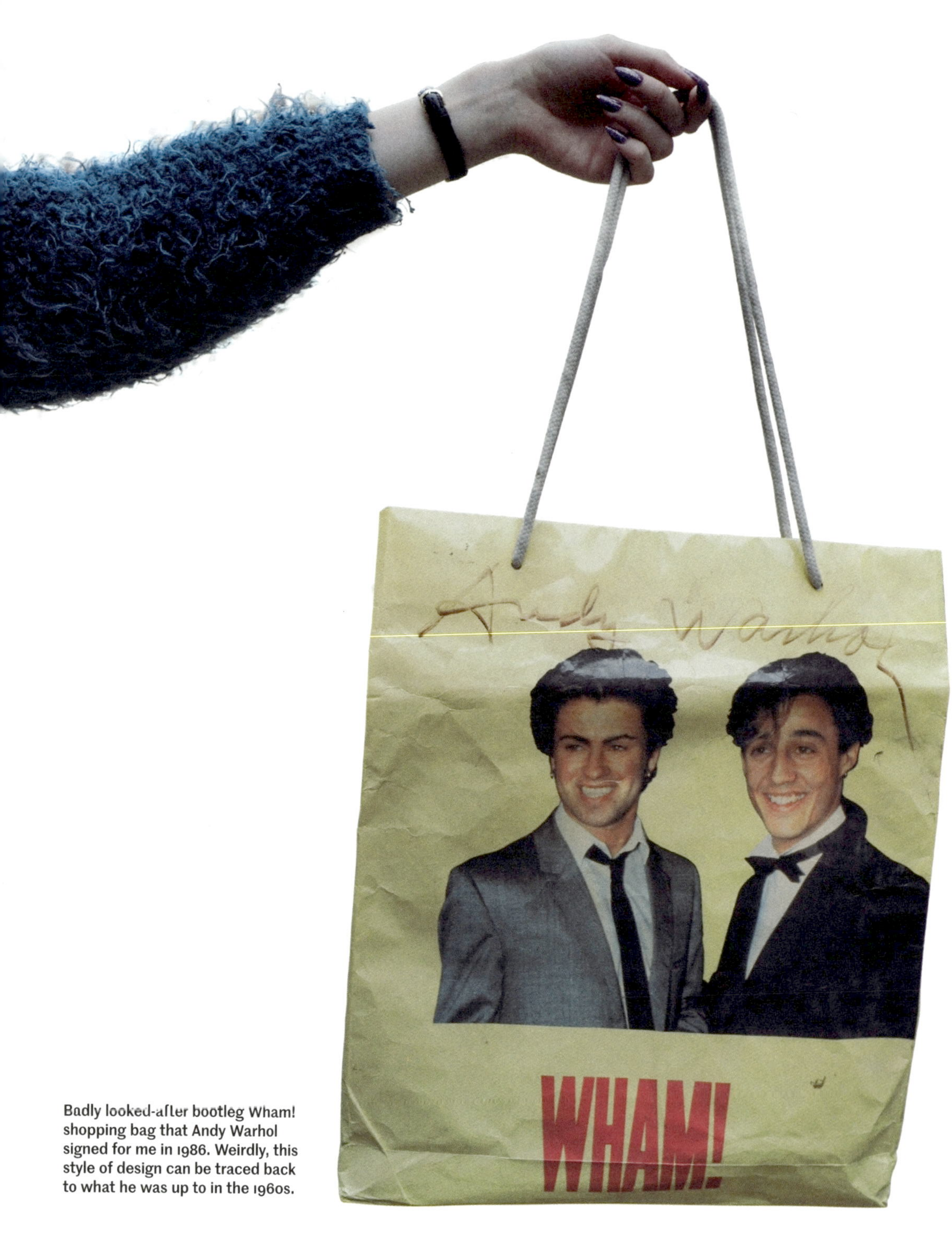

Badly looked-after bootleg Wham! shopping bag that Andy Warhol signed for me in 1986. Weirdly, this style of design can be traced back to what he was up to in the 1960s.

Chapter 13

Benny Hill with the sound turned down

A brush with Andy Warhol

It goes without saying that, as a young person, encountering your idols can have a profound and, hopefully, positive effect on your life, which was something which happened to me in 1986. I vowed to retire this story a few years ago as it was so tired, but my editor insisted I give it one last airing before it goes to the home for extended anecdotes. So, here goes:

Andy Warhol was somebody I was aware of in secondary school, as much for the Velvet Underground connection as for the art itself – not that I'd heard their music at that point. For teenagers, Warhol is a very attractive figure: he remained something of a teenager himself throughout his career in how he interacted with the press as well as with the public. He sent a look-alike, for example, to the University of Utah in 1967 on a lecture tour in his place – just being naughty because he could. I can totally see his appeal: wanting to be cool but being awkward at the same time is the essence of life when you are a teenager. In 1986, he had an opening of self-portraits at the Anthony d'Offay Gallery off Bond Street. I didn't have an invite myself, but was shown one by a tutor at the Courtauld Institute of Art where I was studying History of Art.

I arrived at the private view as soon as it opened. I didn't know anyone there which was not a surprise. It was busy and people had dressed up; I think I was wearing something that looked like a school uniform or a white suit I bought from a jumble sale. At one point a table was set up for Warhol to sign whatever people brought to him: soup cans, copies of *Interview* magazine, books. A scrum ensued. The act of signing was deeply connected to his childhood, in which he had written to Hollywood stars for their autographs. He clearly understood our desire to have something signed; he saw it as a form of benediction and here he was, returning the gesture he had so appreciated as a young person.

I took along a bag featuring a photo of George Michael and Andrew Ridgeley. When I got this signed, I felt it was mission accomplished. The bag had been chosen because it had '*Wham!*' written on it (I assumed the band were

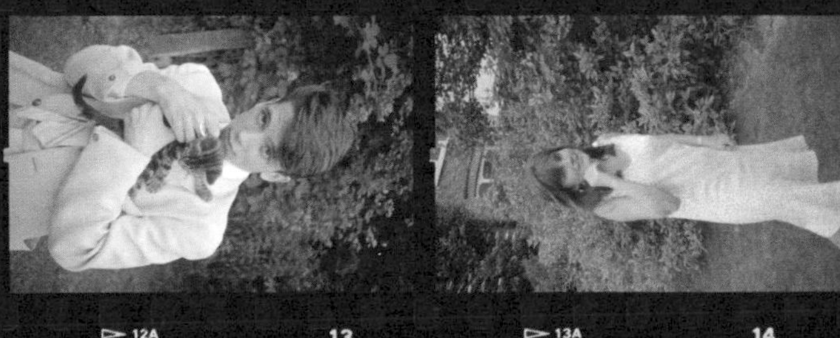

Larks. I'd bought the psychedelic hats at a jumble sale, like everything else I was wearing that night.

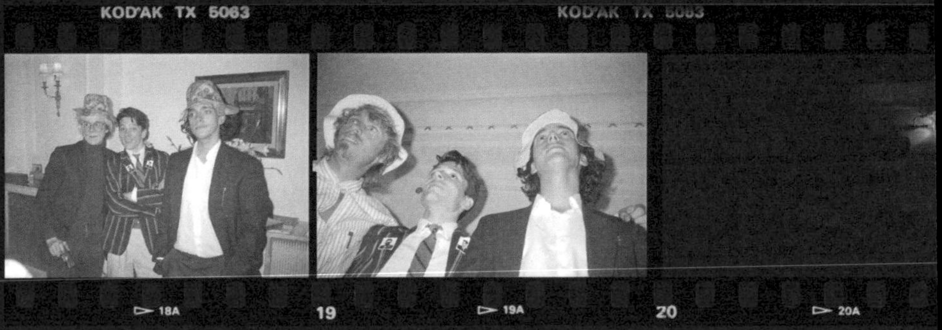

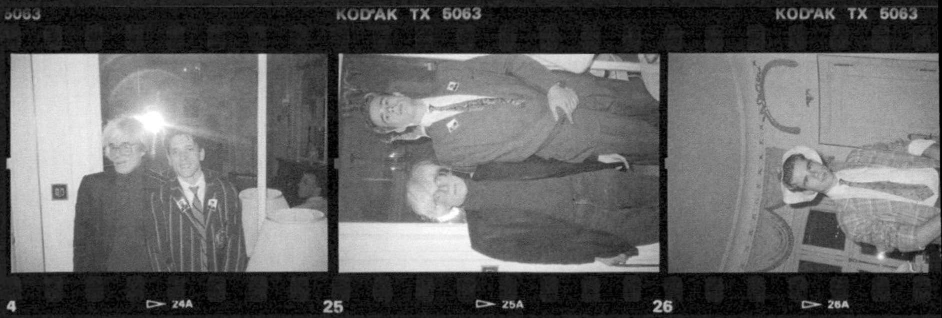

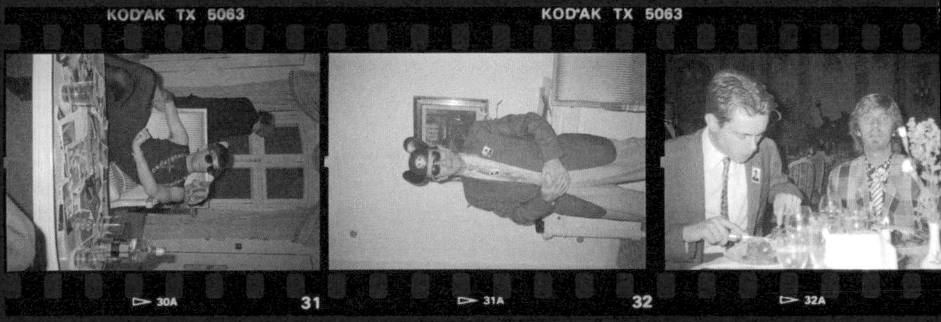

Jewellery designer Billy Boy. I think he was a bit irritated by us.

Lucio Amelio. He ran an eponymous gallery in Naples which also showed Joseph Beuys.

The posh meal that me and my friend Chris Solbé (pictured left) were in no position to pay for.

Contact sheet of a fun night out at the Ritz, 10 July 1986. I was ruined after this. A career in art history not surprisingly lost its appeal (note images before this meeting of me in the garden with Rupert the kitten). The weird thing is that as I write this, I am more or less the same age as Warhol is in these photos.

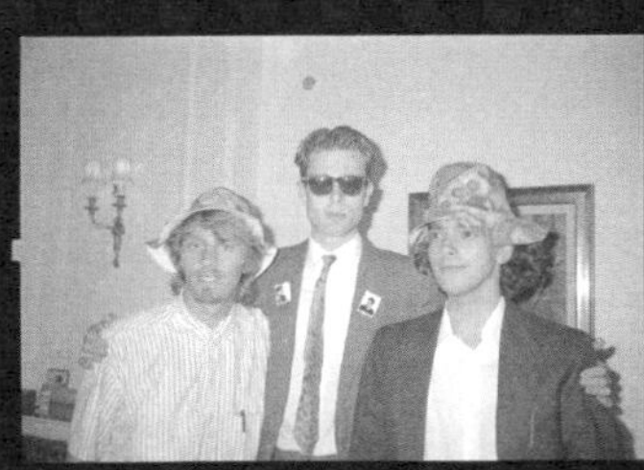

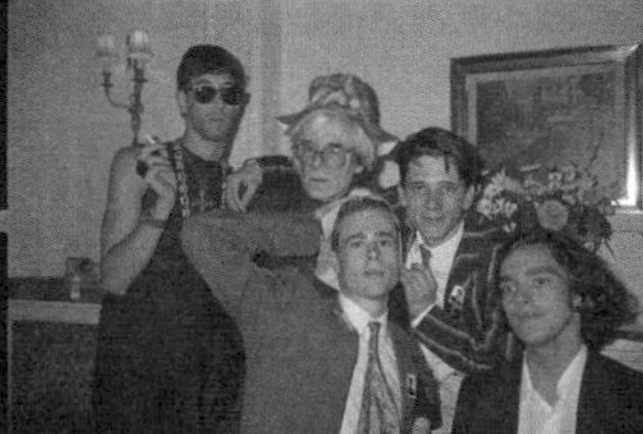

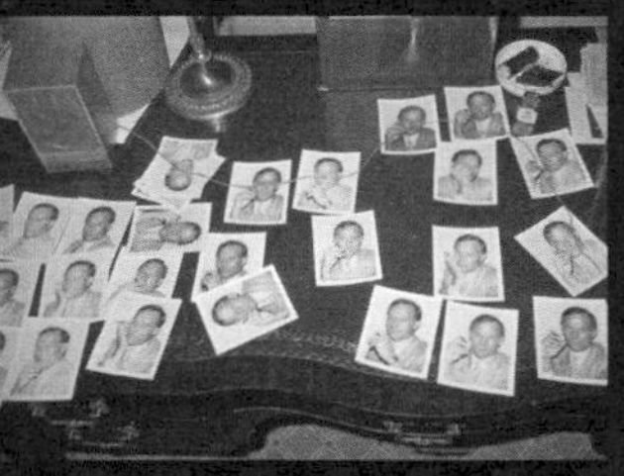

Polaroid headshots, presumably for a portrait commission.

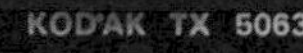

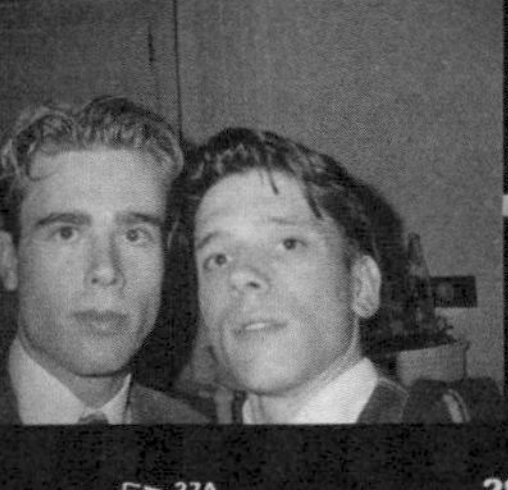

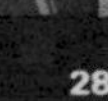

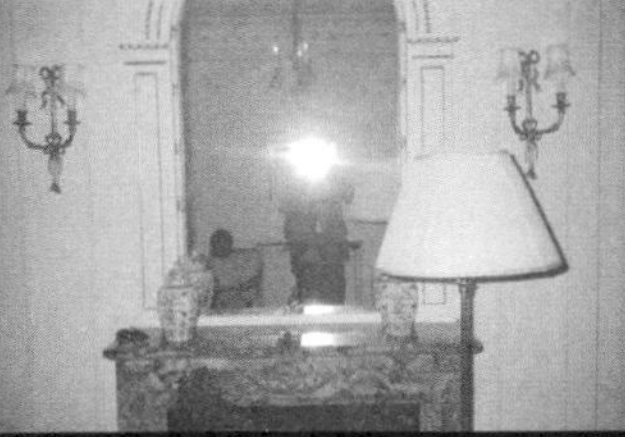

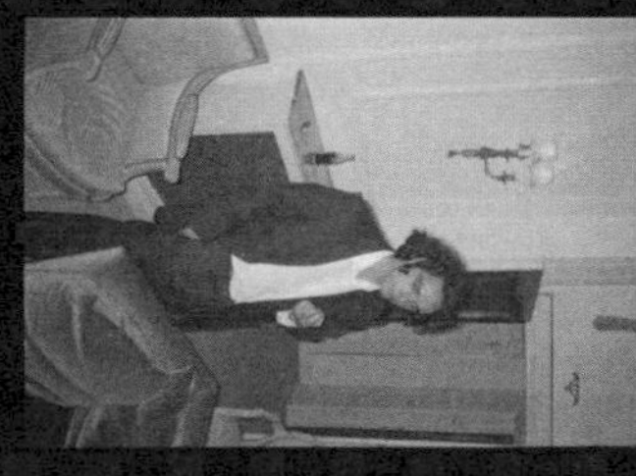

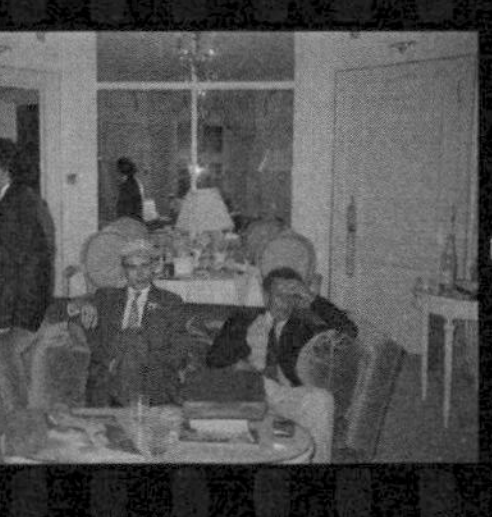

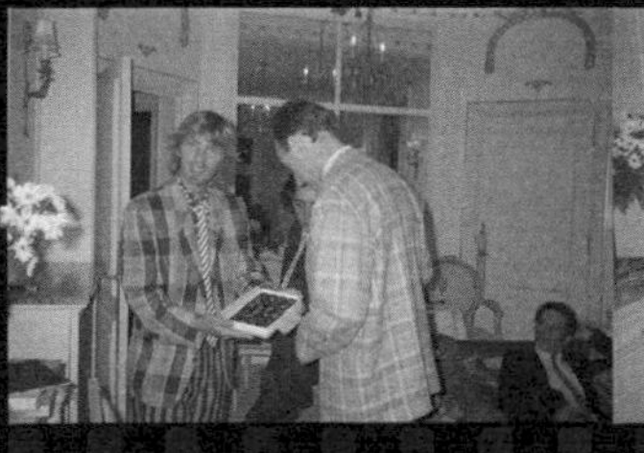

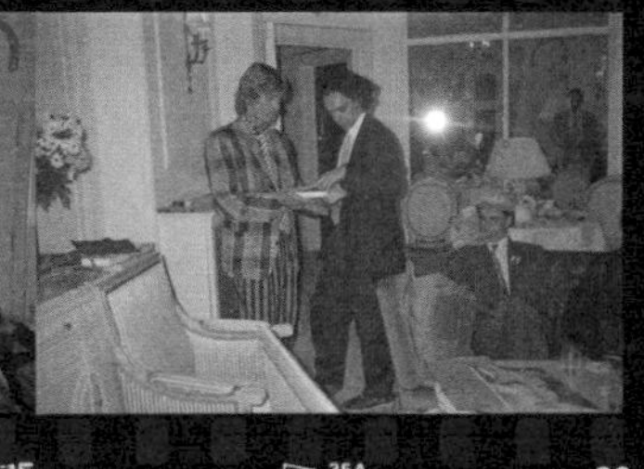

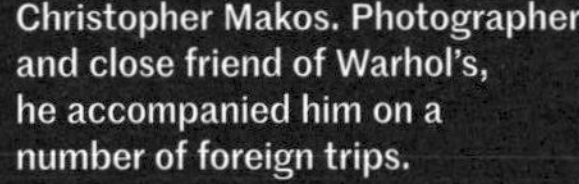

Christopher Makos. Photographer and close friend of Warhol's, he accompanied him on a number of foreign trips.

named after the pop art painting by Roy Lichtenstein). Thought he'd like the joke. Then a grown-up sidled over for a chat. His name was Christopher Makos, a photographer who worked with Warhol. He invited me to come and meet them all at their hotel the next day. Which I did, taking along my friend Chris as support, as the whole incident seemed so preposterous.

So, Chris and I found ourselves standing outside room 321 of the Ritz, in hysterics, about to knock on a door and have our lives changed. Certainly mine, at least. We had no idea what to expect on the other side – possibly a scene of unimaginable debauchery – but it was in fact half a dozen men sitting around watching Benny Hill with the sound down while listening to a Roxy Music greatest hits album on a ghetto blaster, a great art installation in itself. The other people in the room were (among others) Warhol's Italian art dealer, an ad executive and a guy who ran some saunas in Amsterdam.

We were basically a bit of light entertainment. Everyone seemed to be taking pictures of each other. Weirdly, that is what it would be like now, in that respect. A table was covered in polaroids of a businessman who was having his portrait painted. We then all went down to the very traditional hotel restaurant – string quartet, lobster, champagne – and all the while Chris and I had no idea who was going to pay for dinner. We were also casually invited out to New York, more out of politeness than anything else I suspect.

Chris and I took them up on their invitation a couple of months later. I had saved money by working in the picture library at the Courtauld, cutting out images from auction catalogues, sticking them on pieces of card and putting them in boxes. An analogue version of the internet, strangely Warholian. The first thing we did when we arrived in New York was to go to Warhol's studio, which was just off Madison Avenue. This was the Factory's last incarnation, and was a sprawling building shared with *Interview* magazine. The art was physically made in the Basement, though we didn't get to see much of that. We did however see Warhol wandering around the place.

Christopher Makos gave us loads of invites to clubs; Chris and I even blagged a meeting at Def Jam with their publicity guy, Bill Adler, where we discussed our rap project, the Nice Boys, a take on the Beastie Boys, who we had heard about but not yet actually heard. We were even filmed for *Andy Warhol's Fifteen Minutes*, his MTV magazine programme, again out of politeness as we had come all that way.

The last time I saw Warhol was on a Saturday afternoon, after he had been shopping for antiques with his friend Stuart Pivar. He was chatty, if not animated, wanting to know what I had been up to. Intelligence gathering, essentially. It is strange to think that as I write this, I am almost the same age that he was then.

Warhol died the following year. This marked the end of my dream where I would have packed in the Courtauld and worked in the Factory as a painting assistant. In truth, I know I would have been terrible at this and almost definitely been given the sack within weeks.

As preparation for the show *Love Is Enough* (see page 140), I had the opportunity to visit the Andy Warhol Museum in Pittsburgh and hang out with one of my favourite people: the much-missed archivist Matt Wrbican, who knew more about Warhol than anyone else in the world. He showed me items from the time capsules, or archive boxes, that Warhol had put together, some of which ended up in the show. The most poignant capsule I saw was put together after Warhol's death and contained the rucksack he took with him to the hospital where he died. It contained a pair of Calvin Klein boxer shorts, a Sony Walkman, the Kitty Kelley biography of Elizabeth Taylor and a wig.

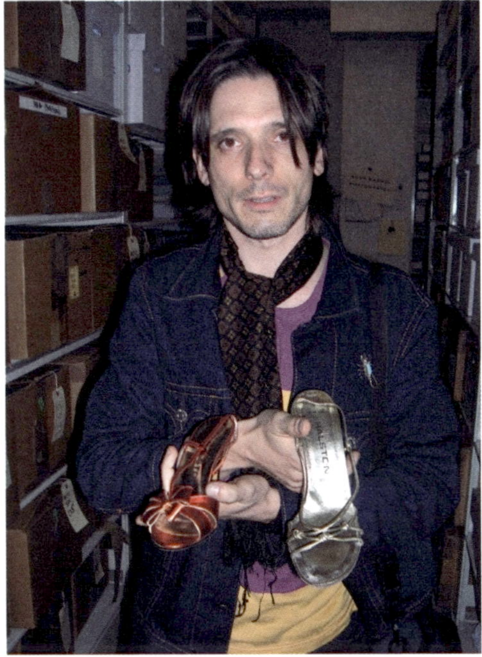

Backstage at the Andy Warhol Museum in Pittsburgh holding two Halston shoes from one of the time capsules behind me, 2004.

Warhol's importance is without question, but his legacy is not straightforward. Towards the end of his career, especially with the print portfolios, he became disconnected from his own ideas as he effectively made art to order. His interest in money and celebrity helped create the beast of the art world (and much of the wider world) we know now. Some people have assumed that that was all he was about and have thus created for themselves degraded versions of this iteration of him, which is far from the full picture.

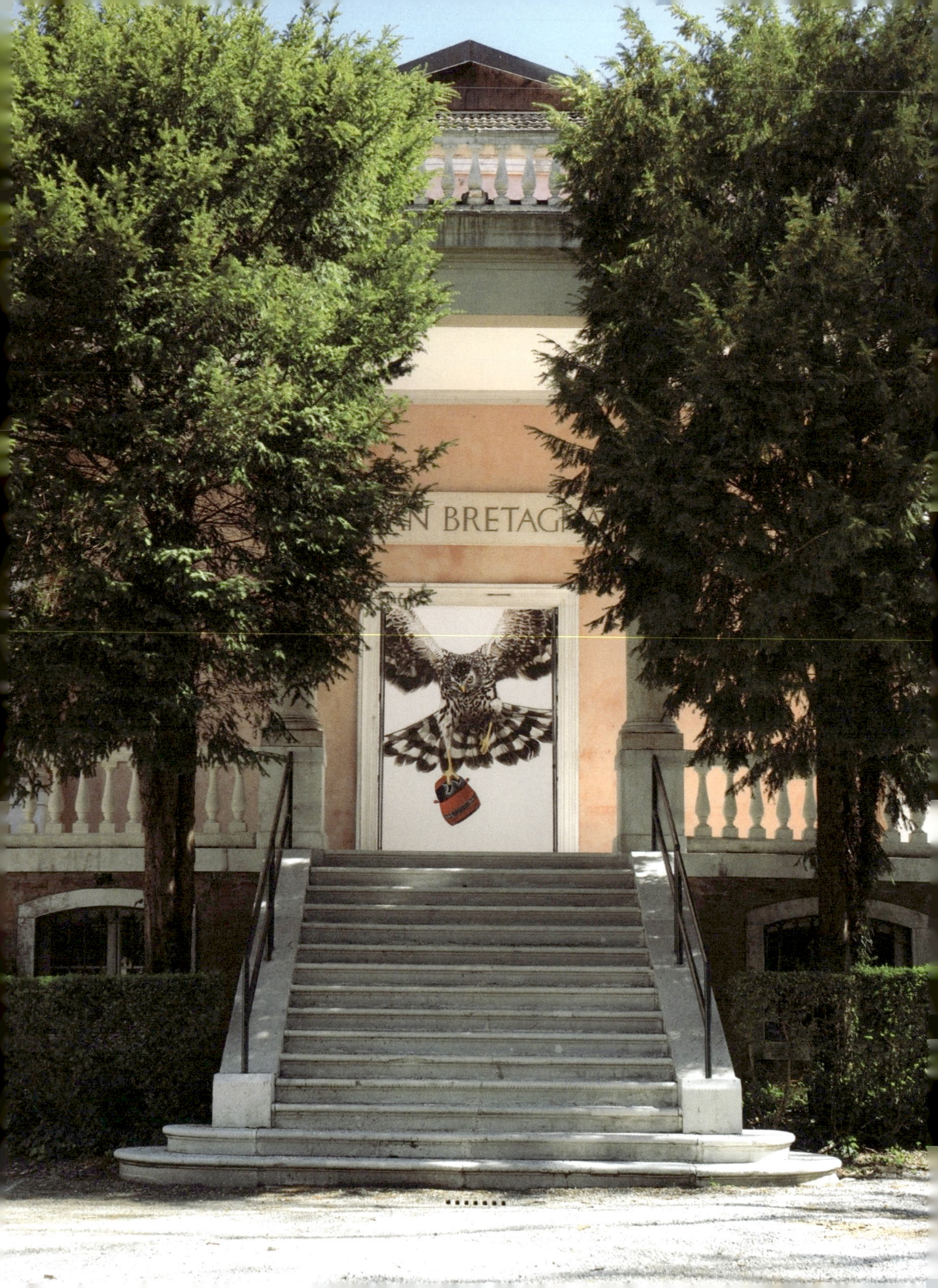

Chapter 14

A Range Rover crushed and made into a bench

English Magic in Venice

The Venice Biennale is a biannual art exhibition which takes place throughout the city but is centred on the Giardini, the gardens, where twenty-nine countries each have their own pavilion. It has been going since 1896, which probably explains why it has something of an old-fashioned character. In many ways, it feels more akin to a world's fair than a contemporary art show.

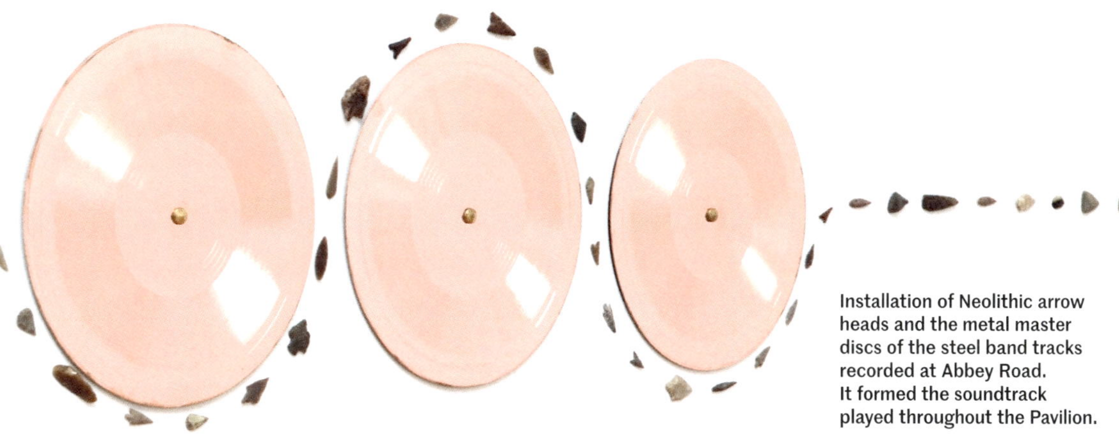

Installation of Neolithic arrow heads and the metal master discs of the steel band tracks recorded at Abbey Road. It formed the soundtrack played throughout the Pavilion.

In 2012, I was invited to represent Great Britain at the following year's Biennale. Initially, I was reluctant to do it and couldn't work out what to fill the huge space with. However, I thought perhaps I had better accept the invitation because if I didn't, someone else would and I'd never know what it was like. Surely the best motivation for taking part in anything. I realised that

← The approach to the British Pavilion is along a slightly inclined path and gives a view to the back wall of the space. It seemed right to put a big image on that wall so the exhibition could be seen from the outside. The mural *A Good Day for Cyclists* by Sarah Tynan, was 10 × 7 metres. We tried to convince the gardeners to prune the trees into the shape of neolithic hand axes, but to no avail.

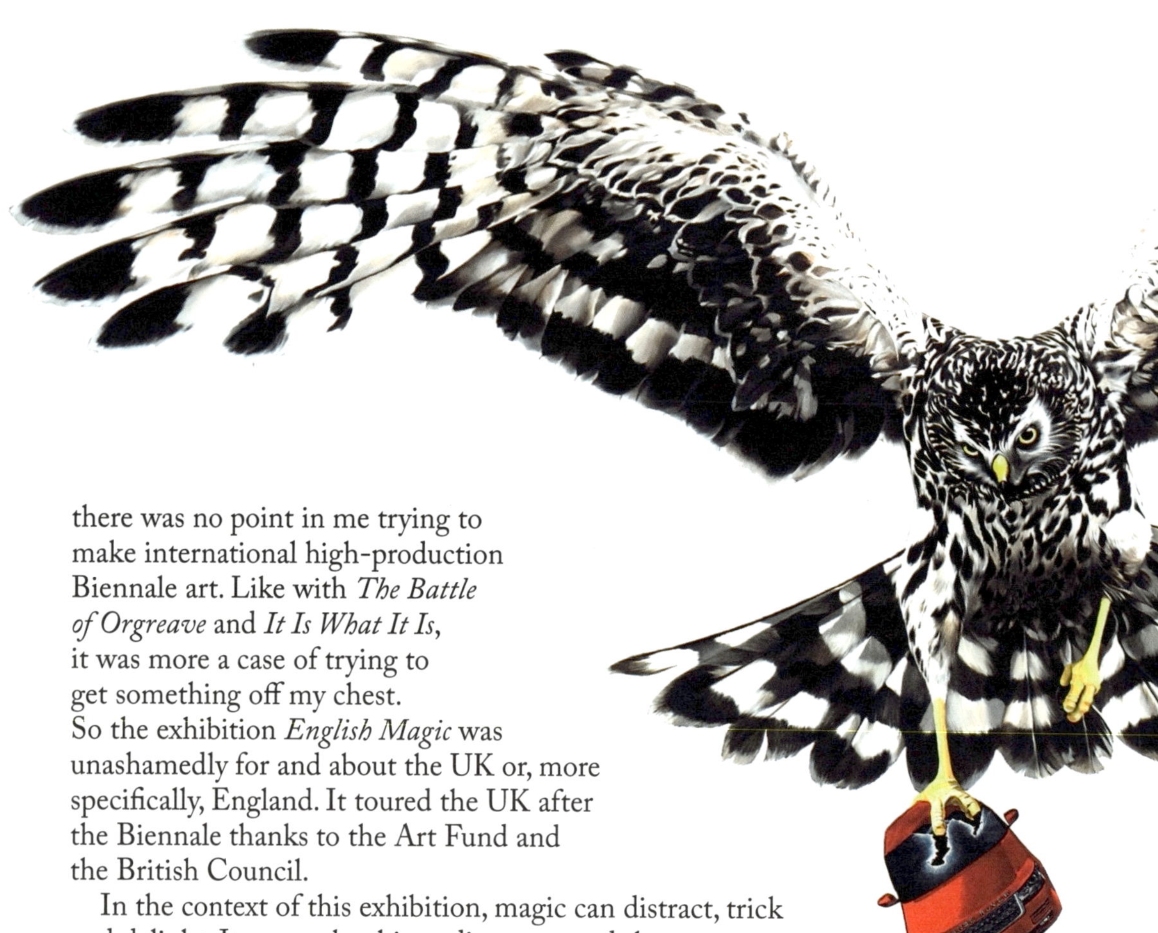

there was no point in me trying to make international high-production Biennale art. Like with *The Battle of Orgreave* and *It Is What It Is*, it was more a case of trying to get something off my chest. So the exhibition *English Magic* was unashamedly for and about the UK or, more specifically, England. It toured the UK after the Biennale thanks to the Art Fund and the British Council.

In the context of this exhibition, magic can distract, trick and delight. It can make things disappear and then reappear (money or chemical weapons). The work had a consciously mythic quality about it which prompted me to create imagery around contemporary events. I approached each room as if it were a chapter of a book. *English Magic* was based around three large murals by artists Stuart Hughes and Sarah Tynan, who were working there for months before the show opened in May. I like paintings: I had after all spent three years at college looking at them. I just can't paint myself, or at least not to the required standard. The works were all painted directly onto the walls of the pavilion, meaning they were covered over at the end of the Biennale – so they too were destroyed, which seems appropriate for images of destruction.

The first room was dominated by a huge mural by Sarah, titled *A Good Day for Cyclists*, depicting a hen harrier carrying a Range Rover in its claws (the Range Rover being the internationally recognised mode of transport for arseholes). The image referred to an event in 2007 when Prince Harry (version 1.0) and

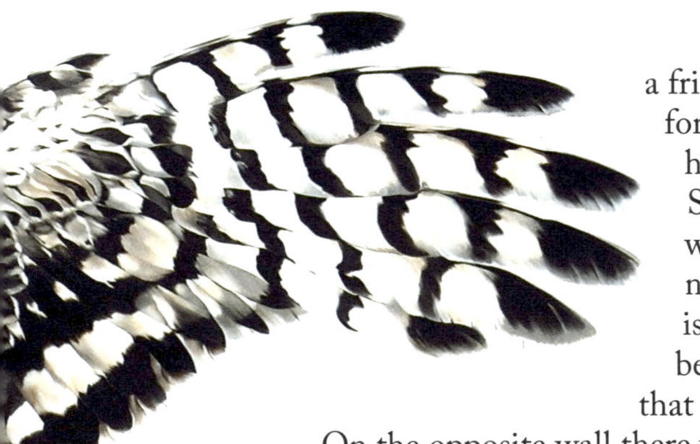

a friend were present at (if not responsible for) the shooting of a rare pair of hen harriers when hunting on the Sandringham Estate, a criminal act witnessed by the park ranger of a nearby bird reserve. The hen harrier is persecuted in the UK by gamekeepers because it preys on grouse chicks, a bird that hunters would rather kill themselves.

On the opposite wall there was a depiction of St Helier, the capital of Jersey in the Channel Islands, going up in flames, after being ransacked by UK taxpayers angry at its status as a haven for money laundering. Jersey is just one of many tax haven jurisdictions around the world that, though nominally governed by the UK, is independent in how it manages its financial services sector – the best of both worlds for investors wanting to conceal their wealth. This painting was flanked by two of Ed Hall's banners of simplified, diagrammatic faces. These images refer to the structure of popular tax-avoidance schemes, one a transfer-pricing device set up by Tesco in Hungary, in which Tesco Hungary is charged fees to trade using its name but via a Tesco subsidiary based elsewhere. This enables Tesco Hungary profits to leave the country with no tax to pay in that domain. It is a perfectly legal and popular device for big companies to pay little tax despite having a huge turnover.

In front of them were two worktables: on one, you could print your own image of the hen harrier and the William Morris image (more of which later); on the other were two hand axes for the public to handle. One of the axes was approximately 6,000 years old and the other was estimated as being at least 300,000 years old, made by *Homo heidelbergensis*, a subspecies of archaic human classified as its own separate

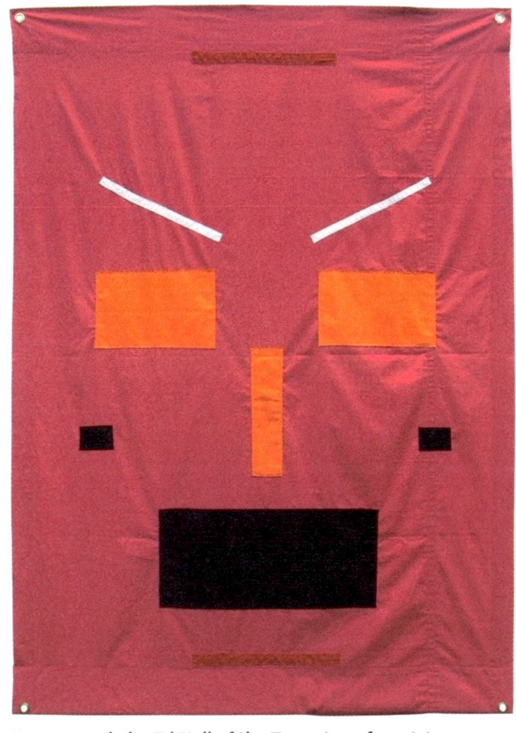

Banner made by Ed Hall of the Tesco transfer-pricing scheme diagram, reconfigured into a mask-like face.

species. That axe was uncanny for its ergonomic properties, fitting perfectly into your hand, like a bodily extension immediately connecting you to someone from so far back into history it is almost impossible to comprehend. Some visitors assumed that the hand axes were copies, reasoning that if real, they would be too valuable to be touched.

On the left-hand wall, the arrowheads curled around the three gold master discs of the tracks composed for the film playing in the show. The discs looked like artefacts from ancient sun worship. On the other wall, titled *The Small Faces*, several hand axes were arranged geographically according to where they were found in London, forming a map of sorts.

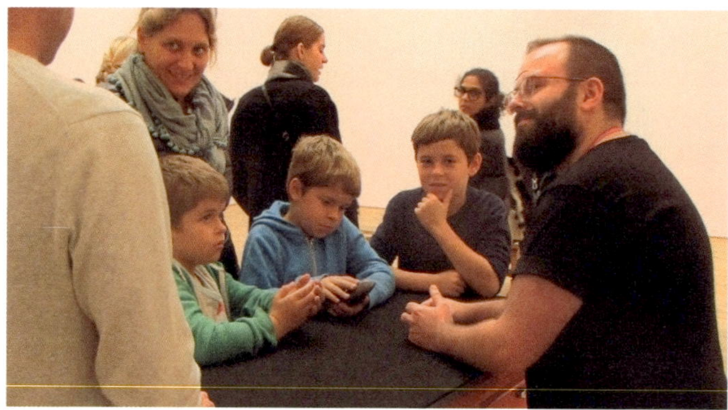

One of the workstations in action. A child holding a Neolithic hand axe connects to the time and person who made it over 5,000 years ago.

The second room was dedicated to William Morris, the fall of the Soviet Union and the rise of the thieving oligarchs, some of whom enjoyed visiting the Biennale. We also included a William Morris tiled panel, for some aesthetic light relief.

The bad magic of deception was the theme of *You Have the Watches We Have the Time* (a saying by the Taliban): an installation of drawings made in prisons around the UK by former soldiers who had served in Iraq and Afghanistan. Facilitated by Koestler Arts, a charity which promotes art, music and writing in prisons through an awards scheme, the project would have been a non-starter without their help.

The room was set out like a traditional picture gallery, with half the images of people involved in the war – most of them responsible for selling it to the public, such as Murdoch, Blair and Richard Dearlove, the Head of the Secret Intelligence Service – and the rest drawings of 'everyday army life', ranging from a depiction of villagers in Afghanistan who were executed the day after British soldiers had given them leaflets (the same leaflets were stuffed in their mouths as a warning from the Taliban), to a self-portrait by a soldier as he took cover under a bed while under mortar fire.

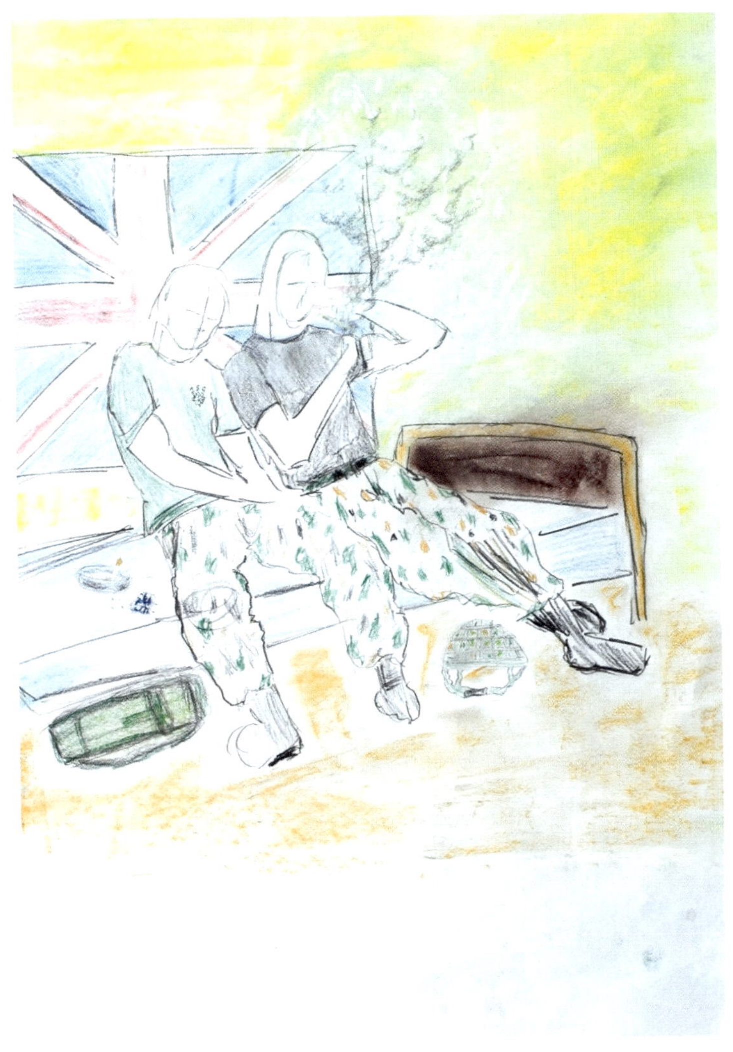

Soldiers smoking crack in Wellington Barracks, London, the night before deployment to Afghanistan in 2001, drawing by Neil, a prisoner at HMP Shotts.

To tie up the loose ends, I made a film to accompany the show. The soundtrack is by the Melodians Steel Orchestra, who make an appearance at the start of the film, arriving at the sacred space of Studio 2 at Abbey Road to record Vaughan Williams' Symphony No.5, 'Voodoo Ray' by A Guy Called Gerald and David Bowie's 'The Man Who Sold the World'. It was a mood piece, with the music heard throughout the exhibition. Visitors watched the film from a bench made from one of the crushed Range Rovers.

Tony Blair by Eddie, a prisoner at HMP Everthorpe.

The last room was concerned with the enchanting escapist magic of pop music. It charted the 1972–3 Ziggy Stardust UK tour by David Bowie, juxtaposing images of the fans at the venues with news stories from the same day. The reality of strikes and unrest in Northern Ireland was set against the parallel fantasy that Bowie was offering up. In a sense, it was risky to put these images next to each other, as it might have looked a bit radical chic, but young people were involved in both popular culture and street-level politics at this time, having formative experiences.

Audience members at Ziggy Stardust Farewell Concert, Hammersmith Odeon, London, 1973.

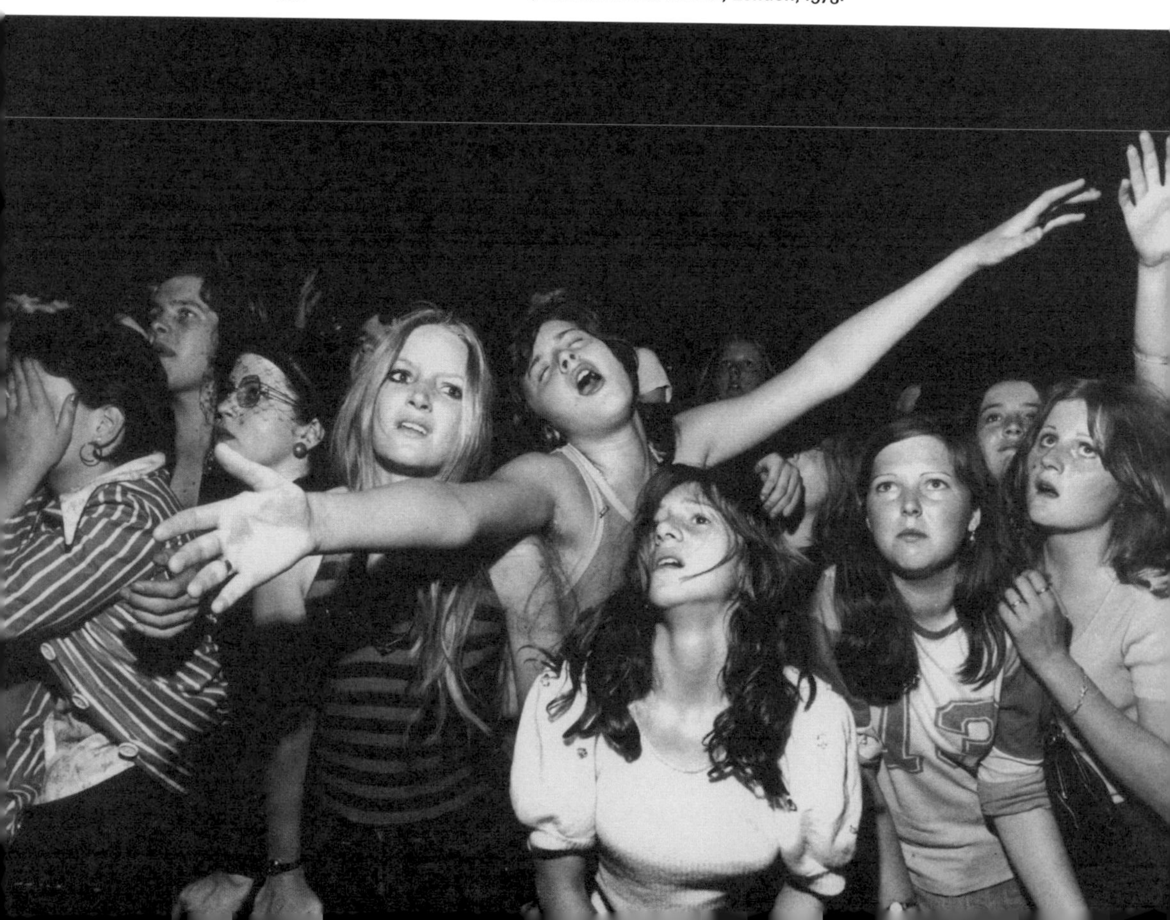

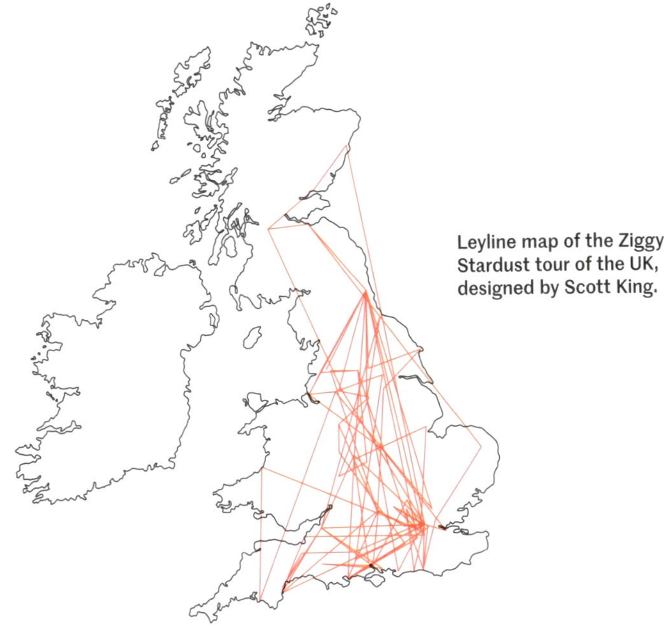

Leyline map of the Ziggy Stardust tour of the UK, designed by Scott King.

Children hijack vehicles to celebrate the shooting of a British soldier by an IRA sniper in West Belfast, April 1972.

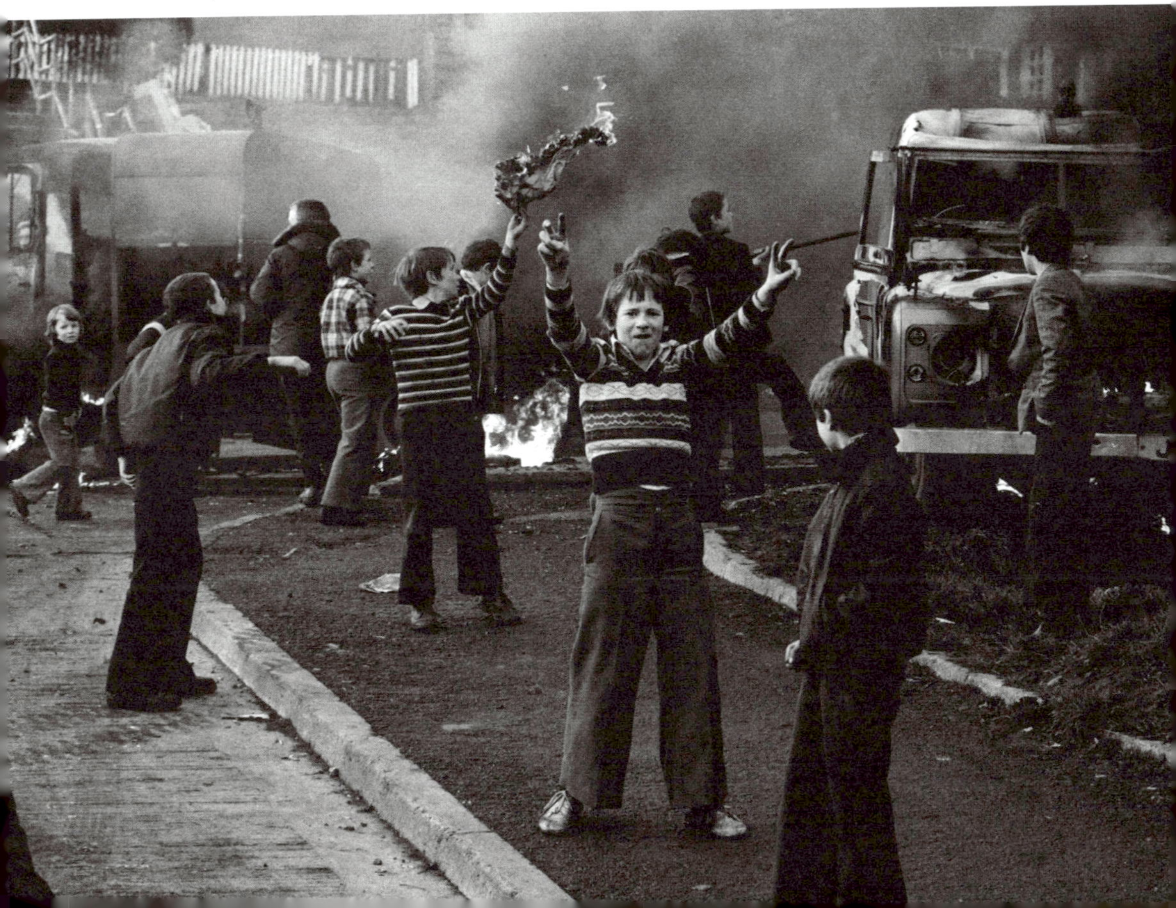

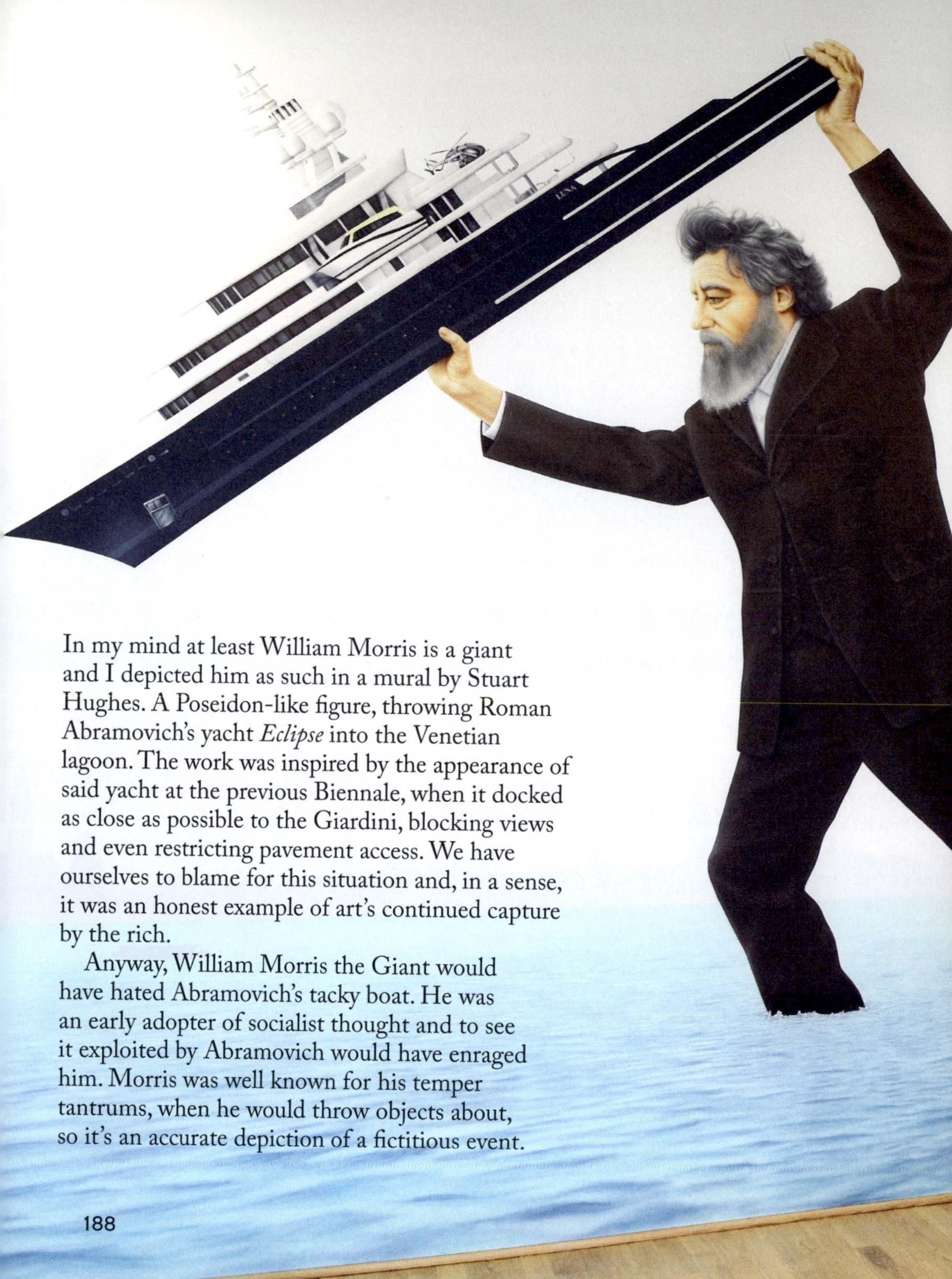

In my mind at least William Morris is a giant and I depicted him as such in a mural by Stuart Hughes. A Poseidon-like figure, throwing Roman Abramovich's yacht *Eclipse* into the Venetian lagoon. The work was inspired by the appearance of said yacht at the previous Biennale, when it docked as close as possible to the Giardini, blocking views and even restricting pavement access. We have ourselves to blame for this situation and, in a sense, it was an honest example of art's continued capture by the rich.

Anyway, William Morris the Giant would have hated Abramovich's tacky boat. He was an early adopter of socialist thought and to see it exploited by Abramovich would have enraged him. Morris was well known for his temper tantrums, when he would throw objects about, so it's an accurate depiction of a fictitious event.

Next to the painting was a series of share certificates issued to state workers after the fall of the Soviet Union, guaranteeing them a stake in their industries, which proved worthless as powerful people like Abramovich took over these industries at knock-down prices, turning themselves into billionaires in the process.

I did see George Osborne, the then Chancellor of the Exchequer, in my pavilion, and if he had read all the text panels, he would have seen himself mentioned in relation to an incident on a yacht belonging to the oligarch/criminal/political operative Oleg Deripaska.

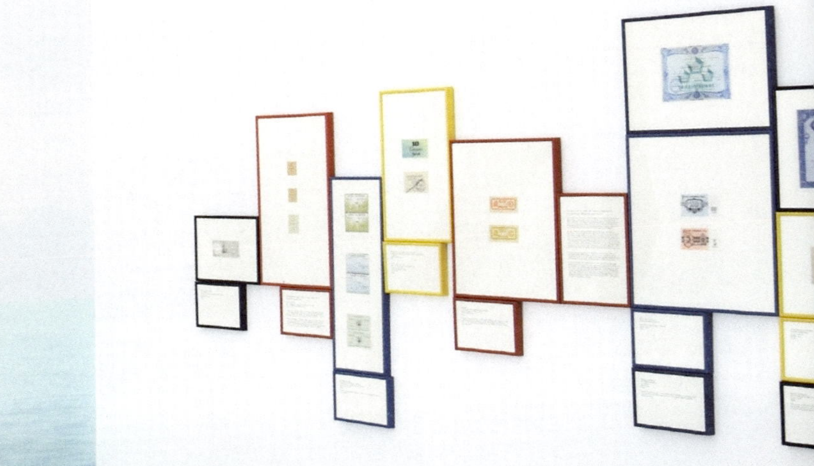

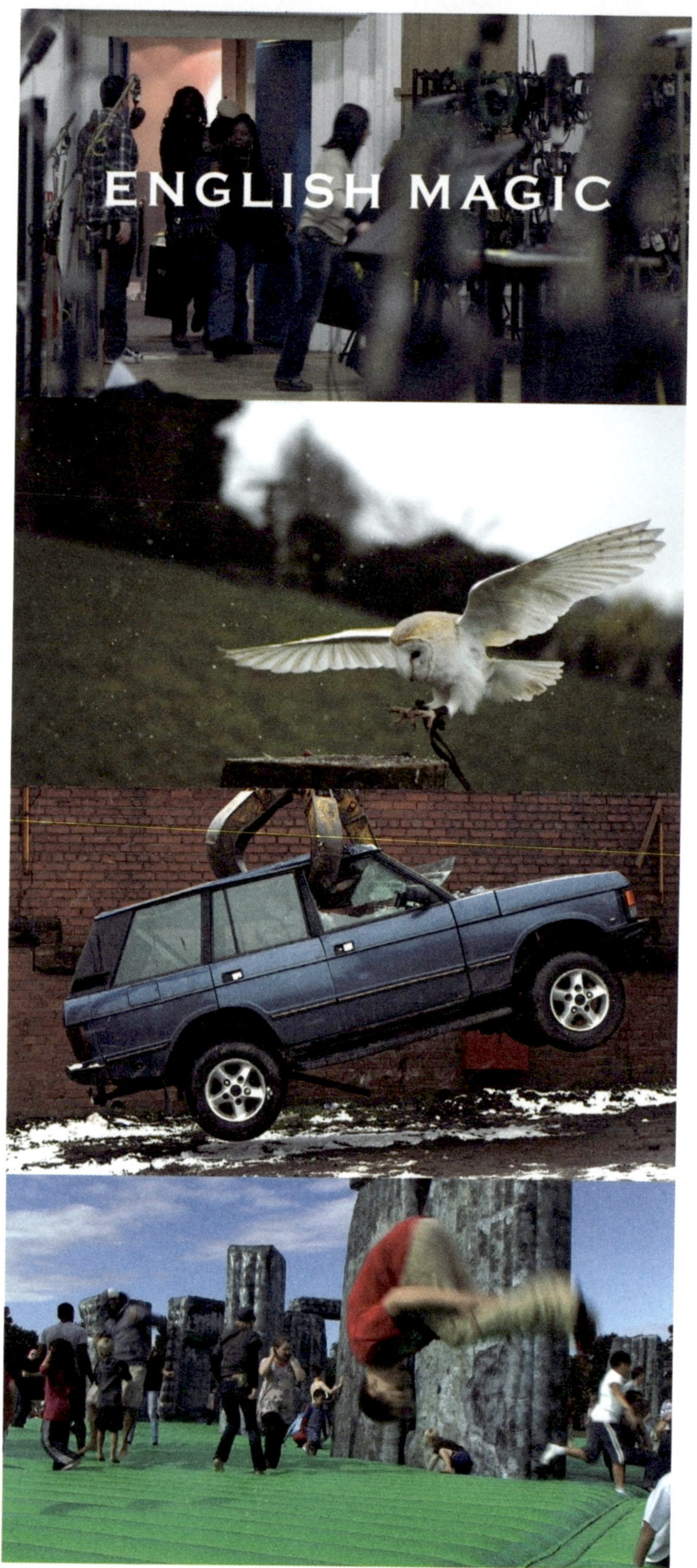

The film *English Magic* was a mystical journey around the UK. It starts with the steel band arriving at Abbey Road Studios.

A spectral Vaughan Williams symphony is played to co-incide with super slow-motion footage of birds of prey.

The talons of the birds are replaced by the mechanical talons at a car breaker's yard where two Range Rovers are crushed. The solid block of metal the cars have become is revealed…

… as air is pumped into the inflatable Stonehenge, which erects itself. The soundtrack for this sequence is 'Voodoo Ray' by A Guy Called Gerald.

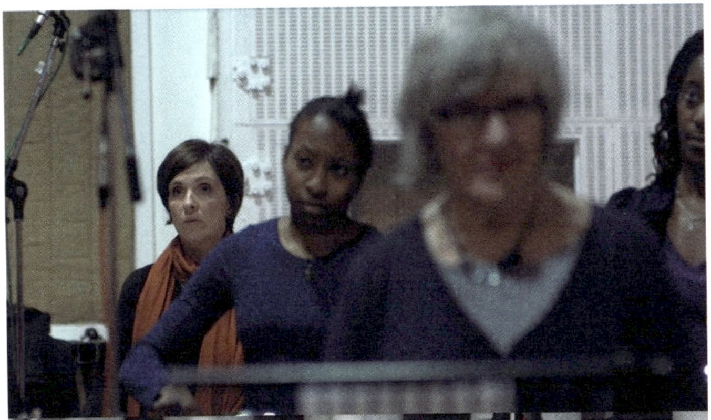

The inflatable then deflates, and we find ourselves back in Abbey Road Studios for a new track, David Bowie's 'The Man Who Sold the World'.

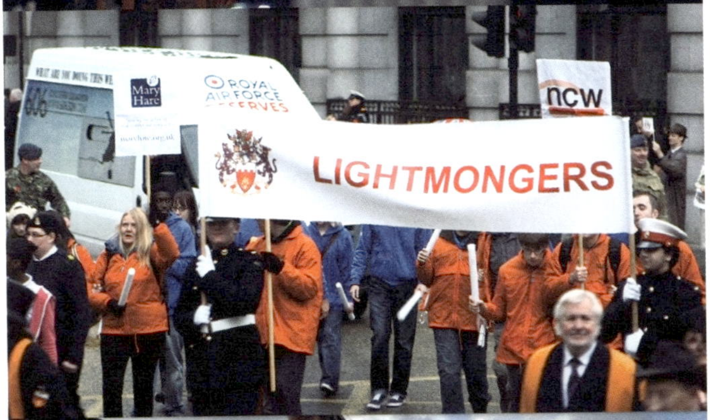

A sequence filmed at the Lord Mayor's Show in London illustrates a strange display of power in the UK. The army are out in force, as are all the Guilds and Societies, from this most opaque borough in the Land.

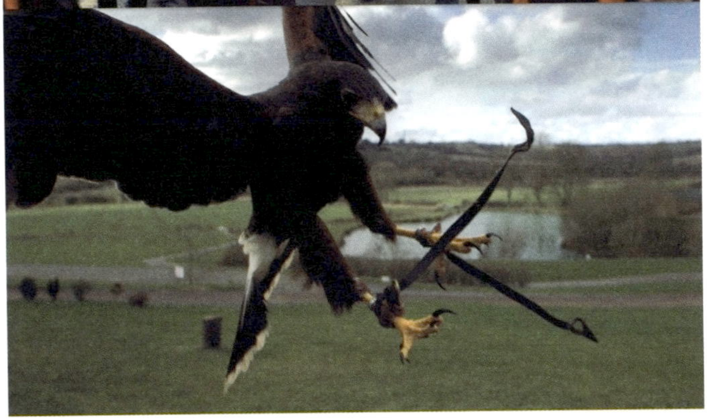

Back to the birds. The hyper beauty of a bird of prey in super slow motion is a reference to the Hen Harrier painting in the main space.

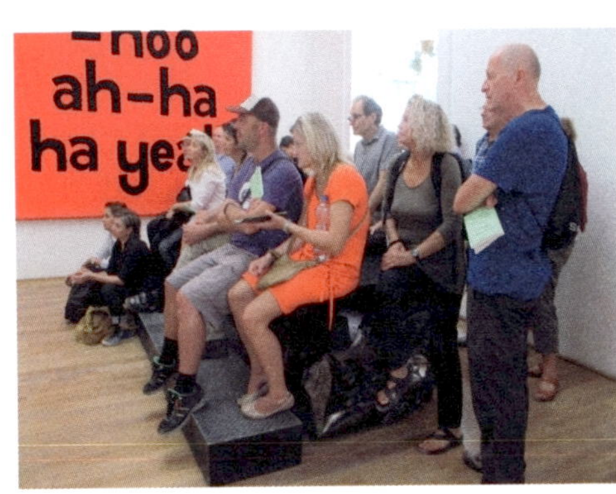

The film was viewed from a bench made out of the crushed Range Rover.

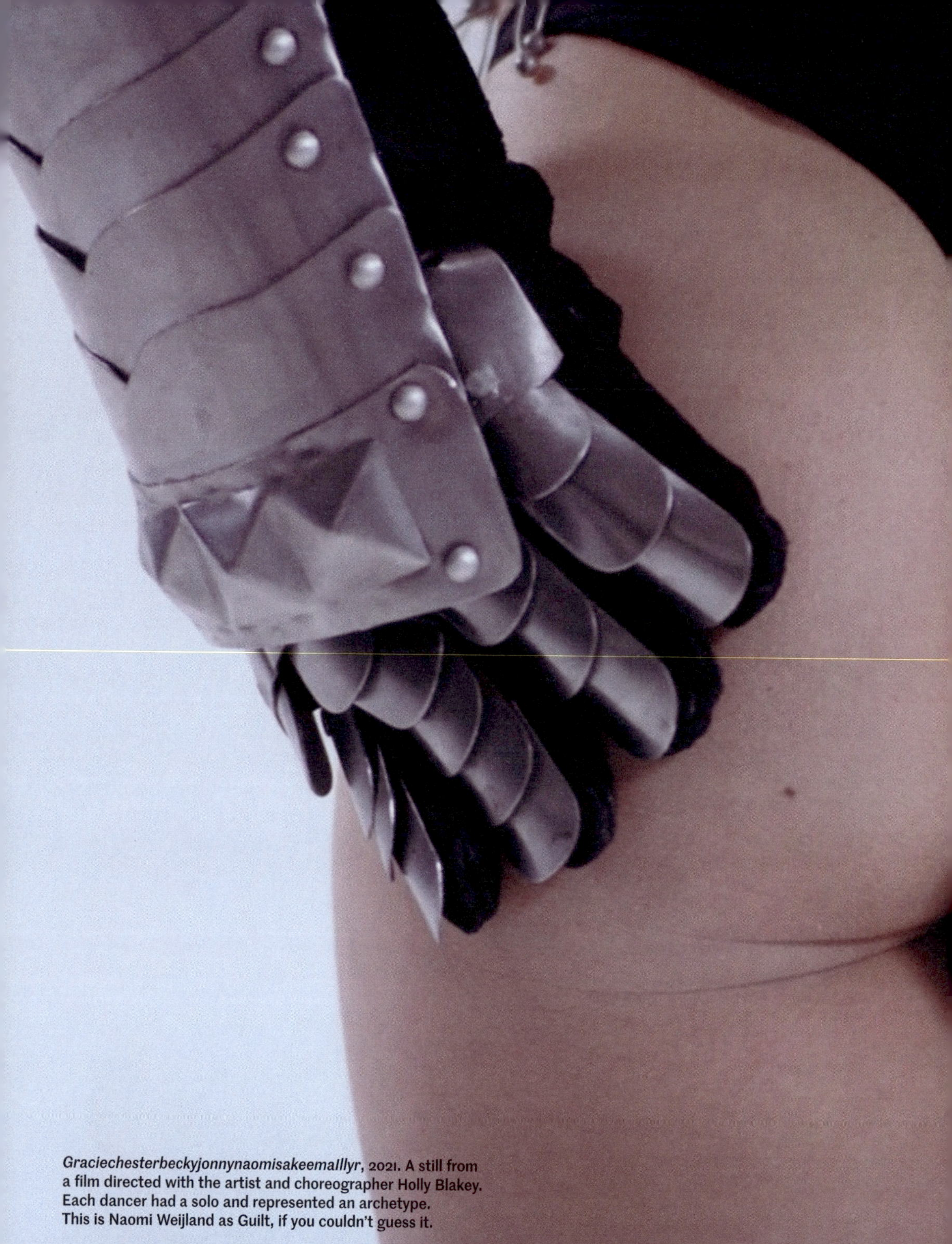

Graciechesterbeckyjonnynaomisakeemalllyr, 2021. A still from a film directed with the artist and choreographer Holly Blakey. Each dancer had a solo and represented an archetype. This is Naomi Weijland as Guilt, if you couldn't guess it.

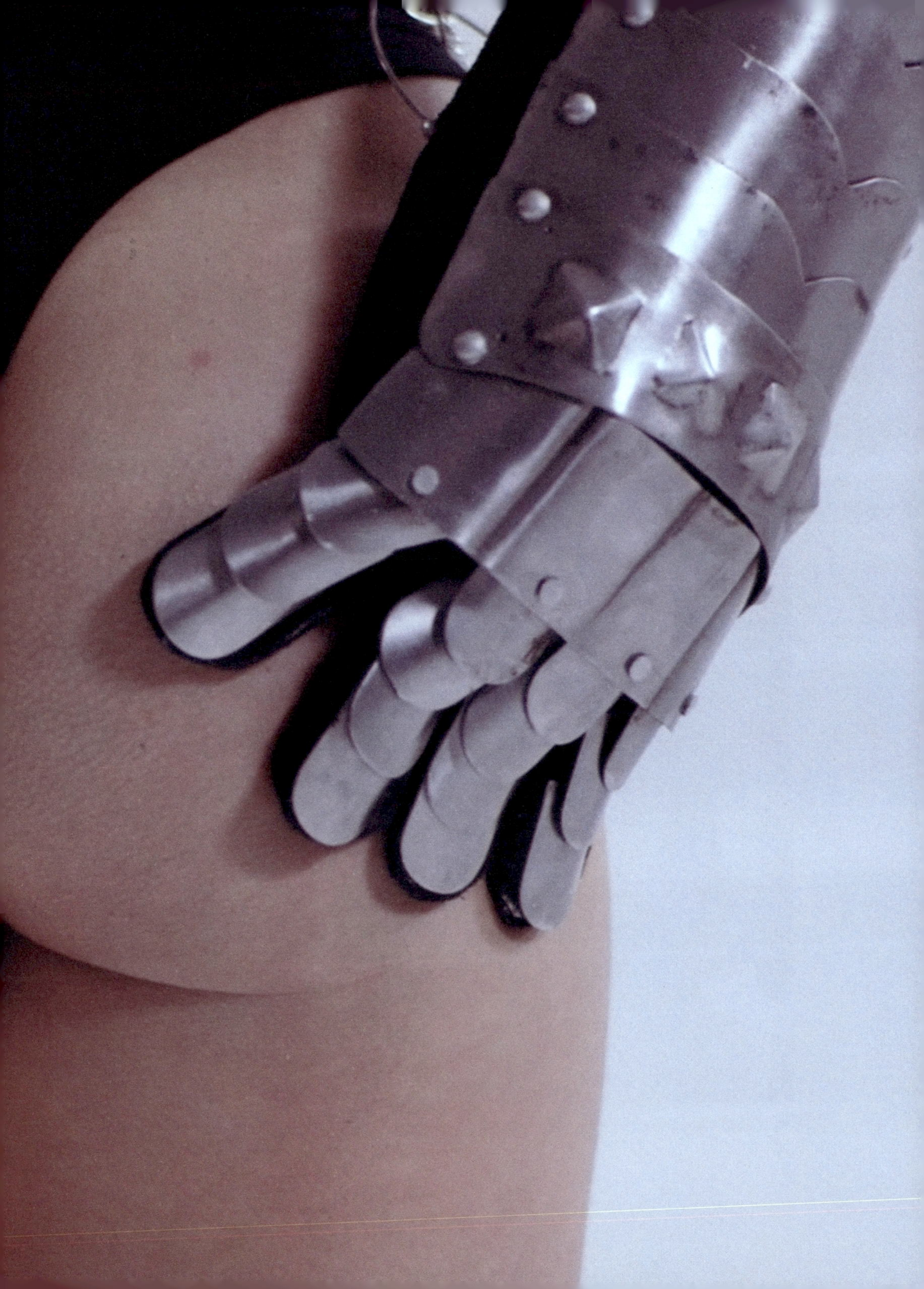

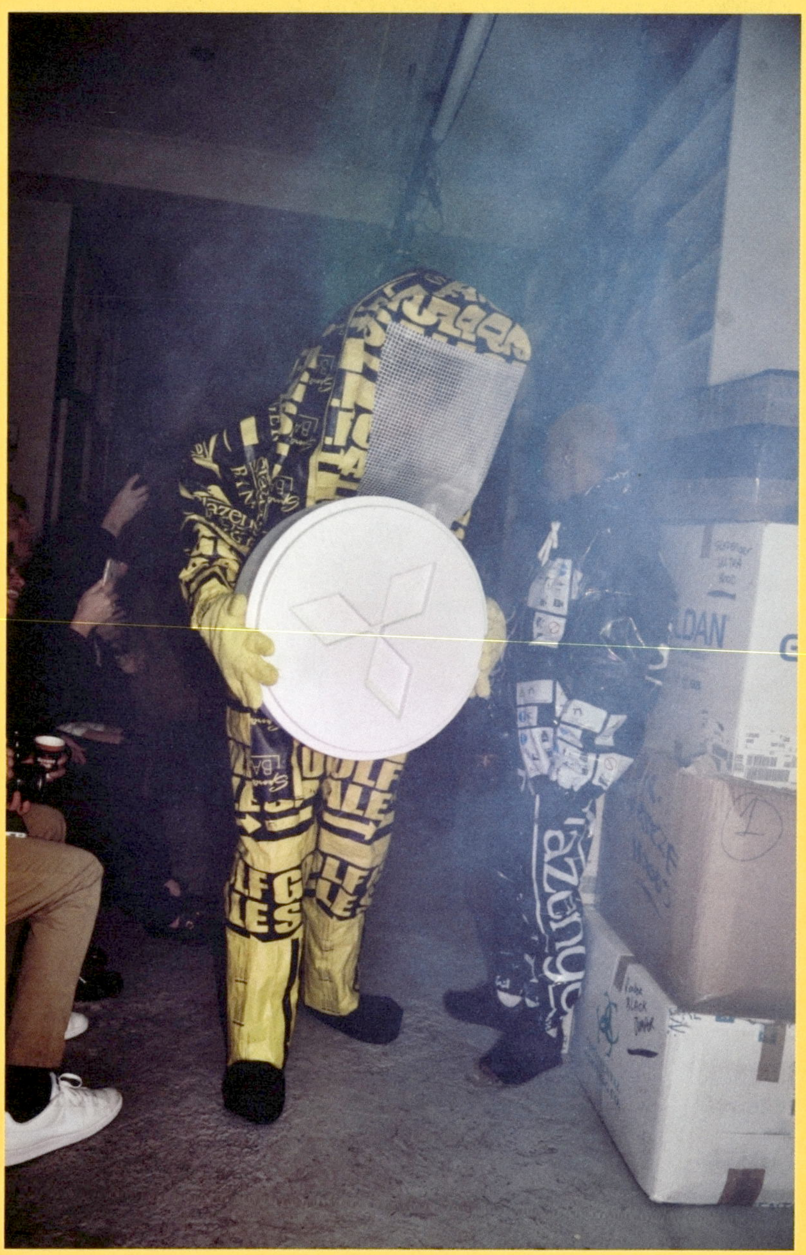

The first Sports Banger fashion show, Seven Sisters, London, 2019.

Chapter 15

The Factory comes to Seven Sisters

Jonny Banger in conversation

Maison de Bang Bang, Seven Sisters. Jonny Banger, AKA Sports Banger, has a practice that is difficult to pin down. On the face of it he runs a business selling streetwear but that is just the starting point of all sorts of multimedia mischief.

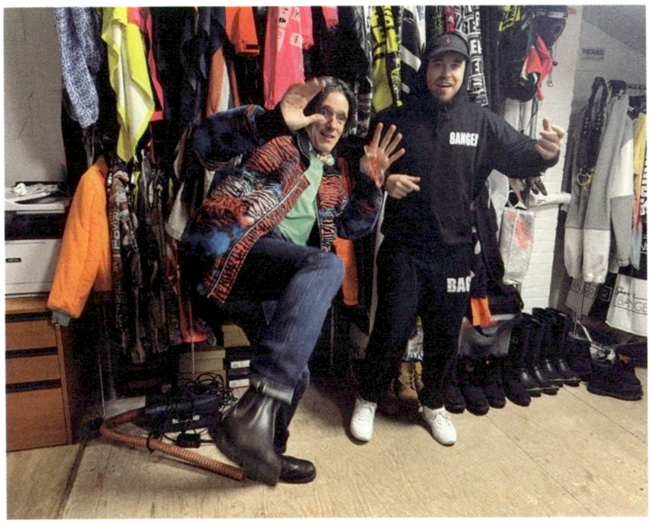

JD and JB at Banger HQ, London, 2022.

Jeremy Deller: So, what are you up to?

Jonny Banger: We are in a new studio, redoing the website, looking towards a fashion show in February. T-shirts are the fun token which pays for everything else. There is a lot of money going out every month before you have even made anything, so we are trying to get a handle on the business side of things.

JD: You have been very good at the creative side. I have always thought that this place and how you work is like Warhol's Factory. Have you ever thought about it in those terms?

JB: I just do things and then they usually explain themselves to me as time goes by. I am trying to get a bit more of a plan now, so that these things will still be here in five or ten years. I certainly didn't know about all these references to do with fashion or art when I was starting out.

JD: Did you study art at school or receive encouragement when you were young?

JB: No, just from a record shop in Colchester where I did work experience. I was raised by the elders there, making zines and selling records.

JD: I remember we once didn't get to the end of a very exciting conversation about a world championship scratching competition?

JB: The DMCs DJ competition. I got to the semi-finals of the Battle for Supremacy at the Scala when I was about sixteen. You had one minute up against another DJ. The other DJs would focus on scratching but I would also have rap records so I could diss them with the snatches of lyrics. Scratching, of course, but making a point rather than just a sound. I also won a DJ battle at the Oliver Twist pub in Colchester when I was fifteen. I was called DJ Newborn because I was the youngest of our crew. There is a flyer somewhere of me as a baby in a crib.

JD: Is that scene your earliest experience of community?

JB: Yes, my mum had died so I was certainly looking for something. You want to be out of the house with like-minded, fun people. I could go round to bedsits and sheds of older people into music, and just sit and observe.

JD: I remember you telling me about being on children's TV when a rave act was on. What was the song again?

JB: Xpansions' 'Move Your Body' on *Motormouth*. Kids could go on this Saturday-morning TV programme and run around in the audience eating popcorn.

JD: If there is a documentary made about your life, that is how it should begin.

JB: I have that whole episode on video, along with all the adverts, so I can see everything we were exposed to in 1992. Ads with rave characters and cartoons with eyes popping out. I look at it now and see that is how I got here.

A selection of Sports Banger T-shirts through the ages.

JD: Your origin story! I came to art by seeing pop music on telly. I wanted to be around it in some way although I had no idea how. Are there any boundaries or limits to what you do?

JB: I think I limit myself. I can't engage with something unless there is a personal connection. In fashion, I have never been one to send clothes to someone in the public eye just because they are doing stuff at that moment.

JD: But of course, you don't have much control over who wears your T-shirts or who likes your music.

JB: Absolutely. You will see somebody wearing one of my T-shirts which might look just plain wrong. Or is that my ego?

JD: I made T-shirts in the early 1990s when I worked at Sign of the Times and it was so exciting when you saw somebody wearing one in a club. And you personally are still relatively in the background. Is that something of a throwback to your earlier career when you were selling stuff, you want some anonymity when you are working on the fringes of copyright?

JB: That was in my childhood years – aged ten to fourteen maybe – when I didn't even know the stuff we were selling was fake. My dad would do loads of car boot sales, and he had a mate with a sports shop who ended up going to jail because all the gear he was selling was fake. On the stall, people would say, 'Is this real Ralph Lauren?' and you would say, 'Yes, the horse is in line with the third button and there is the classic tapered back.' All the spiel. None of it was real. You would go to markets and see things called Tommy Sports and you would think, 'Is this proper Tommy Hilfiger?' when it looked shit. Then the penny drops.

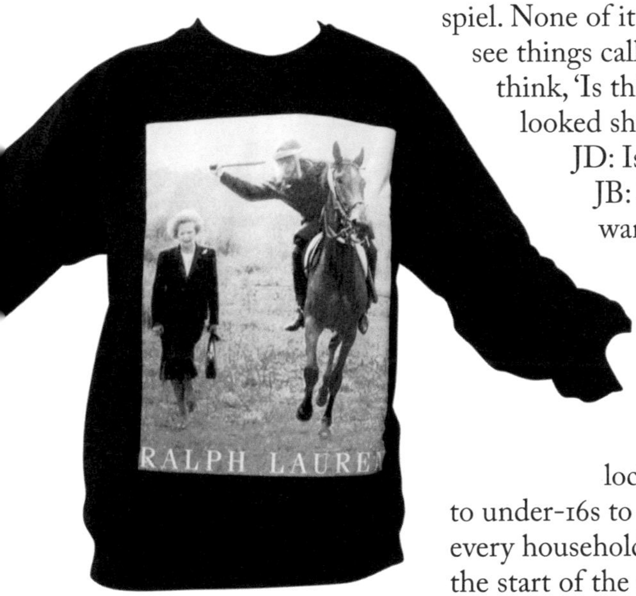

JD: Is there an ethos around what you do?

JB: I suppose it is simply to do what you want. A lot of people have ideas and I just follow them through, otherwise I would be beating myself up about it. Ideas are ten a penny, but you just have to grab it.

JD: Which goes on to your brilliant idea you had during lockdown: *The Covid Letters*, a call-out to under-16s to draw, paint or adapt the letter that every household received from Boris Johnson at the start of the pandemic, which nearly gave me a nervous breakdown: I thought – you bugger! That's what I want to do!

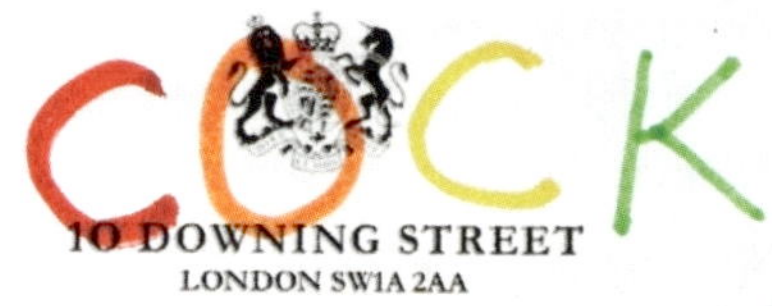

10 DOWNING STREET
LONDON SW1A 2AA

THE PRIME MINISTER

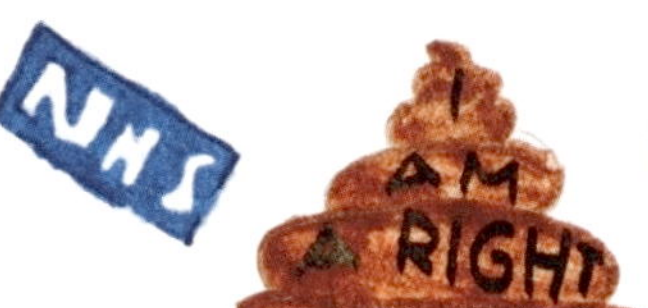

I am writing to you to update [illegible] taking to combat coronavirus.

In just a few short weeks, everyday life in this country has changed dramatically. We all feel the profound impact of coronavirus not just on ourselves, but on our loved ones and our communities.

I understand completely the difficulties this disruption has caused to your lives, businesses and jobs. But the action we have taken is absolutely necessary, for one very simple reason.

If too many people become seriously unwell at one time, the NHS will be unable to cope. This will cost lives. We must slow the spread of the disease, and reduce the number of people needing hospital treatment in order to save as many lives as possible.

That is why we are giving one simple instruction – you **must** stay at home.

You should not meet friends or relatives who do not live in your home. You may only leave your home fo[illegible] purposes, such as buying food and medicine, exercising once [illegible]ng medical attention. You can travel to and from work but should work from home if you can.

When you do have to leave your home, you should ensure, wherever possible, that you are two metres apart from anyone outside of your household.

These rules must be observed. So, if people break the rules, the police will issue fines and disperse gatherings.

Drawing by Honor, 10, London.

I thought it was an elegant and unfiltered idea which I knew would enable you to find out about the children and their lives. When you do something like this you always hope that the public tend to make things better because they do things you cannot imagine yourself.

Daniel Scott: Had that been a Deller project, what would your version have been like?

JD: I don't think it would have been that different. The best ideas are often the simplest ones.

JB: One point I did labour over was breaking down the project to its simplest idea – so did this mean it should only include under-16s or under-18s – the voting age. But I eventually did it with under-16s as this made more of a distinction between adults and kids.

JD: It must have been amazing to see the work coming in.

JB: Initially, the parent or guardian would send photos of the works through but then we needed to see it for real. We got nearly 300 replies.

JD: I was very impressed by what you sent to the kids – a certificate, two T-shirts, a pirate *Blue Peter* badge, and even a self-addressed stamped envelope. Must have cost you thousands.

JB: Yes. Because we reached a lot of people, it meant something, and it kept me busy. It's best when I am doing something for the public, for other people. When it's a project for yourself – like a new website, working on a Sports Banger book – it's much harder.

JD: It's a community which you have created from the people who buy your clothes or records, people who post things about you online.

JB: At the heart,it's something to believe in. There has always been a point to everything we do. It has never been the case of just flipping the logo or making student-y parody T-shirts. There is a narrative behind the work. I think I have got a really quick editing process in my head and can see how seven different people might view a design. I used to host some raves and pirate radio, and with that, each time you are trying to say something. If you are in a packed rave with a mate, you can manage to say, 'So and so is playing in room 3, another of our friends has just arrived, let's go to the bar' – in three words and a nod and a wink. A case of editing down a big thing into the smallest possible number of words.

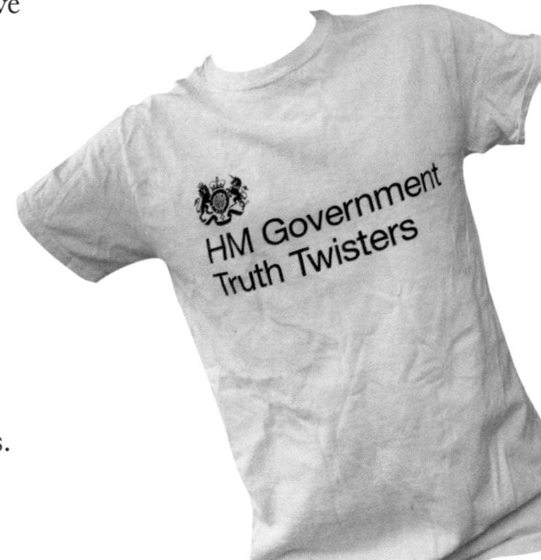

JD: So, what feels right for you is right for the brand.

DS: Have you ever tried to work with a brand you couldn't take through the Sports Banger prism?

JB: No. If there is some personal connection, it can work. I will never be defeated!

DS: When did you two meet?

JB: I went to a talk Jeremy was doing as I liked the public side to the work, across loads of different media.

I like the way you translate everything. With my stuff, you don't need to be into fashion or art but just need to be conscious of the outside world generally. Your work and mine are a celebration of people's relationships with each other and their surroundings.

JD: I just saw a kindred spirit, especially when I went to his first 'catwalk show'. It was so good it felt illegal. There was great music, and it felt very 'London' but not in an elitist way. It was my best night out that year. Fashion, like art, can be too much about money, but this was about ideas and performance in the same tradition as a rave.

JB: As a raver, I have a duty of care. That doesn't stop just because you are not at a rave – that's why we did food banks and stuff like that. If you see somebody passing out at a rave, you'll check they are all right. Everyone's looking out for each other – hopefully that is the same in the rest of my work. You don't want to play to the same crowd all the time. I see Sports Banger as touching on lots of different worlds. At the shows, there will be pattern cutters, vogue dancers, runway models, drug dealers. Peace, love, unity, respect. Duty of care.

JD: I saw how you did that with the participants in the *Covid Letters* show – you made them feel special.

JB: It wasn't a case of 'We will take all your artwork and then it becomes Sports Banger.'

JD: It was a really good example to the children, giving life and inspiration to ideas. At a risk of bigging you up massively, it is giving them the experience you had on the TV programme. It is continuing that tradition of grown-ups showing children a different version of the world.

JB: We want the Maison to come to life. Open the door and anything can happen here.

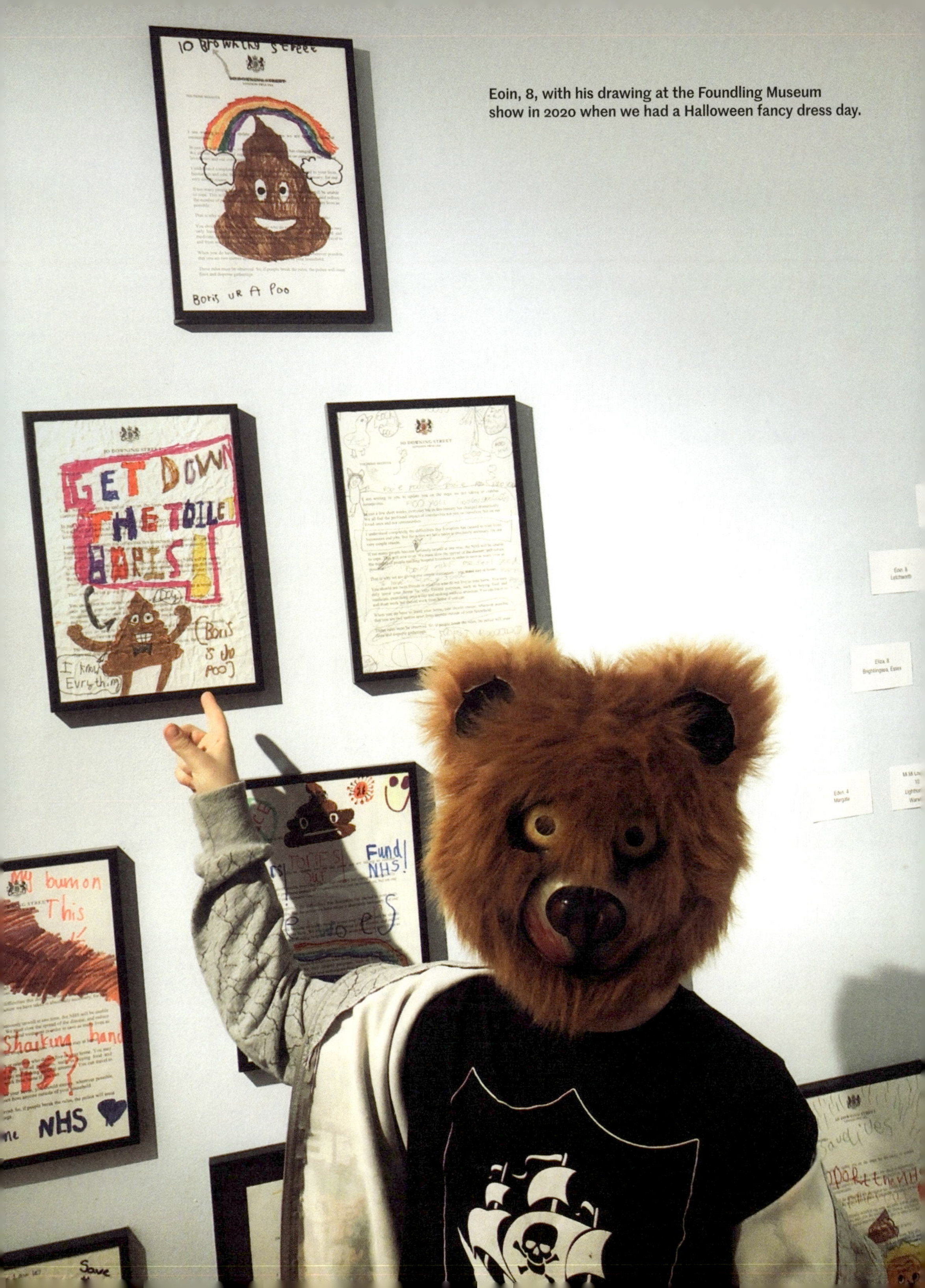

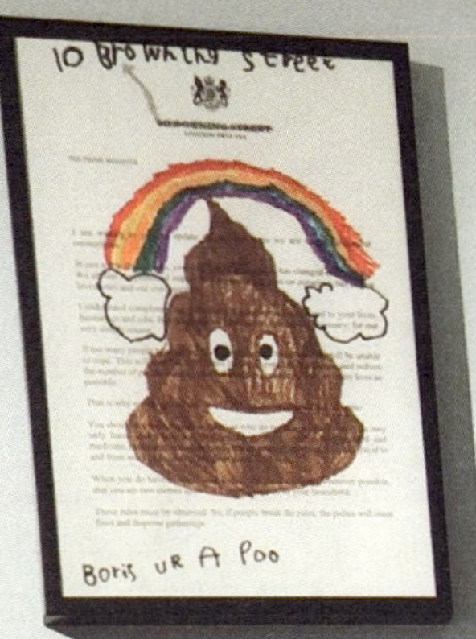

Eoin, 8, with his drawing at the Foundling Museum show in 2020 when we had a Halloween fancy dress day.

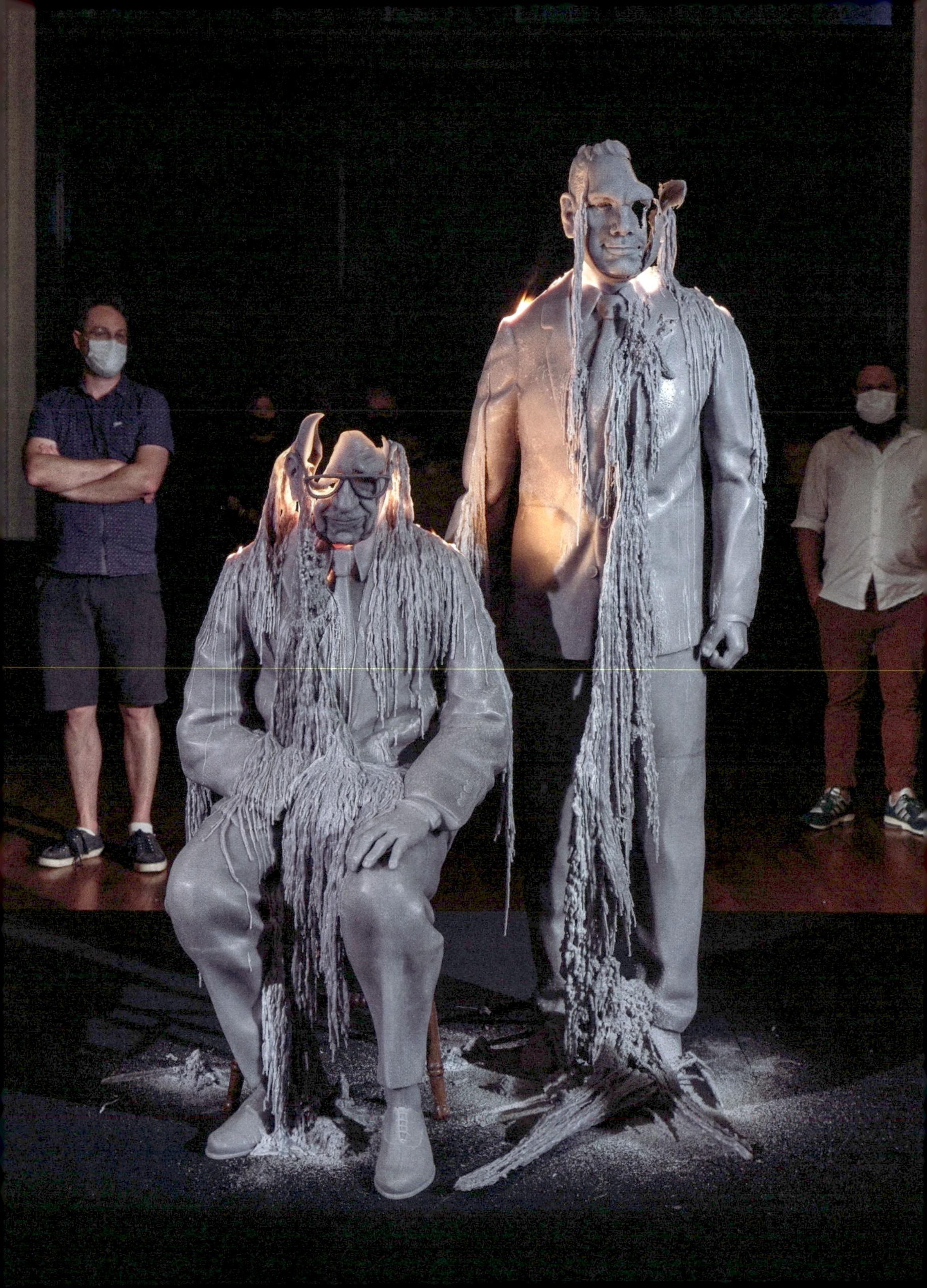

Chapter 16

I burnt Rupert Murdoch

A cover version

Throughout 2019 and 2020, large parts of Australia were destroyed by a number of bushfires: 46 million acres of land were burnt and it is estimated that up to 3 billion animals were displaced or killed. The Murdoch media in the country had initially attempted to ignore the story. When it became clear that they couldn't, they were happy to repeat accusations that environmentalists had started the fires.

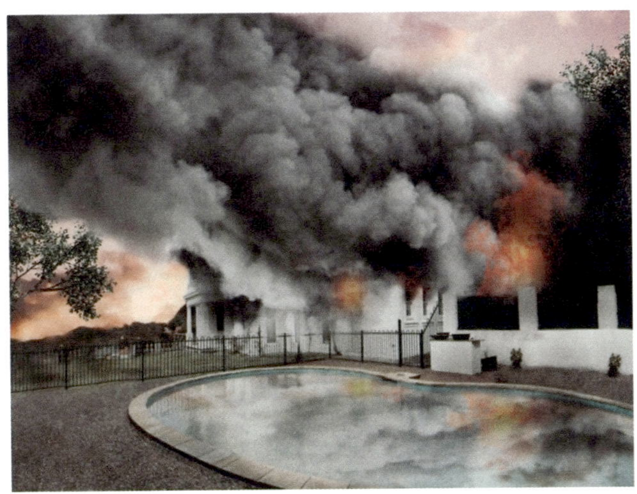

The Offending Print, or, to give it its full title: *Artist's Impression of the Sydney Home of Lachlan Murdoch Being Engulfed by a Bushfire*, 2020. The response to this by the family still puzzles me. But then I'm not a billionaire, so how would I know how tough it is.

Along with a bunch of other artists, I was invited in 2019 to make an editioned print to be sold to raise funds for a charity to help the human and non-human victims of the fires. I made an image of Lachlan Murdoch's villa in Sydney being consumed by a bushfire. Hardly subtle, but to the point. It was printed on a textured grey metallic paper to give it a painterly feel.

I put an image of it on Instagram, and very soon was getting messages from outraged Murdoch family members. Some of Rupert Murdoch's grandchildren were very angry with me. Their main complaint was that Lachlan's children

← Like *The Battle of Orgreave*, *Father and Son* was very much a public event. The audience completed the work. I wanted there to be a sense of calm around the restrained chaos of the work itself.

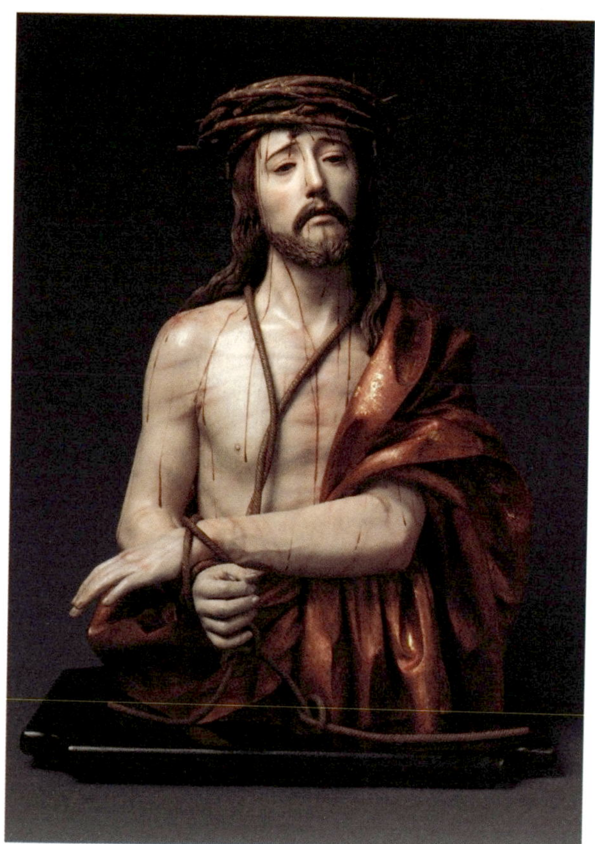

Ecce Homo by Pedro De Mena. I spent three years at college looking at images like this. It clearly rubbed off on me, as in my mind at least *Father and Son* made sense art-historically.

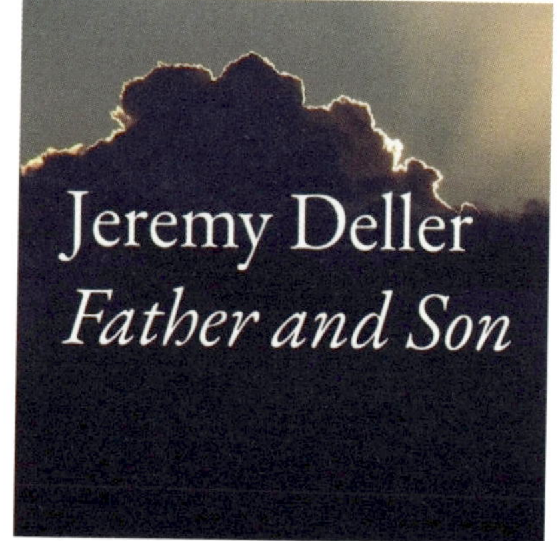

"For what will it profit a man if he gains the whole world and forfeits his soul?"

— Matthew 16:26

Online marketing material for the event strongly referenced the Bible and the aesthetic of religious tracts.

might be in the house. To reiterate: this was a print. So, despite (or maybe *because* of) their riches they seemed to be incapable of understanding the difference between a two-dimensional print and the real world. I turned off online comments as they seemed to be getting out of hand, though I wish I had taken screenshots of this billionaire pile-on. In truth, I felt a bit sorry for them, trying to gain some sympathy for themselves from the situation. Little did the Murdochs know that, for later that year, I had a work in the pipeline where a likeness of Bad Grandpa and Uncle Lachlan would literally be burnt.

I had been asked to make a work for the Melbourne Festival and, with the bushfires uppermost on people's minds, I suggested a sculpture of Rupert and Lachlan Murdoch which destroys itself over a period of time, not dissimilar to a sacrifice or offering of some sort. I wanted it to have all the violence and beauty of a religious artwork.

It quickly became apparent that candle wax would be the best material to work with, as opposed to ice or a sort of effigy. Wax would take time to burn, would create interesting shapes as it melted and has clear ecclesiastical resonances. Oddly enough, there was little chance of Rupert or Lachlan sitting to be moulded for the portrait sculptures, so we had to create a 3D model from 2D images of them.

Rupert has something of an iconic 'look' – I guess his face looks a bit like it's melting anyway. Lachlan was trickier. His weight, his hair and his overall look seem to change from year to year. So we spent hours poring over photos of them – something I am glad I won't have to do again.

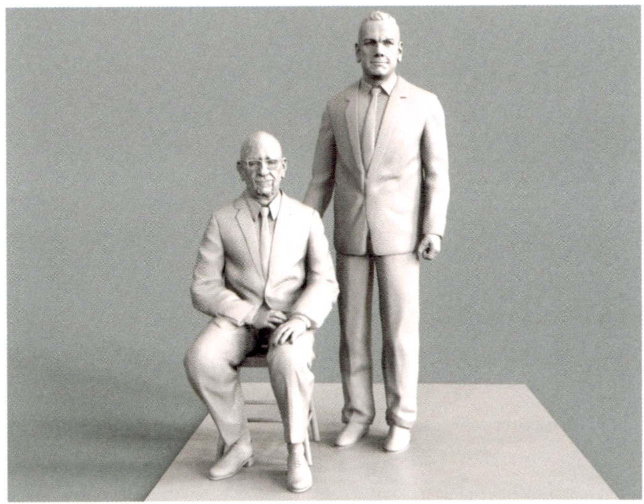

Computer renderings of Lachlan and Rupert. We spent hours studying them both, their faces especially, trying to get Rupert's ears and wrinkles right. Lachlan seemed to look different in every photo.

The candles were made in Australia from moulds, and great care was taken not just with their likenesses but also with details such as their shoes and their gait. Cumulatively, I hoped that these almost imperceptible details would add up to something convincing, uncanny even. We took a great deal of care with something that, paradoxically, was going to be destroyed. The whole process happened remotely, during lockdown. It was kept a secret because of the reach of the Murdoch press in Australia, particularly in Melbourne, which is where Rupert was born. His main paper in the town is the *Herald Sun*, and I was thinking of calling the work *Herald the Son* but decided this was perhaps a bit too antagonistic and smart-arse: the marketing material referred to the work as a vigil burning through the night, and ending in the early morning. The teaser ads led with biblical quotations over images of the sky and sunsets, mimicking the look of those Christian pamphlets you are occasionally given in the street. I'd always liked these for their uncompromising design, demanding the reader's attention by asking big questions.

The presentation was delayed a number of times, but it was eventually shown on the first weekend after the end of a 262-day lockdown, and so became a thanksgiving event of sorts for the lifting (albeit partial) of Covid restrictions, as well as a contemplation on mortality.

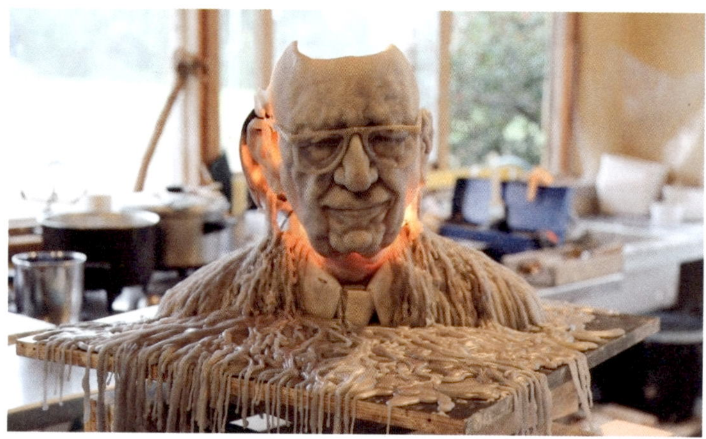

Test burn of Bad Grandpa. Reminds me of Ian Holm's character in *Alien*, post-decapitation.

The venue for the event was a deconsecrated church with very understanding hosts. The Murdochs burnt for twelve hours. By the end, Lachlan's face had fallen off. Rupert's stayed on, but now bowed slightly.

Although I didn't see the work in person, I watched the live stream and spent the day in the knowledge that an odd and foolhardy event was taking place simultaneously on the other side of the world. The detritus has since been melted down and recycled. If ever restaged, the Murdochs would ideally be lit in a functioning church during a service. Mini versions were produced to pay for the inevitable overspend, giving the public the opportunity to burn their own right-wing chaos merchants at their leisure.

Overleaf: *Monarchs of the Glen*, 2012. Dear reader: avert your eyes if you are a bit squeamish. Here is a fantasy painting of former MP Richard Benyon being eviscerated on his grouse moor by some angry birds of prey, including the much-persecuted hen harrier, hated by gamekeepers and grouse-killers alike. Benyon was an Under Secretary of State at the Department for Environment, Food and Rural Affairs between 2010 and 2013, where he consistently sided with landowners (of which he is one) over the rights of wildlife. I think that is why the birds are so angry with him. We just have to be thankful that animals can't communicate with each other because if they could they'd probably conspire to kill humans off as a matter of some urgency.

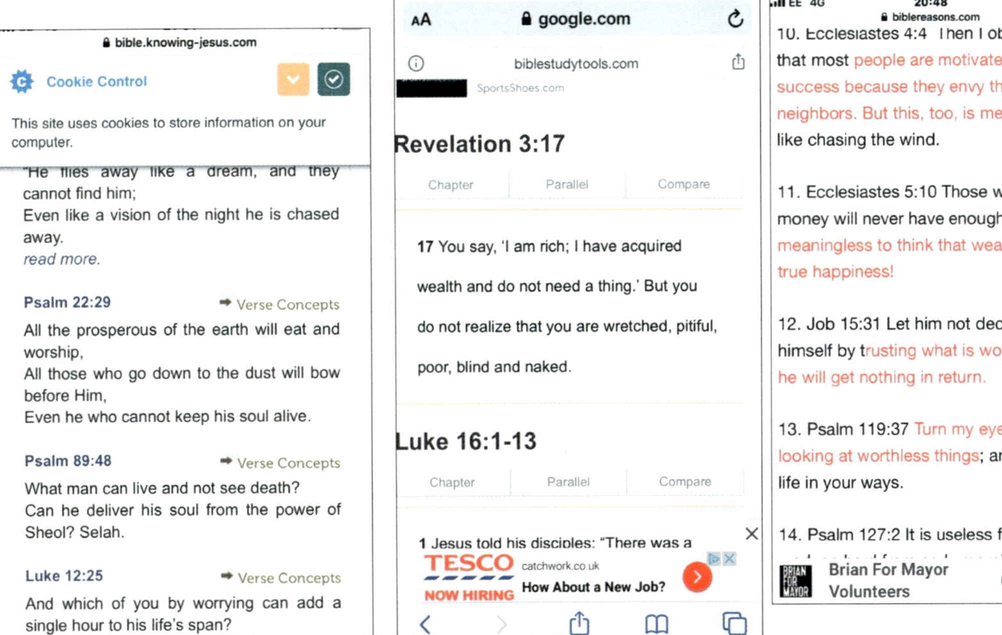

Psalm 103:15-16

As for man, his days are like grass;
As a flower of the field, so he flourishes.
When the wind has passed over it, it is no more,
And its place acknowledges it no longer.

Screenshots of the many Bible verse websites I scoured for suitable quotes for the marketing. I spent hours on these sites while looking for words of wisdom about power, vanity and mortality. I intended to use biblical quotations if challenged about the work. I definitely wanted to project *Father and Son* as a religious artwork.

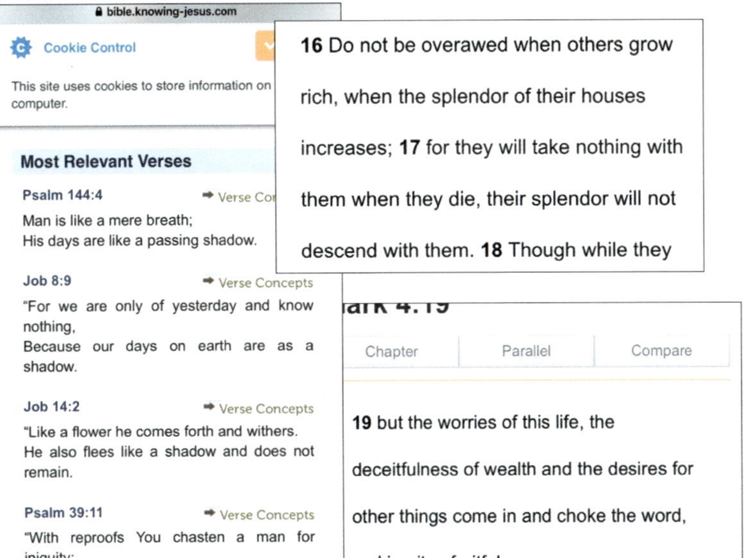

EE 4G 21:15 4%
openbible.info

John 5:19 ESV / 267 helpful votes

So Jesus said to them, "Truly, truly, I say to you, the Son can do nothing of his own accord, but only what he sees the Father doing. For whatever the Father does, that the Son does likewise.

Proverbs 22:6 ESV / 132 helpful votes

Train up a child in the way he should go; even when he is old he will not depart from it.

Malachi 4:5-6 ESV / 96 helpful votes

"Behold, I will send you Elijah the prophet before the great and awesome day of the Lord comes. And he will turn the hearts of fathers to their children and the hearts of children to their fathers, lest I come and strike the land with a decree of utter destruction."

John 3:35 ESV / 70 helpful votes

The Father loves the Son and has given

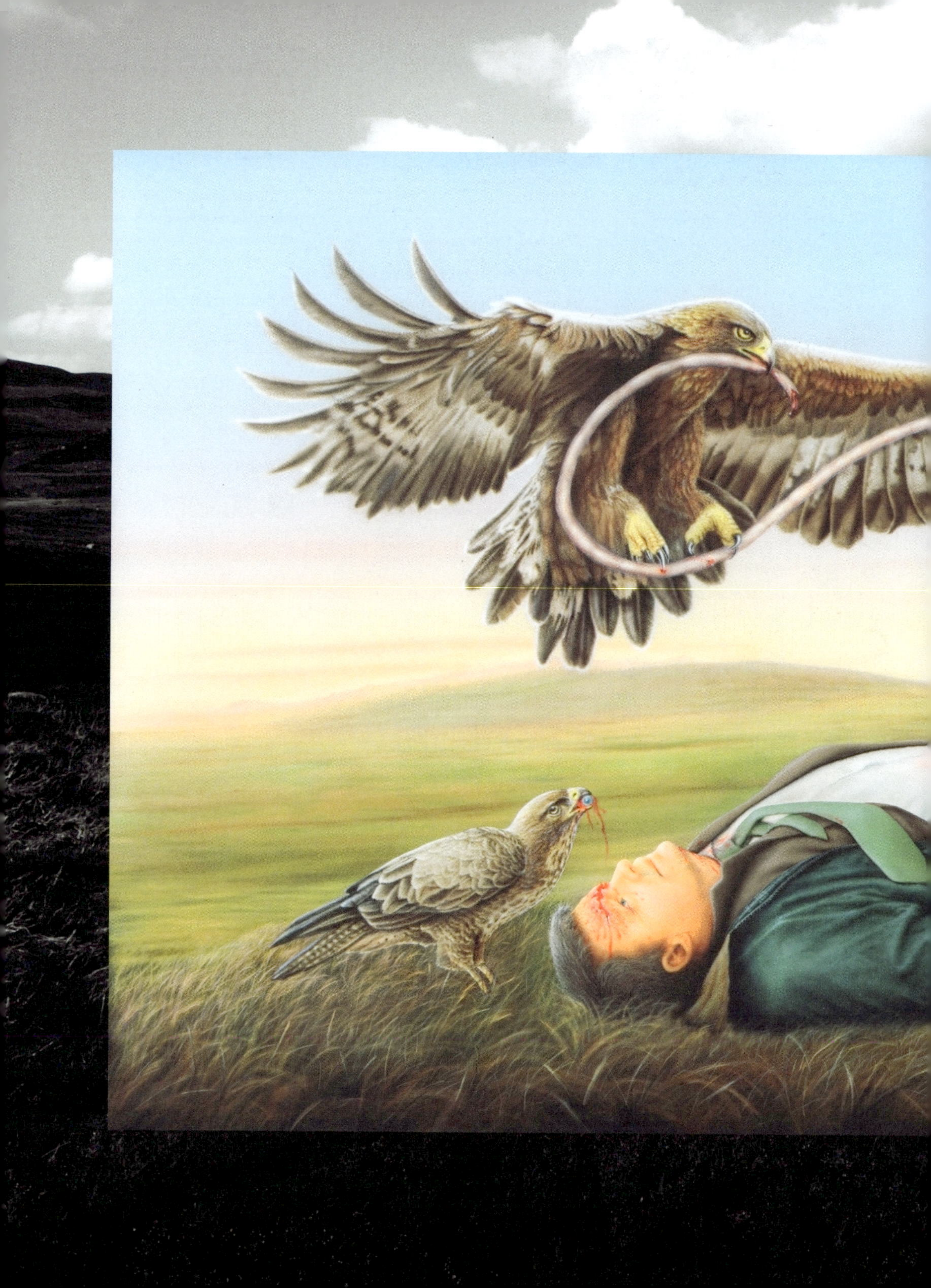

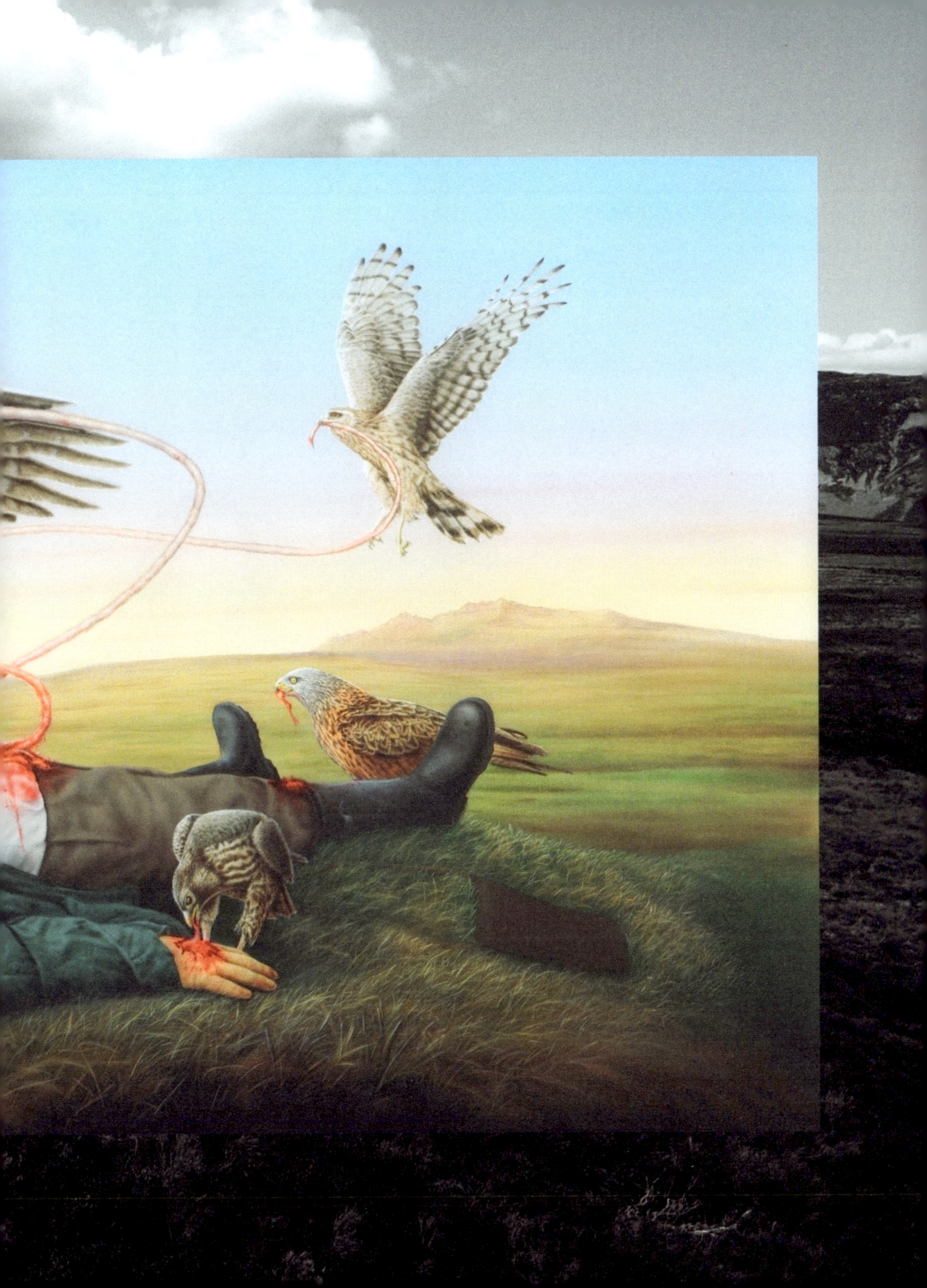

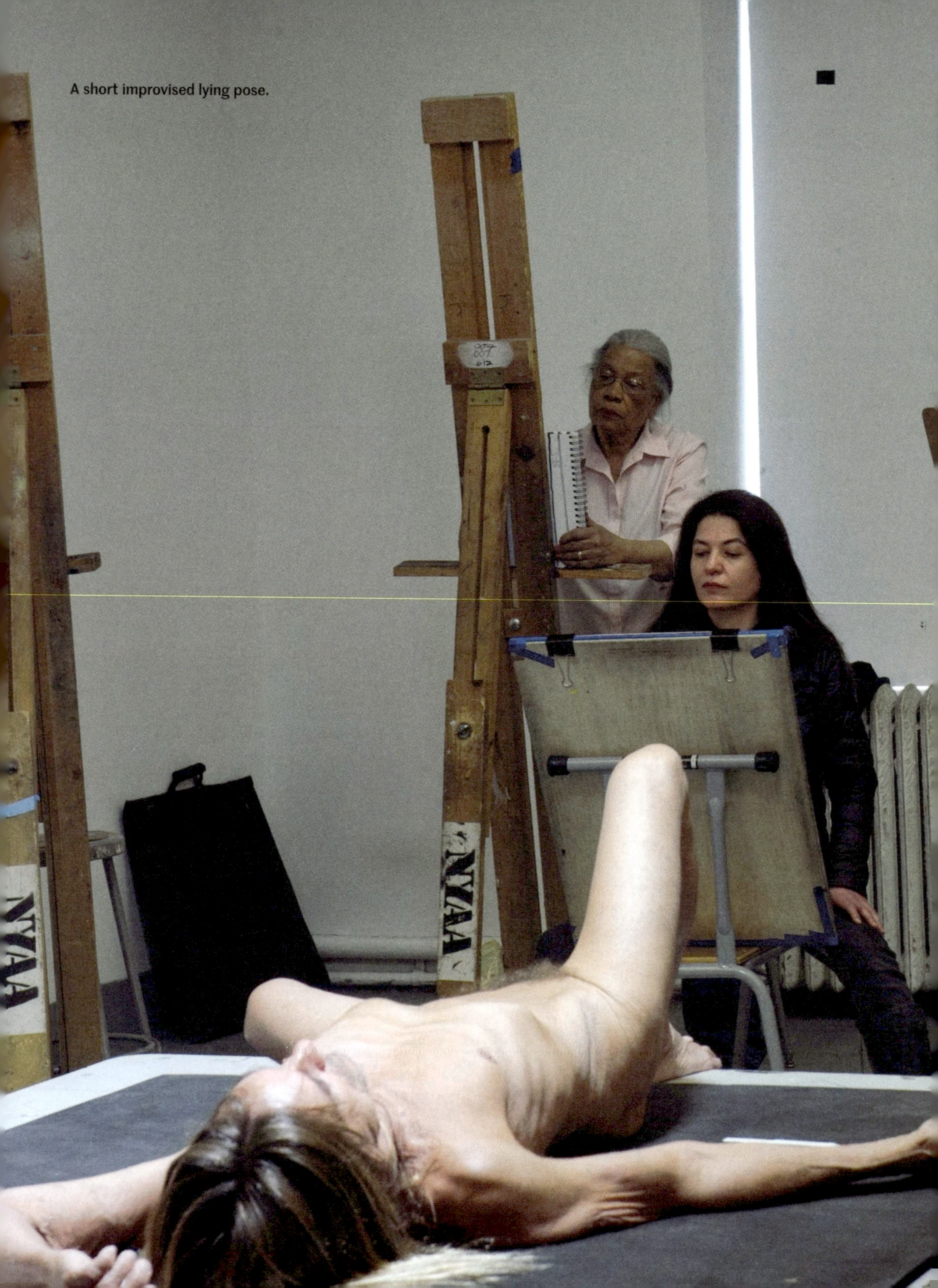

A short improvised lying pose.

Chapter 17

Iggy Pop Life Class

Iggy Pop's body is emblematic of rock 'n' roll. As important as any instrument, it's part of the mythology of popular music. It has borne witness to so much – sex, drugs, self-harm, chaos. We have watched this body age in public over a period of fifty years; few other men in the public eye have allowed us such scrutiny. The art-historical significance of his body fits into the canon of the male nude, somewhere between classical Greek statues and dangerous performance art. I wanted to take his body seriously and document it accordingly, creating a resource for the future, an alternative archive of the most significant male body in music.

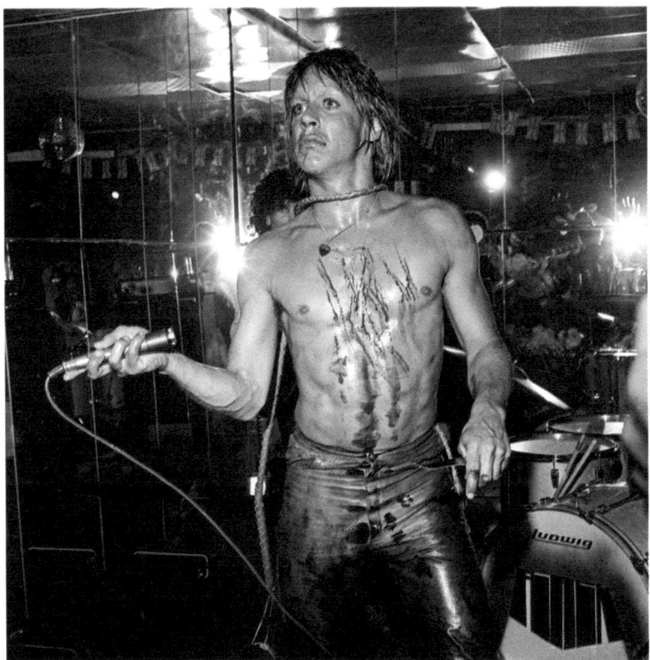

Iggy Pop performing in Los Angeles, 1973. His insistence on semi-nudity and sometimes self-harm places him as much in the tradition of body art performance as it does popular music.

I had the idea for the life class when walking round an installation by the artist Mike Kelley at the Louvre. I asked myself, what would be the most Mike Kelley artwork I could make? By the time I had left the museum, the obvious answer was a life class with Iggy Pop as the model. Like Kelley, Iggy was from the Detroit area. Kelley said that one of the greatest experiences of his life was going to see the Stooges live, in a club full of Michigan biker gangs. Iggy came on stage wearing a dress.

Overtures were made to Iggy in 2007 introducing the idea, and, somewhat remarkably, he did express some interest, though not enough to want to pursue it any further. He was sent some books and enjoyed the *Folk Archive* catalogue. I guess it had elements of ritual, the bizarre, and the unexpected, which must have resonated with him. In 2015, it was suggested I should give the project another go.

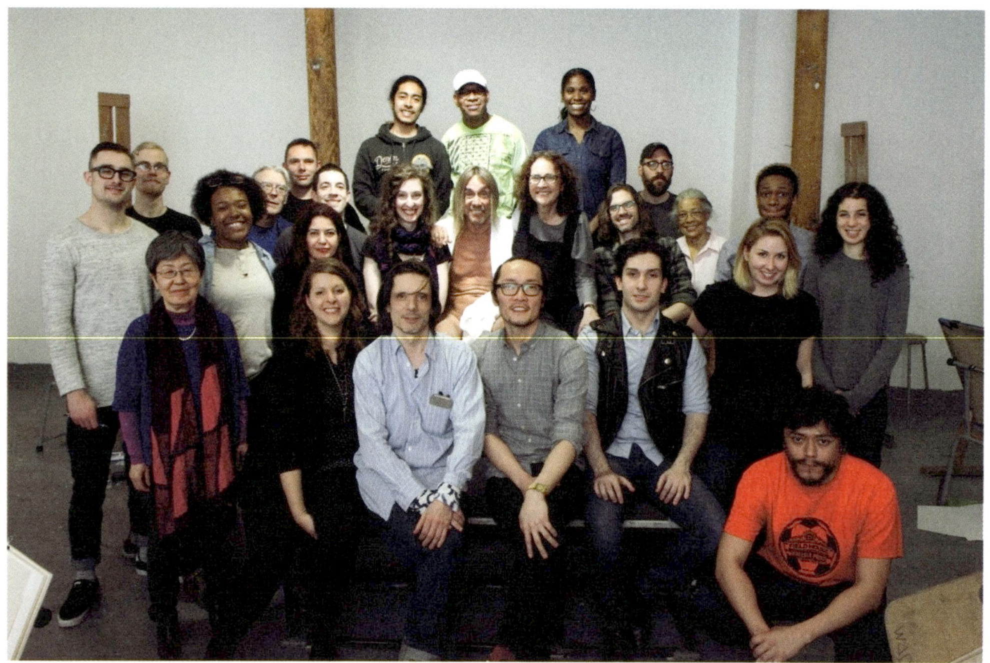

The model and the class, which I wanted to look like a cross-section of America.

By this stage, I had totally written it off – even including it in an exhibition in a section titled 'My Failures'. This time, he emailed back within a day. Things then started to move quickly. It would take place in the United States, and the Brooklyn Museum was the institution I spoke to about hosting it that showed the most enthusiasm. The project had to be aligned with an institution as it needed this recognition and a home after the class. The drawings would then become part of the collection of the host institution automatically. None of the work would find its way onto the market.

Iggy liked the idea that the work was going to be held in Brooklyn, rather than Manhattan. He knew the museum and its collection of African and ancient classical art, some of which were included in the exhibition alongside the drawings.

The plan was to have Iggy provide a range of poses over a four-hour period. In terms of selecting the artists, I worked with the curator Sharon Matt Atkins in reviewing work from art classes around Brooklyn and elsewhere in New York. We settled on twenty participants, from seven colleges, covering a range of experience. They were to be paid $500 for their time and their works, but they didn't know much more about the project than that. We met them the night before the class. They were aged between eighteen and eighty and we felt they represented a broad group of Americans, who would be looking at a fellow American. When I announced the name of the model, about a third knew who he was and got very excited, a third had a vague idea and the rest wondered who the bloke in the photos with his top off was.

On the day itself, the model, unsurprisingly, seemed totally comfortable in his nakedness. All-over tan, no tattoos. Students came in, I did a quick intro and off we went. For most of the session, I sat biting my nails in the corner, not quite believing what was happening. We started with short poses of five and ten minutes, so at least we would have something to show for the day in case he got sick of it and wanted to clear off. We then moved to longer poses. He found standing stationary for a long time quite wearing as one of his legs is slightly shorter than the other on account of arthritis he had as a consequence of the combination of an old sports injury and his exertions on stage.

The long pose was held for about two hours in twenty-minute blocks, with breaks. The model would know to within a few seconds when the session was scheduled to end as, while staying still, he was playing his albums in his head. In this way, he could work out how much time had elapsed. The long pose was seated, quite regal. He remarked that it was similar to that of a painting of Mars by Velázquez in the Prado. For the model, the biggest challenge was not being naked, but remaining still and accepting that he had no control over how he was portrayed. Of the drawings, those he liked the most were ones which were reminiscent of German expressionist art, which didn't idealise him.

There is no film of the class, just a few photographs and of course the drawings themselves. It was effectively a closed set. As soon as the drawings were made, they were taken away by museum staff wearing white gloves and put in portfolios to be accessioned as part of the Brooklyn Museum collection.

Throughout the whole class, I couldn't quite get my head around the fact it was finally happening after all those years. It was a very relaxed, if not studious, atmosphere, rather like that of a library. During the breaks between sittings, Iggy wandered around and chatted to people about their drawings. At one point I asked him why he agreed in 2015 having turned the project down eight years before. He said that at sixty, he was simply too young to be posing naked and being scrutinised.

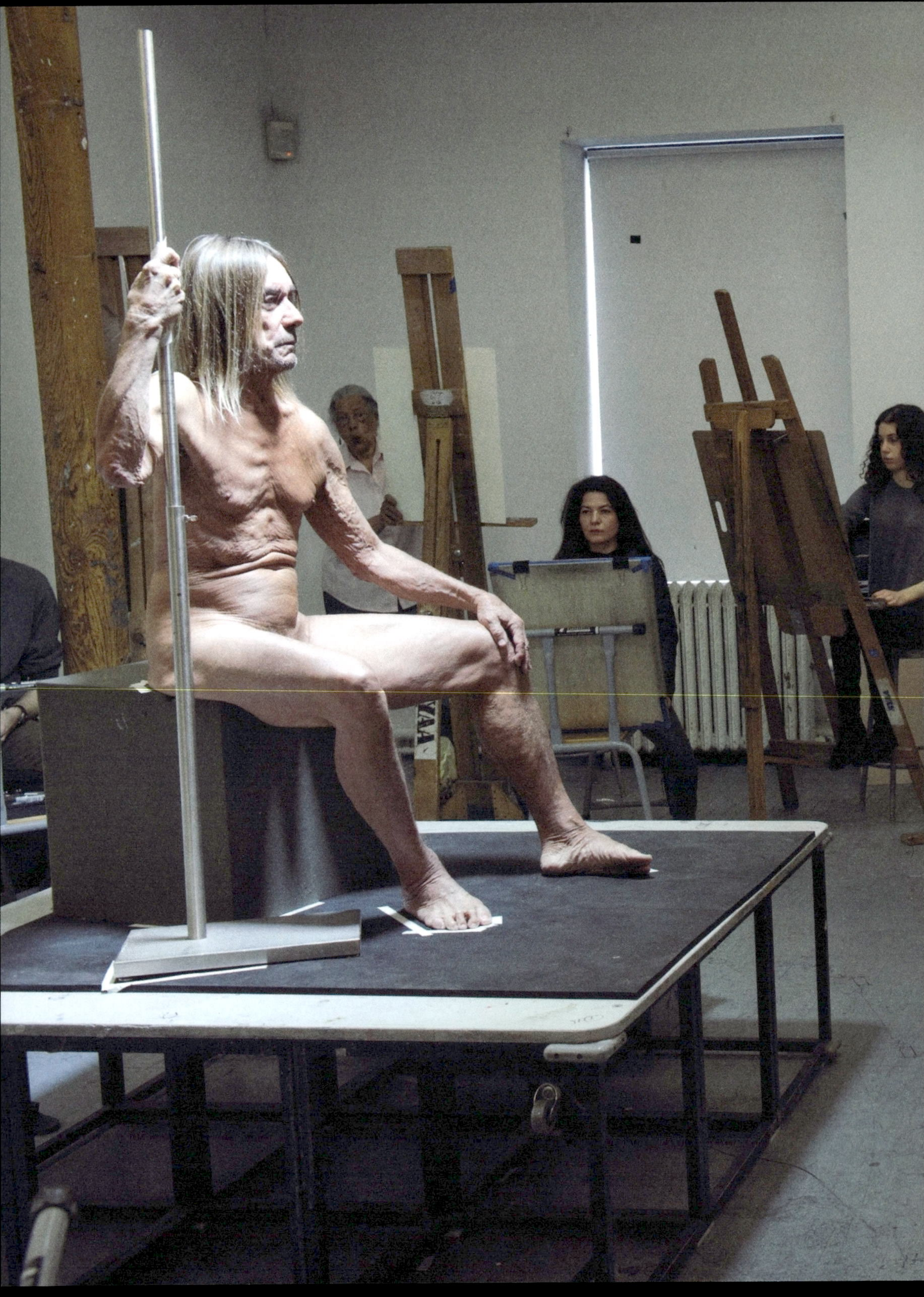

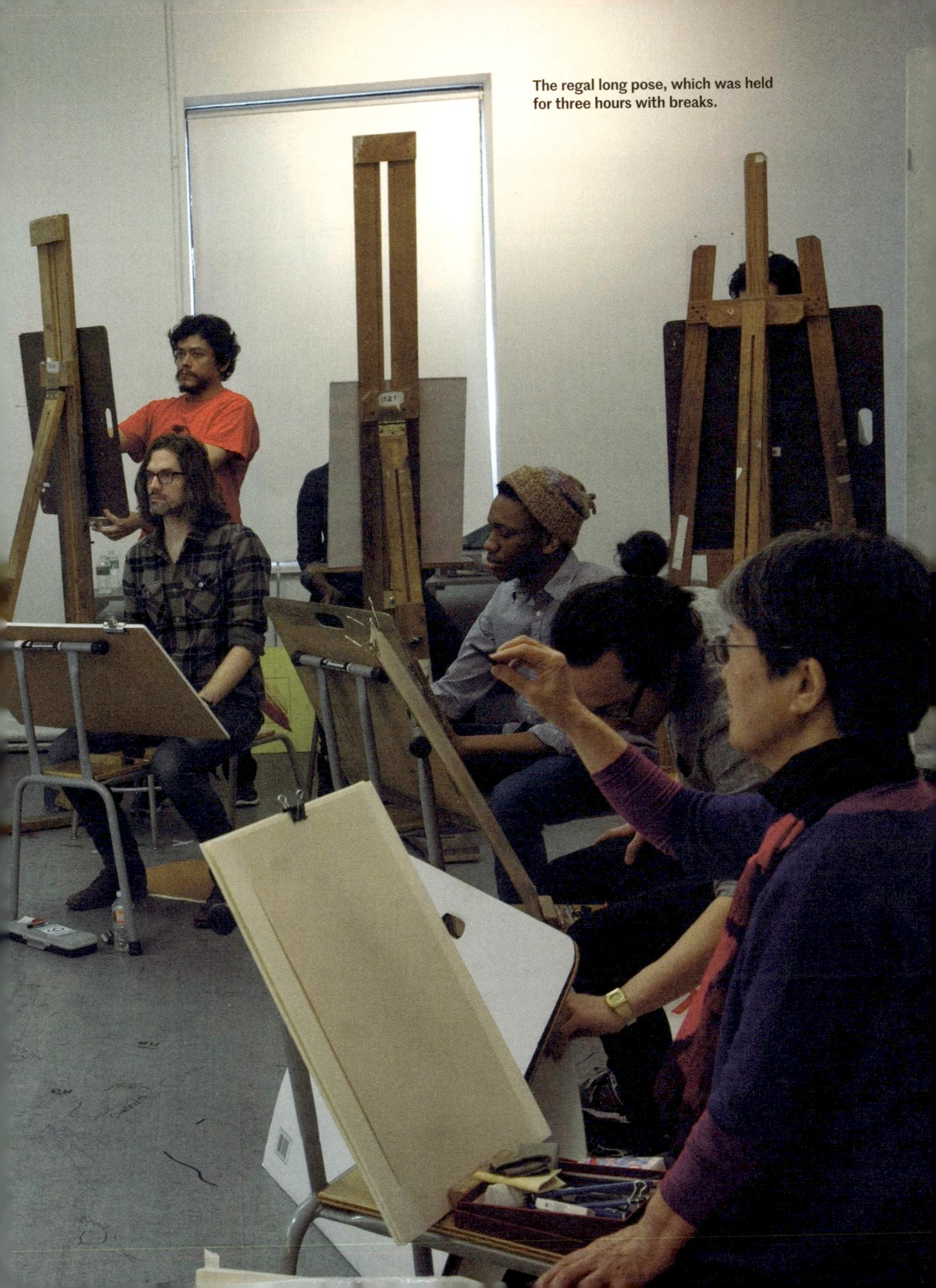

The regal long pose, which was held for three hours with breaks.

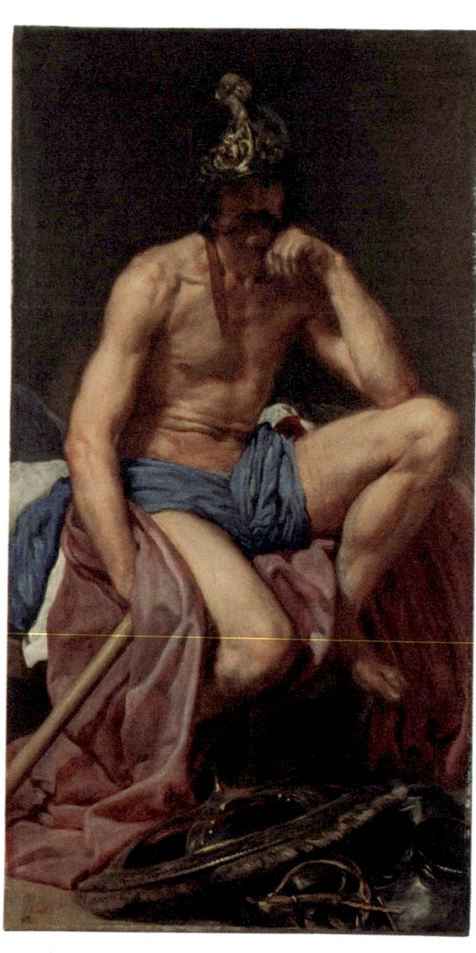

Mars by Velázquez, 1640, Museo del Prado, Madrid.

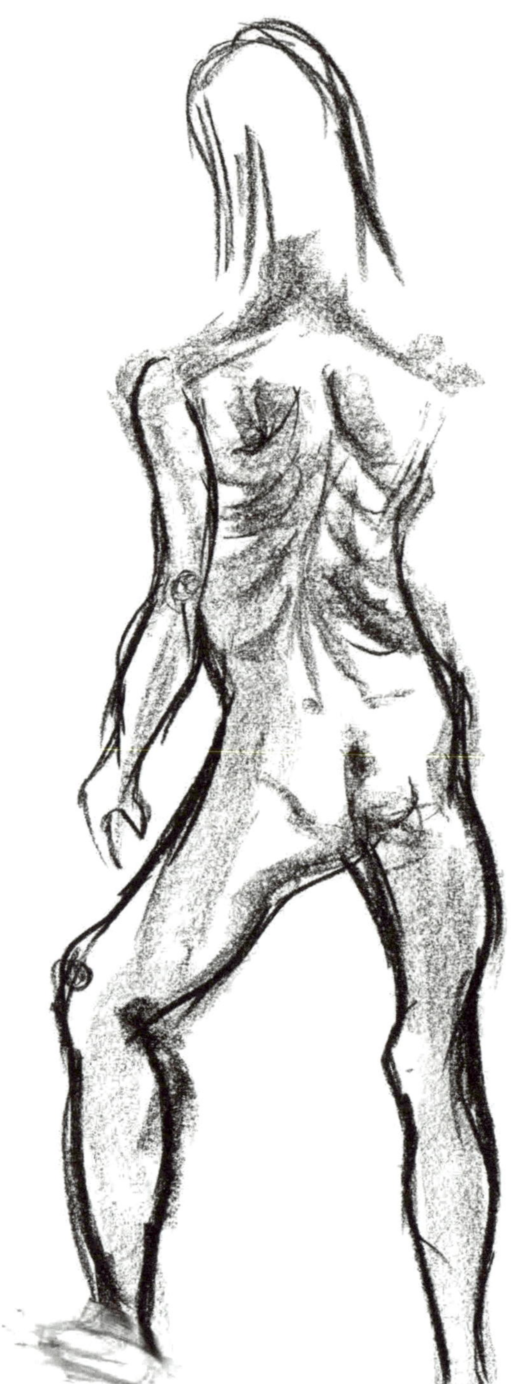

This drawing by Kalliyah Merilus, a novice, was one of our favourites. Unidealised, it has a German expressionist feel to it, which is no bad thing.

The installation of the drawings in 2016 at the Brooklyn Museum had to be old school. The artworks were shown alongside exhibits from the Museum collection, depicting 2,000 years of the male nude.

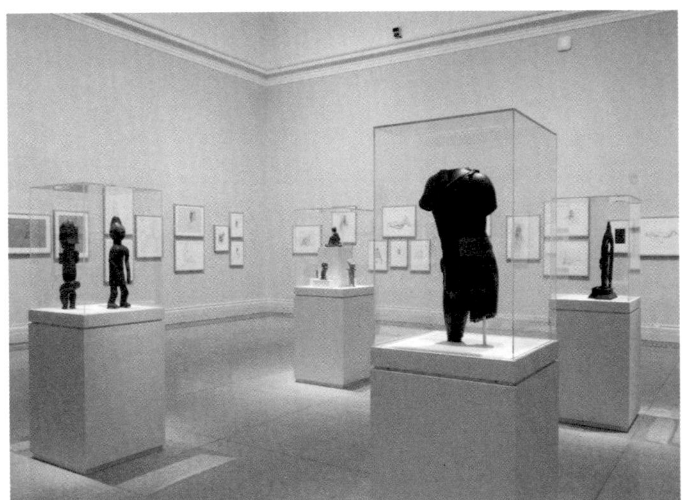

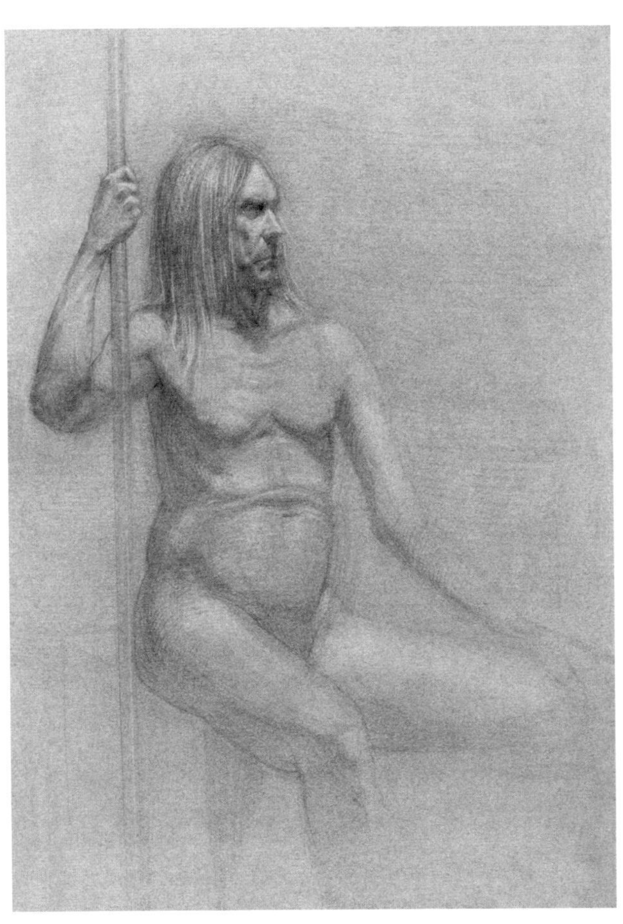

Long pose drawing by Taylor Schultek.

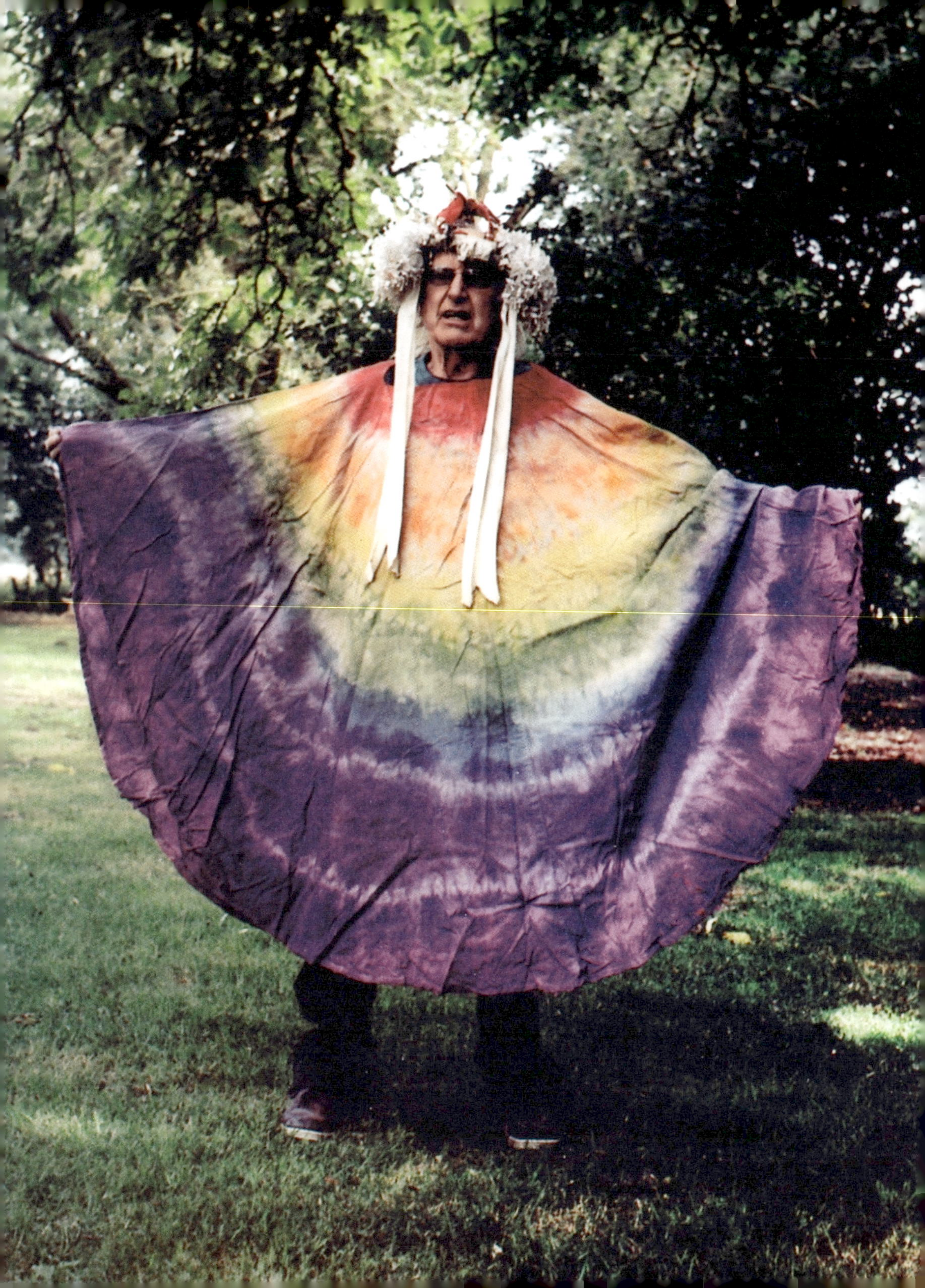

Chapter 18

Lest I forget

Some work I managed to miss out in the excitement and the chaos of putting the hardback together

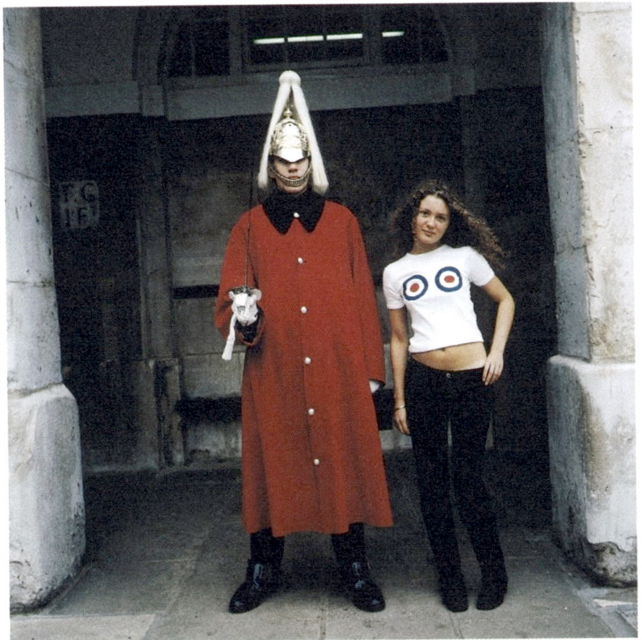

T-shirts. Between 1993 and 1996 I was the 'shop boy' at Sign of the Times, a clubbers' boutique and all-round pre-internet meeting place. I started making T-shirts to be sold in the shop as a way to get ideas out. There is a democratic element to T-shirts which appealed to me. I loved the random nature of selling the shirts as they would literally have a life of their own once bought, a mix of kinetic and public art moving through space.

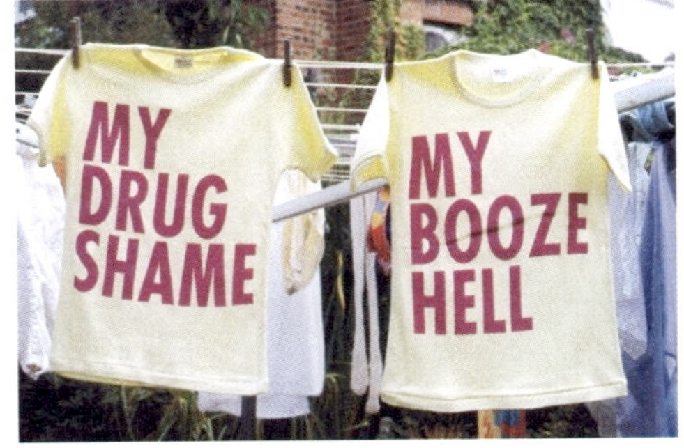

My most successful shirts were two that poked fun at tabloid shaming. They were most often worn on hedonistic nights out, which was sort of the point.

← The artist Bruce Lacey had an incredible decade-spanning career that incorporated, among other things, anti-establishment satire, robotics, children's happenings and mystic performances. In a sense he was a punk twenty years before it had been named. His story is almost one of the UK itself and it tries to work out its history and future. Nick Abrahams and I made a quite chaotic film about him. Here he is pictured in his garden with costumes for rituals he made with his wife at the time, Jill Smith.

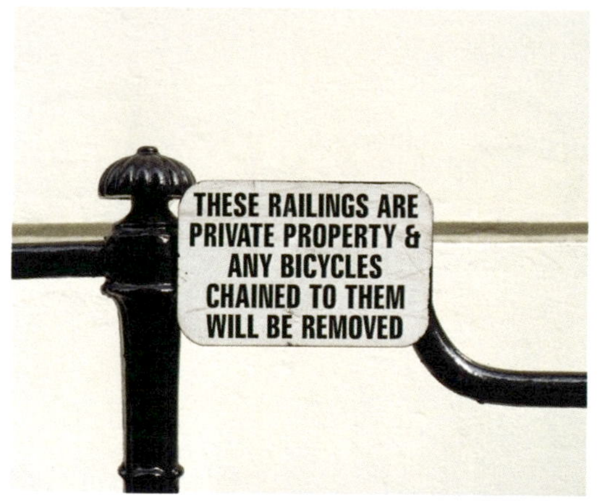

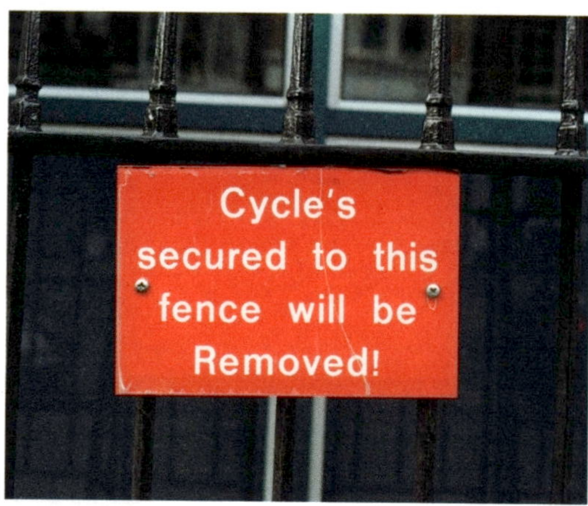

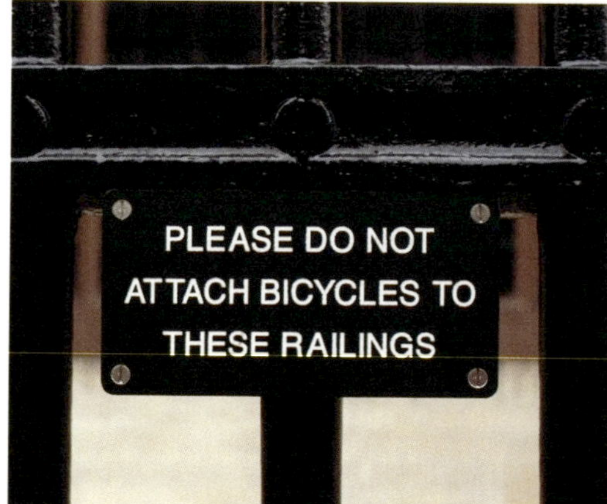

The War on Terror, 2006. Signs like this are all over the City of London and inevitably the more wealthy parts of the capital.

Barbeque Summer, 2007.
The damage done by disposable barbeques in my local park obsessed me for a time – they remind me of Constructivist paintings, and also of satellite images of environmental destruction. I wondered what, if anything, went through the barbequers' minds when they saw what they had done.

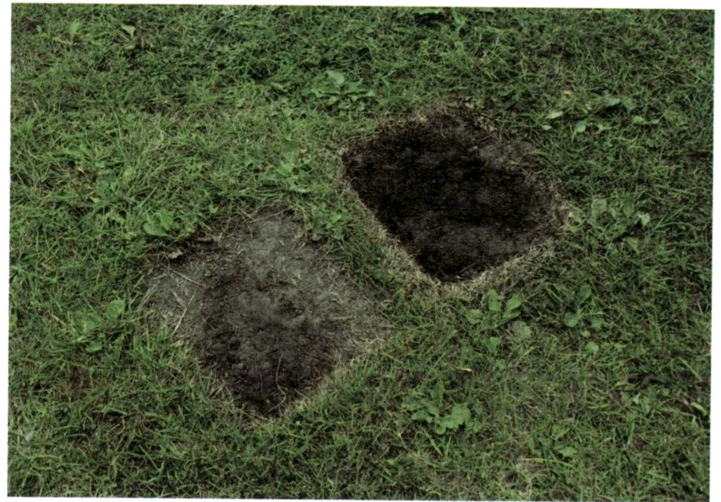

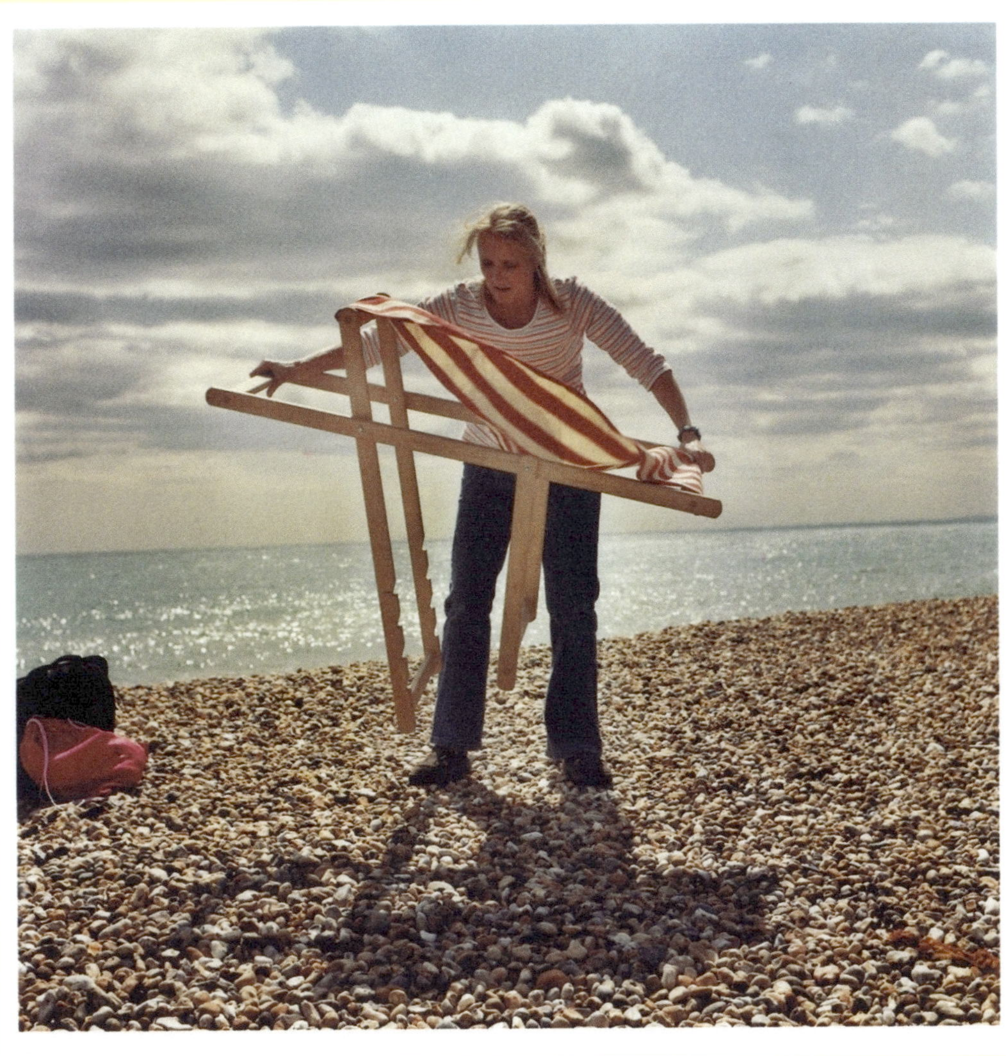

Risk Assessment, 2007. Made for the Folkestone Triennial, this was a series of random encounters for the public with a group of locals trained in slapstick interventions, tripping over, getting tangled in a deckchair and struggling to read a newspaper in the wind. Like so much of performance art, it was an homage to early cinema.

Procession, 2009

I was asked to make a public artwork for the Manchester International Festival and I thought a procession would be a good way to tell a story about or at least project a town in a fantastical way.

I'd always liked seeing town parades in *The Simpsons* and wanted to make something as entertainingly odd as those. There were about twenty or so elements, including a funeral cortege for deceased nightclubs, a group of former millworkers (the last of the Industrial Revolution), *Big Issue* sellers, some local goths who hung around Cathedral Gardens, and a working replica of Valerie's Cafe from Bury Market. There was a lot of music: a local goth band, a Sikh bagpipe band and Steel Harmony, a local steel band that played cover versions of Manchester classics including 'Ever Fallen in Love (With Someone You Shouldn't've)' by Buzzcocks.

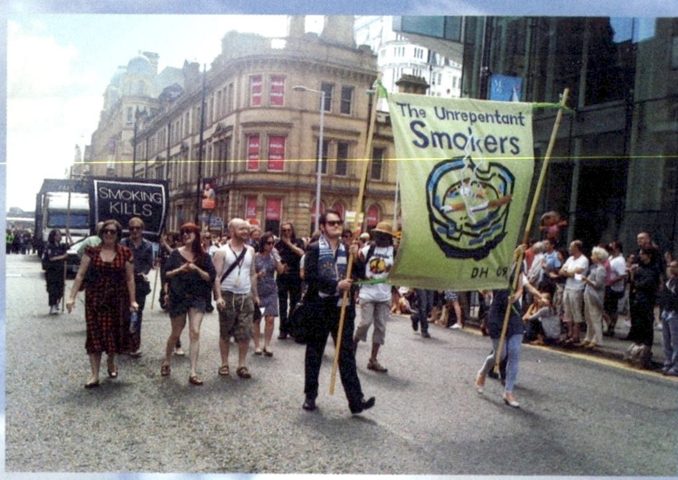

The Unrepentant Smokers proved to be controversial participants with their David Hockney-designed banner (made by Ed Hall). A councillor got on his very high horse and tried to cancel the whole event; in the end we compromised and had a second banner that read 'Smoking Kills' follow the group.

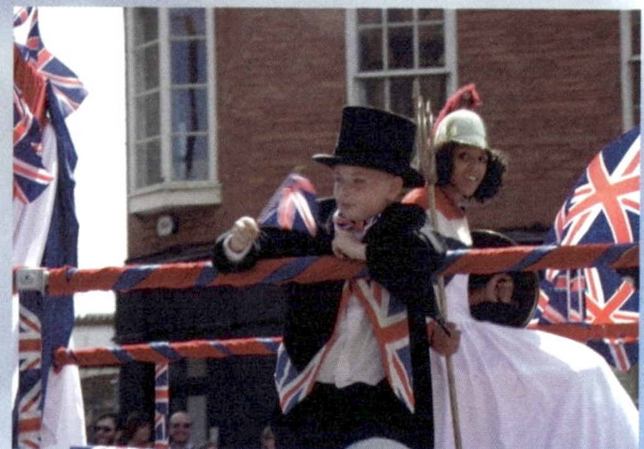

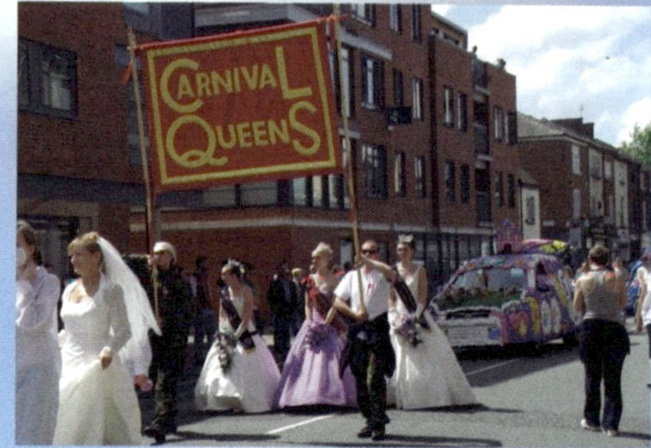

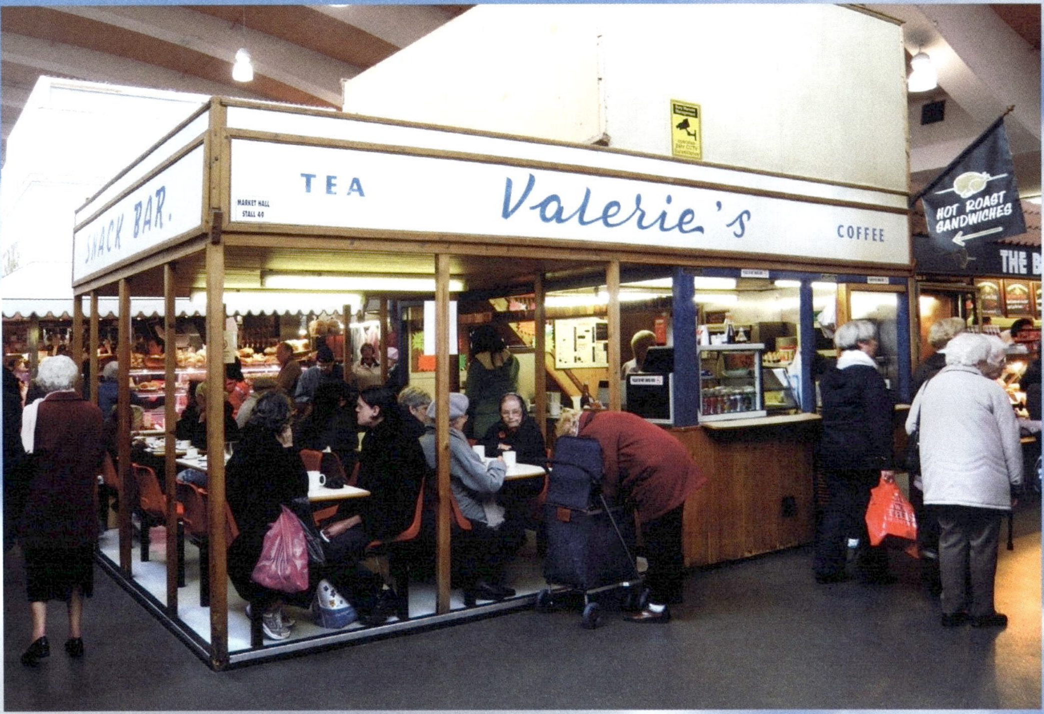

SNACK BAR.
MARKET HALL
STALL 40
TEA
Valerie's
COFFEE
HOT ROAST
SANDWICHES
TEA 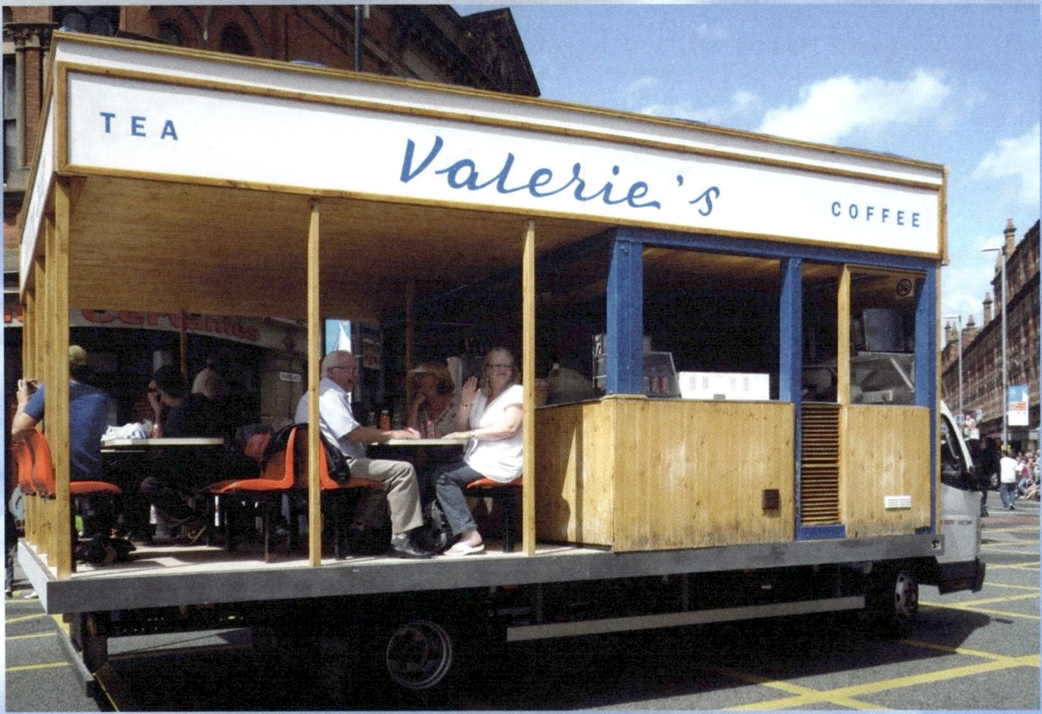
Valerie's
COFFEE

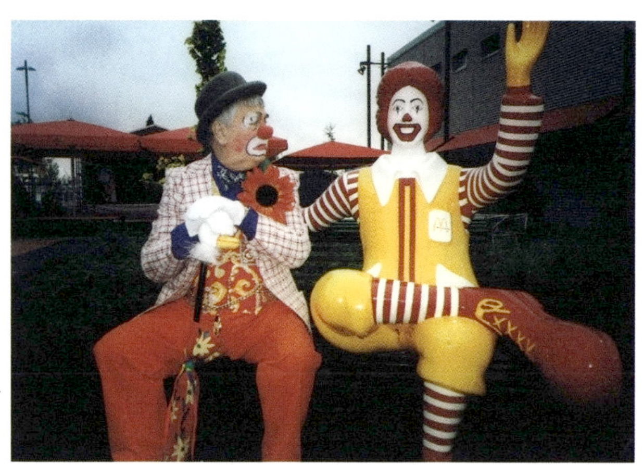

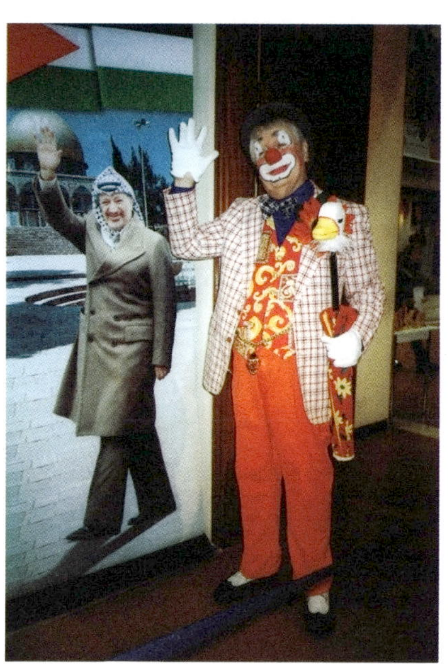

Has the World Changed or Have I Changed? I spent a very tiring day at the World's Fair in Hanover with a clown in 2000: I was trying to see the world through his eyes as he sought to make sense of the world. He hated Ronald McDonald – 'not a real clown'.

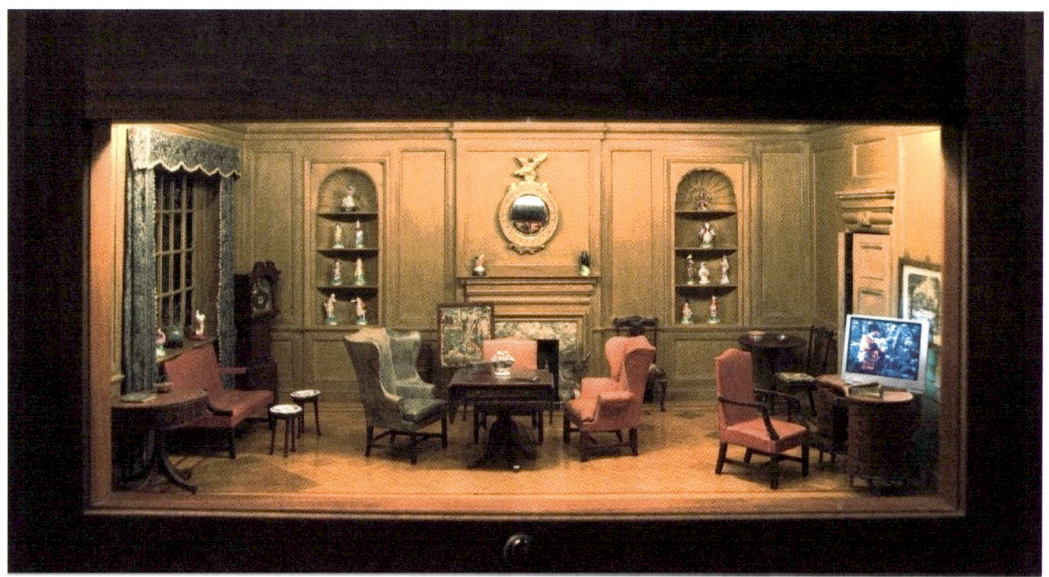

Breaking News, 2004. Possibly the world's smallest video installation. It was made for a series of historically accurate miniature interiors at the Carnegie Museum in Pittsburgh. I filmed battle re-enactments that related to the rooms' era and put them on tiny screens in the spaces as if it was the news.

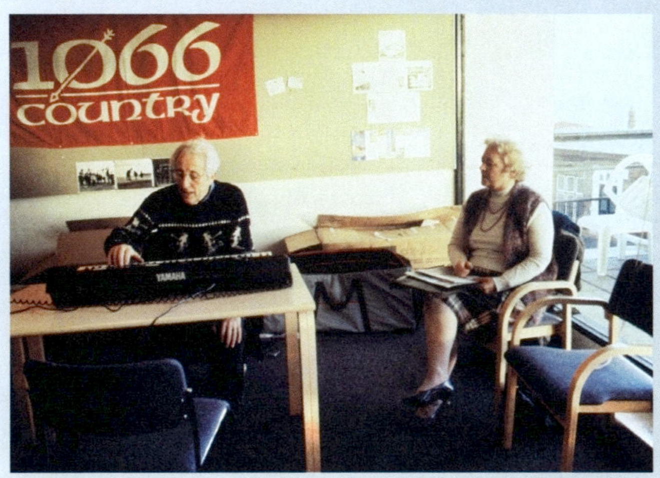

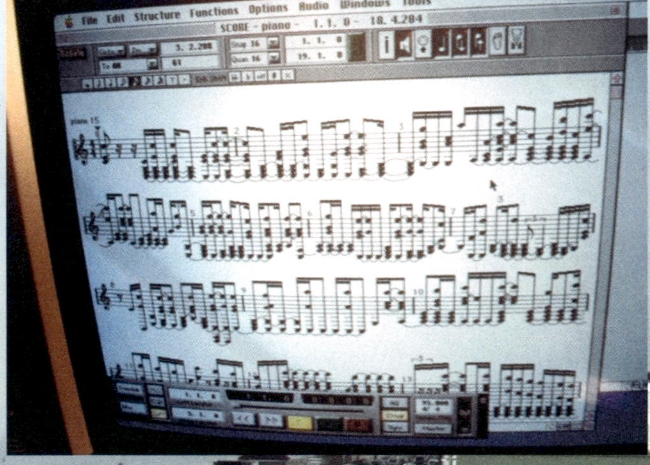

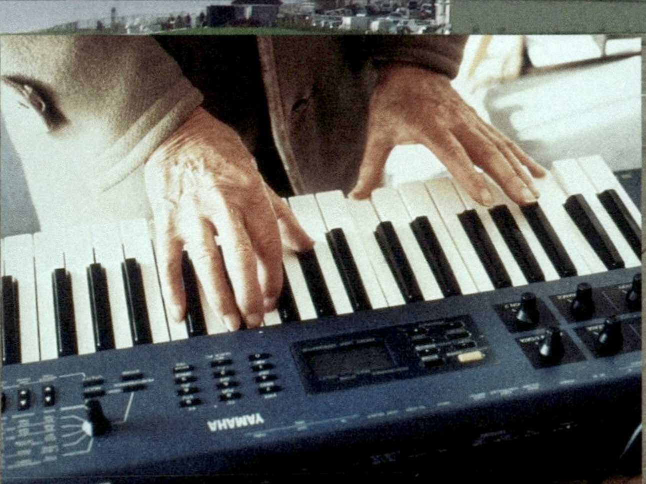

'We are the mods, we are the mods, we are, we are, we are the mods.' In 1998 I set up a recording studio in the De La Warr Pavilion in Bexhill-on-Sea, a Modernist masterpiece. I then invited retirees to try out the samplers and synths. I wanted the technology of dance music to be used in different ways; I also suspected it would be visually interesting.

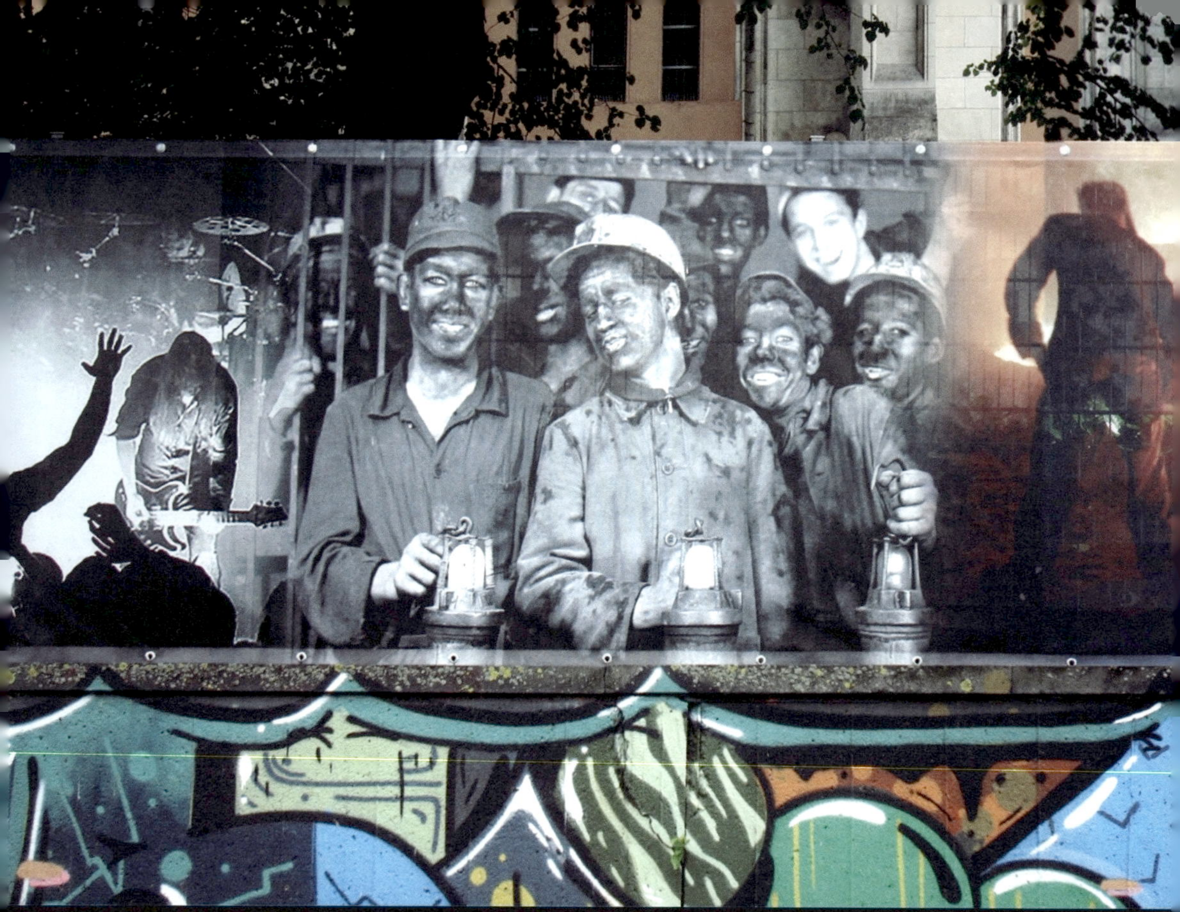

The Folkwang Museum in Essen celebrated its centenary in 2022 and I made a few works for a public project in the town. One was to offer free tattoos of some of their masterpiece expressionist woodcuts by Ernst Ludwig Kirchner and Erich Heckel; the imagery of these artworks seemed to work well on bodies. Another piece, *Hard Work*, was a long frieze-like banner combining imagery of the town's industrial and heavy metal heritage.

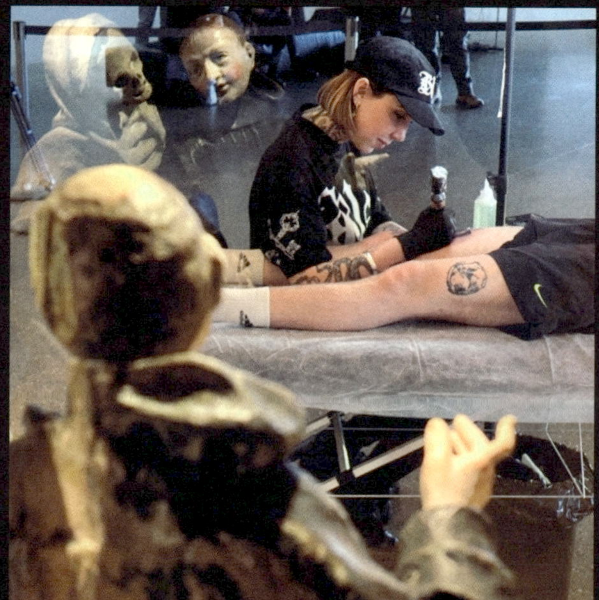

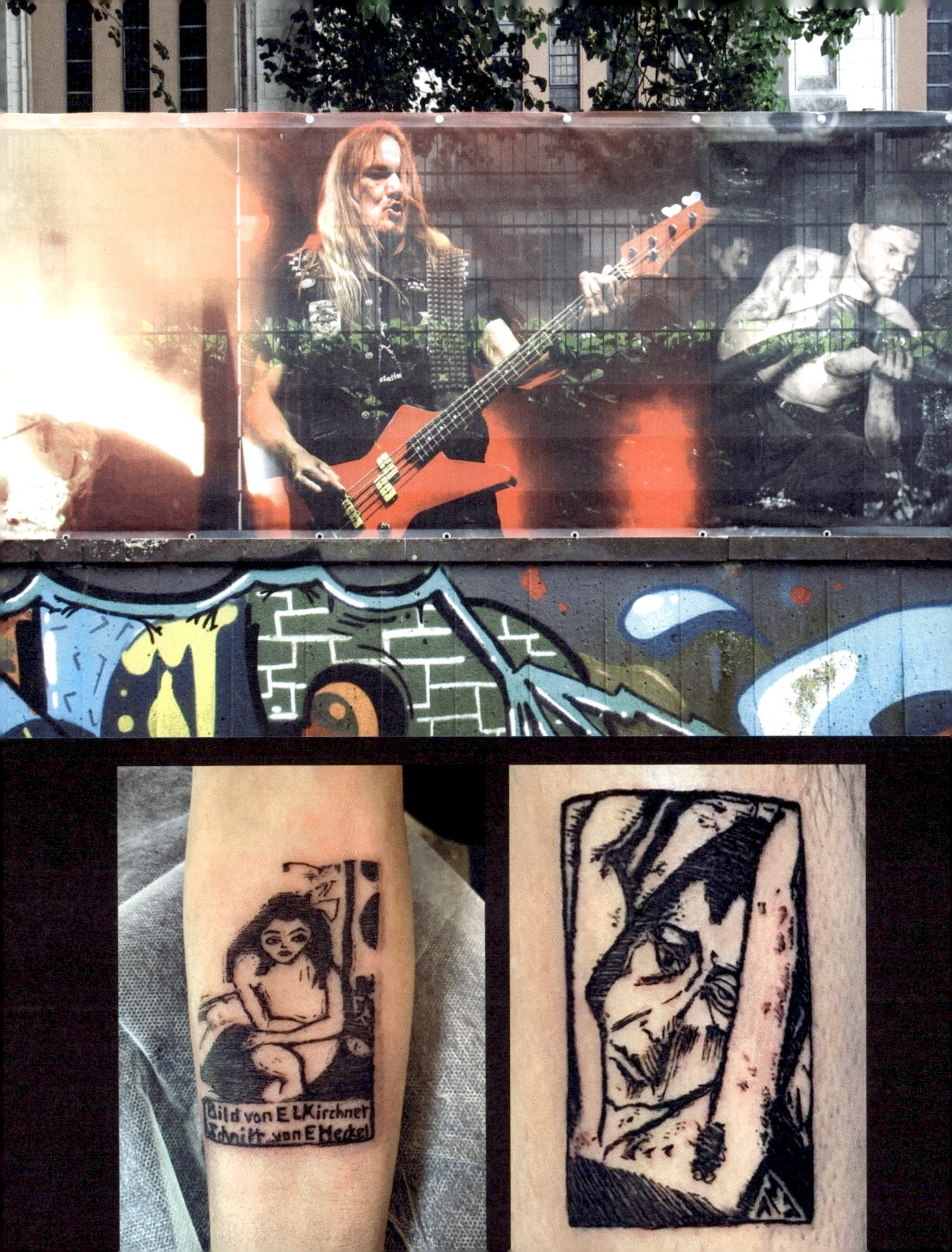
Bild von E L Kirchner
Schnitt von E Heckel

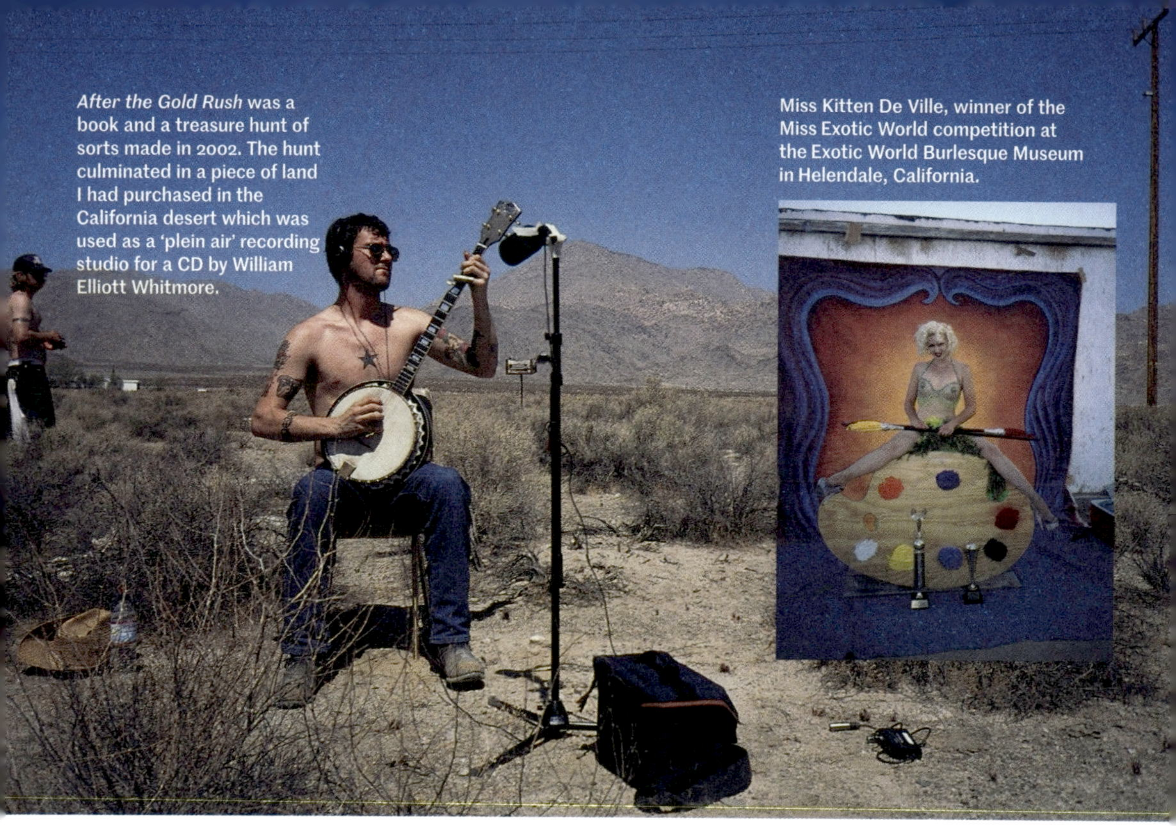

After the Gold Rush was a book and a treasure hunt of sorts made in 2002. The hunt culminated in a piece of land I had purchased in the California desert which was used as a 'plein air' recording studio for a CD by William Elliott Whitmore.

Miss Kitten De Ville, winner of the Miss Exotic World competition at the Exotic World Burlesque Museum in Helendale, California.

Mission Accomplished, 2004. A 1:1 scale facsimile of the banner that hung behind George W. Bush on the USS *Abraham Lincoln* on 1 May 2003 when he declared that combat operations were over in Iraq, when in actual fact they had only just begun. It was originally meant to be attached to the exterior of a museum in 2004 but it seemed too soon to be doing that sort of thing. I was hoping it would go on a tour of the US. Here it ended up in PS1 in New York seven years later.

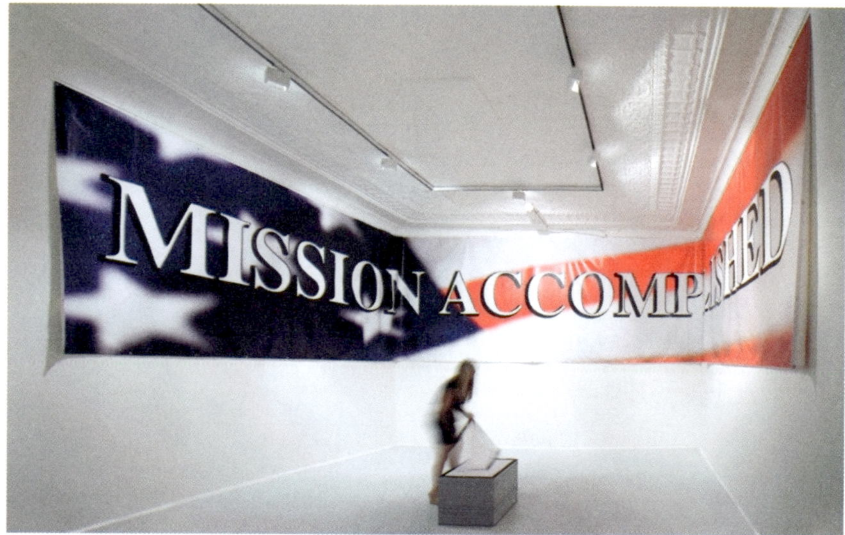

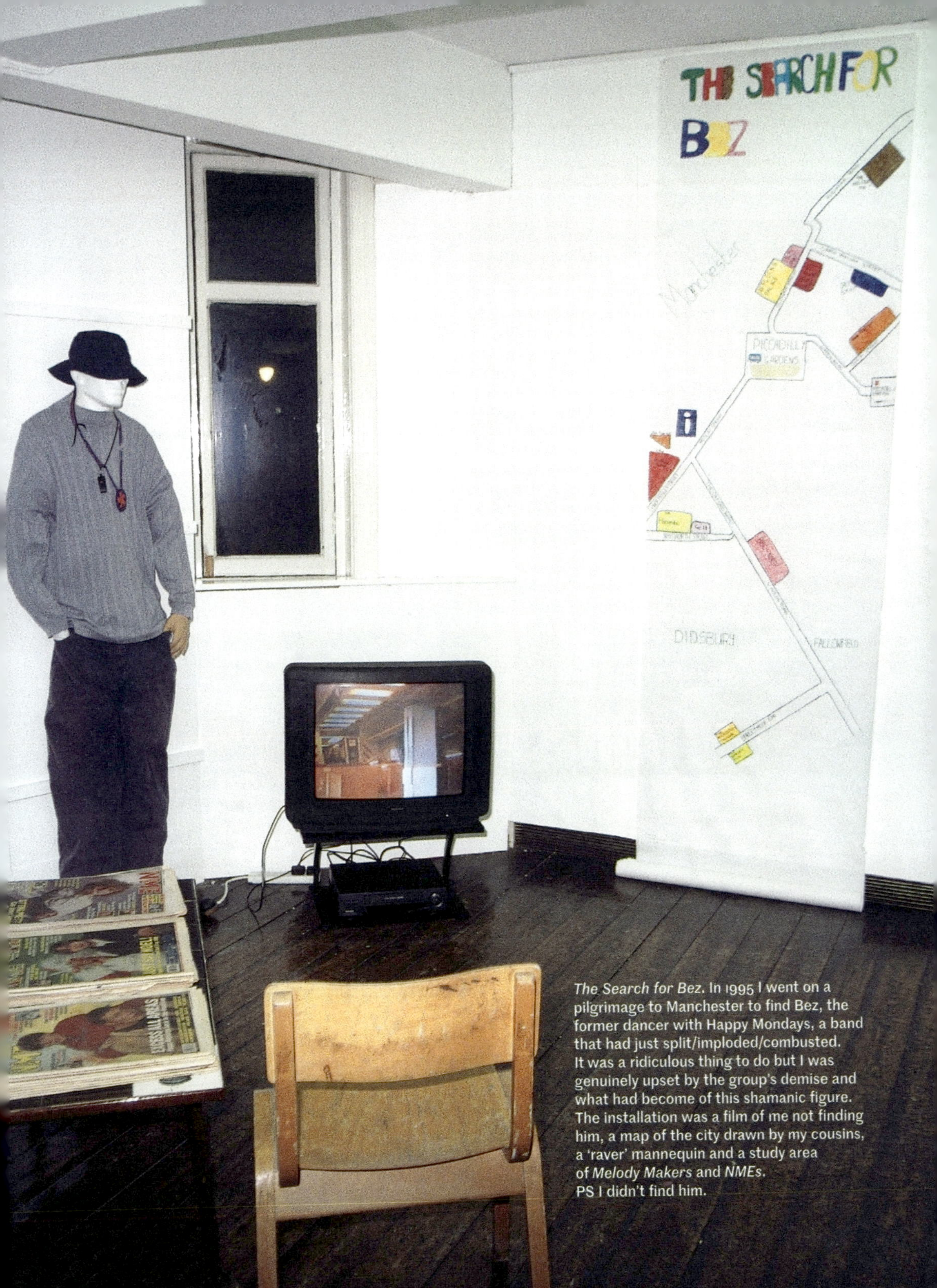

The Search for Bez. In 1995 I went on a pilgrimage to Manchester to find Bez, the former dancer with Happy Mondays, a band that had just split/imploded/combusted. It was a ridiculous thing to do but I was genuinely upset by the group's demise and what had become of this shamanic figure. The installation was a film of me not finding him, a map of the city drawn by my cousins, a 'raver' mannequin and a study area of *Melody Makers* and *NMEs*.
PS I didn't find him.

Karl Marx at Christmas. For some of his time in London Marx lived with his family in a small room in Soho. In December 2000, I was asked to make a work close to this location. I thought why not have the philosopher give each visitor to the opening a chance to meet him and receive a Marxist Christmas card. Geoff the KM lookalike appeared as Santa in an ad the following year.

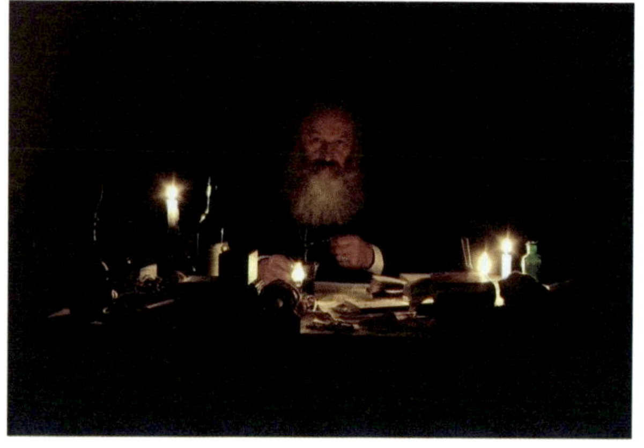

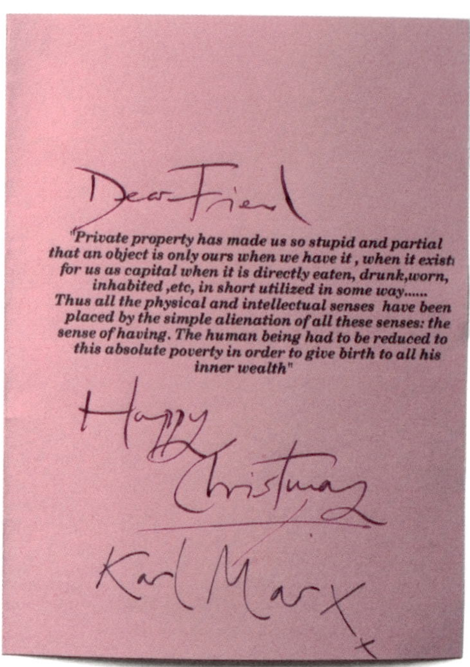

Dear Friend

"Private property has made us so stupid and partial that an object is only ours when we have it , when it exists for us as capital when it is directly eaten, drunk,worn, inhabited ,etc, in short utilized in some way...... Thus all the physical and intellectual senses have been placed by the simple alienation of all these senses: the sense of having. The human being had to be reduced to this absolute poverty in order to give birth to all his inner wealth"

Happy Christmas

Karl Marx
x

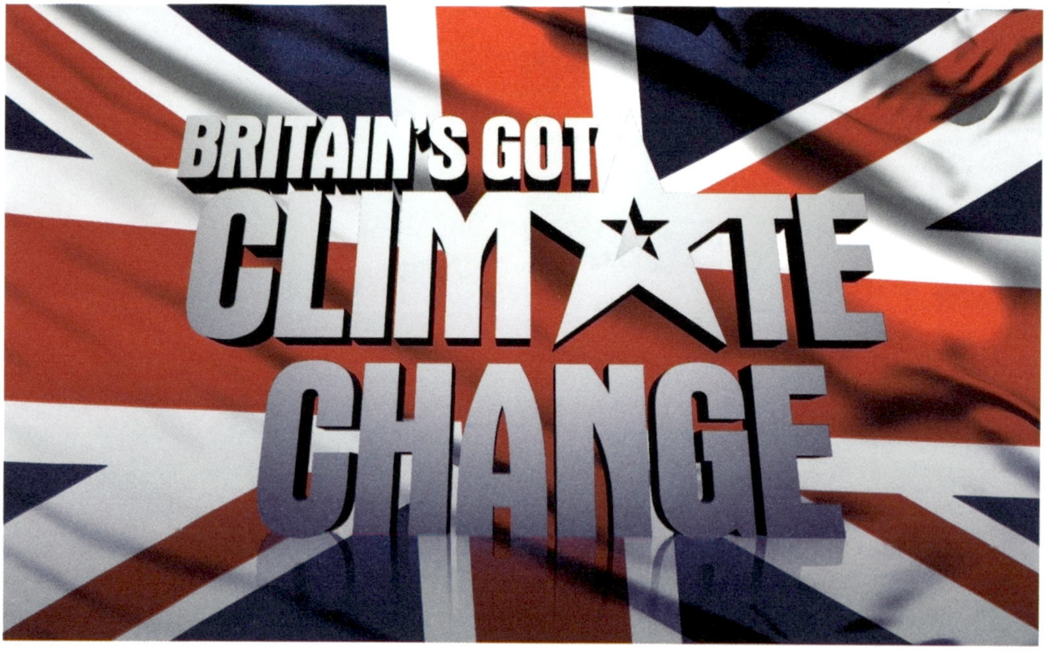

Britain's Got Climate Change, 2023. Self-explanatory pop appropriation. Would make a good animation.

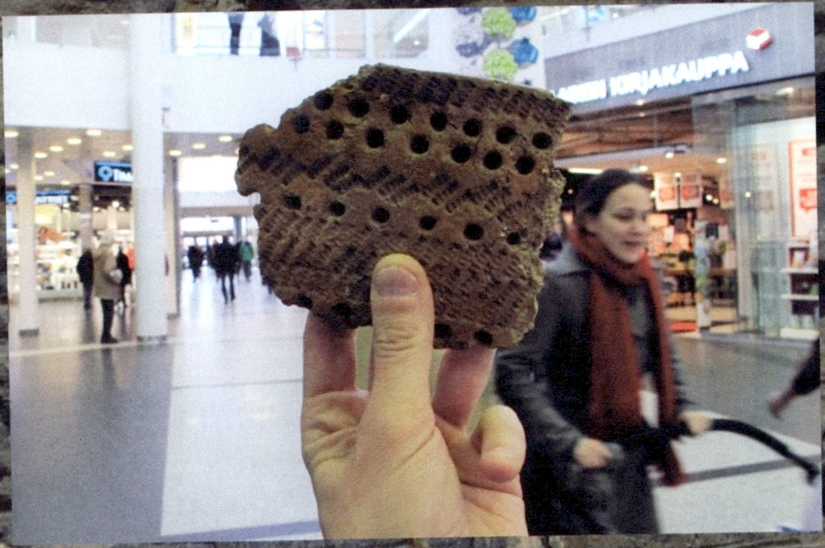

Do Touch was an unexpected encounter for Helsinki residents with objects from museums in their city organised in 2014. Shoppers and commuters were encouraged to handle the objects which ranged from fake Viagra from the Customs Museum to a meteorite fragment.

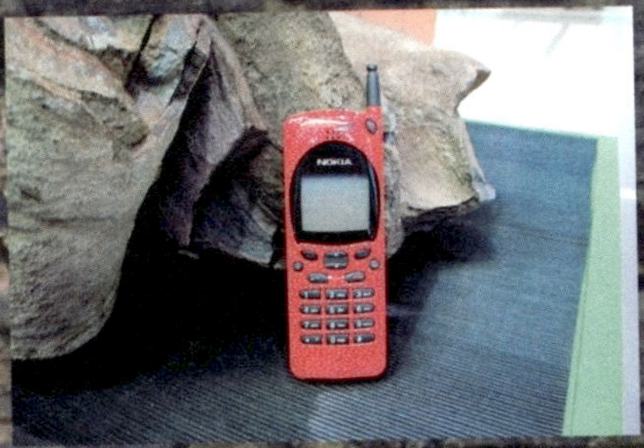

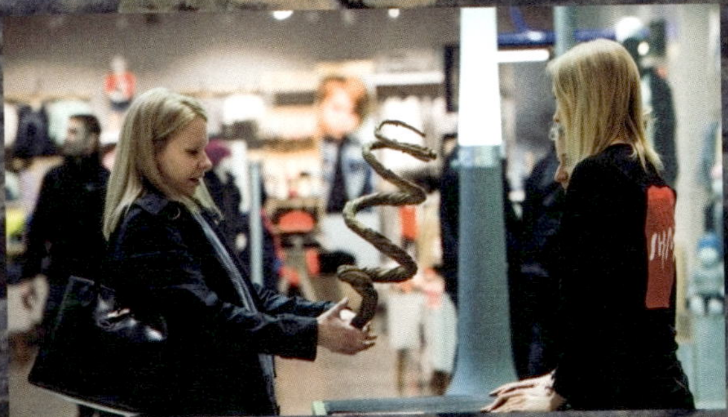

This object is a springy screw that was used in shipbuilding.

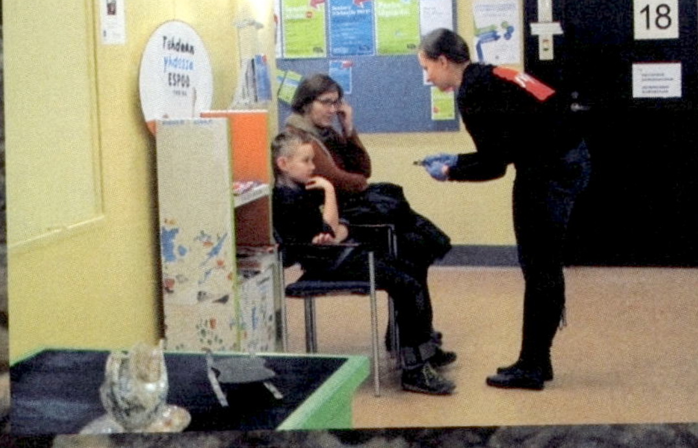

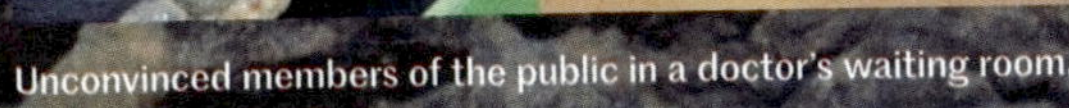
Unconvinced members of the public in a doctor's waiting room.

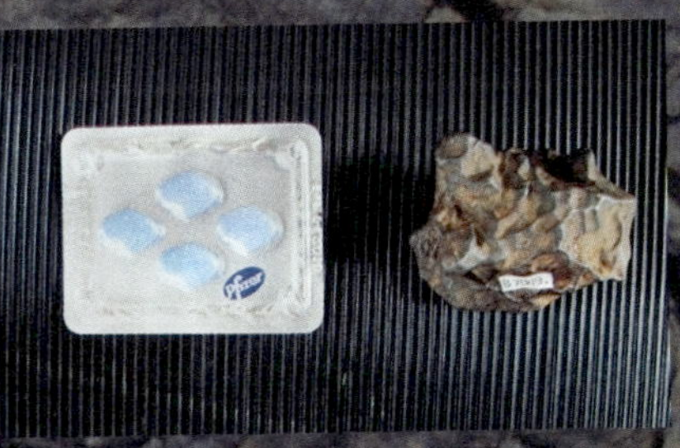

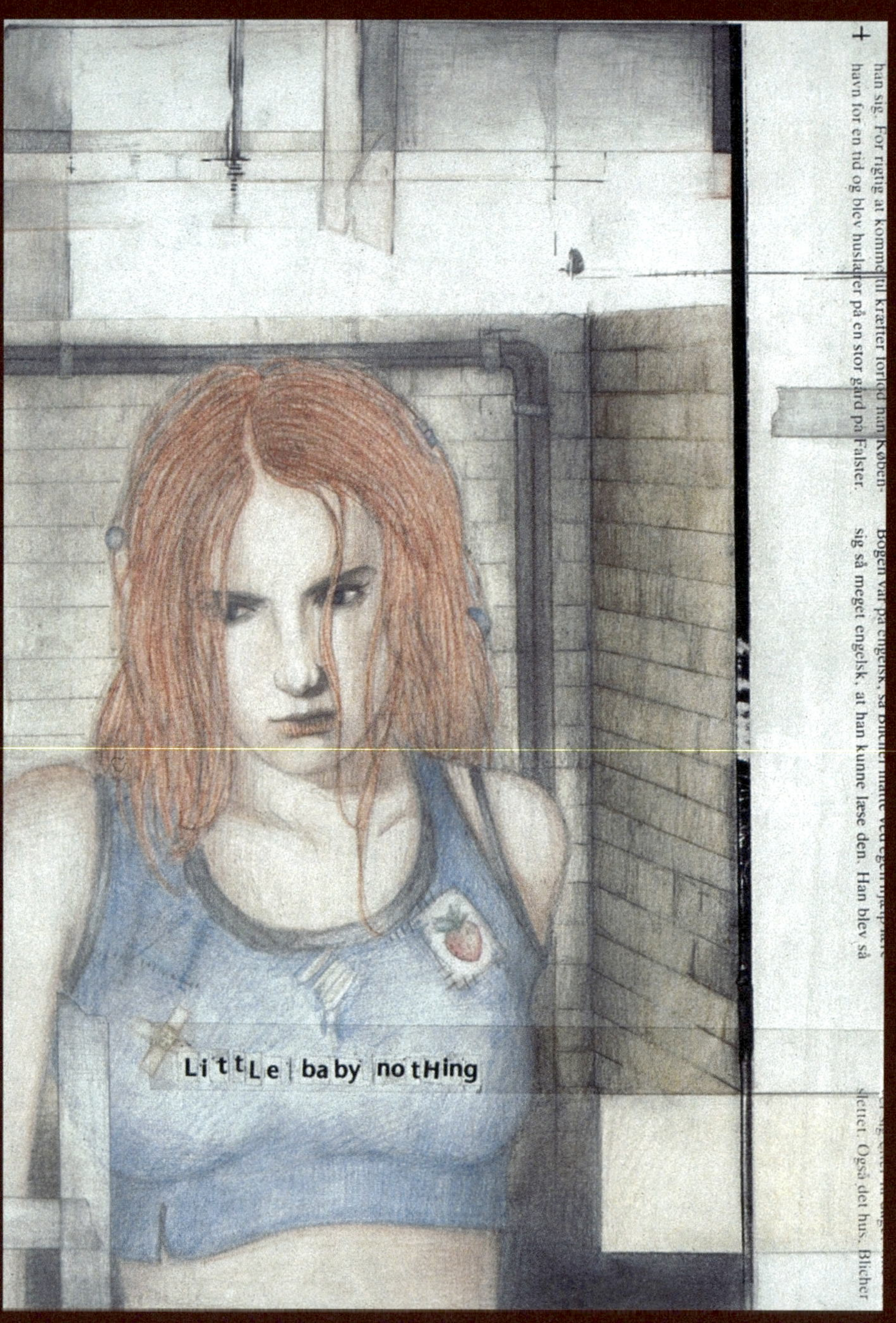

The Uses of Literacy was an exhibition of artwork made by fans of the rock group Manic Street Preachers in 1997. As I suspected, the band (especially at this point in their career) had fans who were artistic and receptive to being creative with their idols. I gave flyers out at a concert to ask for submissions and word quickly spread among fan groups. The final exhibition was a display of devotional teenage folk art, like the above drawing by Lotte Petersen.

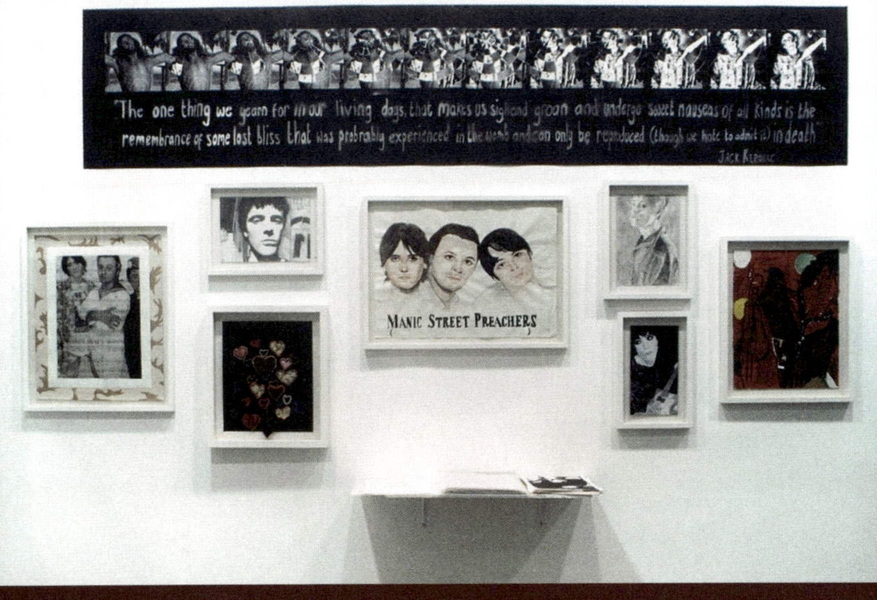

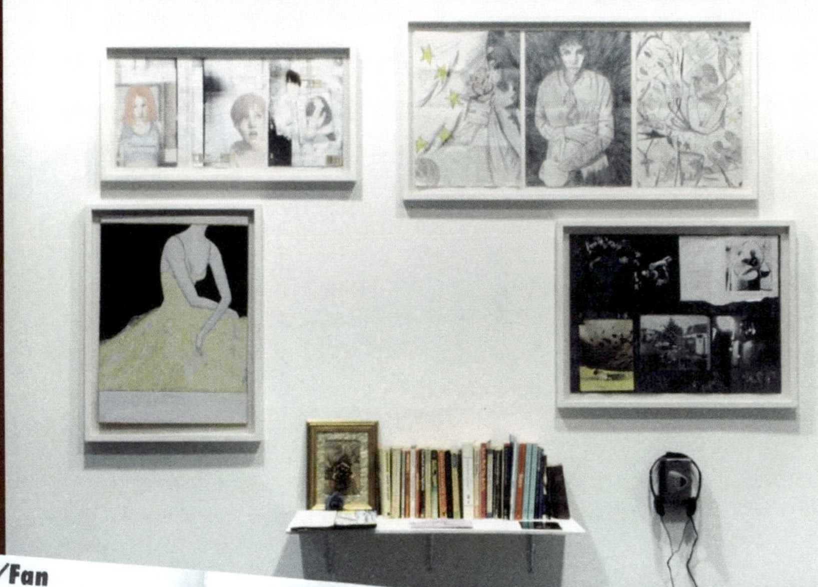

Dear Friend/Fan
I'm currently collecting material for a Manics exhibition next year . If you are interested in taking part or you need more information please get in touch . Thanks
Jeremy

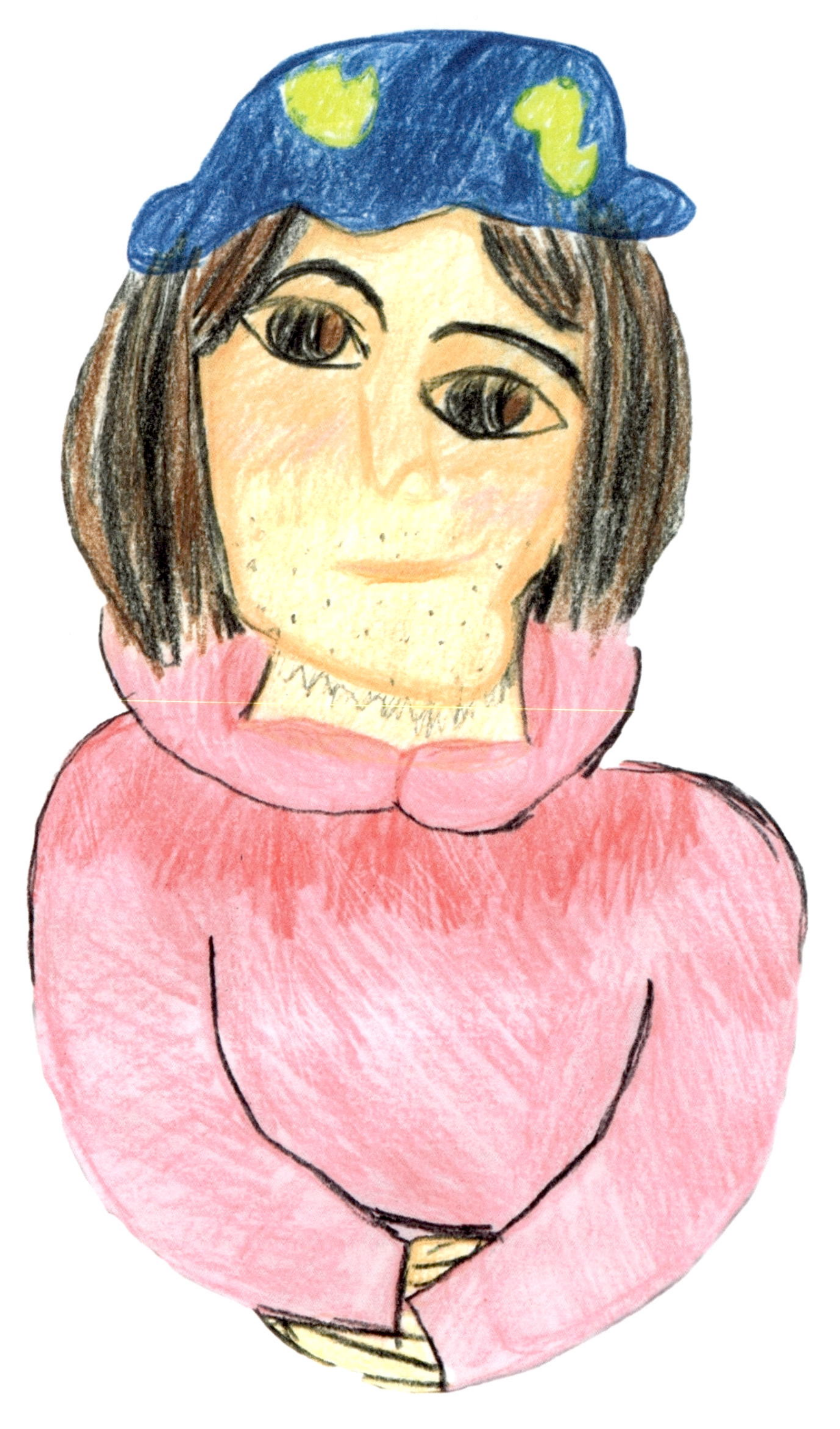

Afterword

Odds and Socks

CHEERIO interview with Jeremy Deller

CHEERIO Publishing: What do you do in your spare time?

Jeremy Deller: I watch a lot of TV. As a child at least it was my real educator. I take it very seriously. I am by nature a nosy person. I like current affairs, *Newsnight*, *Channel 4 News*. So, all in all, I average around five hours' worth of news intake a day through radio and TV, online, etc. I like to know what's going on. Or at least think I do.

C: Do you work from a studio?

J: I have a room. A cross between an office and a bedroom without a bed. The focus of the room is inevitably a computer. It's not necessarily an inspirational space. Inspiration comes from elsewhere. My room is filled with 'things'.

C: Do they inspire you?

J: Not as much as they should, they oppress me!

C: What's your favourite book?

J: *Albert Speer: His Battle with Truth* by Gitta Sereny. I read it again during lockdown to take my mind off things. An epic book. A great history of the Second World War. And, also, it's about an apparently artistic person who becomes thoroughly corrupted by power. Initially, Speer staged spectacles and rallies. He understood crowds. And then during the war he worked with bodies again as Minister of Works, only this time the bodies were expendable as they were slave labour.

C: Why were you shocked by the film *Tommy*, directed by Ken Russell?

J: A teacher at my secondary school ran a film club at school and showed all sorts of unsuitable films to the boys. We watched *The Servant* and *Performance*. These films were way above my understanding but so powerful. I loved *Tommy* in particular because of the mix of pop art, history, religion, music, sacred imagery. It was rich, dense with symbolism and I was ready for it. I could not believe what I was seeing.

C: And how was your cultural life as a child?

J: My dad used to take me to museums and occasionally art galleries.

← *Portrait of the Artist* by Iris Valentine King, 9, 2020.

We were not sporty at all, and I was not particularly musical. We lived near the Horniman Museum in Forest Hill. It's something of a wunderkammer, with stuffed animals and an anthropology collection. I am very at ease in museums and churches. With churches you never know what you are going to find.

C: Why do you always wear lovely socks?

J: I think everybody wears lovely socks. I just wear shorts a lot so it means you always see my socks. That's a metaphor for something.

C: The collaborative nature of your work appears to break down notions of ego, auteur and primary self. Has this occurred organically or is it deliberate?

J: I've heard this said before, but it's not quite accurate. In the process and the planning of a project, I am the equivalent of a film director. So, there is a lot of ego in the preparation, but I am not a 'shouter'. I do of course have to retreat from the work at some point, otherwise I get overwhelmed. With *We're Here Because We're Here*, Rufus Norris saw it exactly as I did. It was a clear idea – the kind of uncomplicated idea that could be explained in a sentence. Which didn't make it easy to make. Likewise *Orgreave*: I wanted to re-enact a battle from the miners' strike in theory. More tricky in practice. I don't want to stand in front of the work. I need to be at the back, not interrupting and not interfering. As I get older, I want my face to be seen less and less.

C: Who would you invite to your dream dinner party?

J: Probably people I know who I don't see enough.

Otherwise, William Blake, Sherlock Holmes, Karl Marx. I would love to invite a Mayan priestess in ceremonial dress. Artemisia Gentileschi, Goya, Bosch (so he could explain his paintings to me), William and Jane Morris. Alternatively, I could simply meet Rod Stewart and Ronnie Wood in a pub.

C: Some of your work evokes English history. Do you see yourself in certain ways as a time-travelling historian as opposed to an artist?

J: I am not a historian, but museums are time-travelling devices. I am working with history, but I am creating something else. With Stonehenge the history is and will remain unwritten. It is history we will never know so there is space to play there.

C: The name of the artist, poet and printer William Blake is often associated with you and your work and yet there are few direct correlations. Do you feel an affinity with him?

J: I don't really understand William Blake as well as I feel I should. His career is so vast, and most people only know him for perhaps 'Jerusalem', and maybe his *Songs of Innocence and of Experience*. 'Jerusalem', however, can be sung by anybody from hardcore socialists to the Women's Institute. It is a universal artwork, a mirror to our beliefs, like Stonehenge: both are public works of art that are also very personal. Everybody can project their feelings onto them.

C: Your work triggers deep feelings in others – whether anger, sadness or joy – yet you profess not to experience those feelings. Do you feel it is only possible to do what you do in a state of emotional disconnection?

J: Yes. In the early days I got too closely involved with the themes and the people. I used to get very, very nervous, and I had to teach myself to walk away and let things happen. The only thing I do worry about is the weather. The one thing I cannot do anything about.

C: Which piece of art do you most admire?

J: Cave paintings. But then I would need the cave. The *Holy Grail* tapestry series by Edward Burne-Jones and William Morris, or the epic *Garden of Earthly Delights* by Hieronymus Bosch. You can't believe how big it is. I would love to know what people thought of it when it was first shown, it must have terrified people! It's effectively the invention of CGI.

C: Do you believe in an afterlife? Or are works such as *The Battle of Orgreave*, *We're Here* and *Everybody in the Place* your version of an afterlife?

J: No. I think this is it. Art and ideas have afterlives though.

C: Does one final act of collective remembering such as a funeral, a memorial service, one of your works of art, allow us finally to forget?

J: No. If anything I'm often trying to make people remember and feel angry. To put those feelings back into the space. *The Battle of Orgreave* was made at a time when Tony Blair was in power, and Labour was erasing its history.

C: How would you like to be remembered?

J: I'd like the work to be remembered.

C: Do you think about your mortality?

J: I am now!

What makes the world go round

On the following pages are some images that have stuck with me; some of them I have pinned to my inspiration board and others just make me happy. Some are challenges almost to the artist, who should always be prepared to be humbled by the art made by people who might not see themselves as artists but actually are.

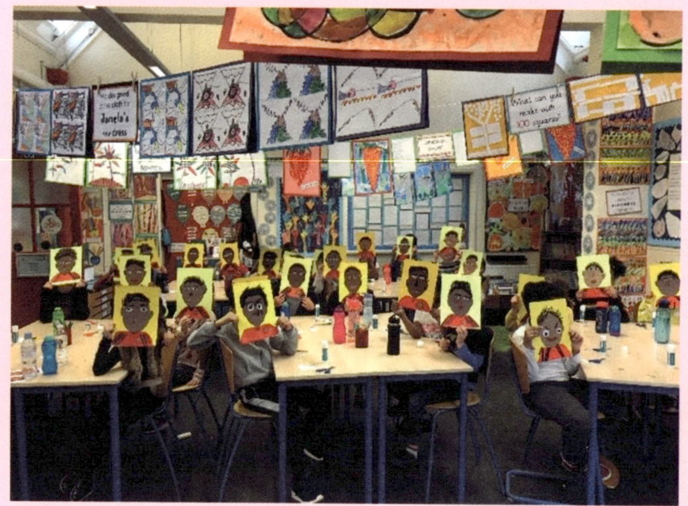

School children in Year 2 class at Reay Primary School in Lambeth, London, hold up their portraits of the footballer and activist Marcus Rashford. This was what the National Portrait Gallery was set up for. As an artist, you'd be pushed to make a better artwork than this.

These petrospheres, found almost exclusively in Scotland, are handmade objects that range in styles but are almost always the same size. Their use is unclear, just as I like it, but just imagine seeing one of these for the first time 4,000 years ago. If there is one thing looking at ancient objects teaches us, it's that everything has been done before and that nothing is new. Not only that, they often were better at it than us.

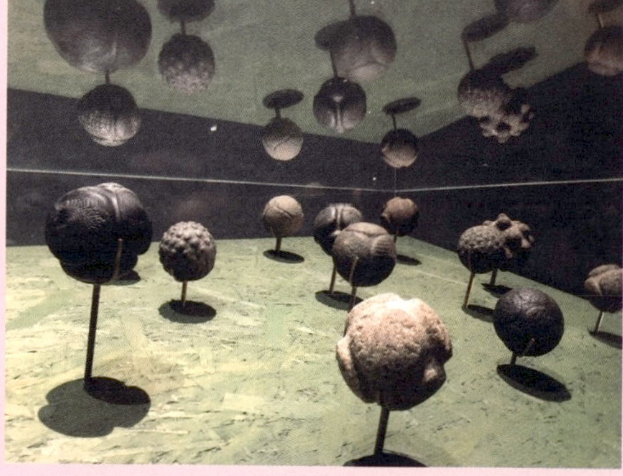

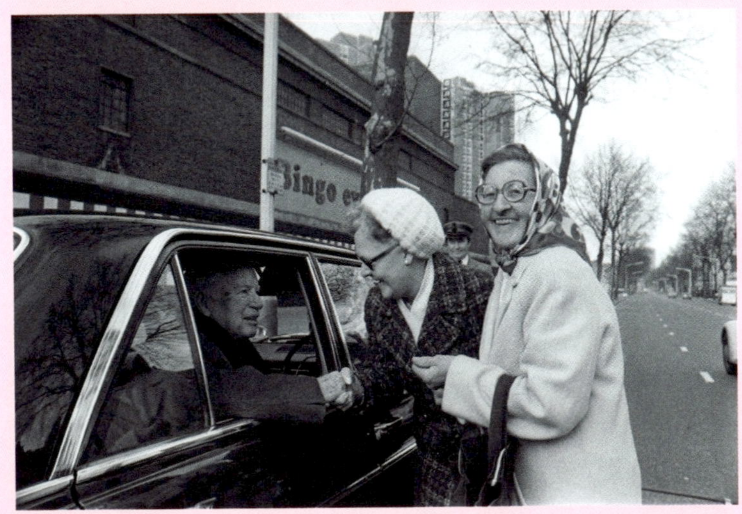

Charlie Chaplin talking to two women opposite his childhood home in Kennington, January 1975. There is so much taking place in this image – time itself is collapsing, their fandom, their joyful regression and mortality all crashing into each other. It's not a stretch to believe that these women actually knew Chaplin as a child in Kennington, their lives taking totally different trajectories before reuniting some seventy years later. Like a time-loop. Their excitement in meeting the most famous entertainer of the twentieth century is palpable.

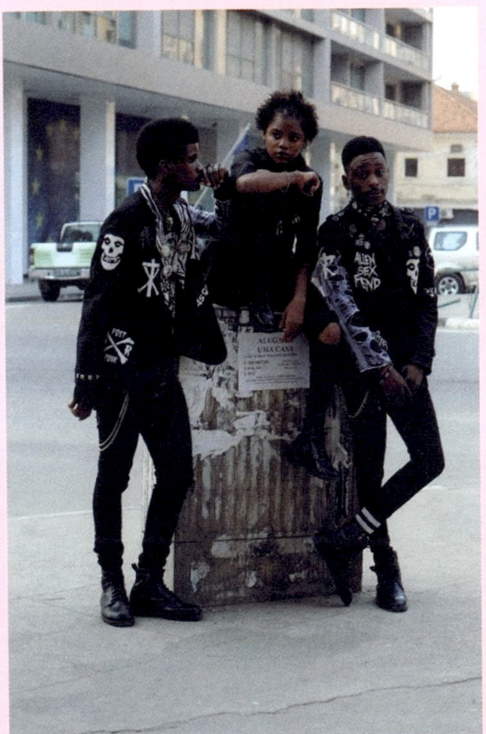

The beauty of these photographs of Goths from Angola gives me hope for humanity.

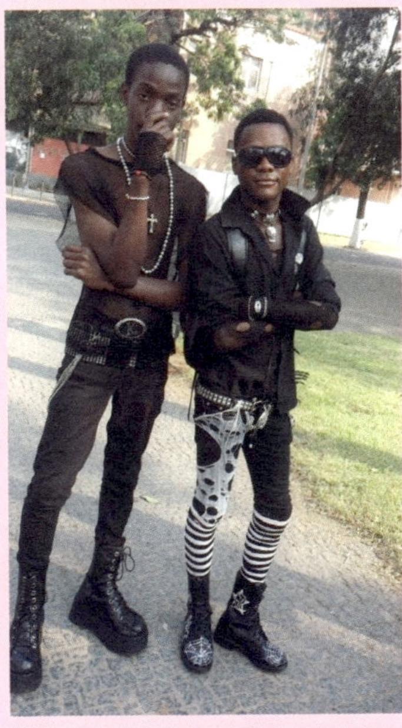

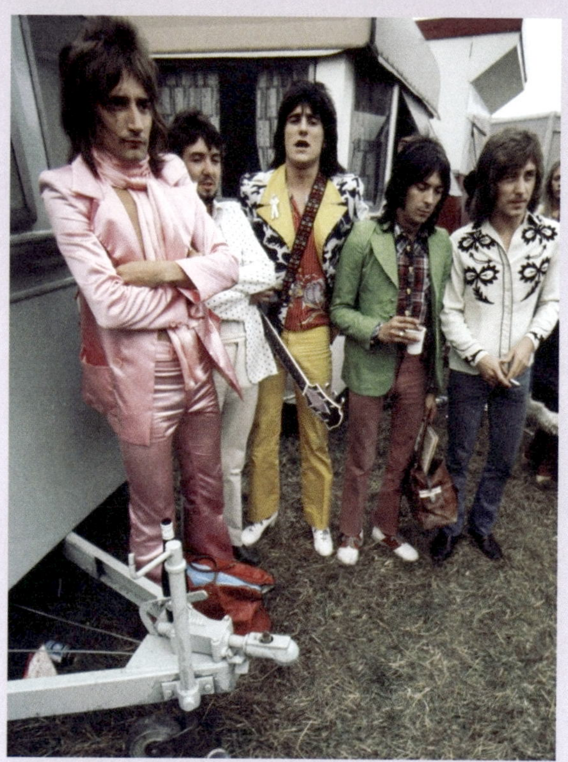

The Faces backstage at the Weeley Festival, Essex, 1971. In the history of Western civilisation has ever a group of men looked so good together? Did they have a stylist, I wonder. Each individual has a subtle take on the other's style, apart from Rod, who understands his role in the band perfectly by projecting his masculinity in pink satin. In a sense, this is a more outrageous outfit than any of David Bowie's, considering their fanbase.

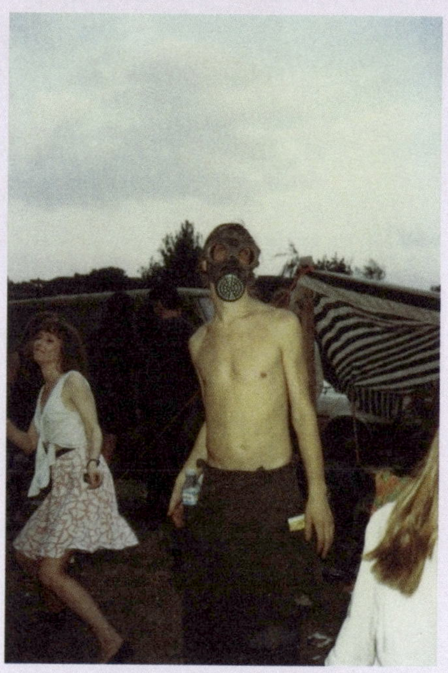

A raver at Deptford Free Festival, 1992. I have always liked it when music takes an absurd turn. Rave had so many possibilities for this. The inherent childishness and escapism explains perhaps why it appealed to so many youngsters, many barely out of primary school.

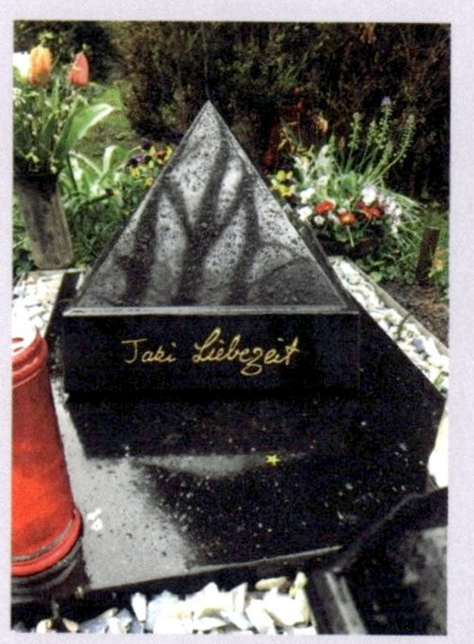

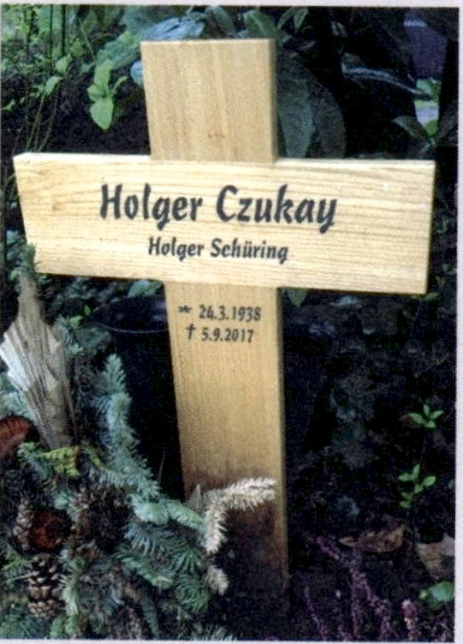

These two members of the band CAN, Jaki Liebezeit on drums and Holger Czukay on bass, are tied with Sly Dunbar and Robbie Shakespeare as possibly the greatest rhythm section of all time. They are still keeping it tight, buried only feet apart in the Melatenfriedhof cemetery in Cologne.

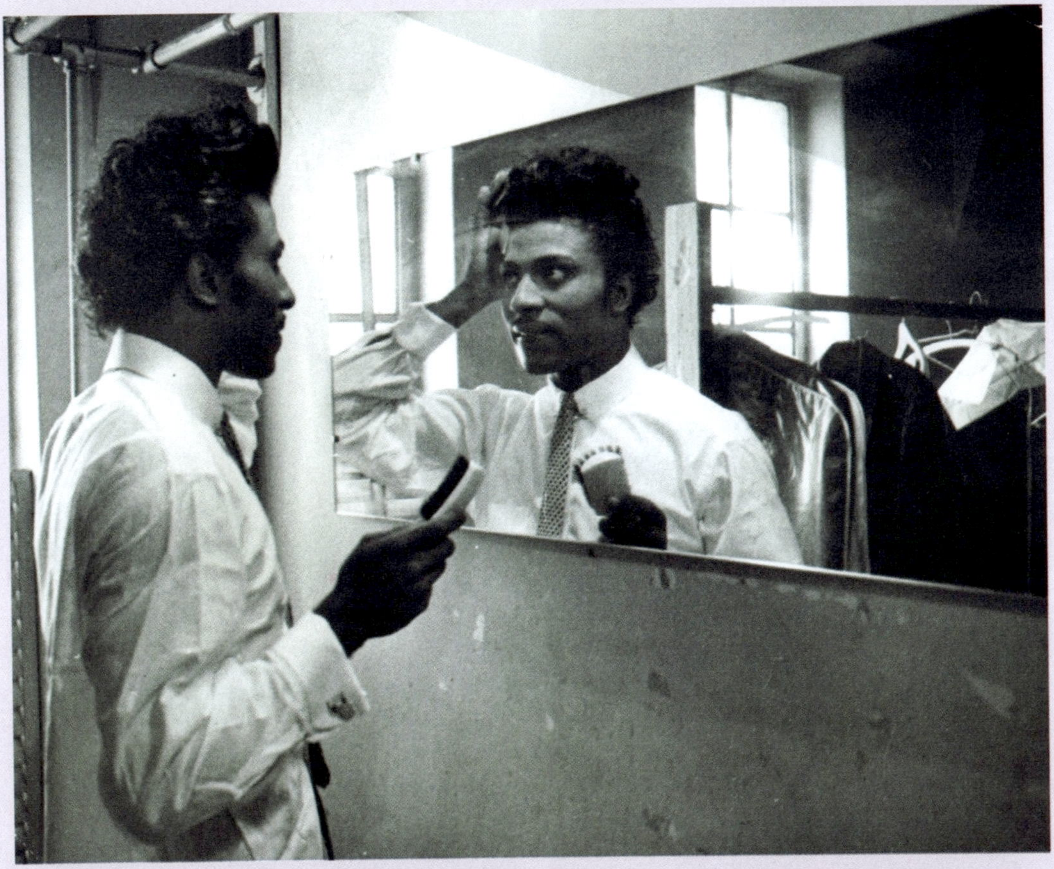

Little Richard backstage, Wrigley Field, Los Angeles, 1956. To understand the twentieth century, you have to know about Little Richard – as crucial a figure to me as Albert Einstein or Sigmund Freud, he liberated millions of people from themselves. Like Einstein, he too was a pioneer in his field of almost unimaginable and uncontrollable power. He was at least sixty-seven when I saw him perform in London, and you could see where everybody else got it from.

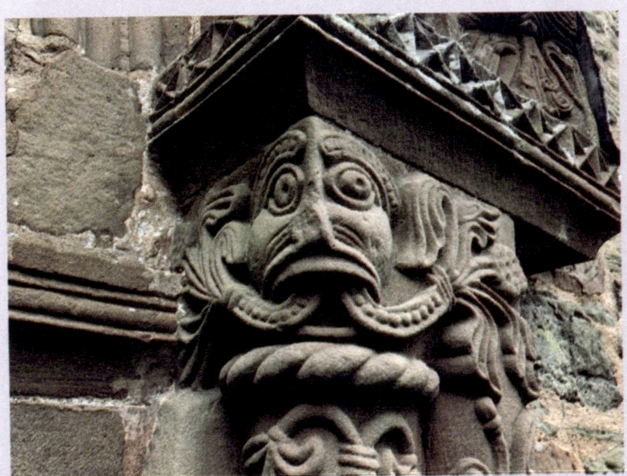

The Church of St Mary and St David in Kilpeck is something of a miracle to have survived the last 700 years. The exterior carvings are in almost perfect condition, portraying musicians, animals (including, I think, an elephant) and an incredible depiction of the pagan figure of Sheela Na Gig. One of the great joys of going to an old church is to discover something that survived the best efforts of that arsehole Henry VIII and the philistine Oliver Cromwell to destroy literally anything that looked remotely interesting.

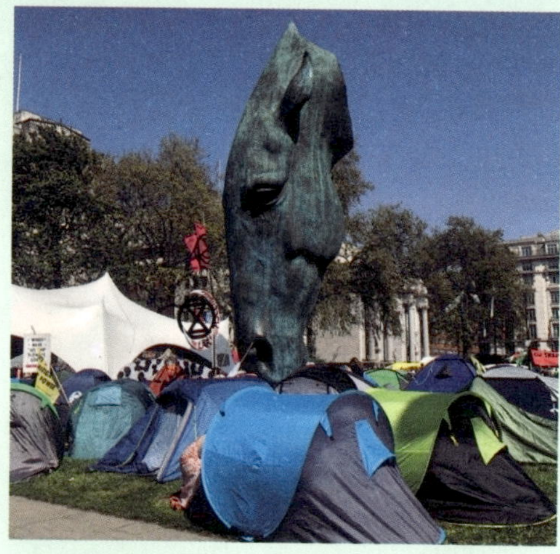

A preposterous artwork suitable only for a thieving oligarch is transformed by Extinction Rebellion's first London encampment at Marble Arch in 2018.

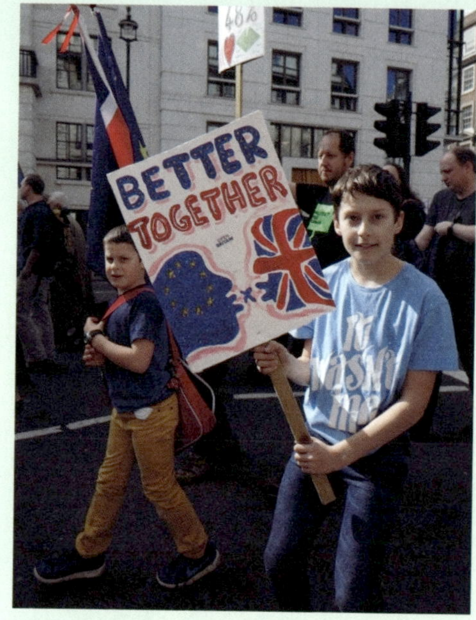

Anti-Brexit demo in 2017. If only this emotion had been stirred for Europe before the vote. I love this youngster's placard. Unsurprisingly, you didn't see many children on pro-Brexit marches.

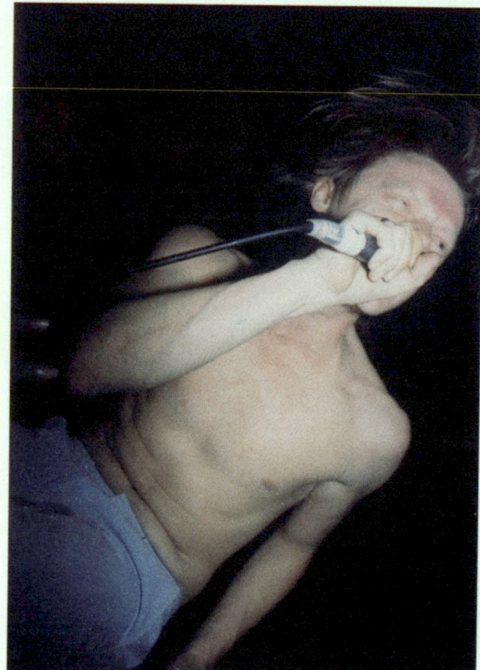

The much-missed band Earl Brutus' live performances were intense affairs, as their love of pop music and frustrations with life came to the boil.

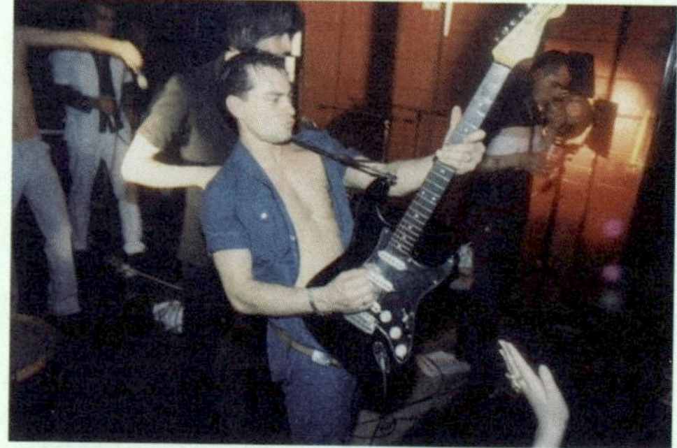

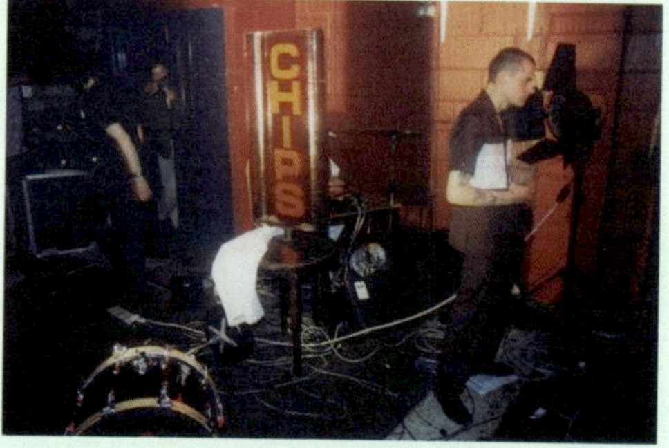

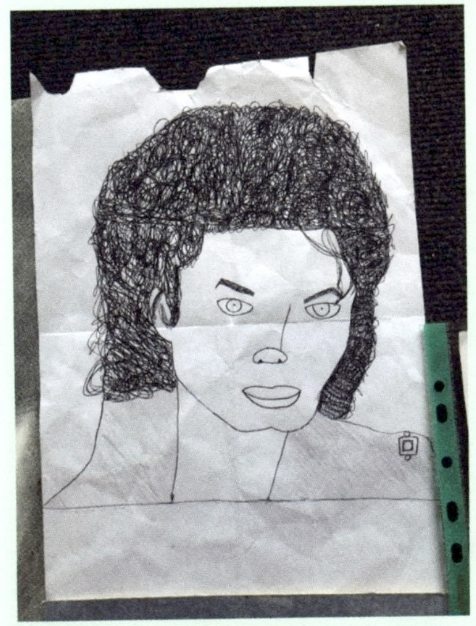

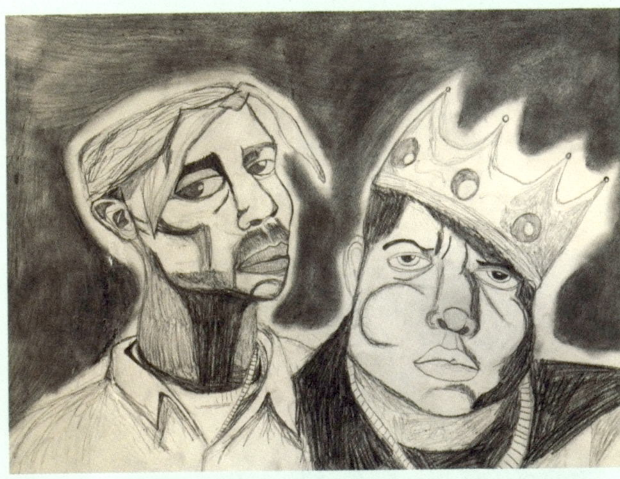

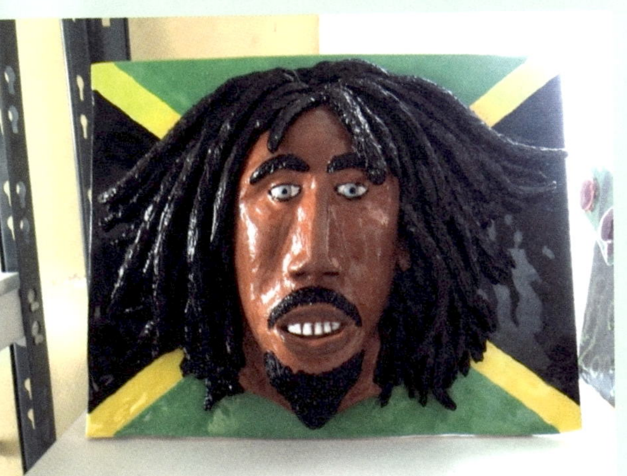

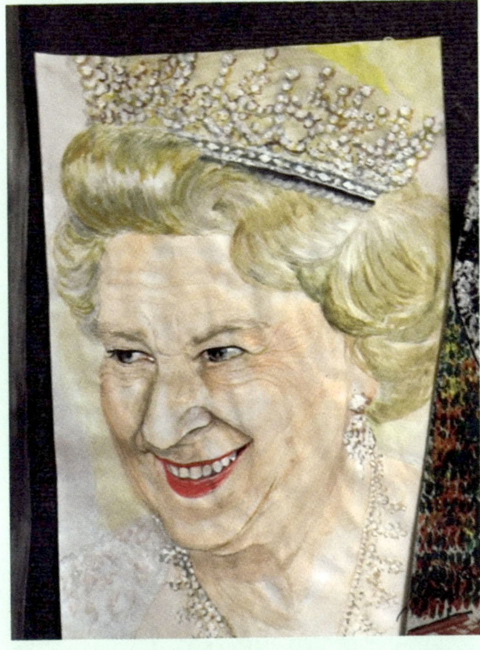

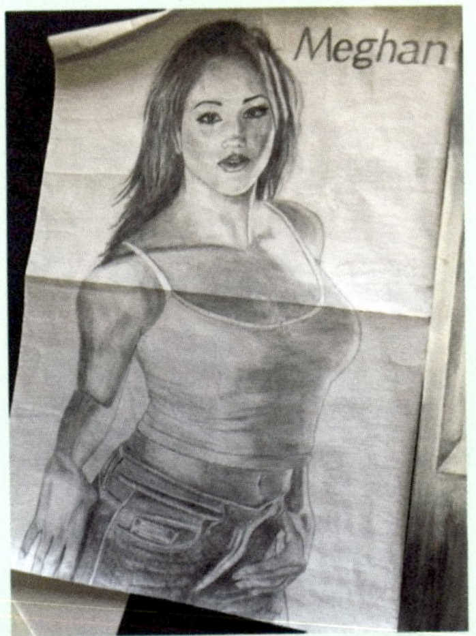

Through Koestler Arts, I have been a judge of work made in prisons and young offender institutes, and was for a while assigned the portrait submissions. Dead musicians are usually the most popular subject. Politicians rarely feature, though there was a portrait of a very buff Hitler once. The Royal Family are frequently depicted. There is a special irony to prisoners sentenced on 'Her Majesty's Pleasure' depicting the Queen. I imagine we can expect more portraits of Charles in the years to come.

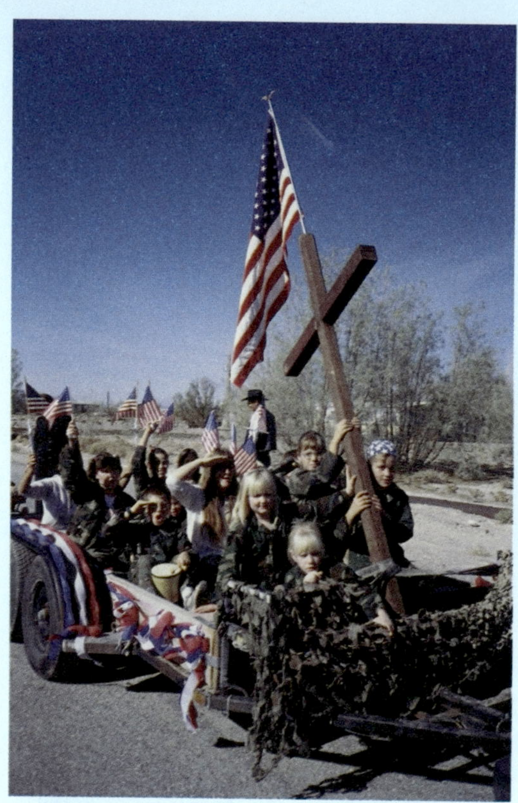

Processions can be a glimpse into the subconscious of societies. They reveal so much about what is actually going on in people's minds. Here is a Veterans Day parade in the small town of Pahrump, Nevada, two months after 9/11. Local children here re-enact the iconic image of the flag being raised at Iwo Jima, substituting it for a crucifix while singing 'Onward, Christian Soldiers'. There was virtually no audience for this parade as the whole village was on the floats, making it more a private ritual than a public event.

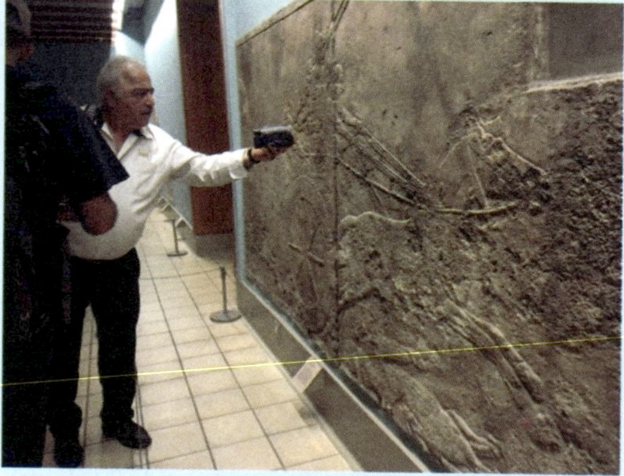

It never fails to amaze me how complex the act of photographing and filming artefacts in the British Museum is by people from all over the world. As a UK citizen, how would it feel to have to go to Egypt to see the Lindisfarne Gospels? I'd like one day to make a film using the footage shot by visitors to the museum as a kind of alternative guide.

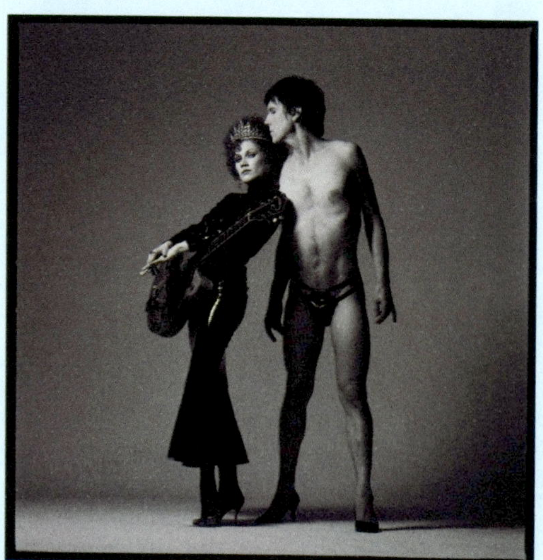

Poison Ivy and Lux Interior of The Cramps are rock's greatest love story, turned into music. They always looked amazing together. They furrowed their own path and tended to get written out of official histories of new wave and punk. The depth of Ivy's sorrow after Lux's death doesn't bear thinking about.

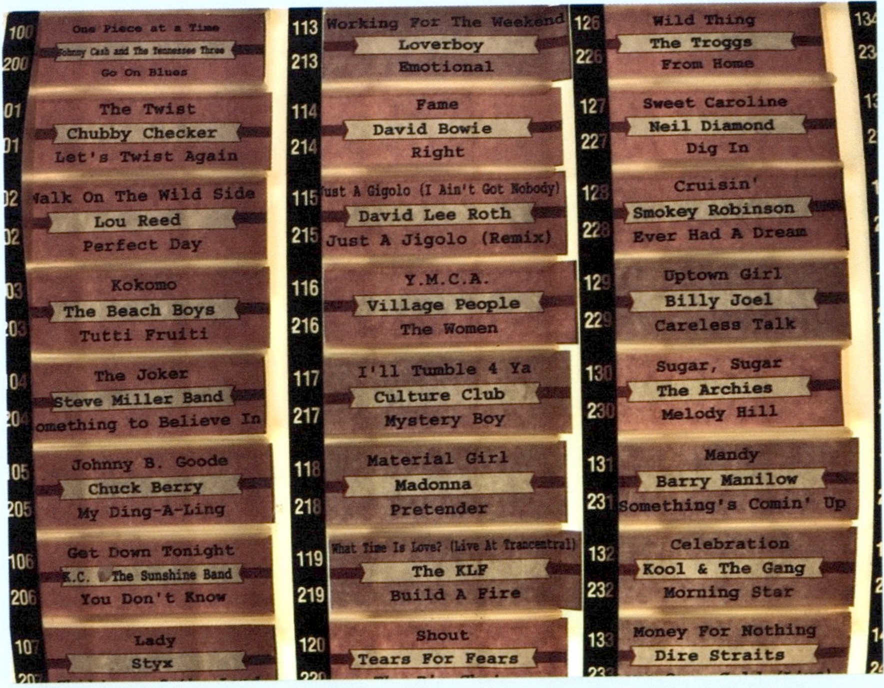

There is almost no joy greater in life than coming across a decent jukebox. I often find myself transfixed in front of them, searching for meanings hidden in the disparate selection of songs. I think this one is from a diner near Nashville, Tennessee, in 2009.

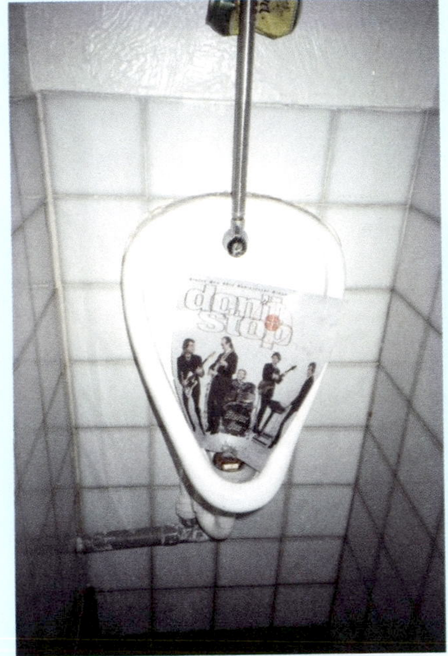

A great piece of public art, in a pub toilet from back in the day.

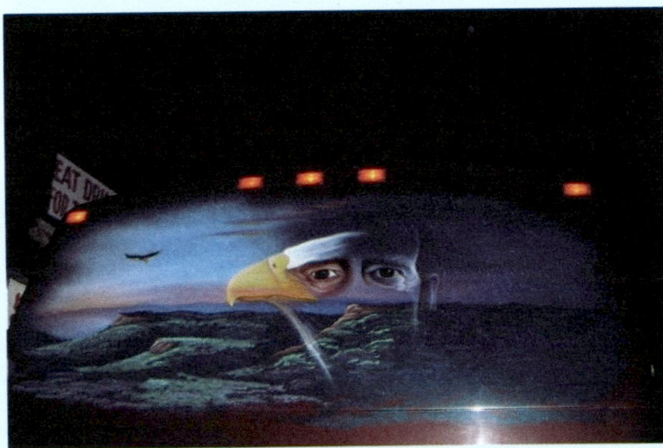

The back of Willie Nelson's tour bus in 2003, featuring his portrait morphing into a bald eagle (or vice versa). As fundamentally American as the landscape itself, Nelson is a living Mount Rushmore.

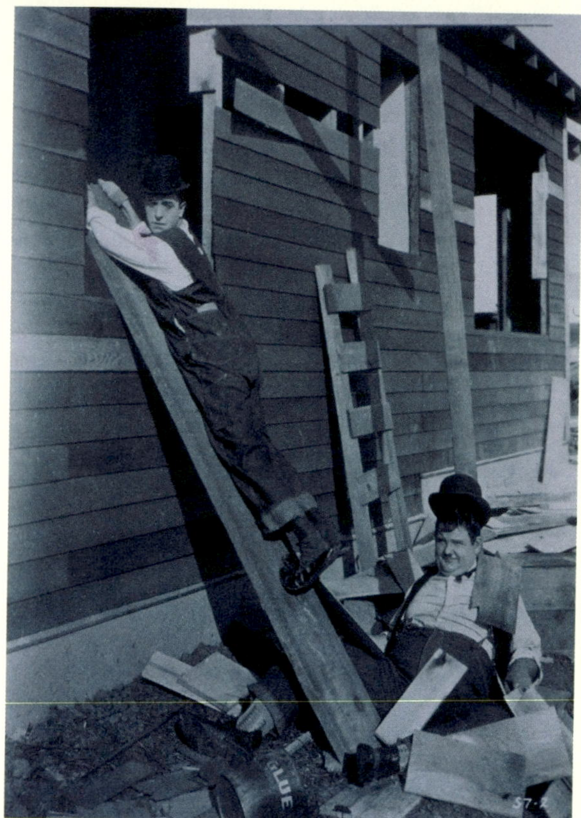

The older I get the more I understand these two. If only children knew that Laurel and Hardy are actually an accurate portrayal of adult life. Also, on the quiet, hugely influential on classic 1970s performance art.

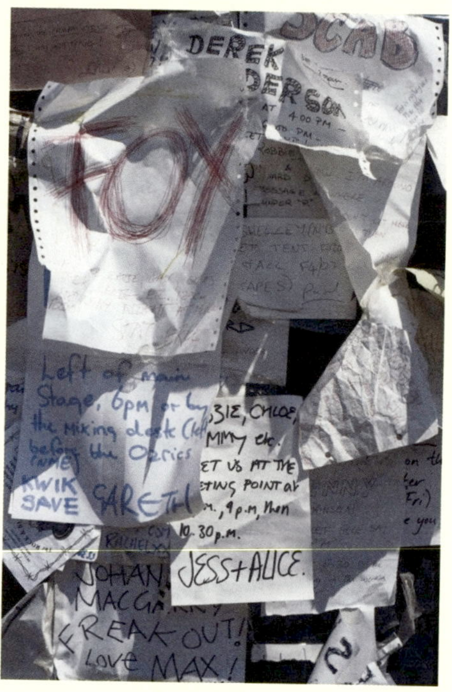

The Glastonbury internet, 1994. Before the mobile phone, if you got lost at a festival, you were on your own. You could, however, write a message and put it up on a central board and offer a prayer to the gods. I know this because I had to do it once myself. A long story, for another time.

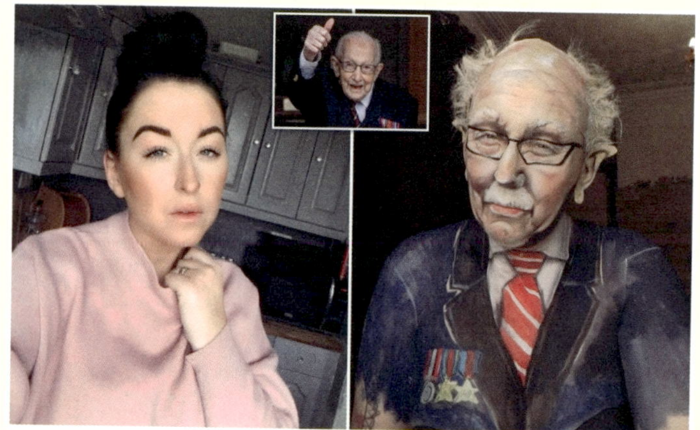

The makeup artist Tara Jenkins transforms herself into Captain Tom Moore in honour of his life. Possibly the greatest (accidental) artwork to come out of lockdown. Not only a brilliant piece of painting, but also presumably a very confusing situation for some men.

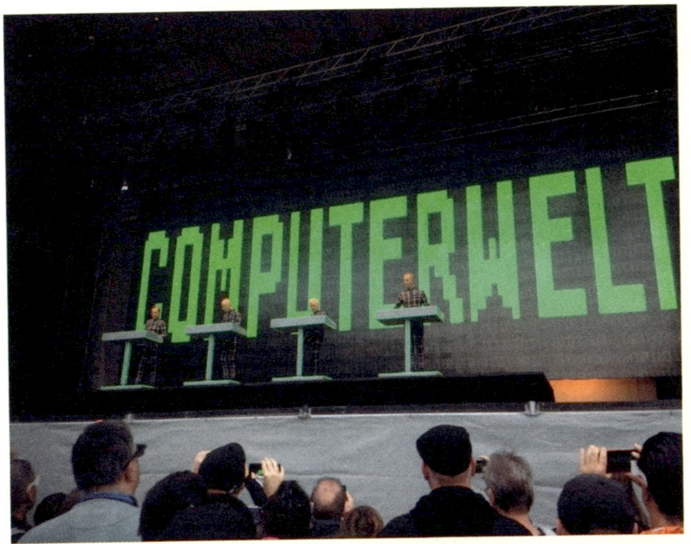

Kraftwerk live in Düsseldorf, 2017. The ongoing art project continues, admittedly with only one founding member. At the risk of sounding like an old man talking about a steam train, the moment in their concerts when 'Numbers' transitions to 'Computerworld' will always be thrilling to me.

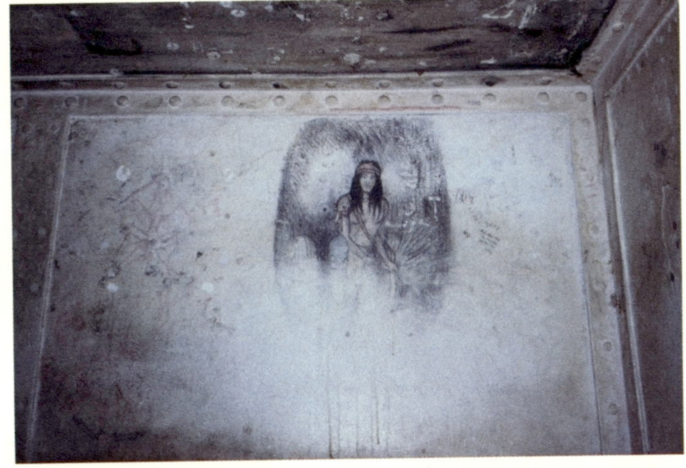

Cell drawings in a courthouse in Arizona, 2002. The creation of beauty from adversity is one of the better abilities of human beings. The eloquence of this artwork speaks for itself, and serves as a perfect complement to the song 'Pocahontas' by Neil Young.

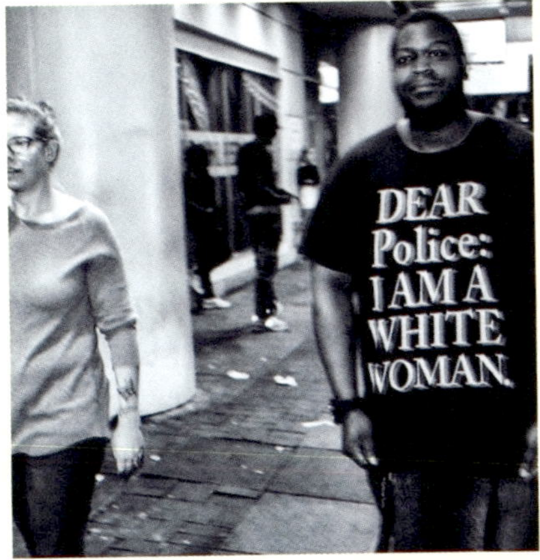

A reality-bending work of necessity and survival in the tradition of Marcel Duchamp, David Hammons and René Magritte.

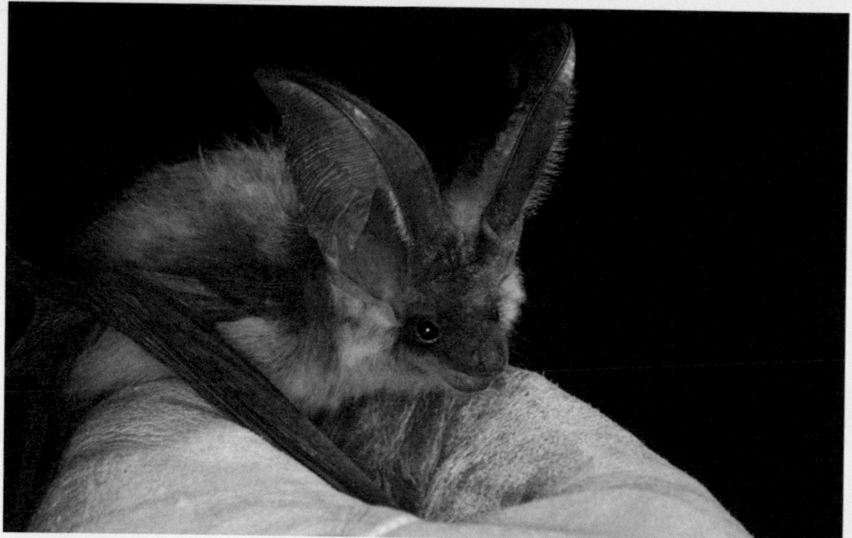

Grey Long-Eared and Greater Horseshoe bats. Portraits of bats have long fascinated me. These mammals have as much personality as any cat or dog, to say nothing of their superpowers: being able both to fly and wipe us off the face of the Earth.

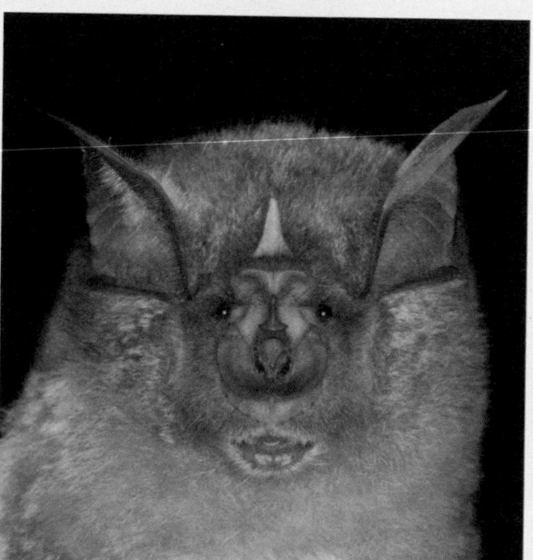

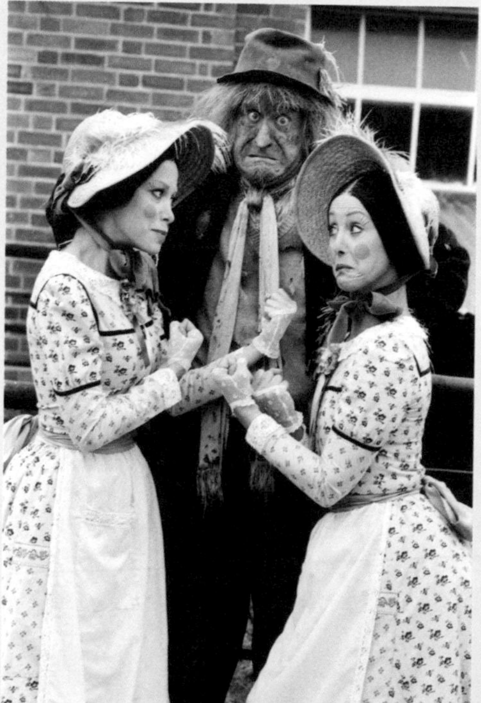

The Scarecrow's dilemma, depicted here; Worzel Gummidge and his complicated love life. That's what you get for being so well-dressed and handsome.

Around 100 years ago, purpose-built bat houses were constructed across the US and Italy to attract bats to assist in the eradication of mosquitoes (and hence malaria), which were decimating local populations. These Mayan temple-like structures are rightfully now listed buildings.

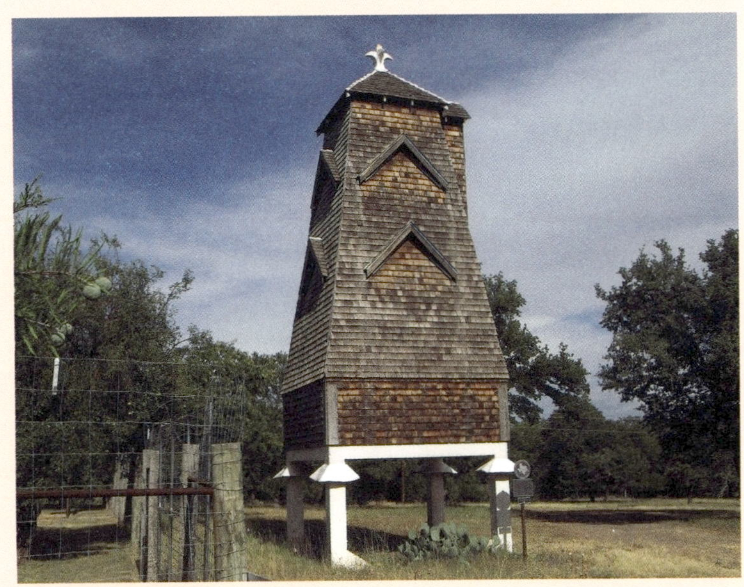

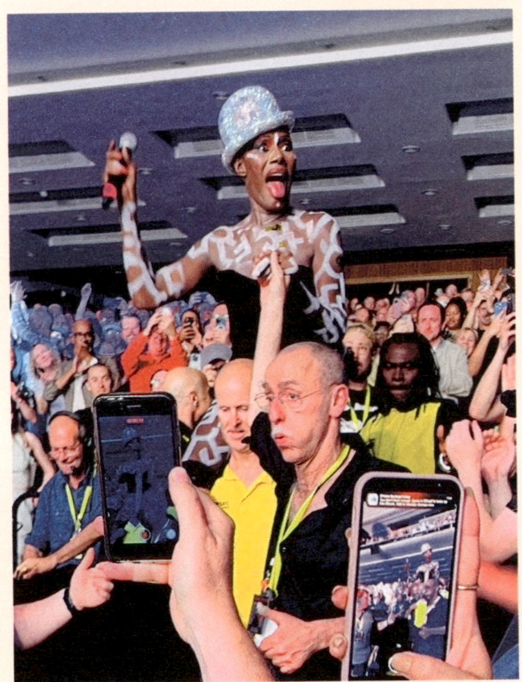

There are few more influential artists than Grace Jones. Her trio of records made at Compass Point are still ten years ahead of their time. I didn't take this photo – my friend Ian did – but I was in the audience for this walkabout at the Royal Festival Hall in London in 2022.

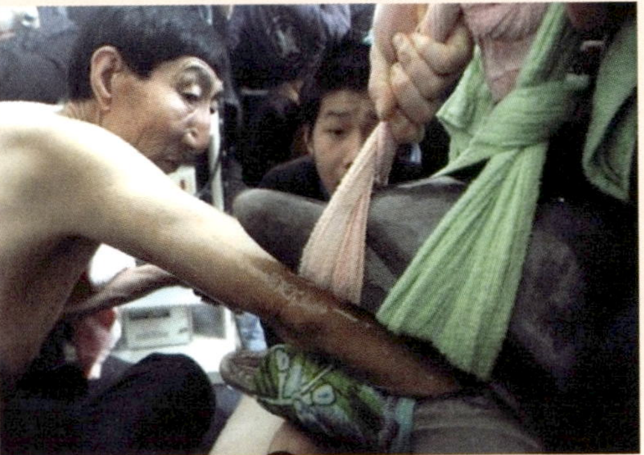

There is something strangely poignant about this inter-species assistance. Xishun Bao, the world's tallest man, saves the life of a dolphin that was sick and showing signs of depression because it has consumed plastic shards. It's like the plot from a Greek myth.

Notes

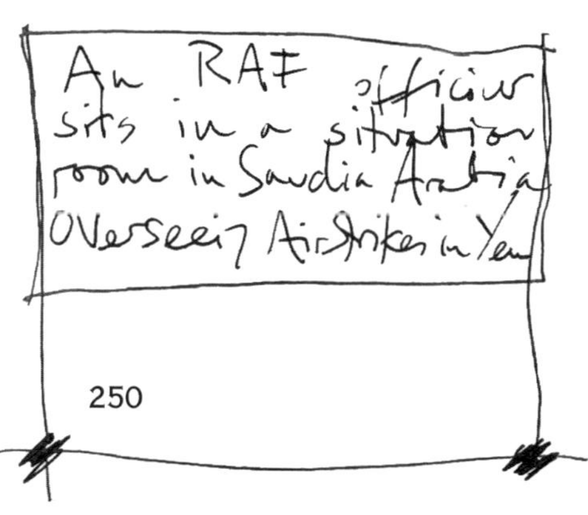
An RAF officer
sits in a situation
room in Saudia Arabia
Overseeing AirStrikes in Yem

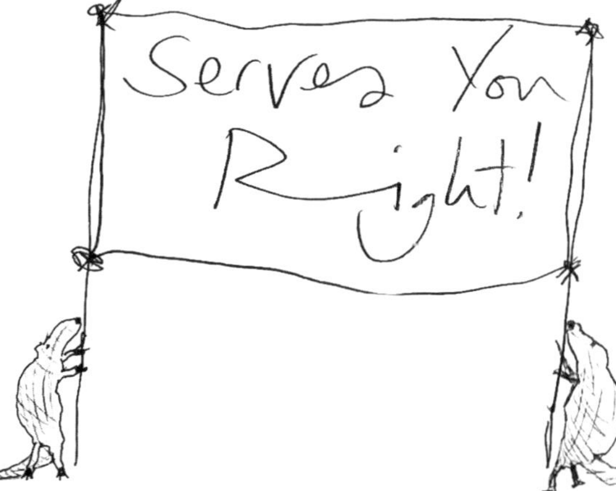
Serves You
Right!

Notes

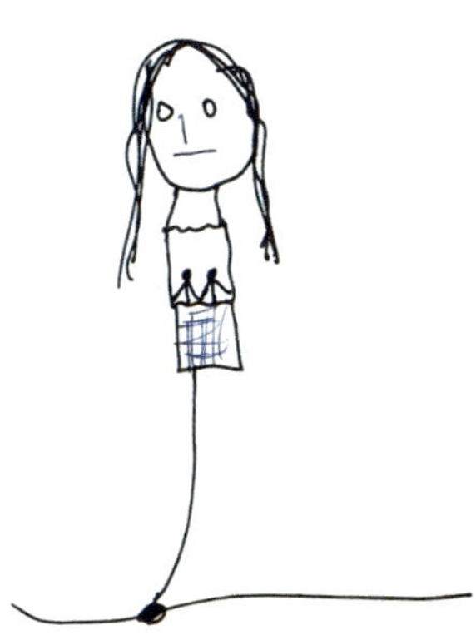

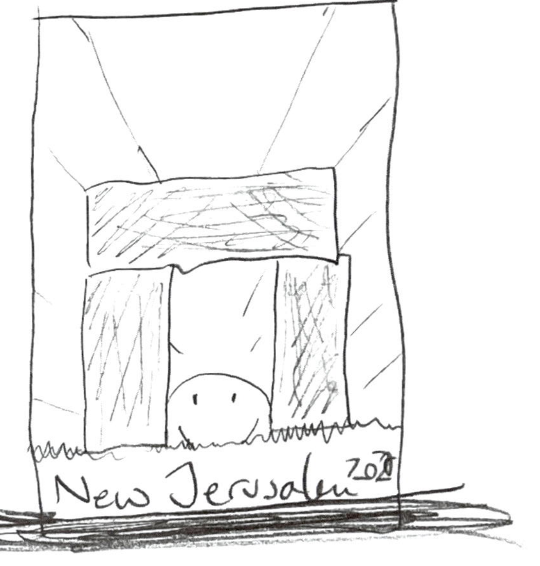

Notes

DIGITALAGE
INDUSTRIAL
IRONAGE
BRONZEAGE
STONEAGE
PALEOLITHIC
MEZOLITHIC
NeoLithic

TAX
AVOIDANCE

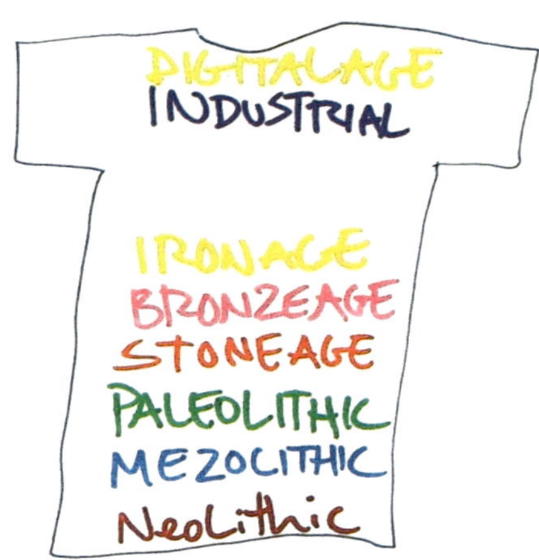

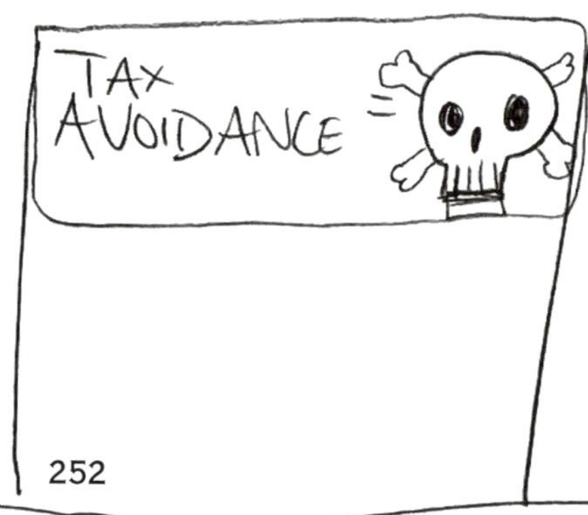

Notes

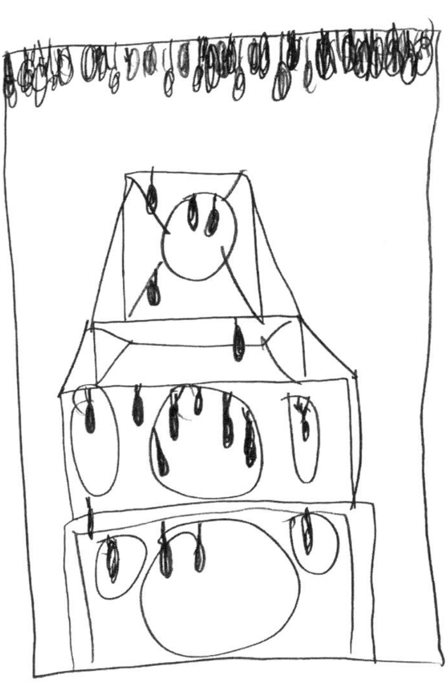

There are many people to thank. Those I interviewed for the book, Jon Banger, Mary Beard and Alan Kane. Manon Veyssière and Fraser for designing the book with me at Fraser Muggeridge studio. At Profile, Claire Beaumont, Peter Jones and Jack Murphy. At Cheerio, Darren Biabowe Barnes, Clare Conville, Ramona Pulsford, Harriet Vyner and, last but not least, my long suffering friend and editor Daniel Scott.

Often the only way something can happen is that someone says yes. Anyway, here in alphabetical order are the people and organisations I'd like to thank for saying yes: Nick Abrahams, Tasha Amini, Olivier Antoine at Art:Concept, Edek Bartz, Cecilia Bengolea, Sean Bidder, Bryan Biggs, Holly Blakey, Brian Boylan, Adrian Burnham, Lizzie Carey-Thomas, Russell Child, Jack Cocker, John Cresswell, Jen Crook, Mitch Crook, Max Delany, Jacqui Edenbrow, Alex Farquharson, Nick Fenton, Flying Leaps and Build Hollywood, Massimiliano Gioni, Bruce Haines, Ed Hall, Matthew Higgs, Ylva Hillström, Laura Hoptman, Caro Howell, Stuart and Val Hughes, Iris Valentine King, Scott King, Koestler Arts, Annika Kristensen, Emily Lim, James Lingwood and Michael Morris at Artangel, Ian MacMillan, John McGrath, Cuauhtemoc Medina, Justin Meekal, Julie Milne, Toby Webster, Andrew Hamilton and Ellie Royle at The Modern Institute, all the gardeners in Münster, Rodney Newton, Thomas Nicolaou, Terry Noel and the Melodians, Rufus Norris, Anne Pasternak, Simon Periton, Christoph Platz, Stephen Pook, Alex Poots, Sofia Prantera, Julian Richards, Andrea Rose, Doc Rowe, Ralph Rugoff, Ingrid Schaffner, Jared Schiller, Sally Shaw, Justine Simons, David Sims, Paul Stolper, Adrian Street, Nato Thompson and Creative Time, Roger Tolson, Sarah Tynan, Herbert Voigt, Jenny Waldman, Toby Webster, the Williams Fairey Brass Band, Volker Zander.

All pictures © Jeremy Deller except those listed below. Courtesy the artist, The Modern Institute / Toby Webster Ltd., Glasgow and Art Concept:Paris.

Inside covers: Installation view, 'Warning Graphic Content', The Modern Institute, Aird's Lane, Glasgow, 2022. Photographer: Patrick Jameson.

pp.34–35: *The Battle of Orgreave* performance image. Photographer: Parisa Taghizadeh. Courtesy Artangel.

p.36: Installation view, 'Joy in People', Wiels Centre for Contemporary Art, Brussels. Photographer: Filip Vanzieleghem.

p.40: © IWM 14–18 NOW; Hub: Birmingham Rep. Location: Birmingham High St. Photographer: Andrew Fox.

p.42, top: © IWM 14–18 NOW; Hub: National Theatre London. Location: London Westfield, Stratford City. Photographer: James Pegg.

p.42, bottom: © IWM 14–18 NOW; Hub: Manchester Royal Exchange. Location: Manchester. Photographer: Chris Payne.

p.43: © IWM 14–18 NOW; Hub: National Theatre Wales. Location: Wales Bangor Trem Elidir. Photographer: Rhian Cadwaladr.

p.44: © IWM 14–18 NOW; Hub: Birmingham Repertory Theatre, Location: Birmingham Bullring shopping centre. Photographer: Andrew Fox.

p.45: © IWM 14–18 NOW; Hub: Salisbury, Location: Salisbury Churchill Way. Photographer: Adrian Harris.

pp.62–63: Entangled children in recording studio from 'Wir Haben die Schnauze Voll'. Photographer: Mareike Tocha.

p.68: June 8 2020, an image of George Floyd is projected onto the base of the statue of Confederate General Robert E. Lee on Monument Avenue in Richmond, VA. Associated Press.

p.69: Aneurin Bevan, the National Health Minister and founder of the NHS, is toured around the 400-bed Park Hospital Davyhulme Lancashire. Sylvia Beckingham aged 13 was too shy to ask him any questions, 1948. Alamy.

p.70: Emperor Vespasian (left) and Emperor Augustus (right) © The British Museum.

p.74: © IWM 14–18 NOW; Hub: Birmingham Rep, Location: Birmingham Photographer: Andrew Fox.

p.106: Installation view 'Aries, Jeremy Deller, David Sims: Wiltshire Before Christ', The Store X, 2019. Photographer: Jack Hems.

p.106, bottom left: Installation crew with sign. Photographer: Daniel Reeves.

p.110: Deller, Kane and Stringfellow in Hyde Park looking for food in a bin with which to feed the ducks. Photographer: Simon Periton.

p.111: Installation view, *Gild the Lily* exhibition, London 1993. Photographer: Simon Periton. Courtesy the artist.

pp.112–123: Photographers: Jeremy Deller and Alan Kane.

pp.124–125: Installation view 'Folk Archive', Palais de Tokyo, Paris. Photographer: Marc Domage.

p.132: Installation view, *Unconvention* exhibition, Cardiff 1999. Features Picasso: *Reclining Nude with Necklace* 1968 Tate.

p.133: Installation view, *Unconvention* exhibition, Cardiff 1999. Features Warhol: *Self Portrait*, 1986 Tate.

pp.142–145: Installation view, *Love is Enough: William Morris & Andy Warhol*, Modern Art Oxford Image: Andy Keate © 2022 The Andy Warhol Foundation for the Visual Arts, Inc. / Licensed by DACS, London.

p.150: © IWM 14–18 NOW; Hub: Birmingham Rep, Location: Birmingham New St Station, Photographer: Andrew Fox.

p.152: Eric Clapton in *Tommy* by Ken Russell, 1975. Alamy.

p.153: Detail of *Father and Son*. Rupert Murdoch. Melbourne 2021. Photographer: Herb Fenton.

p.156: 30 March 1972: A newspaper seller outside the British Museum selling copies of *The Evening Standard*. The headline – 'The Treasures of the Boy King' – a reference to Tutankhamen, the Egyptian Pharaoh. Photographer: William Milsom / Evening Standard / Getty Images.

p.157: Slade perform on BBC TV show Top of The Pops, London, 1973. Photographer: Michael Putland / Getty Images.

pp.160–161: Adrian Street, Welsh professional wrestler, pictured with his father, a coal miner, 2nd November 1974. A.k.a. Kid Tarzan Jonathan, The Nature Boy, Hell's Angel #1. Alamy.

p. 187, bottom: Children hijack vehicles to celebrate the shooting of a British soldier by an IRA sniper in West Belfast, 12 April 1972. Photographer: Alex Bowie / Getty Images.

p. 202: Installation view, *Father and Son*. Melbourne 2021. Photographer: Christian Capurro. Courtesy the photographer and ACCA.

p. 210: *Iggy Pop Lifeclass* New York 2016. Photographer: Elena Olivo.

p. 211: Iggy Pop at the Whisky a Go Go on Sunset Blvd., Hollywood CA. © James Fortune.

p. 212: Class Portrait with Iggy Pop. Photographer: Elena Olivo.

pp. 214–215: *Iggy Pop Lifeclass*. Photographer: Elena Olivo.

p. 216: *Mars* by Velázquez. © Photographic Archive Museo Nacional del Prado.

p. 238: Schoolchildren's portraits of Marcus Rashford, All Reay Primary School, Lambeth 2019. Photographer: Alice David-Jekyll.

p. 239: English comic actor and filmmaker Charlie Chaplin meets fans, 13 January 1975, near the 'Granada Bingo' on Kennington Road, London. Photo by Evening Standard / Hulton Archive / Getty Images.

p. 240, top: The Faces in 1973. From left: Rod Stewart, Ronnie Lane, Ronnie Wood, Ian McLagan and Kenny Jones. Alamy.

p. 241, top: Little Richard backstage at Wrigley Field, Los Angeles, 2 September 1956. Alamy.

p. 244, bottom: Lux Interior and Poison Ivy of the Cramps, 1990 © Michael Lavine.

p. 246, top: Laurel and Hardy in *Finishing Touch*, 1928. Alamy.

p. 248, top: Grey Long-Eared and Greater Horseshoe bats © Daniel Hargreaves.

p. 248, bottom: Wurzel Gummidge with two Aunt Sallies 1981. Alamy.

Every effort has been made to trace the copyright holders of material featured in this book. Any omissions which are pointed out to the publisher will be amended in future editions.

First published in Great Britain in 2023 by Cheerio.
www.cheeriopublishing.com
info@cheeriopublishing.com

Designed by Fraser Muggeridge studio.

1 3 5 7 9 10 8 6 4 2

Printed and bound in Italy by Puntoweb.

A CIP catalogue record for this book is available from the British Library.
ISBN 978 1 73944 0558

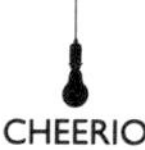